Vorwort

Crossover 1 – 6th edition, Ausgabe Baden-Württemberg ist konzipiert für Englischlernende an beruflichen Schulen, insbesondere an beruflichen Gymnasien. Band 1 bietet Stoff für die Klassenstufe 11 und bereitet dabei schon auf die Abiturprüfung vor.

Die vier auf die Themen des Bildungsplans abgestimmten **Topics** sind wie folgt aufgebaut:

- **Overview** – Hinführung zum Thema und erste Themenwortschatzarbeit
- **Sections** – Texte und audiovisuelle Materialien mit vielfältigen kompetenzorientierten Aufgaben:
  - **Warm-up** – Anregung zum Sprechen
  - **Working with the text** – Leseverstehen und erweiterte Textarbeit
  - **Working with words** – Wortschatzerarbeitung
  - **Skills training** – prüfungsrelevante Aufgaben und anwendungsbezogene Tipps
  - **Looking at language** – Grammatikthemen mit funktionalem oder formalem Ansatz
  - **Crossover TV** – Hör-/Sehverständnistraining
- **Project** – schrittweise Anleitung zu selbstständiger Projektarbeit
- **Skills** – intensives Methodentraining zu Lernstrategien und Prüfungsaufgaben
- **Consolidation & Evaluation** – Rückschau auf das *Topic*, Bewertung des eigenen Lernstands und (in der PagePlayer-App) Aufgaben zur Vertiefung

W0266090

In allen *Sections* gibt es zahlreiche Möglichkeiten zur **Differenzierung**, die Sie an folgenden Hinweisen neben den Aufgaben in der Randspalte erkennen:

D ▸ More help	Zu diesen Aufgaben stehen im Anhang Varianten mit Hilfestellungen zur Verfügung.
D ▸ More practice	Hier stehen im Anhang weitere Übungsmöglichkeiten auf demselben Niveau zur Verfügung.
D ▸ More challenge	Hier finden Sie im Anhang Erweiterungsmöglichkeiten oder Transferübungen.
○	kennzeichnet Übungen in den Sections für leistungsstärkere bzw. schnellere Schülerinnen und Schüler.

Ebenso in der Randspalte befinden sich Übersetzungen anspruchsvoller **Vokabeln**, die mit Zeilennummerierungen versehen sind.

8 **rise** *Aufstieg*	Fett gedruckte Wörter sind Lernwortschatz.
17 quirky *eigenwillig, unangepasst*	Nicht fett gedruckte Wörter dienen lediglich zum Verständnis des jeweiligen Textes.

Weitere Symbole und Verweise

🔈	Hörverstehen/Tracknummer
▶	Hör-/Sehverstehen / Nummer des Films
▯	Zusätzliches Material auf der PagePlayer-App
S ▸	Verweis auf *Skills*-Inhalte
G ▸	Verweis auf die *Grammar summary*
Exam preparation	Aufgaben, die auf die Anforderungen der Prüfung ab 2024 vorbereiten

Zusatzmaterialien in der PagePlayer-App

Crossover 1 – 6th edition bietet eine neue Dimension des individuellen Lernens. Die zusätzlichen Materialien können zu Hause, unterwegs oder auch im Kurs mit dem Smartphone oder dem Tablet direkt aus dem Buch heraus angesehen und -gehört werden.

Und so können Sie die Materialien abspielen:

1. Laden Sie die kostenlose PagePlayer-App herunter. Sie können die Inhalte zu **Crossover 1 – 6th edition** kapitelweise auf Ihrem Smartphone oder Tablet speichern und jederzeit aufrufen.
2. Scannen Sie mit Ihrem Smartphone oder Tablet die ausgewählte Buchseite, die Verweise auf Audio- und/oder Videomaterialien enthält, sowie Seiten mit diesem Icon. Das Material wird angezeigt und Sie können es direkt starten. Alternativ können Sie auf die Inhalte der App über das Medienmenü zugreifen.

Auf der PagePlayer-App finden Sie die folgenden Materialien:

- alle Audios und Videos zum Schülerbuch
- auf den Overview-Seiten (Auftaktseiten der *Topics*): Audiodateien mit *Background information* zu den einzelnen Sections, auch als Lesetexte verfügbar
- Checklisten zu *Writing*-Aufgaben
- auf den *Consolidation & Evaluation*-Seiten: Vertiefungsaufgaben zu jedem *Topic*
- zum *Skills*-Teil „Eine argumentierende bzw. bewertende Schreibaufgabe bearbeiten": Hilfestellung zum Verfassen einer Stellungnahme
- zum *Skills*-Teil „Eine kreative Aufgabe schreiben": Kriterien, Tipps und *language help* für Textsorten, die angefordert werden können

Topic 1 – We are Gen Z

Topic 2 – Cities and regions in anglophone countries

Topic 3 – British and American political systems

Topic 4 – The media

Topic 1 We are Gen Z

Section A
Identity and values

our back-grounds

our youth culture

"Multiculturalism is one of the most prominent markers of [Gen Z]. Not only is there more racial diversity, but there is also greater overlap in cultures, making personal identity multi-layered and complicated." – rpa.com

adolescence

Fact: About a third of American Gen Z'ers know someone who goes by gender-neutral pronouns (source: Pew Research).

Section E
Educational possibilities

our decisions

our future

"I have dreams but I'm very scared of failing."
– Anant, b. 1999, USA

Fact: American Gen Z'ers say they care more about earning money and having a successful career than about having close friends, being in a romantic relationship, getting married or travelling (source: Morning Consult).

Good to know

Generation Z, or Gen Z for short, were born between the mid-1990s and the early 2010s.

1 Read ...

a the facts about young people. Does your experience confirm them?
b the quotations. What are your opinions on these statements?

2 The mind map shows you a preview of Topic 1. Copy it onto a piece of paper and add words and phrases from ...

a the facts and quotations above (the highlighted words).
b the Word Bank box opposite.
c your own ideas.
d Sections A–E (skim them to find words you think are important).

Your teacher may give you a time limit for each step a–d.

Section B

Well-being

Fact: For mental well-being, the biggest challenges facing young Europeans today are risky sexual behaviour, drinking and smoking, lack of physical activity, inadequate nutrition and obesity (source: World Health Organization).

Find information on each Section in the PagePlayer app!

our relationships

our conflicts

Section C

Generational conflict

"They [Gen Z] might not necessarily feel comfortable with talking to their parents or authority figures. But to be in front of the camera, ironically, makes them feel comfortable."
– Megan Bycell, Head of Talent Relations, AwesomenessTV

our working life

Section D

Gap years

Fact: In Norway, Denmark and Turkey, half of the students take a year off between school and university (source: gapyearassociation.org).

"I'm terrified of growing up."
– Lorde, musician

3 Rank the Sections A–E based on how interested you are in them.

4 Make a "KWL" (Know, Want to know, Learnt) list for the Topic.

5 With a partner, compare …

a your mind maps. Say why you put words where you did.
b your rankings from exercise 3.
c your "Want to know" lists.

Then compare with another pair.

6 Save your work for reviewing when you've finished the Topic.

Word bank

approval *Anerkennung*
belief *Überzeugung*
commitment *Engagement, Leistungsbereitschaft*
degree *Schul-/Universitätsabschluss*
education *(Schul-/Universitäts-)Bildung, Unterricht*
gap year *freies Jahr zwischen Schule und Universität*
habit *Gewohnheit*
identity *Identität*
profession *Beruf*
value *Wert, Wertvorstellung*
volunteering *ehrenamtliche Arbeit*

Section A Identity and values

Warm-up

1 Which social media platforms do you use? What do you think of how people present themselves there? And how do you present yourself?

How to say or write it

authentic ◂▸ fake
confident ◂▸ shy
interested in causes ◂▸ uninterested in causes
fun ◂▸ boring
honest ◂▸ dishonest
nice ◂▸ obnoxious
normal ◂▸ weird
popular ◂▸ introverted
serious ◂▸ silly
smart ◂▸ stupid

2 What adjectives from the How to Say or Write It box would you use to describe Joseph Park's profile?

< **Joseph Park** ...

4 **posts** | 46 **followers** | 145 **following**

Identities: Korean-American, San Franciscan (go 49ers!), queer activist, progressive politics, music lover, Christian, future nurse

Values: family, spirituality, activism

Motto: This is who I am today. Tomorrow I may be different.

San Franciscan *jd aus San Francisco*
progressive *fortschrittlich*
to **identify as sb/sth** *sich als jd/etw bezeichnen, sich als zu jdm/etw zugehörig erklären*
to **identify with sb/sth** *sich mit jdm/etw identifizieren*
affinity *Neigung, Vorliebe*

Listening

02

3 Listen to Joseph's conversation at a party. What subjects do he and the other partygoers mention? Name some key words.

4 Complete the sentences with the phrases for talking about identity.

identifies as | identify with | part of ... identity | shows ... identity | sure about ... identity

1 The partygoers ... their hometown.
2 Joseph ... a music lover.
3 Korea is ... Joseph's ethnic ... .
4 Joseph sometimes ... his ... with flags and emojis.
5 Joseph is not really ... his professional ... .

5 The table below shows aspects of identity. What examples of these aspects can be found in Joseph's profile? Copy and complete the table.

affinity	ethnic	gender/ sexuality	ideological/ political	local	national	professional	religious
music							

Writing

6 Would you like to be friends (IRL) with Joseph? Comment on this question.

Exam preparation

S ▸ *Eine argumentierende/bewertende Schreibaufgabe bearbeiten*, pp. 35–40

S ▸ *Operatoren*, pp. 33–34

How to say or write it

I think I could be friends with him because …

… is important to both of us.

We share … as a value.

… makes him likeable.

We're both interested in …

I don't think I would be friends with him. My friends are …

Working with the text

7 Complete the questionnaire on values.

What are your values?

1 **How important are the following to you? Rate each one on a scale of 1 to 10.**
1 = not important at all 10 = I couldn't live without it/them

- a Activism/Causes
- b Being/Looking cool
- c Family
- d Fashion/Clothes
- e Friends
- f Good grades at school
- g Humour
- h Image, followers and likes on social media
- i Local/National sports teams
- j Music
- k Popularity at school
- l Spirituality
- m Work–life balance

2 **How honest were you with your answers?**
1 = not honest at all 10 = totally honest

8 In small groups, compare your answers and explain the reasons for your choices.

9 In your group, agree on the three most important and three least important values. Then compare your results with the rest of the class.

How to say or write it

Why did you rate that so high/low?

The reason why I said that is …

… is more important to me than … because …

It's difficult to be honest, because …

Looking at language

10 State your opinions using the phrases below.
Example: *Joseph is* ***a person who*** *values his online image too much.*

1 a person who
2 a person whom
3 a person with whom I
4 a person whose
5 an online profile which
6 a profile with which he
7 an identity that
8 a value that I

Then put brackets around the relative pronouns that could be left out (as shown in the Remember box). Check with a partner.

G ▸ Relative clauses, p. 175

D ▸ More challenge, p. 145

Remember

If the relative pronoun refers to the object of the verb, you can leave it out.

Kindness is something (that/which) more people should value

Speaking

11 On a sheet of paper, write three sentences about yourself for people to guess who you are – but don't make it too easy. Crumple the paper up into a ball. When your teacher says "Go!", have a ten-second "snowball fight" with your class. Then pick up a paper ball, read the description aloud, and guess who it is.

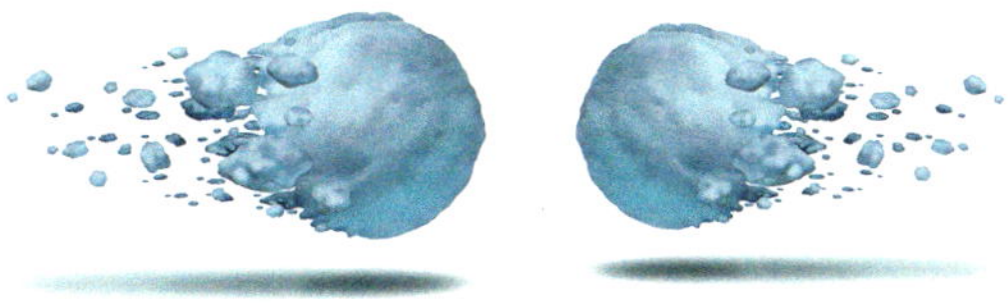

Section B Well-being

Warm-up

How to say or write it

- close your eyes
- take a deep breath
- ask yourself how you're feeling
- give your mind a break
- let go of tension
- bring your attention to your … (calves, thighs, rear end, belly, chest, neck, jaw, forehead)

1 What is your stress level right now on a scale from 1 to 4?

1 2 3 4

2 Let's see if we can reduce your stress level by doing a short meditation. Before you do it, make sure you understand the words and phrases in the How to Say or Write It box.

03

Sit on a chair with your weight evenly distributed. Put your feet flat on the floor. Rest your arms on your lap. Then start the meditation.

3 How do you feel now, having completed the meditation?

Working with the text

4 Work with a partner. Make two lists: 1) causes of stress, and 2) ways of reducing stress. Try to think of as many as possible. Your teacher will give you a time limit.

5 Skim the article "Living with stress". Which paragraphs 1–12 are a) causes of stress or b) tips for dealing with stress?

S ▸ *Schwierige Texte lesen*, pp. 72–73
D ▸ More help, p. 145

6 Read the article, then work with a partner to create a heading for each paragraph.

04

Living with stress

Stress has a huge impact on everyone's mental and physical health. What are the causes of stress? More importantly, what can you do about it?

1 We live in a visual society and are bombarded by images of perfect bodies we can't compete with. The result? About 50% of people are or have been on a diet. Eating disorders are on the rise. Gyms are full of young men and women desperate to change their bodies.

2 Just sitting quietly for ten minutes a day can reduce your stress levels. If you've never tried meditation before, give it a try. How does it work? One thing meditation does is bring you into the present moment. Stress and suffering are usually connected to thoughts about the past or the future.

impact *Auswirkung(en), Folge(n)*
to do sth about sth *etw gegen etw unternehmen*
to **be on a diet** *eine Diät machen*
eating disorder *Ess-Störung*
to **be on the rise** *(ständig) zunehmen, auf dem Vormarsch sein*
to **be desperate to do sth** *etw was unbedingt (aus Verzweiflung) tun wollen*
stress levels *pl Stress-niveau*
suffering *Leiden, Leid*

3 It's not the end of the world when a romantic relationship breaks up – but it can seem like it. Friends change and develop different interests. Losing a friend is painful.

4 Natural disasters, wars, terrorism, economic problems and threats to the environment fill the news. Just as teens are trying to find their place in the world, it seems the world is not a safe place.

5 Keeping active is a great way to fight stress, especially if you do it with others. Physical activity gives you more energy and promotes positive feelings. It's a great stress-buster. If kicking a ball around isn't your thing, try yoga: it calms the mind and exercises your body.

6 Think positive. They also say that laughter is the best medicine. Research shows that laughing can lead to a more positive outlook on life. Looking on the bright side definitely helps reduce stress.

7 Teens place high value on their social lives. Trying to fit into a group can cause anxiety. Peer pressure is an additional stress for teens, with many feeling they have to say or do things they are not wholly comfortable with to be accepted.

8 When you feel run down, your defences are low, which leads to more colds and illnesses. That's why healthy eating is so important. A varied diet that includes fruit and vegetables boosts your immune system so can help you deal with everyday life.

9 We all face conflict, too. It's a normal part of social relations. However, learning how to deal with conflict is difficult. An extreme form of conflict, of course, is bullying.

10 School-related stress can also include worrying about grades, meeting deadlines for coursework, keeping organized and living up to parents' and teachers' expectations.

11 Students can spend too much time on social media and answering text messages and phone calls. If you do this late in the day, sleep can suffer as a result. Getting enough sleep is essential.

12 Teens enjoy their independence and behave differently to children. This can cause issues at home. Parents may also be going through difficult times. Divorce, money problems, job worries and illness in the family can trigger stress.

(493 words)

to **be painful** *wehtun*
natural disaster *Naturkatastrophe*
threat (to sth) *Bedrohung (von etw)*
laughter *Lachen*
outlook on life *Lebensperspektive*
the bright side *die positiven Aspekte*
wholly *völlig, hundertprozentig*
to **feel run down** *sich schlapp fühlen*
defences pl *Abwehrkräfte*
varied diet *abwechslungsreiche Ernährung*
to **live up to sb's expectations** *jds Erwartungen erfüllen*
sth suffers *etw wird in Mitleidenschaft gezogen*
to **behave** *sich verhalten*
to **cause sth** *etw verursachen*
to **trigger sth** *etw auslösen*

Working with words

Skills training: Diagramming vocabulary

Collocations are fixed, common phrases – for example, *take your time*. You can diagram collocations using tables, drawings or mind maps.

▸ Phrases for writing and discussion, inside front cover

7 In the following tasks, diagram the collocations in ways that make sense to you.

D ▸ More practice, p. 145

1 *Fight stress* (paragraph 5) is a collocation. Find four other collocations with the word *stress* in paragraphs 2, 6, 10 and 12.
2 The text mentions feeling *run down* (paragraph 8). Find three other ways one can feel in paragraphs 1, 4 and 7. These words all collocate with *feel*.
3 The text mentions problems one can *worry about* (grades, paragraph 10), *face* (conflict, paragraph 9) or *deal with* (conflict, paragraph 9). Find nine other potential problems in paragraphs 4 (5x) and 10 (4x). These words can be used with *worry about*, *face* and/or *deal with*.

How to say or write it

I/We think exercising is (not very) helpful because …

I … and this helps me to relax / forget my problems.

I often/sometimes/rarely/never …

Speaking

8 With a partner, make a list of "Top ten stress-busting tips" using the headings you created in exercise 6 and adding tips of your own. Then explain your rankings to another group using the phrases in the How to Say or Write It box.

Writing

Exam preparation

S ▸ *Eine kreative Schreibaufgabe bearbeiten*, pp. 41–42

9 Write an article for your school magazine in which you give your "Top ten stress-busting tips" using your personal experience and opinion as well as the advice given in the text.

Looking at language

Remember: Adverbs of frequency

Single-word adverbs of frequency like *always* or *sometimes* go between the subject and the verb. This is different than in German!

*I **occasionally** take time to relax.*

Phrasal adverbs of frequency like *once a year* go at the end of the sentence. The standard order for adverbs is 1) place, 2) frequency and 3) time.

*I relax in the sauna **once a week**.*

G ▸ Word order – positions of adverbs of time, place and frequency, p. 174

10 As the text on pages 12–13 states, some habits help reduce stress, others can worsen it. Make sentences about habits using the words in the table below in the correct order.

Example: *Marion always eats healthy food.*

	Subject	Verb	Object	Adverbs / Adverbial phrases
1	Marion	eat	healthy food	always
2	James	exercise	–	three times a week
3	Christopher	meditate	–	for ten minutes often on the sofa
4	My mother	worry	about things	after she watches the news on TV sometimes
5	My brother	play with	his phone	before going to sleep every evening in bed
6	My parents and I	take	a walk	after dinner in the neighbourhood occasionally
7	You	take	a break to go outside	never when you're working at home

D ▸ More practice, p. 146

11 Modify each sentence so that it is true about you.

Example: *I always eat healthy food at lunchtime.*

Working with words

12 Match each personality type to a description of the typical behaviour.

easy-going | moody | outgoing | selfish | sensible | shy | stubborn

1 These people only think of themselves.
2 They're happy one minute, then angry the next.
3 People say bulls have this quality. It's impossible to change their minds.
4 People like this have no problem introducing themselves to strangers.
5 Others are the opposite. They're nervous when they meet new people.
6 Someone like this won't mind anything you do.

13 Decide which personality types are most and least prone to stress.

D ▸ More challenge, p. 146

Listening

Skills training: Intercultural awareness

What do Americans consider the "typical high school"? Here are some basic facts.

- High school lasts four years (grades 9–12).
- About 40% of Americans attend high school in the suburbs, where the average school size is about 650 students.
- Everyone in a district attends the same school, regardless of their academic performance.
- After high school, there will be students who plan to attend university (usually called "college"), others who choose to go to a vocational school *(Berufsschule)* and others who will go straight into the workforce.
- Most high schools have at least one professional guidance counsellor who takes care of the students' emotional well-being.

14 Listen to part 1 of an interview with Lori Mann, a high school guidance counsellor in the US. How typical is her school?

05

15 Look at this diagram and make sure you understand all the stress factors. Then listen to part 2 of the interview. Which of the factors are mentioned? How much does Lori Mann's experience confirm the findings of the survey?

06

Lori Mann

We asked teens: How much pressure do you feel to ... ?

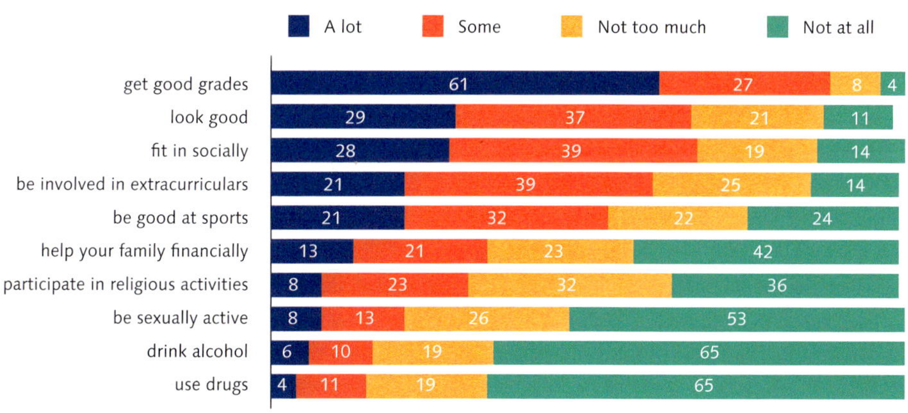

(Source: Pew Research Center)

D ▸ More help, p. 147 07

16 Listen to part three of the interview and answer the following questions.

1 What kind of advice does Lori Mann give for dealing with academic stress: practical advice, emotional advice, or both?
2 Which students tend to be the most stressed out about their grades?
3 What is the "cake" metaphor and what advice about "intentions" does it illustrate?
4 Do you agree with Lori Mann that the student is always the one in control of their grades? What is your opinion of her advice in general? Do you think many students at your school would benefit from the help of a guidance counsellor?

Speaking

S ▸ *Diagramme beschreiben u. analysieren*, pp. 70–71

Skills training: Describing and analysing diagrams

1. Description
Say what the diagram shows without adding any interpretation.
The diagram shows the percentage of teens who … different stressors.
The biggest stressor is …, followed by …
Only a small number of teens say they're stressed by …

2. Analysis
What conclusions can you draw (without giving your personal opinion)?
What questions remain?
There are about five stressors that are very common. They are …
Very few teens are stressed out by …. Either they don't care about these things or they do them without feeling stress.

Exam preparation

17 Read the Skills Training box. Then, with a partner, practise describing and analysing the diagram on page 15.

D ▸ More challenge, p. 147

18 Partner A, turn to page 157. Partner B, turn to page 159.

Speaking

▸ Creating a podcast, pp. 126–127

19 In a group of 3–4 people, create a podcast about dealing with stress in one of the following contexts: at school, at home, in a relationship.

Start by describing/showing a concrete stressful situation, e.g. an argument between two people. Then give three tips for how to deal with it. The episode should be 5–7 minutes in length.

Section C Generational conflict

Warm-up

1 Look at the cartoon and choose the best interpretation.

- **a** The cartoon is a criticism of families that communicate poorly.
- **b** It makes fun of how overly dramatic teenagers are.
- **c** The humour comes from the fact that rows between teenagers and parents are often very emotional and yet are about unimportant issues.
- **d** The message is that family arguments distract from school work.

"When I left for school this morning, were we getting along, or did I promise never to talk to you again?"

2 What do parents fight about with their teenage children? Write down your ideas, as you will need them later.

Skills training: Understanding through context

When you read texts in English, you're sure to come across words and expressions you don't know. It's a normal part of the learning process.

You can often work out the meaning of a word or an expression from the context. Here are some examples from the text on pages 18–19.

So why is it so difficult? Much of it is, of course, ***down to*** **(1)** *biology.* (l. 7)
The sentence with *down to* is clearly an answer to the question before it, so you can guess that the expression is used to give a cause or an explanation.

... you're standing right next to the speakers at a concert. It's a lot harder for you to ignore the ***racket*** **(2)**. (ll. 45–46)
This describes a situation with a lot of loud noise, which is what *racket* means.

... the parts of your brain that ***crave*** **(3)** *independence and control, as well as* ***novelty*** **(4)** *are* ***being ramped up*** **(5)**, *meaning you're driven to do things your way,* ***on your terms*** **(6)**, *and seek out new experiences.* (ll. 60–62)
Think about what you know about teenage brains. They want (3) more independence and control. The meaning of the word *novelty* (4) is found at the end of the sentence: new experiences. You can guess that ramping up moves something up (5) or makes more of it. In the same way, crave refers to new experiences, *on your terms* (6) refers to independence and control.

In this book the words you're not expected to know are translated or explained in the margin. Don't rely on this help too much. First, guess the meaning based on the text only, and then check to see if your hypothesis is correct. The words printed in **bold** as well as any words that are not in the margin should be learned.

Your hard work will pay off. Research shows that when we are introduced to new words in a meaningful context (e.g. a text), we remember them better.

S ▸ *Schwierige Texte lesen, pp. 72–73*

3 Keep the tips in the Skills Training box on page 17 in mind whilst you read the following article by neuroscientist Dan Barnett.

'Tidy your room!': a teenager's guide to arguing with your parents

So, you're a teenager [...]. You probably have lots on your mind, and are feeling pretty stressed thanks to all the expectations and demands you have to deal with. Then there are the drastic and chaotic changes occurring in your body and brain.

But at least you can rely on your parents to see things your way, to support your decisions, no matter what. Right? In fact, your teens are usually when you argue with your parents more than ever.

[...] So why is it so difficult? Much of it is, of course, down to biology, specifically the differences between your developing brain and your parents' more rigid ones. But it's not hopeless: there are things you can do to get along better. Here are a few of the arguments you might typically have with your parents – and how best to deal with them.

'Get up! You're missing the best part of the day'
Finding it a struggle to get out of bed in the morning? Do you also stay up late at night? Most teens do – but parents rarely approve of this, accusing you of laziness.

The good news is that you're not lazy. Far from it. Those biological changes you're undergoing can play havoc with typical sleeping patterns, and while adults usually start feeling sleepy at around 10pm, studies suggest that for teens it's more like 1am. [...]

Also, you need more sleep because your brain is developing more and working harder. While eight hours' sleep may be enough for adults, you might need nine, or more. [...]

Sadly, school and work start when they start, so opportunities for sleeping in are restricted. But try explaining some of these biological facts to your parents, and emphasising that insufficient sleep can affect your school work by obstructing learning and memory, for instance. They may be more willing to let you have those weekend lie-ins.

You can also help yourself. Regular exercise makes it easier to get to sleep. And after the early evening, try avoiding stimulating activities such as video games, social media and knocking back energy drinks – these can keep your brain awake even longer.

'Stop being so dramatic about everything'
Has there ever been something you think is vitally important, like being at a certain party, [...] but when you explain this to your parents they just look confused? [...]

It's not that your mum and dad are choosing not to feel the same as you. [...] They can't. Their brains aren't wired that way.

Your teenage brain is constantly maturing, but not every part matures at the same rate. Those that produce emotional responses mature quickly, so they are operating at peak performance for much of your teens. But the more logical parts of your brain that keep your emotions under control? They aren't fully ready until your mid-20s.

---

to **tidy sth** *etw aufräumen*
to argue with sb *sich mit jdm streiten*
2 **demand** *Anspruch, Forderung*
5 **no matter what** *was auch (immer) passiert*
8 **rigid** *starr*
13 **sb finds sth a struggle** *jdm fällt etw (sehr) schwer*
14 to **approve of sth** *etw gutheißen*
14 to **accuse sb of sth** *jdn einer Sache beschuldigen, jdm etw vorwerfen*
14 **laziness** *Faulheit*
15 **lazy** *faul*
16 to **play havoc with sth** *etw komplett durcheinanderbringen*
16 **sleeping pattern** *Schlafrhythmus*
22 to **sleep in** *ausschlafen*
24 to **emphasise** *betonen, hervorheben*
24 **insufficient** *unzureichend*
24 to **affect sth** *sich negativ auf etw auswirken*
24 to **obstruct sth** *etw behindern, etw hemmen*
26 **lie-in** *langes Schlafen, Ausschlafen*
28 **stimulating** *aufputschend*
29 to knock back *(Getränk) hinunterkippen*
35 wired *verkabelt, geschaltet*
36 to **mature** *reifen, sich entwickeln*
38 **peak performance** *Höchstleistung, Hochtouren*

The result is that teens have far more powerful emotional reactions, that require extra effort to keep under control. That's why you are prone to emotional outbursts, and why you get so passionate about stuff that baffles your parents. [...]

Think of emotions as like music: your parents are listening to tunes on the radio while driving the car, but you're standing right next to the speakers at a concert. It's a lot harder for you to ignore the racket. [...]

If something upsets you, try to put off responding until you feel calmer. But also, don't feel you should constantly bottle up your emotions. Any chance you get to vent or scream or punch a pillow, take it. As long as nobody, including yourself, gets hurt.

'My house, my rules!'
A lot of arguments revolve around who does what in the family home. It's not uncommon to experience blazing rows over where to put wet towels, who washes the dishes or messy bedrooms.

Ironically, arguments are often about something that both you and your parents insist is "no big deal", and yet you're both yelling about it. Why? One big factor is how your teenage brain is suddenly responding differently to familiar events.

The parts of your brain that process rewards and pleasure have been updated and overhauled, so what used to make you happy – such as toys and colourful cartoons – no longer does. Simultaneously, the parts of your brain that crave independence and control, as well as novelty, are being ramped up, meaning you're driven to do things your way, on your terms, and seek out new experiences.

Meanwhile, your parents have just spent more than a decade providing and caring for a small child who depended on them entirely. That's how they understand your relationship. But now, your changing brain is throwing all that out of the window. [...]

Some research suggests that these arguments can be a good thing, helping everyone reach a newfound understanding much faster – so long as they're not just about the negatives. [...]

'So, how was school?'
Parents often complain that their teenagers are closed off and reluctant to talk to them about school. Can anyone blame you? School is a huge part of your life. You're there all the time, absorbing knowledge constantly, to pass exams you'd rather not do on subjects you're not bothered about, [...]

Then there are all the social pressures. Never is the human brain more sensitive to approval and respect than during your teenage years, so being at school and surrounded by hundreds of your friends (and enemies) is exhausting and stressful.

Come the end of the day, you just want to forget about school. But, no, here come your parents with questions, nagging and reminders.

Actually, one solution is to give in and just tell them something – anything – about your day. Opening up about issues can take the edge off them. But do it when you're ready, on your terms, not the moment they demand – usually when you've just walked through the door. [...]

(981 words) From: *Why Your Parents Are Driving You Up the Wall and What to Do about It*, by Dean Burnett

42 to **be prone to sth** *zu etw neigen*
43 **passionate** *leidenschaftlich, begeistert*
43 to **baffle sb** *jdn vor ein Rätsel stellen*
46 **racket** *Lärm, Krach*
47 to **put sth off** *etw (auf später) verschieben*
48 to **bottle sth up** *etw unterdrücken*
49 to vent *Dampf ablassen*
52 to **revolve around sth** *sich um etw drehen*
53 **row** *Streit*
54 **messy** *unordentlich, unaufgeräumt*
57 **familiar** *bekannt*
58 **reward** *Belohnung*
58 **pleasure** *Vergnügen*
59 to **overhaul sth** *etw überholen, etw neu instandsetzen*
60 **simultaneously** *gleichzeitig, zur selben Zeit*
60 to **crave sth** *sich nach etw sehnen*
61 **novelty** *Neuartigkeit, Abwechslung*
61 to ramp sth up *etw intensivieren, etw hochfahren*
62 **on sb's terms** *zu jds Bedingungen*
63 **to provide for sb** *für jdn sorgen*
74 **sb isn't bothered about sth** *jdm ist etw (völlig) egal*
75 to **be sensitive to sth** *auf etw empfindlich reagieren, empfänglich für etw sein*
76 **approval** *Anerkennung*
79 **nagging** *Genörgel, Gemeckere*
81 to **take off the edge** *die Schärfe nehmen*
82 to **demand** *fordern*

Working with the text

4 Copy and complete the diagram based on information from the text.

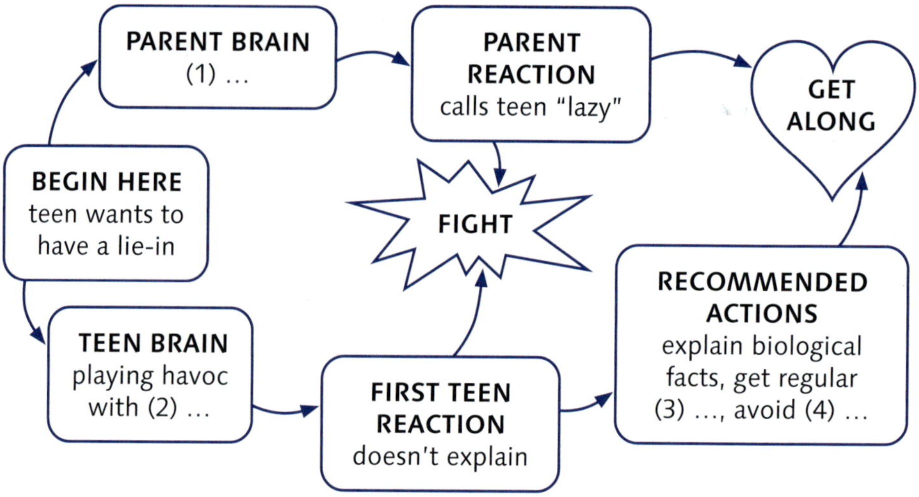

Writing

Exam preparation

S ▸ *Eine Aufgabe zum integrierten Leseverstehen bearbeiten*, p. 76

S ▸ *Operatoren*, pp. 33–34

5 Outline the typical reasons for conflicts between parents and children given in the text.

Speaking

How to say or write it

- I think you should …
- It often helps to …
- Try (not) to …
- We recommend you …
- One useful tip is to …
- It's (not) a good idea to …

6 Discuss with a partner whether you think the text offers good advice. Would it work in your family?

7 Look back at the list(s) you made in exercise 2 on page 17. What advice would you give in these situations?

Working with words

Skills training: Learning new vocabulary

Learning a word depends on two things: 1) the number of times you see or hear the word, and 2) the attention you give to the word.

This means it's a good idea to read a lot. You should choose interesting texts that are not too difficult. When reading, it's a very good idea to try to guess the meaning of words you don't know. On the other hand, looking up words can be good if this helps you pay attention to them more.

D ▸ More practice, p. 148

8 Find the opposite of these words and expressions from lines 57–77 of the text on pages 18–19.

1 unknown
2 punishment
3 pain
4 at different times
5 partially
5 open, accessible
7 ready, eager
8 occasionally
9 friend
10 energizing

Put all the words and phrases into three categories: *positive*, *negative* and *neutral*.

Looking at language

9 Sort the excerpts (1–7) from the article on pages 18–19 into one of two categories.

a *permanent* states, actions and processes **b** *temporary* states, actions and processes

1 ... you're not lazy. (l. 15)
2 ... while adults usually start feeling sleepy at around 10pm, ... for teens it's more like 1am. (ll. 16–18)
3 ... your parents are listening to tunes on the radio while driving the car, but you're standing right next to the speakers at a concert. (ll. 44–45)
4 ... your teenage brain is suddenly responding differently to familiar events. (l. 57)
5 The parts of your brain that crave independence and control, as well as novelty, are being ramped up (ll. 60–61)
6 But now, your changing brain is throwing all that out of the window. (l. 65)
7 Parents often complain that their teenagers are closed off and reluctant to talk to them about school. (ll.71–72)

Which present tense is used for category a, and which for category b?

Remember: Talking about the present

The verb *have* is often used in the simple present, even if it describes a temporary state.

So, you're a teenager [...]. You probably ***have*** *lots on your mind, and* ***are feeling*** *pretty stressed.* (ll. 1–2)

However, *have* can be used in the present progressive in expressions like *have a meal* or *have a good time*.

10 In each sentence, translate the verbs into the simple present or the present progressive. Watch out for the exception with *have* (see Remember box).

G ▸ Simple present, p. 163; present progressive, p. 163

D ▸ More practice, p. 148

Example: Ich liebe meine Eltern, aber gerade kommen wir nicht so gut miteinander aus.
I ***love*** *my parents, but we****'re not getting along*** *right now.*

1 Sein Sohn geht zurzeit sehr spät ins Bett, und Jugendliche brauchen viel Schlaf.
2 Im Moment streitet sich Jamie selten mit seinen Eltern, aber ihr Verhältnis ist grundsätzlich schwierig. (grundsätzlich ▸ *basically*)
3 Lärm stresst meine Großeltern, weshalb ich jetzt die Musik leiser mache. (weshalb ▸ *which is why*)
4 Ich habe gerade keinen schönen Urlaub mit euch, weil ihr mich andauernd kritisiert.
5 Ich rede nicht gern über die Schule, aber wir haben gerade ein Problem zu lösen.

11 Write an article for your school magazine comparing your personal experience with the neuroscientist's comments and advice. Refer to the text and the cartoon on page 17.

Exam preparation

S ▸ *Eine kreative Schreibaufgabe bearbeiten*, pp. 41–42

Section D Gap years

Warm-up

1 Find someone in your class who …

- would like to travel around the world.
- knows what they want to do after they leave school.
- doesn't know what they want to do after they leave school.
- has done some volunteer work.
- thinks it's a good idea to earn some money before university.

Working with the text

Skills training: Collecting arguments for an argumentative writing task

In this Section you'll learn many pros and cons of doing a gap year after leaving school. Collect the pros in one list and the cons in another, and decide what are the strongest arguments for and against gap years. You'll use this preparation for a writing exercise on page 25.

08

2 Read the webpage about taking a gap year. As you read, write down notes about the advantages and disadvantages of taking a gap year.

Plan a gap year to remember with the experts!

Our years of experience will help you have an unforgettable year. If you're thinking about taking a year out but don't know what to do, or if you're overwhelmed by the hundreds of options, we can help. Our fabulous range of adventures and experiences can give you the inspiration you need for a fantastic year. Want a year in Australia? Fancy combining the fabulous beaches and jungles with the exotic cities of Thailand? Something completely different? No problem. We've been there, done it and got the T-shirt!

What to do in a gap year

If you've only just started to look into the possibility of taking a gap year, you'll find there's a huge number of options out there. Research is crucial to ensure that your experience is everything you've ever hoped for – and more! Here are some ideas for your gap year.

Animal care

These projects are popular with those interested in a career working with animals. The programmes typically involve working in shelters, surgeries and centres alongside vets and rehabilitation staff. You might care for elephants and monkeys in Malaysia, rescue street animals such as dogs and donkeys in India, or volunteer to work with lions and giraffes in South Africa. One thing is sure: you'll gain experience of local wildlife and learn valuable skills from resident professionals.

Care and community

Care volunteering includes social and youth work, childcare, au-pairing and spending time in schools and orphanages. Community work covers everything from agriculture to building projects where you might dig a well or build a school in an African village. Whatever you do, you will make a difference to someone else's life, and you'll gain pride and self-sufficiency.

2 to **overwhelm sb** *jdn überwältigen*
3 **option** *Möglichkeit*
4 to **fancy sth** *auf etw Lust haben*
9 **crucial** *entscheidend*
14 **(animal) shelter** *Tierheim*
14 **surgery** *Arztpraxis*
20 **resident** *ortsansässig, vor Ort*
24 **orphanage** *Waisenhaus, Kinderheim*
25 to **dig a well** *einen Brunnen bohren/graben*
27 to **make a difference** *etwas bewirken*
28 **pride** *Stolz*
28 **self-sufficiency** *Eigenständigkeit*

Conservation
Are you passionate about saving the planet? If so, then conservation work is for you. A conservation project will give you the chance to work with endangered wildlife, protect rainforests or conserve marine life, all while learning about the issues affecting local communities.

Cultural programmes
For those with a love of culture – particularly art, dance, drama or music – there's a special gap year for you. Indeed, you can select from a number of travel destinations and get involved in pursuits such as teaching arts and crafts to young women, or drama and music to children in underprivileged communities.

Sports and adventure travel
If you're into sports and fitness, how does coaching football in Ghana, Nepal or New Zealand sound? Alternatively, adventure thrill-seekers can take on a trekking expedition, safari or an adrenalin challenge. You'll gain teamwork and leadership skills while testing your commitment capabilities.

Travel
Explore the world, discover new cultures, and learn how to live independently – all at the same time! You could go backpacking across South East Asia, InterRail through Europe, buy a round-the-world plane ticket, or just enjoy the easy life on a tropical beach. You decide!

(484 words)

[29] **conservation** *Naturschutz, Umweltschutz*

[30] **to be passionate about sth** *sich (leidenschaftlich) für etw begeistern*

[33] **to conserve sth** *etw erhalten, etw schützen*

[39] **pursuit** *Aktivität, Beschäftigung*

[45] **thrill** *Nervenkitzel*

3 **Read the nine statements and say whether they are true or false. Correct the false sentences to make them true.**

1. The text advertises services.
2. Gap years can be done spontaneously, without much planning.
3. The proposal for an animal-care gap year involves taking care of house pets.
4. Care work may involve working with children.
5. Social problems are relevant to wildlife conservation.
6. In a cultural-programmes gap year, you will attend classes at your destination to learn about art, dance, etc.
7. The main reason for doing a sports-and-adventure-travel gap year is to increase your physical fitness.
8. The text cautions against expensive trips.
9. The text suggests you can also be lazy in a gap year.

to **caution sb against sth** *jdn vor etw warnen*

4 Match each of the FAQs (Frequently Asked Questions) to the correct answers.

Plan a gap year to remember with the experts!

FAQ

1 How common are gap years?
2 I don't know what I want to study. Is a gap year for me?
3 Isn't it a lot of work to plan and organize a gap year?
4 Will I be able to deal with my studies afterwards?
5 Won't universities and future employers think I was lazy for taking a year off?
6 I am so attached to my family. Do I have to leave them?
7 This sounds expensive! How can I afford it?

a How much it costs depends on what you do. After all, it's possible to spend a fortune jetting around and staying in hotels! So you'll have to budget and be careful not to run out of money. However, there are inexpensive options such as travelling by bus and staying in simple accommodation. Most gap years involve work of some kind, and some jobs also offer free board and lodgings or even pay you money. Other people actually do gap years to save up money, so that it won't be so tight at uni.

b Maybe! In a gap year, you can explore your interests, mature a lot, and increase your motivation to study. This may be better than studying something you're not committed to.

c This is an understandable concern, as travelling for long periods of time can be uncomfortable, with emotional challenges. It's certainly possible to do a gap year close to home, but one advantage of travelling is that you learn to be independent.

d According to the University College and Admissions Service in the UK, approximately 30,000 British students each year choose to defer entry to university.

e Probably not. Many even view taking a year out as an asset. However, if you don't incorporate any constructive activities into your year, they may in fact disapprove of your choice to just "goof around".

f In a word, yes. You don't want to spend a year floundering aimlessly! You'll want to explore several options, and you'll have to be persistent to ensure you get all the information you need.

g This is a real concern, as some people fall in love with their new homes and don't want to return to the life they had planned. Some have trouble re-adjusting to life in education, especially when studying complex theoretical subjects like maths or physics.

inexpensive *billig*
accommodation *Unterkunft, Bleibe*
free board and lodging(s) *freie Kost und Logis*
tight *(Geld:) knapp*
to **be committed to sth** *von etw überzeugt sein*
to defer sth *etw verschieben, etw aussetzen*
asset *Pluspunkt, Vorteil*
to **incorporate sth into sth** *etw in etw einbinden, etw in etw aufnehmen*
to **disapprove of sth** *etw missbilligen, etw ablehnen*
to goof around *(tatenlos) herumhängen*
to flounder aimlessly *ziellos herumwursteln*
persistent *beharrlich, hartnäckig*

Listening

Remember
Continue collecting pros and cons of gap years for your argumentative writing task.

5 **Before you do the listening task, solve this puzzle.**
Alice, Ben, Cindy and Dan are four students. They each had a gap year doing different things.

1

building a school in Uganda

2

working on a vineyard in Australia

3

helping a vet treat injured elephants in India

4

enjoying beach life in Thailand

The person who went to Australia was a man. Alice worked, but not in Africa or Australia. The person who went to Thailand didn't want to work. Cindy worked, but not with animals. It was a woman who helped build a school in Africa. Ben didn't spend time on the beach.

Who did what?

Listen to the audio from exercise 6 to get the solution.

Skills training: Dealing with multiple matching tasks

The challenge with this task is listening and reading at the same time, so read the entire task as thoroughly as you can before you listen to the audio. Identify key words in the possible answers.

6 **Listen to Alice, Ben, Cindy and Dan talk about their gap years. Match each speaker (1–4) with one of the opinions (a–e). For each speaker there is only one correct answer. There is one more opinion than you need.**

Exam preparation

09

Opinions: Gap years ...

a are great for networking.
b are very difficult to finance.
c can be risky if you have nothing to do.
d are full of intercultural difficulties if you go abroad.
e are only good if you get experience relevant to the profession you want to pursue.

Copy and complete the table.

Speaker	1 Alice	2 Ben	3 Cindy	4 Dan
Opinion				

Writing

7 **Replace the *italicized* expressions in these sentences with words and phrases from the box to make the arguments more interesting or precise.**

an asset | crucial | disapprove | discover | fall in love with | flounder aimlessly | fortune | gain | however | issues | become more mature | select | valuable | view

1 You could end up spending a *lot of money*.
2 You can *get very good* skills and also *grow up*.
3 Some people *really like* their gap-year locations.
4 You can *find* new cultures and *things* affecting local communities.
5 It is not good just to *do stupid things*. Later on, potential employers may *think this was bad*.
6 *But* some employers *take* candidates who have done gap years, because they *think this is something good to have*.

S ▸ *Eine argumentierende/bewertende Schreibaufgabe bearbeiten*, p. 35–40

8 **Assess the pros and cons of taking a gap year.**

Exam preparation

Scan this page with the PagePlayer app to get a helpful checklist for this writing task.

Section E Educational possibilities

Warm-up

1 Read the quotations about education. Pick one and explain how you can relate to it.

"Let us pick up our books and our pens [...] They are our most powerful weapons. One child, one teacher, one book and one pen can change the world." – *Malala Yousafzai, Pakistani activist for female education (1997–)*

"The most important thing we learn at school is the fact that the most important things can't be learned at school." – Haruki Murakami, Japanese writer (1949–)

"Education is for improving the lives of others and for leaving your community and world better than you found it." – Marian Wright Edelman, American activist for children (1939–)

"Education is the passport to the future, for tomorrow belongs to those who prepare for it today." – Malcolm X, American human rights activist (1925–1965)

"Educating the mind without educating the heart is no education at all." – Aristotle, Greek philosopher (385–323 BC)

Working with the text

Good to know

The film *An Education* stars Carey Mulligan as 16-year-old Jenny, a smart schoolgirl who falls in love with a wealthy, older man called David, played by Peter Sarsgaard. The film is set in 1961, but was produced in 2009. It was nominated for three Academy Awards.

2 Read Scene 3 from the screenplay *An Education*. This is near the beginning of the film, before Jenny's boyfriend David enters the story. What is her life like? How does she spend her time, and what is her goal?

AN EDUCATION

3. Interior. Jenny's house – day

Title: TWICKENHAM LONDON 1961

Jenny, her mother and father are finishing Sunday lunch. Jenny's father Jack is in his forties; Marjorie, her mother, is slightly younger than Jack, but every bit as middle aged. The food is grey and brown, in keeping with the colour scheme of the house. [...]

JENNY

I've got an English essay to do by tomorrow morning.

JACK

Right. So, the only sound I want to hear coming through the ceiling this afternoon, is the sound of sweat dripping onto textbooks.

JENNY

Cello?

JACK

No cello.

screenplay *Drehbuch*
1 interior *innen*
5 in keeping with sth *einer Sache entsprechend, wie etw*
5 colour scheme *Farbgebung*
10 **sweat** *Schweiß*
10 to **drip** *tropfen*

JENNY

I thought we agreed that cello was my interest or hobby.

JACK

Well, it already is your interest or hobby. So when they ask you at the Oxford interview 'What is your interest or hobby?', you can say, 'the cello' and you wouldn't be lying. But you don't have to practise a hobby. A hobby is a hobby.

JENNY

Can I stop going to the youth orchestra, then?

JACK

No, no, no. The youth orchestra's a good thing. Shows you're a joiner-inner.

JENNY

Ah. Yes. But. I've already joined in. So now I can stop.

JACK

No, no. Well, that just shows the opposite, don't you see? That shows you're a rebel. They don't want that at Oxford.

JENNY

No. They don't want people who think for themselves.

JACK

(missing the sarcasm [...])

Course they don't.

Carey Mulligan as Jenny

19 **interview** *Vorstellungsgespräch*

25 a joiner-inner *(etwa:) ein guter Teamplayer*

27 to **join in** *(bei etw) mitmachen, (Verein usw.) beitreten*

30 **rebel** *Rebell/in*

34 to **miss sth** *etw nicht mitbekommen*

34 **sarcasm** *Sarkasmus*

3 What is the conflict between Jenny and Jack in Scene 3?

4 What would you say or do in Jenny's situation?

D ▸ More help, p. 149

5 Read Scene 76. How have Jenny's plans changed since the beginning of the film?

76. Interior. Headmistress's office – day.

HEADMISTRESS

How far advanced are these ridiculous plans? Have you set a date? Have you decided on a church?

JENNY

We won't be getting married in a church. David's Jewish.

The headmistress stares at her, dumbfounded.

HEADMISTRESS

Jewish? He's a Jew? You're aware, I take it, that the Jews killed our Lord?

JENNY

(beginning to feel less intimidated by her surroundings)

And you're aware, I suppose, that our Lord was Jewish?

The Headmistress snorts scornfully.

Emma Thompson as the headmistress

1 **headmistress** *Direktorin*

3 **advanced** *fortgeschritten*

3 **ridiculous** *lächerlich*

7 to **stare at sb** *jdn anstarren*

7 dumbfounded *sprachlos, verblüfft*

11 **intimidated** *eingeschüchtert*

13 to snort scornfully *verächtlich schnauben*

16 **excuse** *Ausrede, Entschuldigung*
16 malicious *böswillig*
17 untruthful *unwahr, verlogen*
28 admission of defeat *Kapitulation*
41 it is just as well *das ist auch gut so*
42 to drop a nuclear bomb *eine Atombombe (ab)werfen*
42 any day now *demnächst*
49 Civil Service *Beamtentum, öffentlicher Dienst*
51 impertinent *unverschämt*
52 to **rehearse sth** *etw proben, etw einstudieren*
53 **point** *Sinn, Zweck*
53 **one day** *eines Tages*

HEADMISTRESS

I suppose *he* told you that. We're all very sorry about what happened during the war. But that's absolutely no excuse for that sort of malicious and untruthful propaganda.

Jenny smiles to herself.

Anyway, I can see you're far more in need of responsible advice than I realised.

The Headmistress moves closer.

Nobody does anything worth doing without a degree.

JENNY

Nobody does anything worth doing with a degree. No woman, anyway.

HEADMISTRESS

So what I do isn't worth doing. Or what Miss Stubbs does, or Mrs Wilson, or any of us here.

Jenny doesn't say anything. The headmistress takes her silence as an admission of defeat.

Because none of us would be here without our degrees, you do realise that, don't you? And yes, of course studying is hard, and boring, and ...

Jenny can't contain herself any longer.

JENNY

Boring!

HEADMISTRESS

I'm sorry?

JENNY

Studying is hard and boring. Teaching is hard and boring. So what you're telling me is to be bored, and then bored, and then finally bored again, but this time for the rest of my life. This whole stupid country is bored. There's no life in it, or colour, or fun. It's probably just as well that the Russians are going to drop a nuclear bomb on us any day now. So my choice is to do something hard and boring, *or* to marry my ... my *Jew* and go to Paris and Rome and listen to jazz and read and eat good food in nice restaurants and have fun. It's not enough to educate us any more, Miss Walters. You've got to tell us why you're doing it.

She has never had to answer this question before.

HEADMISTRESS

It doesn't have to be teaching, you know. There's the Civil Service.

JENNY

I don't wish to be impertinent, Miss Walters. But it is an argument worth rehearsing. You never know. Someone else might want to know the point of it all, one day.

Jenny leaves the office.

6 What is the conflict between Jenny and her headmistress?

7 Based on the screenplay, what has changed since 1961 for 16-year-olds, and what is the same nowadays?

8 Interview a person at least 20 years older than you about their educational options when they were your age. Report back to the class on the following.

- What accomplishments or circumstances provided them with these options?
- Did anything limit their options?
- Do they think their lives would be different if they had been born in Gen Z?
- How do you think things have changed since they were your age?

Looking at language

9 Look at the results of the survey of American high school students. Do you think the results would be the same in your class?

Which of the following best describes what you would like to do after leaving high school?

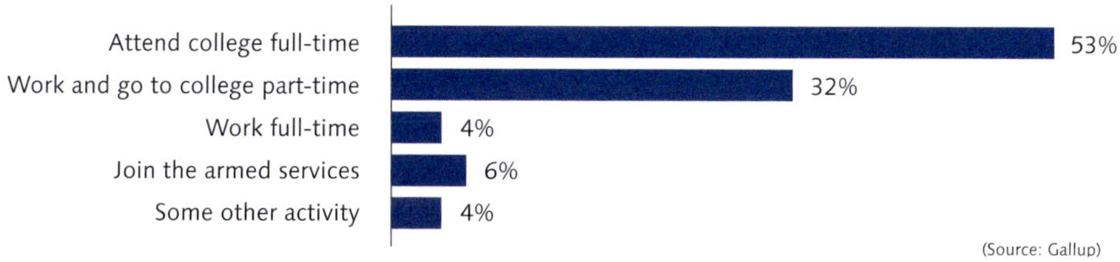

(Source: Gallup)

Remember: Talking about the future

When we name a deadline, we use the preposition ***by*** (not *until*).
*Jenny has an English essay to do **by** tomorrow morning.*

When we make a prediction based on knowledge or previous experience, we usually use ***will/won't***.
*(6 p.m.) If Jenny doesn't start writing now, she **won't** finish in time.*

Signal words for ***will/won't*** include *think*, *hope*, *expect*, *probably*.

When we predict something will happen soon based on a clear sign, we usually use ***(not) going to***.
*(10 p.m.) Jenny's written nothing! There's no way she**'s going to** finish in time.*

10 Read the Remember box, then complete these sentences with *will*, *won't* and *(not) going to*.

G ▸ The future, p. 166

1 It's official: I'm hired! I ... work full-time, starting Monday.
2 We ... probably work and go to college part-timeto earn some extra money.
3 No, of course Jane .... join the armed forces. She's in poor health, and she's not a citizen of this country.
4 No, I'm afraid they ... be able to attend college full-time. It's too late to apply now.
5 College? Work? Military? In my opinion, none of these are for you. I think you ... do some other activity.

How to say or write it

Two of us think they'll …

Three people are sure they're going to …, because …

He's (not) going to …

The majority of us will probably / probably won't …

11 In a group, share your own personal responses to the survey question in exercise 9, then report to the class.

Skills training: Intercultural awareness

School systems vary from country to country, especially when it comes to the school leaving qualifications *(Abschlüsse)*. If you told someone from another country that you had the *Abitur* you would probably need to explain it. To someone from North America you could say, "It's a bit higher than a high school diploma"; in the UK, "It's comparable to A levels".

Working with the text

10

[4] **comparable (to sth)** *vergleichbar (mit etw)*
[9] torn *zwiegespalten*
[11] to **postpone sth** *etw vertagen, etw verschieben*
[16] **breadth** *Breite*
[16] **depth** *Tiefe*
[17] a mixed bag *eine bunte Mischung*
[18] **fairness** *Gerechtigkeit*
[19] **similarly** *ebenso, in gleicher Weise*
[21] **marking** *Benotung*
[21] **harsh** *streng, rigoros*
[21] nationally *landesweit, bundesweit*
[23] **bright** *gescheit, intelligent*
[33] required subject *Pflichtfach*

A levels vs the *Abitur* – two interviews

Miriame Kaba, teacher in Freiburg, Germany

What is the *Abitur*?
The *Abitur* is the higher school-leaving qualification in Germany, and it's comparable to A levels in Great Britain. You can only study at university if you have the *Abitur*, and to get the *Abitur* you have to take a series of exams at the end of the 13th grade.

What's your opinion of the *Abitur*?
Well, I'm a bit torn about the wide range of topics the students have to study. On the one hand, I feel it's important for them to try lots of different things before they decide what their careers will be, and our programme allows them to postpone this decision until after they leave school and keep their options open. On the other hand, occasionally I have a student who has a very strong interest in a specific profession, and the programme doesn't allow them to specialize in this. Luckily, vocational grammar schools are an option that offer a good compromise between breadth and depth.

The exams are also a mixed bag. Having both written and oral exams offers variety, but also helps students with different learning preferences, which ensures fairness. Similarly, I think it's good that students have a choice of questions to answer when it comes to the actual exam, so they can focus on their strengths and preferences.

However, I think the marking is quite harsh: nationally, less than 5% of students get the best possible grade. That compares badly with other countries and might give the impression that our students are not as bright, which is just not true. In addition, the exams are long – can anyone really concentrate fully for three hours, especially in a high-stress situation like an exam?

Mark Garner, teacher in Birmingham, England

What are A levels?
"A level" is short for "advanced level", and it's the school-leaving qualification you need here to get into a university. Students spend two years at secondary school or sixth form college studying for their A level exams, generally from the age of 16 to 18. Most students choose three subjects, occasionally four, from a long list, depending on what interests them. There are no required subjects.

What's your opinion of A levels?
Well, I like the fact that students have the chance to follow personal interests in depth. That simply isn't possible if you have to study 6–10 subjects, which is what happens in some educational systems in other countries. When our students get to university, they are often already quite specialized in the subject(s) they have chosen to study, so the level is generally quite high. One consequence of this is that the drop-out rate from university is relatively low in the UK. I've heard it can be pretty high in other countries.

Does anything worry you about A levels?
Of course, I'm not saying that A levels are perfect or that they suit everyone. They are very academic: you can't get an A level in many vocational subjects – there are other pathways for that. And some people would argue, correctly in my opinion, that not all teenagers are ready to make good choices at the age of 15 or 16 about what three or four subjects to study. Often they'll go with their friends, or choose what they find easiest, not what interests them, or what could be useful in the future.

To do some degrees you need to have particular A levels. For example, you can't study chemistry at university if your A levels are in art, Spanish and economics! So when you choose your A levels, you will be ruling out some university options.
(615 words)

35 **in depth** *gründlich, eingehend*
39 **level** *Niveau*
40 drop-out rate *Abbrecherquote*
45 pathway *Weg*
52 to **rule sth out** *etw ausschließen, etw unmöglich machen*

12 With a partner, make a list of similarities between the *Abitur* and A levels, and a list of differences. Include the following points.

- what the exams qualify you for
- preparation time and age when finished
- subjects
- flexibility or individualization
- possible disadvantages compared to other countries

13 What's your opinion of A levels? Tell your partner whether you would prefer them to the *Abitur* and why.

Writing

14 Give your opinion of the *Abitur* and A levels.

Exam preparation

S ▸ *Eine argumentierende/bewertende Schreibaufgabe bearbeiten,* pp. 35–40

Speaking

15 Work in groups of six. You are English time travellers from 1961 (groovy, man!) and you have just arrived in modern-day Germany. Use the information in partner files to figure out or explain the new educational options.

Partner A, you are a time traveller. Turn to page 157.
Partner B, you are an expert on apprenticeships. Turn to page 158.
Partner C, you are an expert on (technical) colleges. Turn to page 159.
Partner D, you are an expert on internships. Turn to page 160.
Partner E, you are an expert on universities. Turn to page 161.
Partner F, you are an expert on voluntary social service years. Turn to page 162.

Project Creating short plays

to rehearse *proben, einstudieren*
to perform sth *etw aufführen, etw spielen*
play *Theaterstück*
director *Regisseur/in*

Working in small groups, you are going to write, rehearse, and perform a short play. Once you have formed your group, choose a director who will make decisions when the group cannot agree. Then choose a subject from the options below, or make up your own.

protagonist *Hauptfigur*
to lose one's mind *den Verstand verlieren*
liveable *lebenswert*

Whatever works for you
Life is so stressful for our protagonists that they almost lose their minds. Then they find an unusual hobby that makes life liveable again.

to dare to do sth *es wagen, etw zu tun*

The kids will never know
In this play, Mum and Dad dare to do something forbidden. Of course the kids find out all about it.

from hell *schrecklich, furchtbar*

Gap year from hell
Some recent graduates meet in a foreign country. They're taking a year off from school. What could possibly go wrong?

act *(Theaterstück:) Akt*
audience *Publikum, Zuschauer pl*
rising action *Steigerung (der Handlung)*
to encounter sth *auf etw treffen, auf etw stoßen*
obstacle *Hindernis*
climax *Höhepunkt*
falling action *Verlangsamung (der Handlung)*
resolution *Lösung (der Handlung)*

Your play should follow a five-act format.

Act 1: Exposition	The audience learns the time, place and protagonists. A conflict is introduced.
Act 2: Rising action	The protagonists begin to encounter obstacles, which they deal with in different ways.
Act 3: Climax	Things start to go seriously wrong, but there is no turning back for the protagonists.
Act 4: Falling action	This is a brief sequence where we discover how the protagonists will meet their challenge.
Act 5: Resolution	You can choose to have a happy or a tragic ending. It can be a surprise, but it must make sense.

story outline *Szenario*
purpose *Zweck, Absicht*

Step 1
Write a story outline. This is a short description of what should happen in each scene (you do not need to write down every word the actors are going to say). For at least one scene, find some background music or a sound effect (e.g. played from a mobile phone). The purpose of the outline is to make sure you follow a clear story.

Step 2
Decide who should play which role(s). Everyone must have at least one role, and everyone must speak.

expression *Ausdruck*

Step 3
Rehearse your play several times. This is an opportunity to practice speaking clearly and with expression.

script *(Theaterstück:) Text, Textbuch*

Step 4
Present your play to the class (without reading from an outline or script).

Operatoren

Ein Operator ist ein Verb in einer Arbeitsanweisung, das Ihnen exakt vorgibt, wie Sie die Aufgabe zu bearbeiten haben. Daher ist es wichtig, dass Sie die gängigen Operatoren kennen und sich ihre Bedeutung genau einprägen.

In der Oberstufe begegnen Ihnen u.a. folgende typische Operatoren, die jeweils verschiedene sogenannte Anforderungsbereiche abdecken. Die fett gedruckten Beispiele beziehen sich auf Lesetexte im Buch.

Gut zu wissen

Der Anteil Ihrer Eigenleistung steigert sich von Anforderungsbereich zu Anforderungsbereich.

Anforderungsbereich I *Reproduktion* (Wiedergabe von vorgelegten Materialien)

Anforderungsbereich II *Reorganisation und Transfer* (Erklären, Verarbeiten und Darstellen bekannter Sachverhalte anhand einer neuen Fragestellung)

Anforderungsbereich III *Reflexion und Problemlösung* (selbstständiges Erarbeiten von Lösungen, Deutungen, Begründungen)

Anforderungsbereich I + II

S ▸ Integriertes Leseverstehen, S.76

Operator	Beispiele	Was von Ihnen erwartet wird
gelenkte Zusammenfassung		
outline darstellen	• *Outline the information given by the author on …* • *Outline the arguments for and against …* ***Outline the typical reasons for conflicts between parents and children given in the text. (p. 20)***	Aspekte auf das Wesentliche reduziert darstellen
describe beschreiben	• *Describe … as depicted in …* ***Describe Mirame Kaba's opinion of the Abitur in the text on p. 30.***	Aspekte präzise und strukturiert beschreiben
point out aufzeigen	• *Point out the author's ideas/opinion on …* ***Point out what gets on Mahmood's nerves at home. (p. 113)***	zentrale Aspekte herausfiltern
state angeben	• *State the reasons/information the author gives for/on …* ***State the main reasons why many people think the US voting system needs to be reformed. Illustrate your text with examples. (p. 89)***	dargestellte Aspekte klar herausarbeiten
illustrate veranschau-lichen	• *Illustrate the way in which … differs from …* ***Summarize the author's experience with the internet and illustrate your text with examples. (p. 123)***	Aspekte mit Hilfe von Textbelegen veranschaulichen
traditionelle Zusammenfassung		
summarize zusammen-fassen	• *Summarize the (main points of the) article.* • *Sum up the text.* ***Summarize the information given in the article about Seattle. (p. 52)*** ***Summarize the main points of the blog entry. (p. 114)***	die wichtigsten Punkte zu einer Fragestellung zusammenfassen

S ▸ Textanalyse, S. 138–143

Anforderungsbereich II

Operator	Beispiele	Was von Ihnen erwartet wird
analyse analysieren	• *Analyse/Examine how the reader's interest in the text is aroused by its content and structure.* • *Analyse/Examine how the author tries to convince the reader of his/her point of view on the issue.* • *Analyse/Examine to what extent the picture/cartoon/graph relates to the text.* ***Examine how the author presents his opinion and analyse the means used to convince the reader of his position. (p. 113)*** ***Examine how the author presents his opinion and analyse the means used to convince the reader of his position. Refer to the article and the picture and the cartoon above it. (p. 125)***	Aspekte ausführlich und mit Hilfe von Fachbegriffen beschreiben und ihre Funktion im Hinblick auf die beabsichtigte Aussage des Texts erklären
examine untersuchen		

S ▸ *Eine argumentierende/ bewertende Schreibaufgabe bearbeiten,* S. 35–40

Anforderungsbereich III

Operator	Beispiele	Was von Ihnen erwartet wird
comment on Stellung nehmen zu	• *Comment on / Give your opinion of the writer's view on …* ***Would you like to be friends with Joseph? Comment on this question. (p. 11)*** ***Comment on Harry and Meghan's decision to leave the royal family. (p. 101)*** ***Give your opinion of the* Abitur *and A levels. (p. 31)***	die eigene Meinung strukturiert und mit Argumenten und Beispielen versehen darstellen
give your opinion die eigene Meinung äußern		
assess beurteilen	• *Assess/Evaluate the impact/development/success of …* ***Assess the pros and cons of taking a gap year. (p. 25)***	nach Untersuchung aller Vor- und Nachteile zu einer sorgfältig abgewogenen Meinung gelangen
evaluate einschätzen, bewerten		
discuss erörtern	• *Discuss the advantages/chances and disadvantages/risks of …* • *Discuss whether … is a blessing or a curse.* ***Discuss the benefits and downsides of using social media for political activism. (p. 121)***	Beleuchten eines komplexen Themas aus unterschiedlichen Blickwinkeln mit den jeweiligen Vor- und Nachteilen
weigh the pros and cons Für und Wider abwägen	• *Weigh the pros and cons of …* ***Weigh the pros and cons of living in a city vs living in the countryside. (p. 65)***	

Eine argumentierende bzw. bewertende Schreibaufgabe bearbeiten

Bei der **argumentierenden Schreibaufgabe** geht es darum, das Für und Wider eines Sachverhalts sachlich abzuwägen und zu einem begründeten Sach- bzw. Werturteil zu kommen. Grundsätzlich handelt es sich dabei um ein Thema, das kontrovers diskutiert werden kann, oder um eine Entscheidungsfrage. Diese Textsorte nennt sich **dialektische Erörterung**.

Dialektik: Die Kunst der Rede und Gegenrede.

Beispielaufgabe:

Discuss the pros and cons of taking a gap year.

Bei der rein **bewertenden Schreibaufgabe** hingegen steht als Textsorte eine begründete persönliche **Stellungnahme** auf der Grundlage eines Sachverhalts oder einer These im Mittelpunkt des Schreibauftrags.

Gut zu wissen

Im **Abitur** haben Sie die Wahl zwischen einer **argumentierenden/ bewertenden** und einer kreativen **Schreibaufgabe**.

Planen

Schritt 1: Analyse

Lesen Sie sich die Aufgabenstellung mehrmals durch und analysieren Sie, ob es sich um eine **argumentierende** oder eine **bewertende** Schreibaufgabe handelt.

Sie erkennen die jeweilige Textsorte vor allem an den sogenannten **Operatoren**, also an Verben, die Ihnen signalisieren, wie man eine Aufgabe bearbeiten soll.

S ▸ Operatoren, S. 33–34

Operator	Beispiele	Vorgehen
Stellungnahme (bewertende Schreibaufgabe)		
comment on / give your opinion	*Comment on the influence a gap year has on young people.*	Formulieren Sie klar Ihren Standpunkt (für – gegen – unentschieden) und begründen Sie ihn ausführlich mit Argumenten.
Erörterung (argumentierende Schreibaufgabe)		
discuss/weigh the pros and cons	*Discuss the pros and cons of taking a gap year.*	Analysieren und wägen Sie detailliert konträre Haltungen oder Aspekte gegeneinander ab und kommen Sie zu einer plausiblen Schlussfolgerung.
evaluate/assess	*Evaluate the pros and cons of taking a gap year.*	Formulieren Sie Ihre Meinung nach sorgfältiger Darstellung und Abwägung gegensätzlicher Argumente.

Weitere Hilfestellung zum Verfassen einer **Stellungnahme** finden Sie in der PagePlayer-App.

Gut zu wissen

Bei '***discuss***' ist eine eigene Meinung nicht zwingend erforderlich.

HINWEIS: Auf den folgenden Seiten wird eine dialektische Erörterung, also eine **argumentierende Schreibaufgabe** gemäß der Aufgabenstellung in der obigen **Beispielaufgabe** im Detail behandelt.

Schritt 2: Brainstorming

Eine Mindmap bietet eine sinnvolle Unterstützung beim Sammeln und Strukturieren von Ideen. Halten Sie dazu die Hauptpunkte *pros (= benefits/advantages)* und *cons (= downsides/disadvantages)* fest, um Argumente zu sammeln.

Übung 1

Übertragen Sie die Mindmap zum Thema *Taking a gap year* in Ihre Unterlagen und vervollständigen diese, indem Sie sämtliche Ideen zu den Hauptpunkten stichwortartig notieren.

▸ Weitere Argumente finden Sie in Topic 1, Section D.

Schritt 3: Aufbau des Hauptteils

Legen Sie die Reihenfolge der Argumente in der Mindmap durch Nummerieren fest. So bestimmen Sie den Aufbau Ihres Textes. Dafür gibt es verschiedene Methoden.

Hinweis: Starten Sie bei beiden Methoden mit jeweils der Position, die Sie selbst **nicht** vertreten. Es ist empfehlenswert, mit dem schwächsten Argument zu beginnen und das stärkste am Schluss zu bringen, da sich das zuletzt Gelesene dem Leser / der Leserin am besten einprägt. Untermauern Sie jedes Argument mit Fakten und Beispielen.

Sanduhr-Methode
1. Einleitung
2. Pro-Argumente
3. Contra-Argumente
4. Schluss

Zick-Zack-Methode
1. Einleitung
2. Argument 1 ➞ Gegenargument 1
3. Argument 2 ➞ Gegenargument 2
4. Argument 3 ➞ Gegenargument 3
5. Schluss

Übung 2

Strukturieren Sie Ihre in Übung 2 gesammelten Argumente.

a) Nehmen Sie dazu ein DIN-A4-Blatt im Querformat und legen Sie drei Spalten mit den folgenden Überschriften an:

Hauptargument	Beispiele	Fakten

b) Führen Sie jeweils drei Pro- und drei Contra-Hauptargumente aus Ihrer Mindmap auf und untermauern diese mit einleuchtenden Beispielen und Fakten.

c) Ordnen Sie Ihre Hauptargumente der Triftigkeit nach und nummerieren Sie sie entsprechend.

d) Entscheiden Sie sich für die Art des Textaufbaus: Sanduhr- oder Zick-Zack-Methode?

▸ Weitere Beispiele und Fakten finden Sie in Topic 1, Section D.

Schreiben

Schritt 4: Einleitung

Generell soll die Einleitung beim Leser Interesse wecken, die Erörterung zu lesen.

Hauptfunktionen sind

1. Vorstellung des Themas durch z. B.
   a) Anekdote
   b) Zitat
   c) provokative Aussage
   d) sachliche Einordnung
2. Überleitung zum Hauptteil durch z. B.
   a) direkte Frage
   b) indirekte Frage
   c) Einladung, weiter zu lesen

BEISPIELE EINLEITUNG:

1. *The prophet Mohammed said, "Don't tell me how educated you are, tell me how much you have travelled."*

2. *When my friend Maria took her gap year …*

3. *When a person waits a year before starting their career or further education, this is called "taking a gap year".*

4. *Let's face it: Studying is awful; work is even worse.*

BEISPIELE ÜBERLEITUNG:

1. *Let's take a closer look at the issue.*

2. *So what exactly are the pros and cons of gap years?*

3. *At this point, you may be asking yourself what the pros and cons really are.*

Übung 3

1 Ordnen Sie jedes Beispiel (Einleitungen 1–4 und Überleitungen 1–3) einer Funktion (1a–2c) zu.

Schritt 5a: Hauptteil – Themensätze

Jedes Argument erhält einen eigenen Absatz, der mit einem **Themensatz** beginnt. Dieser vermittelt das Thema des jeweiligen Absatzes.

Zur Entfaltung des Themas schließen Sie an den Themasatz eine plausible Erklärung und ein bis zwei Beispiele zur Veranschaulichung an. Fügen Sie, soweit möglich, auch Faktenwissen ein.

Wichtig: Im Hauptteil ist Ihre eigene Meinung tabu. Diese stellen Sie erst im Schlussteil dar.

BEISPIELE EINLEITUNG:

Gap years abroad are an excellent chance to improve your foreign language skills.

The first and foremost reason for taking a gap year is to have fun.

The biggest con of taking a gap year is likely to be financial.

Unfortunately, some people enter into a gap year without a solid plan, and this can result in wasted time.

first and foremost *wichtigste/r/s, Haupt-*

Übung 4a

1 **Ordnen Sie dem folgenden Absatz den korrekten Themensatz zu.**
... Often people in this situation go to university and focus on a subject they have limited interest in, with the consequence that they have to restart their education when they're older. What they should really be doing is trying out new things and getting to know themselves. A gap year can provide these opportunities.
a) *A gap year may be the best option for school-leavers who don't know what they want to do with their lives.*
b) *For adolescents who are very much attached to home and family, a gap year away from home may be the best way for them to mature and gain independence.*

2 **Schreiben Sie für einen der oben aufgeführten Themensatzbeispiele den kompletten Absatz mit Erklärung, Beispielen und Fakten zu Ende.**

Gut zu wissen

Diese Strukturwörter können Sie auch für Präsentationen nutzen.

Schritt 5b: Hauptteil – Strukturwörter

Verdeutlichen Sie Ihre Gesamtargumentation durch **Strukturwörter**. Diese verbinden Ihre Absätze und helfen Ihnen, Ihren Text logisch und nachvollziehbar zu schreiben und somit den roten Faden nicht zu verlieren.

Außerdem geben Strukturwörter beim Lesen eine Richtung vor, sodass der Leser Ihrem Gedankengang leichter folgen kann.

BEISPIELE FÜR STRUKTURWÖRTER:

Argumente gliedern
First, / Second, / Next, / Further, / In addition,

Beispiele anführen
For example / For instance / To illustrate

Vergleiche anstellen
On the one hand / On the other hand / Despite / In spite of / Alternatively, / However,

Begründungen geben
As / Since / The reason for ... is that

Ergebnisse und Konsequenzen aufzeigen
As a result, / Consequently, / For this reason

Ein Fazit ziehen
All in all, / To sum up, / To conclude,

Übung 4b

1 **Übertragen Sie die Kategorien für Strukturwörter spaltenweise mit den jeweiligen Beispielen auf ein DIN-A4-Blatt im Querformat und ergänzen Sie die folgenden Beispiele**

a) *In conclusion then, it's clear that*
b) *Finally,*
c) *Moreover,*
d) *This fact sounds convincing, but*
e) *Besides,*
f) *In brief,*
g) *Therefore,*
h) *On the whole,*
i) *Additionally,*
j) *By contrast*
k) *Let me start with*
l) *On the contrary,*
m) *Lastly,*
n) *To begin with,*
o) *Another point*

2 **Schreiben Sie Ihren Hauptteil. Stellen Sie dabei sicher, dass Sie den Aspekt der Themensätze berücksichtigen und passende Strukturwörter verwenden.**

besides *außerdem*
in brief *kurz gesagt*
by contrast *dagegen, Im Gegensatz dazu*
on the contrary *(ganz) im Gegenteil*

Schritt 6: Schlussteil

Im letzten Absatz ziehen Sie Ihr Fazit. Dies kann die *Pro*-Position oder die *Con*-Position sein oder auch einen Kompromiss darstellen. Sie müssen sich jedoch klar positionieren.

Außerdem empfiehlt es sich, zur Abrundung der Erörterung auf die Einleitung Rückbezug zu nehmen und einen Blick in die Zukunft zu werfen.

Wichtig: Führen Sie im Schlussteil keine neuen Argumente ein, sondern unterstreichen Sie Ihren Standpunkt kurz und knapp.

BEISPIELE:

~~*Everybody has to decide what opinion he or she has.*~~

Weighing up the pros and cons, it becomes clear that ...

The pros clearly outweigh the cons.

Tu sum up, it's very hard to say whether the pros outweigh the cons or vice versa.

Looking to the future, ...

As I stated at the beginning, ...

My personal opinion is that ...

to **weigh up sth** *etw (gegeneinander) abwägen*

to **outweigh sth** *(gegenüber etw) überwiegen, schwerer wiegen als etw*

vice versa *umgekehrt*

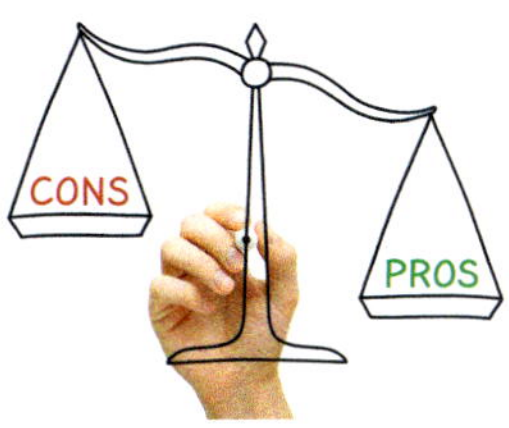

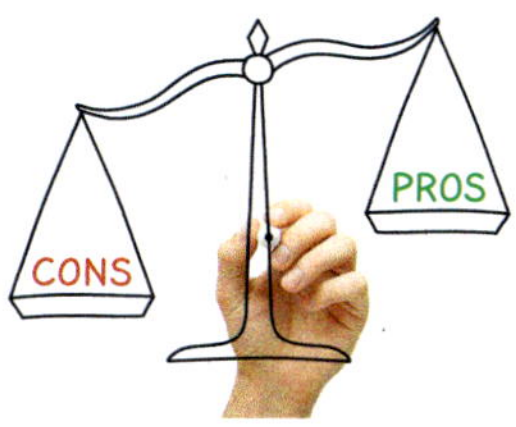

Übung 5

Schreiben Sie Ihren Schlussteil. Überprüfen Sie dabei, ob ein Rückgriff auf Ihre Einleitung machbar und ein Blick in die Zukunft sinnvoll ist.

Überprüfen

Gut zu wissen

Auf S. 72 wird dargestellt, wie man einsprachige Wörterbücher sinnvoll nutzt.

S ▸ Wörterbücher verwenden, S. 106–107

Schritt 7: Korrekturlesen

Überprüfen Sie Ihren Entwurf auf:
- Rechtschreibfehler
- Grammatikfehler
- Wortwahl
- Satzbau
- Gedankenführung

Tipp: Nutzen Sie dazu vor allem ein einsprachiges Wörterbuch, dort finden Sie viele Hilfestellungen zur sprachlichen Verbesserung Ihrer Erörterung.

HÄUFIGE FEHLER

Rechtschreibung:

there ◂▸ their
who's ◂▸ whose
it's ◂▸ its

Übertragungsfehler aus dem Deutschen:

find a ~~work~~ job
~~it makes~~ it's fun
be interested ~~on/for~~ in sth
spend money ~~for~~ on sth
~~in the~~ be near / close by
~~At~~ First (of all), …
~~Also~~ Another reason is …
What~~'s~~ about …?
~~the~~ most (of the) people
~~a small/big part of~~ most (of the) people
I ~~mean~~ think/believe

Übung 7

Nachdem Sie Ihre eigene Erörterung überprüft haben, tauschen Sie diese mit einem Partner aus, korrigieren gegenseitig Ihre Entwürfe und geben sich Feedback.

Verwenden Sie dazu folgende Checkliste und Korrekturzeichen:

Feedbackkultur – wichtige Regeln

Komplimente haben Vorrang! Bleiben Sie positiv und machen Sie sich klar, dass es darum geht, die Arbeit eines Mitschülers / einer Mitschülerin zu verbessern. Seien Sie konkret und formulieren Sie Vorschläge zur Verbesserung.

Korrekturzeichen

R Rechtschreibung
G Grammatik
A Ausdruck (z. B. unpassendes Wort)
V Auslassung (hier fehlt etwas)
> Beginne einen neuen Absatz
? Ich verstehe nicht, was du sagen möchtest
! sehr wichtiger Aspekt in deinem Text
☺ sehr gelungen (z. B. Inhalt oder Stil)
[ ] Dieser Teil ist unnötig (z. B. passt nicht oder wiederholt sich).
~ Dieser Teil muss überarbeitet werden.
( ) Dieser Teil ist nicht überzeugend.

Eine kreative Schreibaufgabe bearbeiten

Bei dieser Aufgabe handelt es sich um sogenanntes textbezogenes Schreiben, d. h. Sie verfassen eine schriftliche Reaktion zu einem vorgegebenen Text. Dabei wird Ihnen explizit genannt, welche Art von Text (**Textsorte**) Sie aus welcher **Perspektive** für wen (**Adressaten**) zu welchem Anlass verfassen sollen. In der Textvorlage können zusätzlich auch noch Diagramme, Bilder oder Karikaturen enthalten sein.
In Ihrer Prüfung kommen für Ihr Schreibprodukt beispielsweise **eine Rede, ein Artikel, ein Brief oder eine E-Mail** in Frage. Achten Sie genau auf diese Vorgabe, denn Sie müssen sich strikt an die formalen Kriterien der jeweils geforderten Textsorte halten.

Gut zu wissen

Im **Abitur** haben Sie die Wahl zwischen einer argumentierenden/bewertenden sowie einer kreativen Schreibaufgabe.

Schritt 1: Planen

Eine sorgfältige Planung ist genauso wichtig wie das anschließende Verfassen des Textes. Folgende Hinweise helfen Ihnen dabei:

- **Brainstorming:** Sammeln Sie zunächst Ideen und notieren diese stichwortartig.
- **Auswahl:** Grenzen Sie den Umfang ggf. ein, indem Sie unwichtige und unzutreffende Aspekte aussortieren.
- **Struktur:** Sortieren Sie Ihre Ideen/Argumente in einer klaren, logischen Abfolge.
- **Visualisierungshilfen:** Nutzen Sie diese zur Vorbereitung. Eine Auswahl finden Sie auf der Folgeseite.

Übung 1

1 Lesen Sie den Artikel des Neurowissenschaftlers Dean Burnett auf S. 18/19.
2 Sammeln und strukturieren Sie Ideen und Argumente mithilfe einer passenden Visualisierungshilfe für folgende kreative Schreibaufgabe:

Write an article for your school magazine in which you compare your personal experience with the neuroscientist's comments and advice. Refer to the text and the cartoon on p. 17.

Schritt 2: Schreiben

Vergewissern Sie sich, dass Sie die **Perspektive**, den **Anlass** und den oder die **Adressaten**, für die Sie schreiben, stets im Blick behalten. Kreativ sind Sie innerhalb dieses Rahmens!

Grundsätzlich folgen Sie unabhängig von der Textsorte dem bewährten Aufbau von Sachtexten: Einleitung – Hauptteil – Schlussteil. Dazu gehört u. a., den Text durch Absätze visuell zu strukturieren, diese mit Themensätzen einzuleiten und passende Strukturwörter zu verwenden.

In der PagePlayer-App finden Sie Kriterien, Tipps und *language help* für relevante **Textsorten**.

S ▸ Eine argumentierende bzw. bewertende Schreibaufgabe bearbeiten (Schritte 3–6), S. 36–39

Übung 2

1 Bestimmen Sie Textsorte, Perspektive, Anlass und Zielgruppe der Schreibaufgabe von Übung 1.
2 Verfassen Sie Ihren Text gemäß der Aufgabenstellung.

Schritt 3: Überprüfen

Überprüfen Sie Ihren Entwurf auf Inhalt und sprachliche Korrektheit.

S ▸ Schritt 7: Korrekturlesen, S. 40

Visualisierungshilfen *(Graphic organizers)*

Visualisierungshilfen unterstützen Sie dabei, Informationen zu organisieren und Beziehungen zwischen verschiedenen Aspekten eines Themas oder Problems aufzuzeigen.

Mindmap

Geeignet für: **Brainstorming, Überblick gewinnen**

Eine Mind-Map hilft bei der Strukturierung der ersten Gedanken und zeigt Beziehungen auf. Vom Thema in der Mitte führen Linien zu den Ideen. Nutzen Sie Farben zur inhaltlichen Markierung, fügen Sie Symbole hinzu – es gibt viele Möglichkeiten zur Ausgestaltung.

Fischgrätendiagramm *(fishbone diagram)*

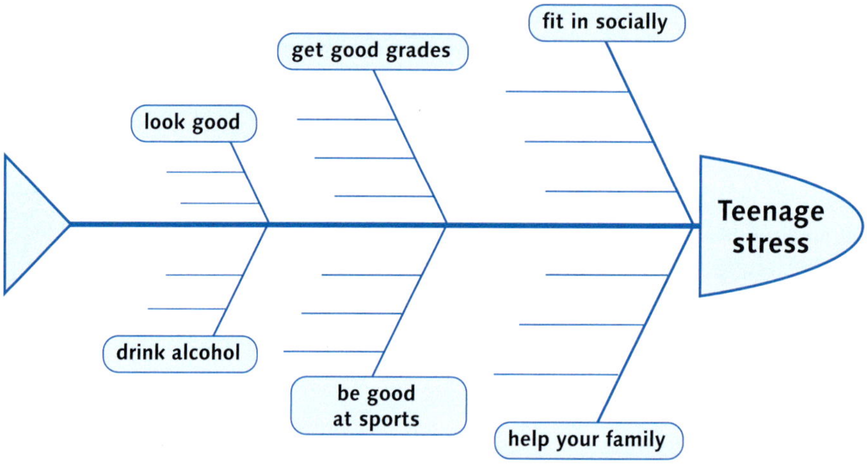

Geeignet für: **Ursachen und Wirkungen beschreiben**

Rechts (Kopf) wird das Problem eingetragen, schräg (Gräten) die Hauptfaktoren. Darauf folgt die Ursachensammlung für jeden Faktor (jeweils weitere Verästelungen). Nach einer Gewichtung der potenziellen Ursachen wird die Hauptursache ermittelt.

Flussdiagramm *(flowchart)*

▸ Working with the text, S. 20

Geeignet für: **Veranschaulichung von Abläufen**

Verbindungspfeile zeigen den Prozess bzw. definieren den Ablauf. Flussdiagramme dienen u.a. zur Entscheidungsfindung, da alternative Pfade erforscht und die Konsequenzen ermittelt werden können. Dazu hat jede Form auch eine Funktion:

- **Formtyp 1:** Anfang und Ende
- **Formtyp 2:** Ja/Nein-Entscheidungsfelder
- **Formtyp 3:** Stationen/Handlungen

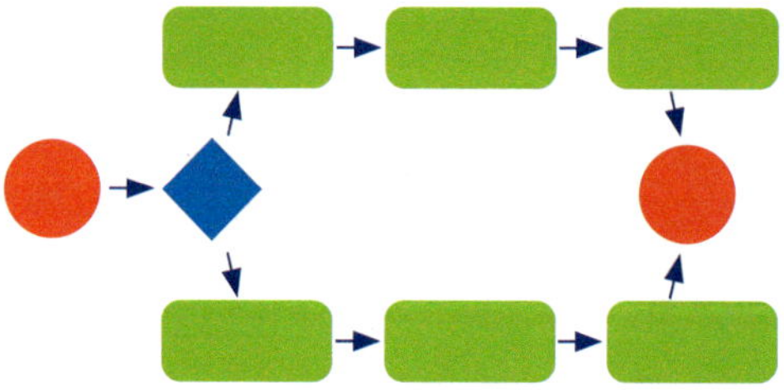

Review

1 Rank the Sections A–E in this Topic based on how interesting they were to you. Then, look back at your work on the Overview of this Topic (pages 8–9) and how you ranked them there (page 9, exercise 3). Have your rankings changed? Share your results with a group, and tell them what you found most interesting.

2 Look back at your KWL list (page 9, exercise 5). Fill out the "Learnt" part of the list. Next, look at your "Want to know" list. What do you still want to know?

3 Make a list of ten words in the Topic that were new to you and you consider important to know. Then collect everyone's words and cluster them into groups. Finally, pick a word group and write a paragraph using all the words.

Evaluate

1 Do this task on your own. How much do you agree or disagree with the statements below? Rate each one on a scale of one to four. The references on the right show you what exercises you can review.

1 = totally disagree **2** = disagree **3** = agree **4** = totally agree

Section		Statement	
A	**1**	I can describe different aspects of a person's identity.	▸ p. 10, exercises 3–5
	2	I can name many values and explain the reasons for my values.	▸ p. 11, exercises 7–9
B	**3**	I can talk about stress, its causes and ways of reducing it.	▸ pp. 13–14, exercises 7–11
	4	I can diagram collocations in ways that help me remember them.	▸ p. 13, exercise 7
	5	I can talk about habits, using adverbs of frequency correctly.	▸ p. 14, exercises 10–11
	6	I can describe and analyse the diagram in this Section.	▸ p. 16, exercise 17
C	**7**	I can guess the meaning of words by their contexts, when possible.	▸ p. 18, exercise 3
	8	I understand some of the neurobiological influences behind typical teen-parent arguments and can give advice on how to manage them.	▸ pp. 18–20, exercises 3–7
	9	I can use present tenses appropriately.	▸ p. 21, exercises 9–10
D	**10**	I understand many advantages and disadvantages of gap years.	▸ pp. 22–25, exercises 2–6
	11	I can deal with multiple matching listening comprehension tasks.	▸ p. 25, exercise 6
	12	I can write an argumentative text on gap years.	▸ p. 25, exercise 8
E	**13**	I can identify the main conflicts in scenes from dramatic literature.	▸ pp. 27–29, exercises 3, 6
	14	I can talk about the future using *will/won't* and *going to*.	▸ pp. 29–30, exercises 10–11
	15	I can talk about German educational possibilities and UK A levels.	▸ p. 31, exercises 12, 13, 15
Skills	**16**	I am familiar with typical task *Operatoren*.	S ▸ pp. 33–34
	17	I can deal with argumentative and evaluative writing tasks.	S ▸ pp. 35–40
	18	I can deal with creative writing tasks.	S ▸ pp. 41–42

Consolidate

You want to go deeper into Gen Z topics and speed up your learning process? Scan this page with the PagePlayer app. There you'll find some suggestions for additional tasks.

Topic 2 Cities and regions in anglophone countries

Section A
London street art

"Fewer people go to art exhibitions nowadays – the art comes to them!"
– Chris Geiger, street artist

street culture

Fact: The London district of ..., which used to be one of the city's poorest, has seen its property prices rise by 25% from 2015 to 2019 (source: Galliard Homes).

Section F
Modern poetry in rural America

hometown

where we live

"No tears in the writer, no tears in the reader. No surprise in the writer, no surprise in the reader."
– Robert Frost, poet

"Poems are like dreams: in them you put what you don't know you know."
– Adrienne Rich, poet

knowing your roots

1 Read ...

a the facts about the cities, regions and countries.
Can you fill in the blanks with the correct place names?
Are these facts new to you?

b the quotations. What are your opinions about these statements?

2 The mind map shows you a preview of Topic 2. Copy it onto a piece of paper and add words and phrases from ...

- the Word Bank on the opposite page.
- the facts and quotations.
- Sections A–F (skim them to find words you think are important).

Section B
Gentrification case study: …

Section C
Urban transport and activism

Find information on each Section in the PagePlayer app!

"Think of bicycles as ridable art that can just about save the world."
– Grant Petersen, bicycle designer

neighbourhood

affordability

Fact: … is the biggest city in Washington State, famous for its coffee culture and big tech companies. More than 70% of "Amazonians" live here.

getting around

Fact: In 2016, … was the most congested area in Europe. The average driver lost 101 hours a year in traffic (source: Eurostat).

discovering cultures

Section D
Geography, culture and history down under

quality of life

Section E
Big city vs countryside in the UK

"I would rather wake up in the middle of nowhere than in any city on earth."
– Steve McQueen, film director

Fact: … is a country with about five million inhabitants and about twenty-seven million sheep. The indigenous people call it the "land of the long white cloud".

3 Rank the Sections A–F on how interested you are in them.

4 Make a "KWL" (Know, Want to know, Learnt) list for the Topic.

5 With a partner, compare …

- **a** your mind maps and say why you added words where you did.
- **b** your rankings from exercise 3.
- **c** what you want to find out about the cities and regions.

Then compare with another pair.

6 Save your work for reviewing when you've finished the Topic.

Word bank

accommodation *Unterkunft*
affordability *Erschwinglichkeit*
commuting *Pendeln (zur Arbeit)*
convenience *(Ort:) gute/günstige Lage*
gentrification *Gentrifizierung*
hometown *Heimatstadt*
industry *Branche, Sparte*
in the middle of nowhere *am Ende der Welt, mitten in der Pampa*
opportunity *Möglichkeit, Chance*
rent *Miete*
vibrant *dynamisch, pulsierend, spannend*
working class *aus der Arbeiterklasse*

Section A London street art

Good to know

Shoreditch is a neighbourhood in London that artists and other creative people have made famous. Today it's a popular and expensive area, filled with public art and a lively street culture.

Warm-up

1 Read these eight comments from people who have just been on a guided tour of street art in Shoreditch. Which of these comments (1–8) could refer to the pieces of street art (a–d) on page 47?

to **take a stand against sth** *ein Zeichen gegen etw setzen*

1 We've seen a lot of wall paintings with political messages. I guess street artists always take a stand against the existing system or at least want to get people thinking.

impressive *beeindruckend*

2 I saw a painting on a door in Princelet Street that I found very impressive – I think it's about the diverse culture in London.

to **grab sb's attention** *jmds Aufmerksamkeit erregen*

mural *Wandbild*

3 Some pieces really grab your attention. This mural was created by an Australian artist who often paints women's faces against a psychedelic background.

evil *böse*

4 This is a masterpiece we saw in Heneage Street. "Hear no evil, speak no evil and see no evil" – that's the message.

large-scale *großformatig*

5 We saw such great art. Look at this large-scale graffiti here, it was done by a British-born artist – bright colourful letters on a black background.

6 What a powerful visual statement! It reminds me of graphics in the '80s with colourful lines, dots and blocks.

creature *Gestalt, Wesen*

to blend into one another *miteinander verschmelzen, ineinander verschwimmen*

7 I just love this black and white fantasy – it's so surrealistic – look at these strange creatures that all seem to blend into each other.

real eye-opener *echtes Aha-Erlebnis*

8 The tour was a real eye-opener. Shoreditch is packed with street-art murals. My favourite is this huge wall painting in 3D style.

a

b

c

d

Watching/Listening

2 Watch or listen to this walking-tour slideshow of Shoreditch and choose the correct phrase to complete each sentence.

1 The guide wants to show them …
- **a** his favourite graffiti.
- **b** a wide variety of street art.
- **c** the best graffiti in London.
- **d** the cultural highlights of Shoreditch.

2 In the last part of the tour, Dave will show them …
- **a** the highlights of graffiti art.
- **b** the highlight of every walk in London.
- **c** some of the highlights of London street art.
- **d** his personal highlight of Shoreditch street art.

3 The guide thinks that part of the charm of street art is that it's so …
- **a** colourful.
- **b** temporary.
- **c** large-scale.
- **d** permanent.

4 Zabou's paintings …
- **a** are a bit scary.
- **b** show cartoons.
- **c** are inspirational.
- **d** have political and religious connotations.

5 The painted bird …
- **a** is a bit frightening.
- **b** was painted on a shutter.
- **c** is the highlight of the walk.
- **d** was created by a British-born artist.

6 When you walk around in Shoreditch, you can sometimes …
- **a** talk to graffiti artists
- **b** see a lot of spray cans.
- **c** see a lot of other tourists.
- **d** come across artists in action.

Crossover TV

Shoreditch walking tour

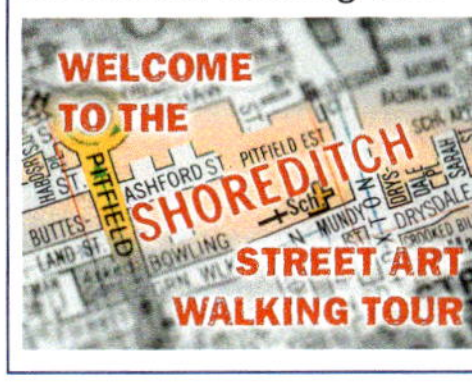

11 01

S ▸ *Richtig mit Hörverstehensaufgaben umgehen*, pp. 104–105

D ▸ More help, p. 149

Exam preparation

Speaking

3 After watching or listening to the tour, tell a partner which piece of art you like best. Which do you find least impressive? Explain why.

Working with words

4 Watch or listen to the walking tour again and note which presentation phrases are used.

1 Welcome to …
2 I'm happy to welcome so many of you here today!
3 If you have any questions during the walk, please don't hesitate to interrupt me.
4 OK, so let's get started.
5 I'd like to start by explaining …
6 OK, let me start by saying that …
7 Now we'll move on to …
8 Let's now look at …
9 The next slide shows …
10 In this photo we can see …
11 I would like to conclude with …
12 Thank you very much for …

Skills training: Guiding people through a talk or presentation

To structure your talk well, we recommend the following steps:

Introduction

1 Welcome the audience and introduce yourself.
Hello / Good morning, everyone.
My name is …

2 Say what you will talk about or do.
I'm going to talk about …
I want to start with …. After that I'll talk about …. And finally, I'll focus on …

3 Tell people when they can ask questions.
If you have any questions, please feel free to ask me at any time.

Main part

4 Use signposting phrases to guide your audience through the talk.
I'd like to begin by saying …
If I can turn your attention to …

5 Describe what people see.
The next image shows …
As you can see here …

Conclusion

6 Summarize the main points and end on a positive note.
I would like to finish by saying …
You've been a great audience!

5 Now look at the presentation phrases in the Skills Training box and on pages 74–75 to make your own list of phrases to use in your talk.

Speaking

S ▸ *Präsentieren*, pp. 74–75

6 Take photos or make a video about public art. Choose a place you know or research one online, then present it to your classmates.
Start by saying who you are. Then explain what you are going to talk about and guide your audience from one image to the next.

Section B Gentrification case study: Seattle

Warm-up

1 Look at these photos. What has changed over the past twenty years? What are some possibilities for how this building could look twenty years from now?

Twenty years ago

Today

Listening

2 Listen to four people saying how their hometown and their lives have changed. Who thinks the changes are generally positive, and who thinks they are negative?

12

1 Laura

2 Ben

3 Jorge

4 Amahle

Exam preparation

3 Copy and complete the table below. Match each speaker (1–4) with the aspect they mention (a–e). For each speaker there is only one correct answer. There is one more aspect than you need.

a crime
b economy
c eating out
d community life
e housing/rental costs

Speaker	1 Laura	2 Ben	3 Jorge	4 Amahle
Aspect				

4 Listen again and check your answers. How do you feel about the points mentioned? Which one would you agree with most?

Speaking

5 Work in small groups. Discuss whether you think gentrification offers more advantages or disadvantages.

Working with the text

Skills training: Creating mind maps for concepts

Creating mind maps is a useful skill. Mind maps can help you collect and sort ideas, thoughts and key words. They are useful tools to get the "big picture". Information shown in mind maps can be easier to memorize than in lists or tables.

1 Write the main topic/idea at the centre of the mind map.
2 Add key words that branch off from the main topic. Connect them with lines.
3 Add further ideas or examples to the key words.

6 **Create a mind map with all aspects of gentrification mentioned by the people from exercise 2 on page 49. Then add other aspects you can think of.**

S ▸ *Schwierige Texte lesen*, pp. 72–73

7 **Read the news article about Seattle on page 51, then go back to your mind map and add further ideas.**

Skills training: Dealing with comprehension questions

1 Read the questions carefully.
2 Look for key words in the questions.
3 Look at the text again while keeping the questions in mind.

8 **After reading the article, note down answers to the questions. Compare your notes with a partner's.**

1 What was Seattle like in the past?
2 Why is Seattle sometimes called *Amageddon*?
3 What does the tech boom mean for people with lower incomes?
○ **4** What's the Seattle "coolness factor paradox"?

9 **Choose the most suitable answer to complete the sentences. Use the Skills Training box to help you.**

1 Many residents of Seattle like to remember the time when …
a the first Starbucks café opened.
b housing prices were lower.
c there was an atmosphere of innovation and creativity.

2 Seattle is known for its …
a quirky neighbourhoods.
b cool suburbs.
c crowded city centre.

3 Seattle's population has grown …
a a lot over the last five years.
b by 40% in three years.
c dramatically since Amazon was founded.

4 Amazon has …
a increased its workers' pay.
b led to income inequality.
c paid every worker $100,000.

5 The rise in housing prices has forced many people to …
a take a second job.
b move into smaller apartments.
c get married to save on rent.

6 In addition to its tech companies, Seattle is also home to …
a National Public Radio
b Boeing
c Universal Studios

10 Create a heading for each paragraph (1–6) of the text.

How the tech boom has transformed Seattle – "The coolness factor paradox"

13

1 Ben Gibbard, leader of the Seattle indie band Death Cab for Cutie, recently said in an interview with National Public Radio: "Seattle has been transformed into an almost unrecognizable city over the past fifteen years with the tech boom, specifically the rise of Amazon and the other carpetbagging tech firms."

2 Most residents of Seattle, the fastest-growing major city in the US, would agree with him. And many of them long for the pre-tech years when Seattle was *the* cool place in the US with a vibrant pop music and art scene, creative lifestyle and innovative business ideas. One of these businesses is Starbucks. This pioneer in American coffee culture opened its first coffee shop in Seattle and now has more than 30,000 locations across the world.

3 Unlike in the late 1990s and early 2000s, when corporations like Microsoft mainly operated from offices in the suburbs, many companies have recently started crowding themselves into the same limited space in the city centre. Paradoxically, Seattle's "coolness factor" and its quirky neighbourhoods attracted many tech firms and affluent people, but, by arriving in large numbers, the very same people destroyed the culture that had attracted them in the first place.

4 Of course, Seattle has some older, more traditional industries such as Boeing, the aerospace manufacturing company, which employs about 80,000 people. But it's the tech companies, above all Amazon, that are the key drivers of change. Amazon has transformed the city so profoundly that some residents now call it *Amageddon*. Since Amazon was founded, thousands of people have moved to Seattle each year, leading to a 40 % increase in the city's population.

5 The tech industry has also brought better-paid jobs, with an average salary of about $100,000. Most non-tech workers in Seattle don't even make half that. This has led to income inequality and a big difference in the economic situation and spending power of Seattle's old and new populations.

6 Those with higher incomes can afford to rent or buy the limited properties available on the housing market, and housing prices have surged by 70% over five years. People with lower-paid jobs find it incredibly difficult to find an affordable place. That is why a lot of people move into smaller and cheaper accommodation, or are forced to leave the city. And many of them end up living on the streets, in parks or tent camps under bridges. Seattle now has more than 11,000 homeless people, which means it has the highest number of people without a permanent home after New York and Los Angeles. (439 words)

Good to know

Carpetbagging is a negative term that means relocating for economic profit.

to **transform sth** *etw verwandeln, etw (grundlegend) verändern*
5 **unrecognizable** *nicht wiederzuerkennen*
8 **rise** *Aufstieg*
10 **resident** *Einwohner/in*
11 to **long for sth** *sich nach etw sehnen*
16 **unlike** *anders als*
19 quirky *eigenwillig, unangepasst*
20 affluent *wohlhabend*
21 **in the first place** *überhaupt (erst), in erster Linie*
24 **key driver** *treibende Kraft, Hauptmotor*
25 profoundly *grundlegend, tiefgreifend*
30 **inequality** *Ungleichheit, Unterschied(e)*
31 spending power *Kaufkraft*
32 **property** *Immobilie(n)*
33 **housing market/prices** *Wohnungsmarkt/-preise*
36 to **end up living in the streets** *auf der Straße landen*

Working with words

D ▸ More help, p. 149

11 Find words and phrases in the text on page 51 that have the same meaning as these below. They are in the same order as they appear in the text.

1 inhabitants
2 companies or firms
3 unusual, strange or weird
4 wealthy
5 established
6 number of inhabitants
7 money a person earns
8 place to live

Writing

Exam preparation

S ▸ *Eine Aufgabe zum integrierten Leseverstehen bearbeiten*, pp. 76
S ▸ *Operatoren*, p. 33

12 Summarize the information given in the article about Seattle.

Looking at language

13 Which of these sentences from the text describes something that:
a happened at a specific time in the past?
b has happened over a period of time that continues to the present?

1 Seattle was *the* cool place in the US with a vibrant pop music and art scene.
2 Amazon has transformed the city in many ways.
3 Thousands of people have moved to Seattle each year.
4 This pioneer in American coffee culture opened their first coffee shop in Seattle.
5 The tech industry has also brought better-paid jobs.
6 Housing prices have surged by 70% over five years.

Remember: Talking about past events with and without present effects

When we talk about things that happened at a certain time in the past, we use the **simple past**.
In the late 1990s, Microsoft mainly ***operated*** *from offices in the suburbs.*
(Microsoft worked there in the past, but this is no longer the case.)
When we talk about things that have happened over a period of time and are still relevant today, we use the **present perfect**.
This ***has led*** *to income inequality. (We still have income equality.)*
In German, when we talk about the past, we mostly use the ***Perfekt***.
In den späten 1990er Jahren ***hat*** *Microsoft von Büros in den Vororten* ***gearbeitet***.

G ▸ The simple past, p. 164
the present perfect, p. 164

14 Use words from the table to make five or more sentences about what happened (simple past tense) or has happened (present perfect tense).

Seattle	change	over the past ten years.
My hometown/village	open	since Amazon set up business there.
Cities across Germany	transform	in 2000.
Amazon	bring	last year.
The tech industry	move	the first coffee shop in 1978.
Starbucks		higher-paid jobs.
The lower income residents		

Speaking

Skills training: Describing diagrams orally

You may be tested on your ability to talk about diagrams, so it is a good idea to prepare how to structure a description and to learn useful words and phrases.

1 First, say what the visual is about.
This chart shows/indicates/illustrates/compares ...

2 Then, summarize the main information.
You can see that ... is/has the biggest/highest ...

3 Describe trends using interesting and expressive verbs.
For upward movement: *rise, grow, increase, surge, go up*
For downward movement: *drop, fall, decrease, slump, plummet, go down*
If there is no movement: *stay at, remain stable, keep at the same level*

4 Make sure you use the correct tense to describe change.
Use the simple past for things that were completed in the past.
Between 2000 to 2015, the numbers of travellers ***fell*** *to a low.*
Use the present perfect for things that are unfinished and have an effect now.
Over the past 10 years / Since 2015, the number ***has grown****.*

5 Include adjectives and adverbs in your description.
To say *how* something develops, use adjectives and adverbs:
rapid/-ly, sharp/-ly, dramatic/-ally, slight/-ly, moderate/-ly, slow/-ly.
In 2020, there was a ***sharp*** *increase in tourists.*
The number of tech workers has dropped ***slightly*** *in the past five years.*

15 First write down some key words and phrases to talk about this chart. Then describe the chart to your partner and compare the language you use.

Exam preparation

S ▸ *Diagramme beschreiben u. analysieren*, pp. 70–71

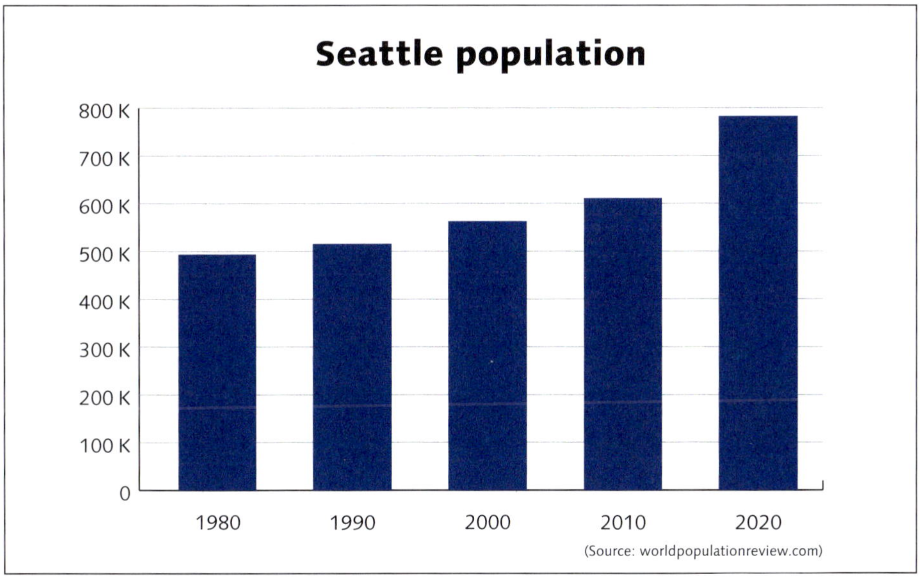

16 ○ Explain the cause of this population growth based on information given in the text on page 51.

Section C Urban transport and activism

Warm-up

1 Discuss with a partner. How was your journey to school today? What did you experience on the way? Do any of these pictures look like your usual trip to school?

Speaking

How to say or write it

- I think … would be a very good idea because …
- In my opinion, … is not useful at all because (there aren't enough/any) …
- I don't think we need (any/more) …
- … would be very effective. They would help us reduce/improve …
- If we had (more) …, more people could …
- Urban areas would (greatly) benefit from …

2 Complete the questionnaire on public transport. Compare your answers with a partner and explain your ratings in the questionnaire.

Which additions to public transport would you find most useful or effective where you live?

1 = not useful/effective 10 = extremely useful/effective

a free car parks
b safe bike lanes
c free or cheap public transport (bus, train, tram, underground)
d park & ride sites
e taxi ranks
f e-scooters
g bicycle hire scheme
h electric vehicle charging points
i electronic signs that guide drivers to available parking
j car-free zones

What other changes or improvements would you welcome?

Looking at language

Remember: Translating *fahren* und *gehen*

The verb *fahren* can be translated as *drive, ride, take* or *go* depending on the mode of transport.

ride a bicycle, motorbike, moped, horse
drive = go by car
take a / **go** by bus, train, taxi, plane = use a means of transport as a passenger

Remember that *drive* automatically indicates travelling by car. Therefore, it is redundant to say *drive by car*.

How did she get here?
She drove.

***Gehen* is translated as *go*, which is often combined with the prepositions *on* and *for*:**

walk / go for a walk	*zu Fuß gehen / einen Spaziergang machen*
go on holiday / a trip / a tour	*in Urlaub gehen / auf eine Reise gehen*
go for a run/swim/walk/hike	*laufen/schwimmen/spazieren/wandern gehen*

"go on holiday"

"ride"

"walk"

"drive"

"go by train"

"go for a run"

3 Complete the sentences with the correct word. Use *ride, drive, take* or *go.* Make sure you use the correct tense and form of the verbs.

D ▸ More challenge, p. 150

1 Anna and her family … on holiday last week.
2 Would you like to … for a walk in the Botanical Garden?
3 I didn't know you can …. When did you pass your driving test?
4 I always … to work by train. It's much faster.
5 It was late when I left the party so I … a taxi.
6 I usually … my bike to the gym.

4 Translate the sentences into English.

1 Ich fahre immer mit dem Bus zur Arbeit.
2 Im Sommer fahren wir oft mit dem Fahrrad.
3 Mein Chef fährt gewöhnlich mit dem Auto ins Büro.
4 Meine Eltern gehen manchmal im Park spazieren.
5 Im Winter fahre ich mit meiner Familie in Urlaub nach Österreich.
6 Fährst du oft mit dem Bus?
7 Fahrradfahren ist was ich in meiner Freizeit am liebsten mache.
8 Sollen wir zu Fuß ins Kino gehen oder mit dem Bus fahren?

5 Look at your English translations of the sentences with *fahren* and *gehen*. Where do you put the adverb of frequency (*immer*, *oft*, etc.) in the English sentences? Where do you put them in the German sentences?

Working with words

6 Before you listen to the podcast about urban transport in London and Stuttgart, match the English words (1–8) and the German words (a–h).

1 congestion	**a** Erkennung
2 charge	**b** Gebühr
3 recognition	**c** Lastschrift
4 direct debit	**d** Plakette
5 penalty	**e** schädlich
6 harmful	**f** Strafe
7 badge	**g** Verbot
8 ban	**h** Verkehrsstau, Überlastung

Listening

14

7 Copy out the table in your notebook. Then listen to the podcast and complete the table.

	Congestion charge London	*Umweltzone* Stuttgart
When it was introduced		
Purpose or goal		
Areas included		
How much it costs		
Payment methods		
How often it must be paid		
Penalty for not paying		

8 Listen again and answer the questions.

1 What would *Umweltzone* be called in English?
2 How are cars driving into the charging zone registered in London?
3 Who can get a green badge in Stuttgart?
4 What is a PCN?

Speaking

How to say or write it

I prefer the congestion charge concept because …

I think the *Umweltzone* is better because it offers …

In my view, both systems help to …

9 Work in small groups. Which of the concepts do you prefer – the congestion charge or *Umweltzone*? Which of them is better for the environment? Explain why.

Working with the text

10 Read the newspaper article and tell the class which of the cyclists' campaigns and activities you like best. Which of these measures would you like to see where you live?

How guerrilla cyclists are solving urban transport issues

15

Across the world, cyclists are concerned and frustrated because transport planning in urban areas often does not take their needs seriously. Cities are still made for cars and, as a consequence, they're not safe for cyclists. In many cities around the world, the lack of proper cycle lanes has resulted in many cyclists being injured or killed in accidents. So now frustrated cyclists have decided to take matters into their own hands – whether the local department of transportation likes it or not! Let's look at some examples and find out if cyclist activism leads to safer streets.

A Cyclists in Sydney, Australia

Following the death of a cyclist who collided with a truck, the Sydney biking community was so frustrated that some of them started painting bike lanes around the city with the words "UNSAFE CYCLE LANE". The aim of the campaign was to highlight the dangers of unseparated lanes where cyclists have to ride between fast-moving traffic and parked cars.

B Bike activists in Los Angeles, USA

Cyclists in Los Angeles have clearly had enough. As a result, you can see homemade signs appearing in many places asking motorists to drive carefully and mind the cyclists. The black-and-white posters have phrases like "CAUTION! PASS WITH CARE" written on them and can be found close to the road. The do-it-yourself signs often come with a bike lane icon, and there are also Spanish versions of the signs in many parts of the city.

C Cycling groups across the UK

For decades, cyclists in the UK have been campaigning for safer roads and improved road surfaces. They say that potholes, although bad for motorists, are even worse for cyclists because they can be fatal. Now some cyclists have come up with creative ideas. An anonymous vigilante sprays graffiti around potholes and posts the photos on social media. Another activist connected his smartphone to a spray tank on the bottom of his bicycle. Every time he rides over a pothole, his phone senses the bump, the spray tank automatically marks it and a report is emailed to the city road department. There is also an app called "Fill that hole", which can be used to report potholes to councils. The councils have to fix these holes once they have been informed, and potholes are repaired more quickly now.

D Bike enthusiasts across the USA

Following a string of serious cycling accidents in San Francisco, frustrated citizens decided to make their city safer and more bike-friendly by putting up pop-up bike lanes. They used traffic cones, or in some cases flowerpots, to separate cycle lanes from cars. In other places cyclists have used equally inventive ways to make infrastructure safer: in Kansas, annoyed cyclists put up a barrier with toilet plungers overnight to draw attention to their situation. Because of these unusual experiments, many city councils have decided to invest in safer bike lanes.

Good to know

The Spanish term *guerrilla* refers to soldiers not in an official army, fighting in small groups. It can also refer to people acting secretly or outside the law. The term *vigilante* (also Spanish) means a person seeking justice without any official authority.

cyclist *Fahrradfahrer/in*
urban transport *Stadtverkehr*
4 **lack (of sth)** *Mangel (an etw), Fehlen (von etw)*
12 **unsafe** *gefährlich*
13 **unseparated lane** *nicht abgetrennte Fahrspur*
18 **motorist** *Autofahrer/in*
22 **icon** *Symbol*
32 **bump** *Schlag, Stoß; Unebenheit, Hubbel*
35 **council** *Stadtverwaltung*
38 **a string of events** *eine Reihe von Ereignissen*
41 **inventive** *originell, einfallsreich*
42 toilet plunger *Saugglocke, Pümpel*

[49] **speeding** *Geschwindigkeitsüberschreitung, zu schnelles Fahren*
[51] to be revealed as sth *sich als etw offenbaren*
[52] to **approach** *näherkommen*

E Guerrilla cyclists in Vancouver, Canada
Cyclist support groups in this Canadian city are protecting cyclists and pedestrians. A group in Vancouver has painted 3D images on the road surface to stop cars from speeding. In some streets, drivers seem to see a child playing with a ball in the distance, causing them to slow down, but the child is revealed as an illusion as the driver approaches. Other innovative images that slow cars down include 3D zebra crossings. (562 words)

Working with the text

D ▸ More help, p. 150

11 **Read the article again and complete the sentences.**

1 Innovative traffic calming may … cyclists and pedestrians.
2 Instead of cars and bicycles sharing the same road, activists want … cycle lanes to make cycling safer in cities.
3 … signs are put up by guerrilla cyclists in Los Angeles.
4 … spraying is used to highlight road problems in the UK.
5 In some places, angry citizens started creating … bike lanes, which later became permanent ones.
6 In many places across the world, cyclists are trying to draw … to the dangers of cycling.

Working with words

12 **Look in the text for the English equivalents of the German words.**

1 Mangel an
2 zusammenstoßen
3 Vorsicht
4 Straßenbelag
5 Schlagloch
6 Pylone
7 Stadtverwaltung
8 vorübergehend
9 Fußgänger/in
10 näherkommen

13 **Read the article again and find all connectives (linking words) in the text that have to do with *effect, consequence* or *reason*. Give line numbers.**

14 **Complete the sentences with a word or phrase from the box in the correct form. Sometimes more than one answer is possible.**

although | as a consequence/result | because | because of | but | effect | lead to | nevertheless | result in | while

1 Last year the council built two new cycle lanes. … there are fewer accidents now.
2 Temporary bike lanes … safer conditions for cyclists over the last five years.
3 The … of better town planning can be seen in this city.
4 … the number of bike lanes has increased, there are still too few of them.
5 We need to improve road surfaces … they are dangerous for cyclists.
6 Cyclist activism … some improvements. … there's a lot of work to be done.
7 London's air quality has improved … the Congestion Charge.
8 … drivers are fined for entering Stuttgart city centre without a green badge, last year about 26,000 drivers had to pay a fine.

Writing

Skills training: Writing a formal email

A formal email is similar to a formal letter. It always includes a subject line, in which you say what the email is about.
Suggestions for improving urban traffic

When you write to a person whose name you know, use *Dear* and the correct form of address:
Mr for men – *Dear Mr Smith*
Ms for women – *Dear Ms Jackson*
At the end of your formal email, write: *Yours sincerely* or *Best regards*
A formal email should have a clear structure and usually consists of three parts:

1 Introduction – say briefly why you are writing
I am writing to draw your attention to a few issues regarding cycle lanes in our city.

2 Main body
1 describe a problem/situation, give details and examples
The dangerous road surface near the main station resulted in three accidents last month.
2 say what the other person should do or what you will do next
For these reasons, I hope you will provide more separated bike lanes in the future.

3 Ending/conclusion
1 summarize your key points
In conclusion, we feel that attention to bike safety is urgently needed, and we are asking you to take immediate action.
2 finish off with a polite sentence
look forward to hearing from you.

15 Which part of an email do the following sentences belong in?

A introduction | B main body | C conclusion/ending

1 That is why I suggest that you …
2 The lack of … leads to …
3 As a cyclist/pedestrian, I have noticed/experienced (that) …
4 To summarize, I can say …
5 I am contacting/writing you to inform you about …
6 Let me give you some examples of …
7 I think it would be a good idea to …
8 The reason why I am writing to you is that …
9 I look forward to your reply.
10 The result of … is that …
11 To improve the situation you could …
12 One problem is that …

16 Read the sentences (1–12) again and match them with their purpose/function.

a give reasons for writing
b describe a situation/problem
c talk about consequences
d recommend ways to solve a problem
e end the email in a friendly way

Exam preparation

S ▸ *Eine kreative Schreibaufgabe bearbeiten*, pp. 41–42

D ▸ More help, p. 150

17 As a cyclist and regular user of public transportation, you decide to write the mayor of your town/city with suggestions for improvements. Start your email with a subject line. Use words and phrases from this section to describe …

- problems in public transport you have experienced/noticed.
- the consequences they have.
- ways of solving them.

Before you start writing you collect evidence of problems in public transport in your town/city.

- Take photographs of the problems you find.
- Select the best photos and attach them to your email.
- Comment on your photos in your email.

How to say or write it

Personally, I think/feel/believe that there are not enough bike lanes …

If you ask me, …

Yes, I absolutely agree.

That's true, especially on the main road.

I see what you mean, but …

Actually, I don't think finding a parking spot is …

Speaking

▸ Phrases for writing and discussion, inside front cover

18 In small groups, discuss public transport problems where you live / go to school. Give your opinion and respond to the other students' opinions.

Section D Geography, culture and history down under

Warm-up

1 Look at these photos. Which region or country are they associated with?

2 In small groups, share what you already know about these aspects of the country depicted above: geography, history, culture, food, sports or other interesting information. Then present the facts to the other groups.

Working with the text

3 Read the text from a travel website and answer the FAQs.

1. I love water sports and adrenaline-rush activities. Where should I go?
2. What's the best way of getting to the fjords?
3. Is it dangerous to travel in New Zealand (animals, climate, weather, etc.)?
4. What is the best time to go if we want to enjoy warm weather?
5. Is Maori culture still present in New Zealand today?
6. I'd like to see whales up close. Where should I go?

Welcome to your dream destination: New Zealand

16

Geography, geology and wildlife

Our beautiful country lies in the southwest Pacific and consists of two main islands: the North Island and the South Island. New Zealand has an extremely varied landscape including dramatic mountain ranges, large lakes, active volcanoes and glaciers as well as endless sandy beaches. It sits on two tectonic plates which are constantly shifting and so the country experiences a lot of earthquakes. While the North Island has subtropical temperatures in the summer, it gets a lot colder as you go south.
NZ weather is very unpredictable (especially in the mountains) and varies wildly. NZ is "down under", so the warmest months are January and February, the coldest July and August. And another fact important for travellers is that unlike in Australia, there are no poisonous snakes or spiders to be scared of in NZ!

[1] **wildlife** *Pflanzen- und Tierwelt, Natur*
[3] to **consist of sth** *aus etw bestehen*
[6] **varied** *vielfältig, vielgestaltig*
[7] mountain range *Gebirge, Gebirgszug*
[8] glacier *Gletscher*
[11] to **shift** *sich bewegen, sich verschieben*
[11] to **experience sth** *etw erleben*
[14] **unpredictable** *unberechenbar*
[14] to **vary wildly** *sehr unterschiedlich sein*
[16] **unlike** *anders als*
[17] poisonous snake *Giftschlange*

Five must-do experiences on the South Island

1 Fjordland National Park

For nature lovers, Fjordland National Park is an absolute must! The park features the spectacular Doubtful and Milford Sounds, which can be reached by air, boat or on foot. Milford Sound, also called the "eighth wonder of the world", has stunning waterfalls and dramatic fjords. Explore the area and discover magical places everywhere. And don't forget to keep your camera handy – you might come across dolphins or the famous mountain parrot, the kea.

2 Adventure and sports in Queenstown

Go wild in Queenstown, the adventure capital of the world! Here's a place you definitely shouldn't miss if you're looking for thrills. There's everything from whitewater rafting to jet skiing and skydiving. And don't forget: you can go bungee jumping in other places, but Queenstown is where bungee jumping originated in the 1980s. So come to Queenstown and take the plunge!

3 NZ history and Maori culture

Experience the rich culture of the indigenous people of New Zealand. The first inhabitants came here from Polynesia between 1200 and 1300 AD, long before Europeans arrived in the seventeenth century. By then, the Maori had established their own unique identity and culture. When Britain claimed NZ as a colony in 1840, the Treaty of Waitangi was signed by Maori chiefs and representatives of the British Crown. This founding constitutional document defines the relationship between – and protects the rights of – indigenous and non-indigenous people. Even today, 6 February, the day the treaty was signed, is a national holiday. Although the Maori struggled to maintain their traditions and language during colonialism, their culture plays a big part in Kiwi life today and has influenced many areas, such as cooking, sport, language and customs. The Haka, a traditional Maori dance, is now famous throughout the world because of its use by the All Blacks rugby team.

4 Marine life

You want to see whales, dolphins and fur seals close-up? Then Kaikoura on the east coast is the place to go! This picturesque town is the perfect base to start a cruise for whale-watching and spotting other extraordinary sea creatures. To make your experience even more memorable, you may have snow-capped mountains as a backdrop in your photos.

5 Film locations

Over the past twenty years, New Zealand has become popular as an international film-making destination. So come and visit the "home of Middle-Earth" where the *Lord of the Rings* trilogy was filmed. Take a guided tour of the movie sets and experience these mythical places and New Zealand's dramatic scenery for yourself.

(574 words)

18 **experience** *Unternehmung, Erlebnis*
20 to **feature sth** *etw aufweisen, etw haben*
21 sound *Meeresarm, Sund*
23 **stunning** *atemberaubend*
24 to **keep sth handy** *etw griffbereit haben*
25 **parrot** *Papagei*
28 **thrill** *Nervenkitzel*
30 to **originate in sth** *von etw (her)kommen*
31 to **take the plunge** *den Sprung wagen, springen*
33 **indigenous people** *Ureinwohner*
34 **inhabitant** *Einwohner/in*
34 AD *(Zeitrech.:) nach Christus*
36 **unique** *eigen, spezifisch*
36 to **claim sth** *etw (für sich) beanspruchen*
37 treaty *Abkommen, Vertrag*
37 **chief** *Häuptling*
38 founding document *Gründungsdokument, -akte*
38 **constitutional** *Verfassungs-*
40 **national holiday** *Nationalfeiertag*
41 to **struggle to do sth** *etw nur mit Mühe tun können; es schwer haben, etw zu tun*
41 to **maintain sth** *etw (aufrecht) erhalten*
43 **custom** *Brauch*
46 **marine life** *Tier- und Pflanzenwelt des Meeres*
47 **whale** *Wal*
47 fur seal *Seebär*
47 **close-up** *aus der Nähe, von Nahem*
48 picturesque *pittoresk, malerisch*
49 **cruise** *Seereise, Kreuzfahrt*
49 **sea creature** *Meerestier*
50 **memorable** *unvergesslich, beeindruckend*
50 snow-capped *(Berg:) schneebedeckt*
51 **backdrop** *Kulisse, Hintergrund*
56 **scenery** *Landschaft*

D ▸ More challenge, p. 150

Speaking

How to say or write it

For me, ... would be exciting because ...

I would (definitely) go to ... because I've never ...

I'd love to see ...

4 Work with a partner to discuss ...

- which activities you would most like to do in New Zealand.
- which of the facts mentioned on the website were completely new to you.

Working with words

5 Look at the text again and list all adjectives and verbs that are used to describe interesting features and activities.

Adjectives	Verbs
exciting ...	*visit ...*

6 Find and list the typical expressions and phrases the brochure uses to promote New Zealand as a holiday destination.

Example: *Welcome to your dream destination*

D ▸ More help, p. 150

Speaking

Skills training: Describing and analysing pictures

When describing a picture, start by focusing on the main message first, then speak about the details.

1. Say what the picture shows.
   The picture shows/depicts ...
2. When you describe things or people in more detail, say where they are in the picture. Work from left to right, or from background to foreground.
   On the left-hand side, there is ...
3. Give an interpretation of the picture.
   The point of the picture seems to be ...
   The drawing symbolizes ...
4. Comment on the picture and give your opinion.
   It has the effect of ...
   It forces you to think about ...

7 Work with a partner. Each choose a picture, then describe them to each other.

Exam preparation

S ▸ *Bilder und Cartoons beschreiben und analysieren*, pp. 136–137

Writing

8 Together with a partner, create a brochure about the place you live or a place where you would like to live.
Use phrases from exercise 6, include some facts about the history and geography, and describe one or two highlights or activities you can do there.

Exam preparation

S ▸ *Eine kreative Schreibaufgabe bearbeiten*, pp. 41-42

D ▸ More help, p. 151

Section E Big city vs countryside in the UK

Warm-up

1 Look at the pictures and work with a partner to discuss the following questions.
- Which of the photos most resembles the place where you live?
- What do you like or dislike about it?
- Where would you like to work in the future – in a city, town or country?

A

B

C

D

2 In an agreed time limit, write down as many questions as you can to which the answer is: *(in) the countryside*. Share your questions with a partner.

Working with words

3 Before you listen to a discussion on life in a city versus in a small village, match the expressions and idioms (1–8) with the definitions.

1 on my doorstep
2 within walking distance
3 in the middle of nowhere
4 couldn't care less
5 live on top of each other
6 all sunshine and rainbows
7 get along well
8 lend somebody a hand

a to be very close together
b not interested at all
c so close you can go there on foot
d a carefree and happy life
e far away from any urban areas
f help another person
g right next to where I live
h have a good and friendly relationship

Listening

17

4 You are going to listen to a discussion between Helen, who comes from London but now lives in Edinburgh, and Tim, who lives in a small village in the south of England. Listen to the discussion and note what a) Helen likes about living in a city and b) Tim likes about living in a village.

D ▸ More help, p. 151

5 Think of the pros and cons of living in a city or in the countryside that are *not* mentioned in the discussion.

Working with words

6 For each of the following words, think of as many antonyms as you can. Then listen again and see if any of these antonyms are used in the discussion.

Example: *boring – interesting, fun, exciting, thrilling ("exciting" is used in the discussion)*

1 terrible
2 empty
3 urban
4 noisy
5 bothersome

Looking at language

Remember: Making comparisons

We use the comparative form + ***than*** to say how things are different.
*London is **bigger than** Manchester.* (short adjective)
*Living in the city is **more exciting than** living in a village.* (longer adjective)

We use ***(not) as*** + adjective + ***as*** to say how things are the same or not the same.
*For me, privacy is **(not) as important as** safety.*

7 Find at least five ways to complete each of these sentences.
- Life in the city is … life in the countryside.
- Life in the countryside is … life in the city.

D ▸ More challenge, p. 151
G ▸ Comparisons, p. 174

Speaking

8 Find a partner who has a different opinion than you about living in a city / the countryside. Discuss your preferences and give reasons. Say where you want to live and work after finishing school, and why.

How to say or write it

I want to live in a big city because I think it's …

I'd prefer to live in …. It's more interesting than …

After finishing school, I want to move to … because it's …

For me, working in … is much more …

I think living in … would be as … as living in …

Writing

9 Weigh the pros and cons of living in a city vs living in the countryside.

Exam preparation

S ▸ *Eine argumentierende/ bewertende Schreib- aufgabe bearbeiten*, pp. 35-40
S ▸ *Operatoren*, p. 33

Section F Modern poetry in rural America

Warm-up

1 Write the phrase *My hometown is* three times on a piece of paper. Now complete the sentences in three different ways, all of them true to your experience.

2 Read your sentences to the class.

3 Discuss which different aspects of your hometowns were mentioned.

Reading

4 Read to yourself what the young American poet Clementine von Radics says about her hometown. Then take turns reading aloud parts of the poem to the class. Before you read, decide which part each student is going to read.

Excerpt from "Hometown"

My hometown makes me very suspicious of anyone
who values education over kindness.
Who cares more about how smart you sound saying something
than what you are actually saying.

My hometown makes me hate people who aren't nice to waiters.

My hometown is mostly called rednecks
as though working all day in the sun to support your family is something
to be ashamed of.

My hometown eats at McDonald's
as though being a single mother who still manages to feed their children is
something to be ashamed of.

My hometown is unimpressed by the hubris of art
and listens to music that actually speaks to them.

[1] to **be suspicious of sb** *jdm misstrauen, jdm mit Argwohn begegnen*
[2] to **value sth over sth** *etw höher schätzen als etw, etw über etw stellen*
[2] **kindness** *Liebenswürdigkeit, Güte*
[7] **as though** *als ob*
[7] to **support your family** *die eigene Familie ernähren*
[8] to **be ashamed of sth** *sich für etw schämen*
[10] to **feed sb** *jdn ernähren*
[12] to **be unimpressed by sth** *sich von etw unbeeindruckt zeigen*
[12] hubris *Überheblichkeit, Anmaßung*

My hometown knows you don't need a college degree to be a decent fucking person.
My hometown has a beautiful view of the mountains.

At night you can see so many stars and it fills you with this bottomless hope,
it is the best lesson on beauty you could ever get.

My hometown understands the word community
and believes in taking care of each other.

My hometown can turn a cooler full of beer
and a backyard into the best fucking party you've ever been to.

My hometown loves you, feeds you, does not shame you for struggling.

My hometown is poor.

My hometown has no library.

My hometown does not apologize.

My home does not apologize. (223 words)

[14] **decent person** *anständiger Mensch*
[16] bottomless *unerschöpflich*
[20] cooler *Kühlbox*
[21] **backyard** *Garten (hinter dem Haus), Hof*

Speaking

5 Watch the video of poet Clementine von Radics. With a partner, discuss the following questions. Then share your answers with the class.

1. What does the poem say about Clementine's attitude towards her hometown?
2. What kind of problems does her hometown have? Name at least two.
3. What does Clementine say about the scenery/landscape in her hometown?
4. What about the language, form and rhythm she uses? How does it contribute to the message of the poem?
5. How do you feel about your own hometown? Do you have a clear opinion, or are you conflicted in your feelings?

Crossover TV

Clementine von Radics performs "Hometown"

02

D ▸ More help, p. 151

How to say or write it

The author uses direct/expressive/vivid language.
The tone/mood of the poem is humorous/depressing/sarcastic.
We also find examples of repetition/irony/slang in the poem.
The poem does/doesn't have a fixed rhyme scheme.
The rhythm of the poem varies / becomes faster / is regular.
This (stylistic device / kind of language) emphasizes the fact that …
I have mixed feelings about my hometown because …

Writing

6 With a partner, create a short poem about your hometown or a town you both know. Then present it to the rest of the class.
Which poems contained vivid descriptions? Were any of them touching? Which one did you enjoy the most? Why?

Project Making an awareness campaign video

awareness campaign *Informationskampagne*

You are going to create an awareness campaign video about an area in your town or region that needs improvement. The video should be about five minutes long, and you are going to work together in small groups to plan, write and produce it.

once *sobald, wenn*

Once you have formed your group, choose the topic you want to work on:

A Public transport
not enough buses or trains, buses or trains always crowded, station or bus stops dirty, no night buses or trains

B Boring for young people
no cultural activities for young people, lack of sports facilities, events are only for older people

C Who would want to live here?
ugly architecture, no green areas or parks, some places feel unsafe, no interesting shops, poor wifi

D Your own idea!

public transport *öffentliche Verkehrsmittel*

sports facilities *pl Sportstätten*

Follow the steps and use the tips to help make your campaign effective.

Step 1: Plan and prepare

A video needs careful planning and preparation. Make sure you have the right equipment (e.g. a camera and editing software) and review carefully the steps you're going to take. Make a project schedule so you stay on track.

editing software *Videoschnittprogramm*
to **review sth** *etw (wiederholt) (über)prüfen*

Step 2: Write a mission statement

Write a short statement (one or two sentences) that outlines the main objectives of your campaign. As you work, this will keep you focused on what you're trying to achieve and who you're trying reach.

mission statement *Leitbild*
to **outline sth** *etw skizzieren, etw kurz darlegen*
objective *Ziel*

Step 3: Create a catchy slogan

To be memorable and successful, your campaign needs a slogan people can remember. A slogan is different than a mission statement: it's a short, catchy phrase that creates excitement around your project.

catchy *eingängig, zündend*
memorable *einprägsam*
excitement *Begeisterung, Spannung, Aufregung*

Step 4: Create a "concept" for your video

Discuss what the video will be about and how it will be structured. Will you tell a story? Will it be funny or serious? Will you interview people or act out scenes? Brainstorm ideas and then decide which ones you want to use.

Step 5: Write a script

Your script should include the following elements:

a the text that will be spoken on screen
b clear indication of who speaks each line of the text
c where the words are spoken (location)
d how they should be said (loudly, quietly, aggressively, emotionally, etc.)
e any titles or words that will appear on the screen

Remember that your script should work towards the goals of the mission statement. At some point in the script, make sure to include your slogan.

indication *Hinweis, Anzeige*

Step 6: Create a storyboard

A storyboard is a sequence of drawings that shows the different scenes of the video. Ask yourself how you can visualize the situation or problem you want to describe, as well as the solution you are proposing. There are many storyboard templates available online, or you can create your own.

solution *Lösung*
to **propose sth** *etw vorstellen*

Step 7: Rehearse

to rehearse *proben*

After the script and storyboard are complete, those who act in the video can rehearse their lines.

Step 8: Find a location

What is the best place to shoot your video? Are you going to shoot inside a room or outdoors? Find a good setting and think about lighting and props. Keep in mind background noise when you choose your location.

setting *(Film:) Handlungsort, Schauplatz*
props *pl Requisiten*

Step 9: Shoot the video

Now that you've done all the planning, you're ready to pull out the video camera! When shooting, keep your script and storyboard close at hand. Follow the plan, but allow your actors to improvise as well.

Step 10: Edit your footage

After importing the footage onto your computer, use editing software to put together your final video. The editing process allows you to arrange clips in a different order, trim footage, add titles, and do colour correction.

to **edit** *(Film:) schneiden*
footage *Filmmaterial*
to **trim footage** *Filmsequenzen entfernen*

Step 11: Add music and sound effects

Music and sound effects are important. They can make your visual message stronger and create a special mood or atmosphere.

Tips for an effective campaign

Define your goals
Think of what exactly you want to achieve. Do you want to *inform people* about things they were not aware of? Do you want to *influence people* who have the power to make changes? Do you want to *find people* who support or fund your ideas?

Target your audience
Have a clear idea of the people you are speaking to. Your story, images and language need to be *right for the target group*.

Define specific actions
Your campaign wants people to take action, so be clear about *what the actions are* and *what steps they should take*.

Permissions and rights

Don't forget to think about permissions and rights when you produce a video – ignoring them can get you in trouble!

Permission to film on private property
If you want to shoot at a private location, you must get written permission from the owner. Shooting private property, e.g. the facades of buildings, from the street or another public, government-owned space requires no permission.

Permission to film a person
Before shooting, prepare a declaration of consent. You should ask every person who will be in the video to sign it. For people under the age of 18, including people in your group, a parent must sign a consent form as well.

Music rights
If you want to use music, there are three options:

- get permission from the composer, record company and musician
- use music that is free for non-commercial purposes
- compose your own music

Diagramme beschreiben und analysieren

Informationen, die auf Zahlen und Statistiken beruhen, können auf verschiedene Arten effektiv veranschaulicht werden. So können die eigentlichen Inhalte viel leichter aufgenommen und verstanden werden.
Welche Art von Schaubild zum Einsatz kommt, hängt maßgeblich davon ab, welche Informationen visualisiert werden sollen. Je nach Art des Diagramms benötigen Sie bestimmte Wörter und Wendungen zur Beschreibung und Interpretation.

Planen

Schritt 1: Art des Diagramms festlegen

Bar chart

wird genutzt, um Werte direkt zu vergleichen

Pie chart **Ring chart**

visualisiert prozentuale Anteile von 100 %

Line graph

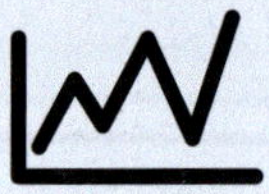

zeigt Entwicklungen über eine gewisse Zeitspanne

Übung 1

Ordnen Sie den folgenden Informationen die jeweils passende Diagrammart zu.

1 *e-bike sales figures over the past 12 months*
2 *bicycle production by EU-countries in 2021*
3 *contribution of different products to a bicycle shop's annual turnover*
4 *share of world's top 10 bicycle brands by sales*

sales figures *Verkaufs-/Absatzzahlen*
contribution *Beitrag, Anteil*
annual turnover *Jahresumsatz*
share *Anteil*

Schritt 2: Diagramme beschreiben

Einleitend geben Sie einen allgemeinen Überblick über Zweck und Inhalt des Schaubilds. Nennen Sie neben der Diagrammart auch Quelle, Autor und ggf. Veröffentlichungsdatum und erläutern Sie kurz, worum es in dem Diagramm geht.

The graph/chart is taken from … by …
It was published on … in …
The graph/chart is about … / deals with … / provides information about … / compares …
The graph/chart gives an overview of …
The graph/chart indicates/shows the development of …

to **publish sth** *etw veröffentlichen*
to **deal with sth** *sich mit etw befassen*
to **provide sth** *etw bieten*
to **indicate sth** *etw anzeigen, etw darstellen*

Übung 2

Bei der Recherche für Ihre E-Mail zur Problematik der aktuellen Straßenverkehrssituation in Ihrer Stadt/Region (siehe S. 60) stoßen Sie im Internet auf interessante Informationen in Form verschiedener Diagramme.
Beschreiben Sie die vier Diagramme, indem Sie mithilfe der gegebenen Formulierungen jeweils
- eine Einleitung zum Diagramm,
- einen Überblick dessen, was es darstellt,
- sowie jeweils eine ausführliche Beschreibung der Informationen verfassen.

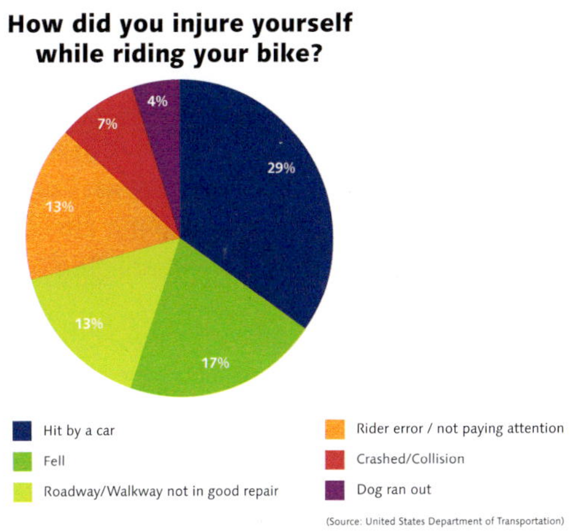

The pie chart is divided into … segments/sections …
Each segment represents …
The sections representing …
and … constitute the majority.
… makes up the biggest/ smallest segment.
more than / roughly / about twice as much as …
far less than …

to **be hit by a car** *von einem Fahrzeug erfasst werden*

to be in good repair *in gutem Zustand sein*

to **represent** *darstellen*

to **constitute** *bilden, ausmachen*

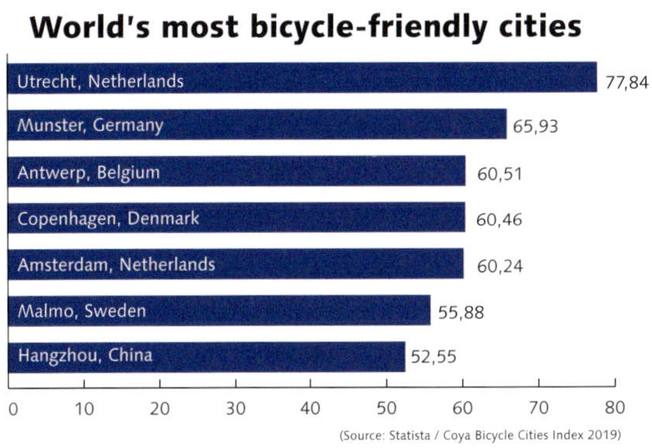

in comparison with / compared with …
in contrast to …
to rank first/second/…/last
the highest/lowest figure/score
no / little / a big difference between … and …
the vast majority of / only a minority of …

to **rank first** *den ersten Platz belegen*

vast majority *überwältigende Mehrheit*

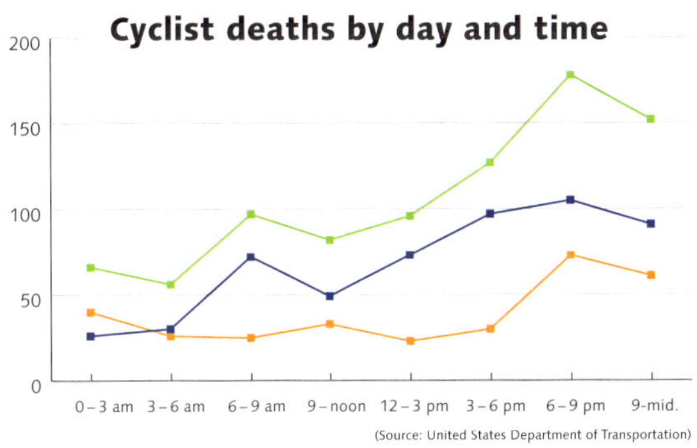

to reach a peak / low point of …
to remain constant/stable
to increase/rise/grow/go up … by … to …
to decrease / fall / drop / go down … by … to …
an increase/rise/growth …
sharp(ly)/steep(ly)/sudden(ly)/ constant(ly)/gradual(ly)/ slight(ly)/slow(ly)

G ▸ Reported speech, S. 168

Schritt 3: Diagramme analysieren

Erläutern Sie, welche Schlüsse Sie aus den Diagrammen ziehen und ordnen Sie diese in den Gesamtkontext ein. Wenn möglich, treffen Sie Vorhersagen für die Zukunft.

By and large, it can be concluded that …
What surprises me most / does not surprise me is that …
The graph could serve as a wake-up call …

by and large *im Großen und Ganzen*

to **serve as sth** *als etw dienen*

wake-up call *Weckruf, Alarmsignal*

Übung 3

1 Analysieren Sie die Diagramme.
2 Nutzen Sie passende und aussagekräftige Informationen aus den Diagrammen, um die Argumentation in Ihrer E-Mail damit zu unterstützen.
Untermauern Sie Ihre Argumentation in der E-Mail mit treffenden und aussagekräftigen Informationen aus den Diagrammen.

Gut zu wissen

Lesestrategien erleichtern das Verstehen von schwierigen Texten.

Schwierige Texte lesen

Das Wichtigste vorab: Geben Sie nicht auf, wenn Sie beim ersten Lesen eines Textes nicht gleich alles verstehen. Oft konzentriert man sich zu sehr auf das, was man noch nicht kann oder kennt, und versperrt sich so den inhaltlichen und sprachlichen Zugang zu einem neuen Text. Dabei haben Sie doch gerade erst angefangen, sich mit einem unbekannten Text auseinanderzusetzen! Haben Sie Geduld mit sich, und arbeiten Sie sich schrittweise voran – es lohnt sich!

Nutzen Sie die folgenden **Lesestrategien**, um Ihre Lesefertigkeit zu verbessern. Mit diesen Strategien trainieren Sie Ihre **Dekodierungskompetenz**, also das selbstständige Erschließen von unbekannten Wörtern und schwierigen Passagen.

Inhaltliche Ebene

▸ *Skills training: Understanding through context*, S. 17

Strategie 1: Den Kontext nutzen

Übung 1

1 **Übertragen Sie die folgenden Begriffe in Ihre Unterlagen. Notieren Sie – soweit möglich – ohne Zuhilfenahme von Wörterbüchern deren Übersetzung.**
cleansing · outgrown · victim · flourish · priced out · closure · venue · storey · layer

2 **Erschließen Sie die restlichen Bedeutungen aus dem Textzusammenhang.**
Lesen Sie dazu den Text über Shoreditch auf der folgenden Seite und ergänzen Sie – soweit möglich – weitere Übersetzungen der oben genannten Vokabeln.

Sie werden feststellen: Allein durch das Lesen von unbekannten Vokabeln in einem Textzusammenhang (und nicht mehr nur isoliert betrachtet) erschließt sich mitunter deren Bedeutung.
Wenn es danach immer noch das ein oder andere unbekannte Wort gibt, so ist das in der Oberstufe nicht unüblich. Letztendlich müssen Sie nicht jedes einzelne Wort kennen, um einen Text zu verstehen.

Gut zu wissen

Auch klassische Techniken wie **Notizen anfertigen, Fragen an den Text stellen, Abschnitte zusammenfassen** oder **Zusammenhänge visualisieren** helfen bei der intensiven Bearbeitung von Texten.

Strategie 2: *Traffic light reading* (Positivlesen)

Fürs Texterschließungstraining empfiehlt sich das Markieren nach dem Ampelprinzip: Grün kennzeichnen Sie, was Sie verstanden haben; Gelb verwenden Sie, um Wörter, Wortgruppen oder Passagen zu markieren, bei denen Sie zwar unsicher sind, aber dennoch glauben, sich diese aus dem Kontext erschließen zu können; und Rot nehmen Sie nur dann, wenn Sie etwas überhaupt nicht verstehen.

Übung 2

Rufen Sie den Text auf der Folgeseite in der PagePlayer-App auf und wenden Sie mithilfe des Textwerkzeugs das *traffic light reading* an.

Ziel des Positivlesens ist es zum einen zu zeigen, dass ein gewisses Maß an Leseverstehen auch ohne die Kenntnis aller Wörter erreichbar ist. Zum anderen wird Ihnen automatisch der Stand Ihrer Wortschatzkompetenz angezeigt – allzu viele rote Stellen sollte Ihr Ergebnis nicht haben!

Strategie 3: Verschiedene Lesestile anwenden

Je nachdem, welches Ziel Sie beim Lesen verfolgen, machen Sie sich neben dem gründlichen, intensiven Lesen weitere typische Lesestile zunutze.

Skimming

Zweck
Überfliegen, um sich rasch über den ungefähren Inhalt zu informieren

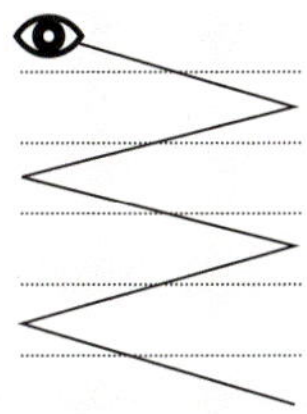

Scanning

Zweck
Suchen nach bestimmten Informationen

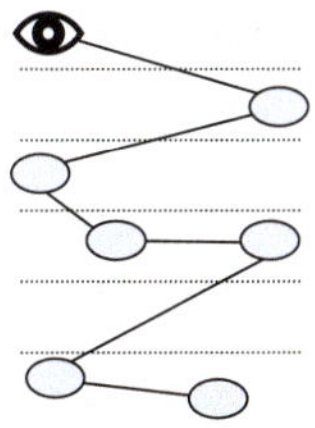

Shoreditch: is hipster heaven now falling prey to 'cultural cleansing'?

It was an edgy part of London, a hipster heaven for artists and clubbers. Now big money is moving in and taking over.

It is the home of hipsterism, the birthplace of a thousand bushy beards, but has Shoreditch outgrown its cool? Has it become an urban victim of its commercial success? It's a familiar cycle: a neglected inner-city neighbourhood is colonised by artists, a cafe culture flourishes, new businesses move in, then rents go up, and the original inhabitants who gave the place its character are priced out of the area.
This week sees the closure of the *Red Gallery*, the idiosyncratic event space, and its sister establishment, the symbolically titled pop-up food and music venue, *Last Days of Shoreditch*. They are to be cleared away for the construction of an 18-storey, 300-bed hotel by upmarket chain Art'otel, by the multinational Park Plaza group. […]
"The good thing about cities like New York and London is that the cool places move on. If you get tired of the white-guy-hipster thing, then there are other layers of the onion to pull back." […]

From: *The Guardian, 22 July 2018*

Übung 3

Wenden Sie für die folgende Frage den passenden Lesestil auf den Text über Shoreditch an.
What is the purpose of the building that will be built by the Park Plaza group?

Gut zu wissen

Im Unterrichtsalltag überschneiden sich ***skimming*** und ***scanning*** häufig.

Wortebene

Strategie 4: Wortbildungsmuster nutzen

▸ *Looking at language*, S. 117

Bestimmte Vorsilben und Nachsilben helfen beim Dekodieren von unbekannten Wörtern.

Strategie 5: Ähnlichkeit zur Muttersprache erkennen

Beispiel: *commercial* (l. 5) – kommerziell → geschäftlich, den Handel betreffend

Strategie 6: Auch einsprachige Wörterbücher nutzen

S ▸ Wörterbücher verwenden, S. 106–107

Besonders bei Redewendungen wie *to fall prey to sth* (s. Titel des Artikels) finden Sie hier Hilfe.

Übung 4

Wenden Sie passende Dekodierungsstrategien auf der Wortebene bei den folgenden Wörtern aus dem Text über Shoreditch an.
to fall prey to sth · *outgrown* · *urban* · *cycle* · *colonised* · *closure* · *symbolically*

Präsentieren

Die Kompetenz, eine wirkungsvolle Präsentation vor einem Publikum zu halten, ist in fast jedem Lebensstadium von Bedeutung, angefangen von der Schule bis hin zum Arbeitsleben. Nicht nur der Inhalt ist wichtig, sondern auch, wie klar und verständlich dieser vorgetragen und vermittelt wird.

Beispielaufgabe:
Halten Sie eine Präsentation zum Thema „Public art in Edinburgh, Scotland".

Recherchieren

Gut zu wissen

Suchen Sie bei Google effektiver mit Suchoperatoren wie *site:*, *related:*, *OR* und *AND*.

Bereiten Sie Ihr Thema sorgfältig vor und vergewissern Sie sich, dass die Webseiten, auf die Sie zurückgreifen, glaubwürdige Quellen darstellen. Schauen Sie im Zweifelsfall auf der *About*-Seite nach, wer die Webseite erstellt hat bzw. für sie verantwortlich ist. US-Webseiten mit Top-Level-Domains wie *.org*, *.edu*, and *.gov* dürften zuverlässig sein.

Halten Sie Ihre Rechercheergebnisse gut strukturiert fest.

Erstellen

Richten Sie Ihre Präsentation in Art und Inhalt auf Ihr Publikum aus. Auf Ihren **Moderationskarten** sollten idealerweise nur Stichwörter stehen, so dass Sie möglichst frei sprechen und Ihre Inhalte mit eigenen Wörtern formulieren können.

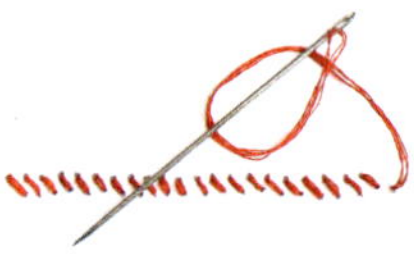

Legen Sie sich auf die wesentlichen Kernaussagen fest und stricken Sie Ihre Präsentation darum herum, so dass ein **roter Faden** entsteht.

🔊 Edinburgh

Edinburgh site:youglish.com

Prüfen Sie die Korrektheit Ihrer Notizen in Bezug auf Informationsgehalt und Sprache. Wenn Sie sich bei der **Aussprache** nicht sicher sind, hören Sie sich Beispiele in einem Online-Wörterbuch an. Suchen Sie notfalls nach Videos, die diesen Begriff enthalten.

S ▸ Bilder und Cartoons beschreiben und analysieren, S. 136–137

Versehen Sie Ihre Präsentation mit geeignetem **Anschauungsmaterial**, um die Inhalte für Ihre Zuhörer/innen einprägsamer zu machen.

- Wenn Sie Ihre Präsentationsfolien erstellen, überfrachten Sie diese nicht mit zu vielen Informationen. Das Hauptaugenmerk sollte auf Ihnen als Vortragendem/r liegen, nicht auf den Folien.

- Wenn Sie ein Flipchart oder Whiteboard benutzen: Überlegen Sie, wie dieses am Ende der Präsentation aussehen soll.

Üben & proben

Sie können gar nicht oft genug üben! Proben Sie Ihre Präsentation vor dem Spiegel oder nehmen Sie sich per Video auf. Sie werden sich wundern, wie schnell Sie Routine bekommen werden!

Üben Sie, ruhig zu stehen, und achten Sie dabei auf Ihre Körpersprache (Mimik und Gestik), auf einen ruhigen Sprachvortrag und klare Betonung.

Verwenden Sie orientierende Redewendungen (sog. ***signposting***), um Ihrem Vortrag Struktur zu geben und den Zuhörern/-innen mitzuteilen, an welcher Stelle Ihrer Präsentation Sie sich gerade befinden und was als Nächstes kommt.

Sagen Sie am Anfang, worum es geht, und wiederholen Sie am Ende Ihre Kernbotschaften.

Introducing yourself and your topic

- Good morning/afternoon. My name is ...
- Today I am going to talk about ...
- The subject of my talk is ...
- My topic today is ...
- If you have any questions, please don't hesitate to interrupt me.
- I'd like to ask you to please save your questions for the end of the presentation.

to **hesitate** *zögern*
to **interrupt sb** *jdm ins Wort fallen*

Beginning your first point

- I'd like to begin by saying something about ...
- I want to start by explaining ...

Guiding your audience through your presentation

- There are a number of points I'd like to make.
- I'll start with .... Then I'll talk about ...
- Firstly .... Secondly ... / First of all ... / And finally, ...
- And now, moving on to ...
- The next topic I'd like to focus on is ...
- Now I'd like to discuss ...
- Now we'll move on to ...
- Let's look at ...
- Why is this important? Because ...
- The significance of this is ...

significance *Bedeutung, Wichtigkeit*
briefly *kurz*
issue *Problem, Thema*
to **cover sth** *etw (Thema usw.) behandeln*

Ending your presentation

- Let's summarize briefly what we've looked at.
- Let me remind you of some of the issues we've covered.
- In conclusion, ...
- I would like to finish by saying ...
- Thank you very much for your attention.
- If you have any questions, I'm happy to answer them now.

Übung

Führen Sie in einer Gruppe das Spiel *Can I have a minute?* durch. Jede/r Spieler/in hält eine einminütige Präsentation zu einem Thema wie z.B. ...

- *How not to get a date*
- *If I ruled the world*
- *Fun things to do during exams*
- *Zombies*

Natürlich sind auch seriöse Themen möglich. Wichtig: Nutzen Sie *signposting*-Phrasen.

Nachdem alle ihre Präsentation gehalten haben, geben Sie Ihr Feedback. Machen Sie sich dazu bereits während der Präsentation Notizen zu *signposting*, Körpersprache, Betonung, visuellen Hilfsmitteln usw.

to **rule sth** *etw regieren, über etw herrschen*

Eine Aufgabe zum integrierten Leseverstehen bearbeiten

Gut zu wissen

Im **Abitur** wird mit diesem Aufgabenformat Ihr **Textverständnis** überprüft.

Bei dieser Aufgabe geht es um das korrekte Verständnis eines Textes. Wovon handelt er? Was sagt er zu einer bestimmten Thematik aus? Je nach Ausrichtung der Aufgabe handelt es sich dabei um eine **allgemeine Zusammenfassung** des Textes (= **Inhaltsangabe**) oder um die **Zusammenfassung bestimmter Aspekte**.

Checkliste für Zusammenfassungen

- Erwartet wird ein zusammenhängender und strukturierter Text im Simple Present.
- Teilen Sie Ihren Text anhand der Argumente des Originaltextes in Sinnabschnitte ein.
- Lassen Sie Beispiele oder Details weg.
- Verwenden Sie keine Zitate, umschreiben Sie stattdessen.
- Bleiben Sie objektiv – verzichten Sie auf Wertungen und bleiben Sie bei den Aussagen des Textes.
- Ihr Text sollte ca. ein Viertel bis ein Drittel der Länge des Originaltextes haben.

G ▸ Reported speech, S. 168

Allgemeine Zusammenfassung (Inhaltsangabe)

▸ Operatoren, S. 33

1 **Lesen Sie die Aufgabenstellung gründlich durch.**
Typische **Operatoren** für Inhaltsangaben sind ***summarize*** und ***outline*** in Verbindung mit dem Hauptthema.

2 **Lesen Sie den Text aufmerksam durch und markieren Sie**
a) die Hauptaussage(n),
b) Argumente und Fakten.

Markieren Sie nur die wesentlichen Begriffe bzw. Satzteile.

Übung 1

Summarize the information given in the article about Seattle on page 51.

Einleitung
The [text type + "title"] written by [author] in [year] informs about / deals with [main topic].

Hauptteil
The author …
… says / states / points out / claims / believes / thinks / describes / explains / argues / suggests that …
… doubts / asks whether …
… criticizes / analyses / tries to express …
… contrasts X with Y / compares X to Y …

Schlussteil
In his/her concluding paragraph/sentence …
The author closes his/her [text type] stating …

Zusammenfassung bestimmter Aspekte

▸ Operatoren, S. 33

In der Aufgabenstellung kann auch eine **Einschränkung** auf bestimmte Aspekte vorgenommen werden. Achten Sie daher besonders auf die **inhaltliche Formulierung** und die **Operatoren**.

Übung 2

Point out the effects of the tech boom on the city of Seattle.

mögliche Operatoren

point out: bestimmte Informationen zu einem Aspekt herausfiltern

describe: einen Aspekt genau beschreiben

state: einen Sachverhalt auf den Punkt bringen (ähnlich wie *summarize / outline*)

illustrate: einen Sachverhalt mit Textbelegen veranschaulichen

Review

1 Rank the Sections A–F in this Topic based on how interesting they were to you. Then, look back at your work on the overview of this Topic (pages 44–45) and how you ranked them there (page 45, exercise 3). Have your rankings changed? Share your results with a group, and tell them what you found most interesting.

2 Look back at your KWL list (page 45, exercise 5). Fill out the "Learnt" part of the list. Next, look at your "Want to know" list. What do you still want to know?

3 Make a list of ten words in the Topic that were new to you and you consider important to know. Then collect everyone's words and cluster them into groups. Finally, pick a word group and write a paragraph using all the words.

Evaluate

1 Do this task on your own. How much do you agree or disagree with the statements below? Rate each one on a scale of one to four. The references on the right show you what exercises you can review.
1 = totally disagree **2** = disagree **3** = agree **4** = totally agree

Section		Statement	
A	**1**	I can talk about pieces of street art.	▸ p. 47, exercise 3
	2	I can guide people through a presentation or talk	▸ p. 48, exercises 4–6
B	**3**	I can collect and sort ideas using a mind map.	▸ p. 50, exercises 6–7
	4	I can understand and summarize the article on gentrification.	▸ p. 52, exercise 12
	5	I can talk about past events with and without present effects.	▸ p. 52, exercises 13–14
	6	I can describe the bar chart in this Section orally.	▸ p. 53, exercise 15
C	**7**	I can translate *fahren* and *gehen* correctly in different contexts.	▸ p. 55, exercises 3–5
	8	I can talk about urban transportation and explain my preferences.	▸ p. 56, exercises 6–10
	9	I can connect sentences using linking words and phrases that express effect or consequence.	▸ p. 58, exercises 12–14
	10	I can write a formal email.	▸ pp. 59–60, exercises 15–17
D	**11**	I can talk about the highlights and attractions of a country or region.	▸ pp. 62–63, exercises 4–6
	12	I can describe the postcard pictures in this Section.	▸ p. 63, exercise 7
E	**13**	I can discuss my preferences on where I want to live.	▸ p. 65, exercise 8
	14	I can make comparisons.	▸ p. 65, exercise 7
F	**15**	I can talk about language and stylistic devices in a poem.	▸ p. 67, exercise 5
Skills	**16**	I can describe and analyse diagrams orally.	S ▸ pp. 70–71
	17	I know strategies to deal with reading difficult texts.	S ▸ pp. 72–73
	18	I can give good presentations.	S ▸ pp. 74–75
	19	I can deal with integrated reading comprehension tasks.	S ▸ p. 76

Consolidate

You want to go deeper into anglophone cities and regions and speed up your learning process? Scan this page with the PagePlayer app. There you'll find some suggestions for additional tasks.

Topic 3 American and British political systems

Section A
Political parties in the US

"To have a healthy government we must have healthy and functioning parties. We must respect each other again in an atmosphere of shared facts and shared values ... We must argue our positions fervently, and never be afraid to compromise." – Jeff Flake, US Senator

two-party system

conservative vs liberal

Fact: In the US, most people with a strong party loyalty talk about politics every day or a few times a week. Swing voters, on the other hand, tend to be younger and less engaged with politics (source: Pew Research).

democracy

Section F
The British monarchy

royal family

Fact: To maintain the royal family, the average taxpayer in the UK pays about £1 a year in direct funding (not including security costs). However, the royal family generates about £550 million annually just in tourism.

1 Read ...
- **a** the facts about the political systems in the US and the UK. Which of them ...
  - are totally new to you?
  - do you find surprising?
- **b** the quotations. What are your opinions about these statements?

2 Rank the Sections A–F on how interested you are in them.

3 The mind map shows you a preview of Topic 3. Copy it onto a piece of paper and add words and phrases from ...
- **a** the facts and quotations.
- **b** Sections A–F you think are important.
- **c** the Word Bank on the opposite page.

Section B

The US electoral system

right to vote

presidential elections

"Free elections don't always result in fair elections." – DaShanne Stokes, author and activist

Fact: Participation in US elections is quite low. In the last fifty years of presidential elections, the average share of eligible voters who cast ballots was 42% (source: electproject.org). By contrast, average election turnout in Bundestag elections is 76% (source: gut-leben-in-deutschland.de).

Find information on each Section in the PagePlayer app!

Section C

Separation of powers in the US

checks and balances

"If men were angels, no government would be necessary … You must first enable the government to control the governed; and in the next place oblige it to control itself." – James Madison, US president

parliamentary democracy

contemporary issues

Section D

Houses of Parliament and the UK

"When people say England, they sometimes mean Great Britain, sometimes the United Kingdom, sometimes the British Isles … but never England." – George Mikes, journalist

Section E

Political parties and voting system in the UK

Fact: The UK's electorate consists of 46.5 million people. In the 2016 Brexit referendum, voter turnout was 72.2%, with the majority voting "Leave". Most young people, however, voted to remain in the European Union.

4 Note a few key words to say what you expect to learn in each Section.

5 Make a "KWL" (Know, Want to know, Learnt) list for the Topic.

6 With a partner, compare …
- **a** your mind maps and say why you added words where you did.
- **b** your rankings from exercise 2.
- **c** what you expect to learn in Sections A–F.

Then compare with another pair.

7 Save your work for reviewing when you've finished the Topic.

Word bank

ballot box *Wahlurne*
to **campaign** *Wahlkampf machen*
constitution *Verfassung*
to **elect sb (sth)** *jdn (zu etw) wählen*
election *(Parlaments-, Präsidentschaft-)Wahl*
electorate *Wahlberechtigte pl, Wahlvolk*
eligible *wahlberechtigt*
representative *(Parlaments-) Abgeordnete/r*
to **step down** *zurücktreten*
turnout *Wahlbeteiligung*
vote *Abstimmung, Wahl, (Wahl-) Stimme*
to **vote** *abstimmen, stimmen, wählen, wählen gehen*

Section A Political parties in the US

Warm-up

1 Who are the people in the photos and what positions have they held in the US government?

2 Which political party – Democrat or Republican – do you associate with each image?

3 Which party is considered more conservative and which more liberal? What does it mean to be "conservative" or "liberal"?

to **align with sb/sth** *mit jdm/etw (in bestimmten Punkten) übereinstimmen*

4 Which political issues are these demonstrations in support of? Which party does each align with?

Good to know

In everyday conversation, *to stick to your guns* means to hold on to your beliefs and not let them be changed.

5 What topics do you think are important in politics today? Which political issues are most relevant to you?

Working with the text

6 Before you read the VOTE-O-MAT text below, look at the highlighted words and match them to the German words.

D ▸ More practice, p. 151

1 Abtreibung
2 Bundesregierung
3 gleichgeschlechtliche Ehen
4 impfen
5 gesetzlicher Mindestlohn
6 Staatsbürgerschaft erhalten
7 Steuern
8 Vorschriften

7 Imagine you are an American and use the VOTE-O-MAT to find out whom you should vote for in the next US presidential election. For each statement, choose *agree*, *disagree* or *don't know*.

VOTE-O-MAT *The easiest way to choose a candidate*

1 Foreigners living in the United States should have the right to vote.

2 The minimum voting age of 18 for general elections should be lowered.

3 The federal government should pay for a four-year university education.

4 Student loans should become much cheaper.

5 The government should raise taxes on the rich.

6 The government should increase the federal minimum wage.

7 The US should not build a wall along the US–Mexico border.

8 The children of illegal immigrants should be granted citizenship.

9 Same-sex marriages should be legal.

10 Parents should be required to vaccinate children, e.g. against COVID-19, measles, etc.

11 All women should have the right to an abortion (I am pro-choice).

12 The government should implement more regulations to slow down climate change.

13 The US should limit or stop offshore oil drilling.

14 Teachers should not be allowed to carry guns at schools.

party affiliation *Parteizugehörigkeit*

3 to **side with sb/sth** *sich hinter jdn/etw stellen, für jdn/etw Partei ergreifen*

6 to **tackle sth** *etw bekämpfen*

6 **social inequality** *soziale Ungerechtigkeit*

7 **social welfare** *Sozialhilfe*

7 **in need** *bedürftig*

8 **abortion** *Abtreibung*

8 to **be pro-choice** *Abtreibungsbefürworter/in sein*

15 to **interfere with sth** *sich in etw einmischen*

17 to **take a tough stance against sth** *eine harte Haltung gegenüber etw einnehmen*

Results: Your party affiliation

If you AGREE with most statements (10 or more):
The more often you chose AGREE, the more you side with *progressive* positions, which means you believe in an open and liberal society and you value diversity. You believe in a strong government which should tackle corruption and social inequality and provide help and social welfare to citizens in need. With regard to abortion, you will likely be pro-choice. You probably also have strong "green" values and want the government to do more to protect the environment. Based on your political beliefs, you should vote for a Democrat.

If you DISAGREE with most statements (10 or more):
The more often you chose DISAGREE, the more you side with *traditional* and *conservative* positions, which means you strongly believe in maintaining traditional ideas of marriage, family, etc. You most likely favour "small government", which you think should interfere as little as possible with citizens' lives. You tend to dislike bureaucracy and inefficiency. You probably believe in law and order and take a tougher stance against immigration. Economic factors are often more important to you than environmental ones. Based on your political beliefs, you should vote for a Republican candidate.

8 Choose the best title for each set of questions in the questionnaire. There is one title that you don't need.

1 Questions 1–2	**a** economic issues
2 Questions 3–4	**b** racial inequality issues
3 Questions 5–6	**c** environmental issues
4 Questions 7–8	**d** social issues
5 Questions 9–11	**e** electoral issues
6 Questions 12–13	**f** educational policy issues
7 Question 14	**g** security issues
	h immigration issues

How to say or write it

According to my result, I would vote for a Democratic/Republican candidate.

According to this, I value …

For me personally, … would be the most relevant issue(s).

Speaking

9 Discuss the questions with a partner.

1. According to your result, would you vote Democrat or Republican? What does your result say about your political beliefs and values?
2. Which of the issues mentioned in the VOTE-O-MAT are most relevant to you?
3. Would you use a VOTE-O-MAT to find out whom you should vote for?

Exam preparation

S ▸ *Eine kreative Schreibaufgabe bearbeiten*, pp. 41-42
S ▸ *Stilmittel*, p.108

Writing

10 Your school will hold an assembly soon, just days before local and national elections. Write a speech explaining to your fellow students why it's important to vote.

Section B The US electoral system

Warm-up

1 Read these quotations. Why do you think the people were motivated to make these statements? Do you agree with them? Discuss in a group.

"A citizen of America will cross the ocean to fight for democracy but won't cross the street to vote in a national election."
– Bill Vaughan, journalist

"Half of the American people have never read a newspaper. Half never voted for president. One hopes it is the same half." – Gore Vidal, author

"Don't boo, vote." – Barack Obama, US president

"If voting changed anything, they'd make it illegal."
– Emma Goldman, political activist

2 If you want to become an American citizen, you must pass the US citizenship test. Answer these questions from the test. Then compare your answers with a partner's.

U.S. Citizenship and
Immigration Services

1 **If you want to become president of the United States, you must ...**
   a be at least 27 years old.
   b be a natural-born citizen of the US.
   c have lived in the US for at least 10 years.
   d have extensive knowledge of American politics.

2 **In what month do Americans vote for president?**
   a January b August c October d November

3 **What is the name of the official ceremony in which the president and vice president take office?**
   a inauguration b election day c party convention d Independence Day

4 **What is the maximum number of years the president can stay in office in the US?**
   a 4 years b 6 years c 8 years d 10 years

5 **Who was the first Black president of the United States?**
   a Martin Luther King, Jr. c George W. Bush
   b Bill Clinton d Barack Obama

6 **What are the two parts of Congress: the House of Representatives and the ...?**
   a Cabinet b Parliament c Senate d House of Commons

Listening

18

D ▸ More help, p. 152

3 **Listen to Part 1 of this podcast for first-time voters about the election process in the US. Then complete the chart with the missing words.**

Electoral College votes | general election | national conventions | president takes office (inauguration) | primaries

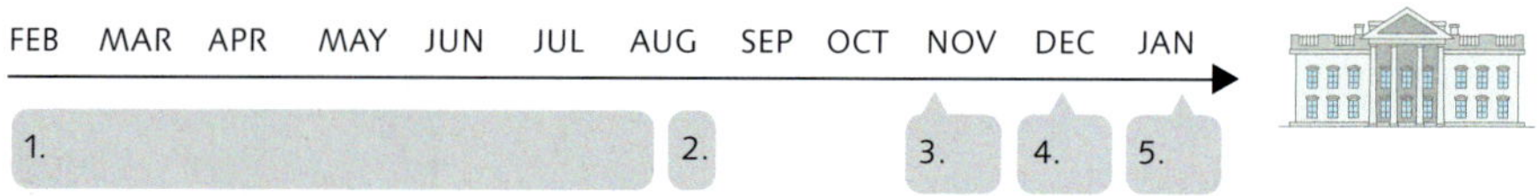

19

4 **Read the podcast summary. Then listen to Part 2 of the podcast and put the questions (a–f) in the order they are mentioned.**

Podcast: *Politics Today: One-on-One*
Host: Ramon García
Summary: Ramon answers voters' questions about the US presidential election
Questions include:

a Do we vote for the president directly?
b How can I become president?
c Swing states – why are they important?
d How many electors are there?
e What's the purpose of national conventions?
f Why vote in the primary?

Exam preparation

S ▸ *Richtig mit Hörverstehensaufgaben umgehen*, pp. 104–105

5 **Choose the right answer. If necessary, listen to Part 2 again.**

1 Primaries are …
a local elections. **b** general elections. **c** elections at the state level.

2 Campaigning across the country as a presidential candidate …
a is very expensive. **b** requires going to all 50 states.
c must be completed by 1 October.

3 If the party is convinced someone is the best person for the job, he or she will …
a win the general election. **b** win the party's nomination.
c receive a lot of funding.

4 The … are a group of 538 people. They choose the president and vice president.
a voters **b** electors **c** conventions

5 A general election is about who becomes president and also who goes to …
a the Senate. **b** The White House. **c** Springfield, Illinois.

6 The number of electors per state depends on …
a the number of voters. **b** the number of inhabitants.
c the geographical size of the state.

7 … are places where the outcome of the vote is uncertain and could go either way.
a Rural states **b** Urban areas **c** Swing states

8 To win a presidential election, the candidate must win …
a at least 25 states. **b** the state of California.
c at least 270 Electoral College votes.

Working with words

6 Match the verbs (1–7) and the expressions (a–g).

1 cast	**a** the party nomination
2 win	**b** money for the campaign
3 vote	**c** for president
4 hold	**d** throughout the country
5 select	**e** a national convention
6 raise	**f** a candidate/nominee
7 campaign	**g** a vote/ballot

7 In groups, use the phrases from exercise 6 to make one sentence for each step of the voting process in the chart on page 84. Then compare with other groups.

Looking at language

8 Complete the sentences with a word from the box. Some words can be used more than once.

announcing | based | casting | given | in which | raising | voting | which | who(m)

1 Primaries are state-level election events … people vote for the candidate … will represent them in the general election.
2 So … in a primary is also about … you want to see in Washington.
3 After … to your party that you want to run for president, you do a lot of campaigning across the country, … costs a lot of money.
4 And that also decides … of these parties wins the majority in the House of Representatives and the Senate.
5 … my vote in the general election means … for the president.
6 And … the fact that Wyoming has fewer than 600,000 inhabitants, it is the least populated states in the USA.
7 … on the election result, the party majority can change in the House of Representatives and the Senate.
8 … funds before and during your campaign would be an important part of the job.

Skills training: Using connective phrases in writing

To create a good flow in texts and present arguments convincingly, connect your sentences in a meaningful way. You can do so by using:

1 relative pronouns: *who*, *whom*, *whose*, *which*, *that*
Many people voted in the primary. The majority support the Republican candidate.
The majority of people ***who*** *voted in the primary support the Republican candidate.*

2 present participles
Many Democrats were elected. This resulted in a majority in Congress.
Many Democrats were elected, ***resulting*** *in a majority in Congress.*

3 past participles
The candidate is supported by young voters. He is likely to win the election.
Supported *by young voters, the candidate is likely to win the …*

D ▸ More practice, p. 152

9 Improve the text by following the instructions on the right.

If somebody votes for a candidate in a primary it means that he or she wants this person to go to Congress to represent his or her interests in Washington.	Replace *if*-clause with a present participle.
After the primaries have been completed in each state, the National Conventions take place. During the National Conventions, the elected delegates cast their vote for a party candidate.	Replace with a present participle.
Many people are surprised to learn that they don't actually vote for a president, but for electors. The electors form the Electoral College.	Use a relative pronoun to connect the sentences.
The electors are appointed by the state. Their task is to support the candidate the voters supported.	Rewrite the sentence using a past participle.
The number of electoral votes in each state ranges from three to fifty-five. The number depends on the population.	Rewrite the sentence using a present participle.

D ▸ More help, p. 152

10 In your own words, give a brief summary of all the events in the US electoral process. Make sure you check the timeline on page 84 and put the events in the correct order.

Speaking

Skills training: Taking part in discussions

To make a discussion interesting and engaging, it's important that you take an active role, listen to other participants, and stick to the topic.

1 **Say what you think and give reasons for your opinion.**
Personally, I think that …

2 **Ask others what they think.**
What do you think about …?

3 **Agree or disagree with what other people say.**
I totally agree with what you said. / I'm not sure I agree with you.

4 **Check whether other people can follow what you are saying.**
Do you see what I mean?

5 **Show that you are listening carefully.**
I see. / Really?

▸ Phrases for writing and discussion, inside front cover

How to say or write it

I think the US voting system is quite/too complicated because …

The US voting system seems rather complicated/simple to me.

What I didn't know was that …

I was surprised to hear that … because …

I was aware that …, but I didn't know that …

11 Discuss what you think about the US voting system. Which aspects of it were new and/or surprising to you? What do you think about the role that fundraising plays in US elections?

Writing

12 ⭘ For an online student magazine, write a blog article that outlines the timeline and steps of the US presidential election process. Use as many of the collocations and connectives from the podcast on page 84 as you can to make your blog article interesting to read.

Exam preparation

S ▸ *Eine kreative Schreibaufgabe bearbeiten*, pp. 41–42

Working with the text

13 Read the interview about the American voting system and answer the questions on page 88.

20

S ▸ *Schwierige Texte lesen*, pp. 72–73

Whoever said democracy was fair?

Malik Johnson interviews author Laura Collins

Malik Laura, you've done a lot of research into the electoral process and have just published a book called *The Electoral Process in the US: How Fair Is It?* Tell me, what was your motivation for writing this book?

Laura Well, recently there have been so many discussions about how fair or unfair the system is that I wanted to figure it out for myself!

Malik And what did you find out? Is it fair?

Laura Well, first of all, it's terribly complicated. And is it fair? I'd say that depends, but let's start with the fact that it's pretty outdated. Remember that the Electoral College was created at the end of the eighteenth century. And basically, it hasn't changed much since then.

Malik Why didn't they set up a system for people to vote on a national level – to vote for the president directly?

Laura To put it simply, a national popular vote would have been practically impossible at that time – just think of the size of the country, the difficulty of communication and so on. So actually, creating the Electoral College wasn't a bad idea at the time, but now we live in the twenty-first century and things have changed. Many people feel the voting process should change too.

Malik OK, so you think we should abolish the Electoral College? Some of my friends are afraid that without the electoral votes there would be chaos and instability.

Laura Honestly, I'm not sure. Perhaps if we didn't have electors and the president were to be chosen by popular vote, we would have loads of presidential candidates running for president. Perhaps too many! This could be confusing for the voters and the outcome might be unclear. But who knows. The biggest problem is that many people think that our voting system itself isn't totally fair.

Malik Why's that?

Laura Because what we have is a "winner takes all" system, meaning the "losers" end up empty-handed. Look, let's say that in the state of Ohio, 49% of the votes go to the Democrats, and 51% to the Republicans. In that case, the Republicans get ALL the Electoral College votes for Ohio, and the Democrats get nothing. That means 49% of the population effectively loses its vote. And the result would be same if the Republican got 90% of the vote and the Democrats only 10%. That's why many people think that the voting system isn't fair.

Malik Right. Let me ask you another question that's been on many people's minds. How is it possible that a presidential candidate can win the majority of the votes nationally, but not become president?

Good to know

The *popular vote* is the total number of votes cast for each candidate in all US states.
The *electoral vote* is the number of votes each candidate receives from the electors.
In 2016, Donald Trump received 304 electoral votes, making him the next president of the United States, despite the fact that he lost the popular vote by nearly three million.

2 **electoral process** *Wahlverfahren*
8 **outdated** *antiquiert, veraltet*
11 **on a national level** *auf Landesebene, landesweit*
13 **national popular vote** *landesweite Volksabstimmung*
19 **to abolish sth** *etw abschaffen*
24 **to run for president** *sich um die Präsidentschaft bewerben*
25 **outcome** *(Wahl-)Ergebnis*
37 **to be on sb's mind** *(Thema, Problem:) jdn beschäftigen*
38 **presidential candidate** *Präsidentschaftskandidat/in*
38 **majority** *Mehrheit*

[53] **competitor** *Mitbewerber/in*

[68] **voting system** *Wahlsystem*

[71] to **question sth** *etw in Frage stellen*

[72] to **serve a purpose** *einen Zweck erfüllen, zweckdienlich sein*

[72] **legitimate** *legitim*

[78] **binary choice** *Wahl zwischen zwei Möglichkeiten*

[79] **appropriate** *angemessen, geeignet*

Laura Yes, many people find that frustrating! The answer is quite simple though. There are 538 members of the Electoral College, and to become president, you need to win at least 270 votes. If you get these, you win, even if your competitor gets more of the popular vote. In our system, only the electoral vote counts when electing a president, the popular vote doesn't.

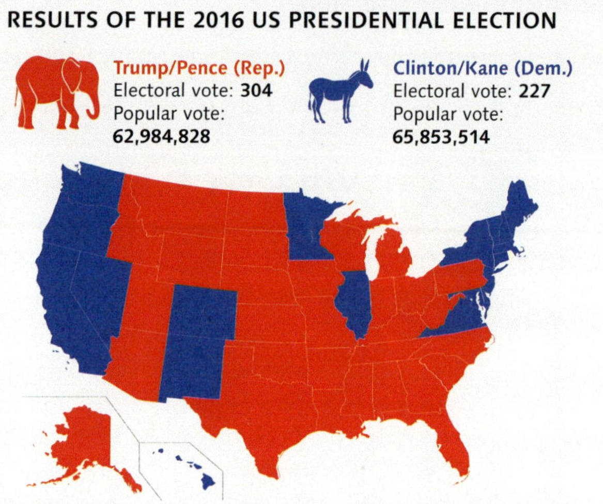

Malik Wow. So how often does it happen that a candidate becomes president without winning the popular vote?

Laura Surprisingly often! It happened three times in the nineteenth century, and more recently, in 2000, George W. Bush won with 271 electoral votes while his rival, Al Gore, had 500,000 more popular votes. And in 2016, it was even worse, when Hillary Clinton had almost three million more popular votes, but Donald Trump won the majority of electoral votes and so he became president.

Malik Would you call this process democratic and fair?

Laura Well, if by democratic you mean that people can vote directly for the candidate of their choice, perhaps it's not extremely democratic. And there are other issues with our voting system: How fair is our voter registration process? Who can vote? Does the number of electors still match a state's population? Is it OK to have two senators per state when the states are so different in population? Many people are now questioning our voting system. Does it serve its purpose? How legitimate is it? Why can't the country as a whole decide who becomes president? These are many questions that need to be answered.

Malik I see. So, in your research, did you come across any positive aspects at all when looking at our voting process?

Laura Yes, I did. Generally speaking, the system works because the Electoral College fits our two-party system. It offers a simple and binary choice – it's absolutely appropriate when you have just two parties.

Malik Thank you very much, Laura. (774 words)

1. Why has Laura written a book about the electoral process in the US?
2. Why was the Electoral College created as it is?
3. What might happen if the Electoral College were abolished?
4. How does the "winner takes all" voting system work?
5. How can a candidate become president without winning the popular vote?
6. With regard to the American voting system, what other problems does Laura mention?
7. What is an advantage of the Electoral College?

Looking at language

Remember: Using adverbs

G ▸ Comparisons, p. 174

There are different ways that an adverb can help make a sentence stronger or more precise.

A to say how you do it (verb + adverb): *vote directly*
B to describe how sth is exactly (adverb + adjective): *terribly expensive* OR (adverb + past participle) *well organized*, *badly written*
C to say how often, when, or in what way sth happens: *recently*, *frequently*, *practically*
D to start a sentence: *Unfortunately*, *Surprisingly*
E in a fixed expression: *to put it simply*

14 Make ten sentences using adverbs in the box. Then compare them with a partner's.

absolutely | actually | basically | directly | extremely | generally | honestly | nationally | originally | practically | recently | simply | surprisingly | terribly | unfortunately | well

Writing

15 State the main reasons why many people think the US voting system needs to be reformed. Illustrate your text with examples.

Before you start, structure your points in a chart.

Exam preparation

S ▸ *Eine Aufgabe zum integrierten Leseverstehen bearbeiten*, p. 76
S ▸ *Operatoren*, pp. 33–34

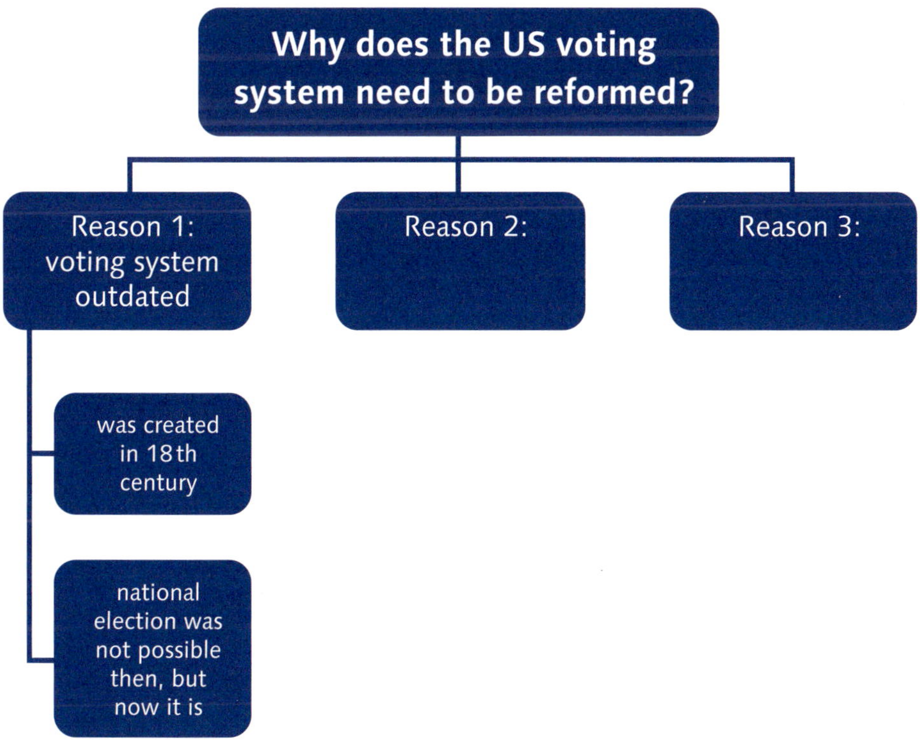

Section C Separation of powers in the US

Warm-up

1 Copy this chart of the US political system and complete it with the words from the box. Work together in small groups.

Cabinet | Congress | Executive Branch | Judicial Branch (Judiciary) | Legislative Branch | President | Senate | Supreme Court | Vice President

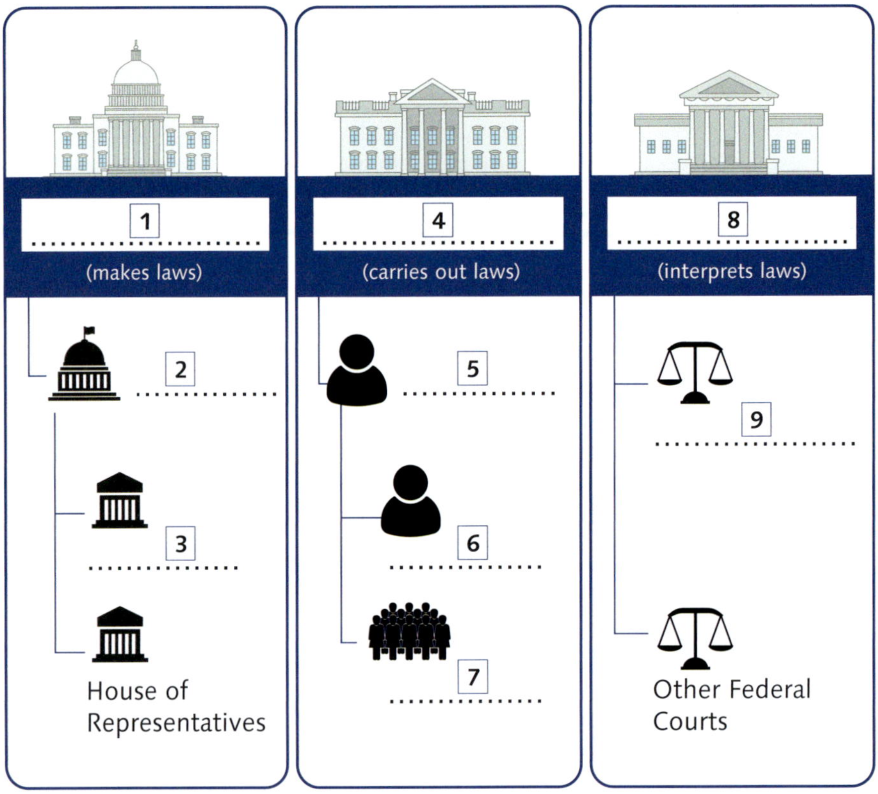

2 Both Germany and the US have three main branches of government. Why is that? What advantages are there to having three branches (as opposed to two, or four, or one)?

Watching

Crossover TV

Separation of powers in the US

03

3 Before you watch the video on the separation of powers in the US, look at the Skills Training box on page 91 for guidance on comprehension. Then watch the video and answer the questions.

1. What are the three main branches of government?
2. What is the purpose of "checks and balances" in the US Constitution?
3. Who makes laws?
4. How many parts does Congress consist of and what are they called?
5. What is the branch called which deals with interpreting the laws?

Skills training: Dealing with listening and watching tasks

Listening and watching tasks are usually divided into two steps: the first step is getting **general information**, the second is focusing on **details**.

Before first listening/watching:

1 The title may give you an idea of what kind of vocabulary to expect.
the separation of powers in the US, branches of government

2 The questions tell you what kind of information you need to look out for.
branches of government, Constitution, checks and balances, Congress

3 Look for key words to tell you what you need to focus on.
question words: *what, who, when, why, how many?*
verbs and nouns: *make laws, interpret the laws*
words such as *purpose, cause, reason, result*

During first listening/watching:

1 It is not necessary to understand every single word.
2 Pictures, graphics, subtitles, and body language will help you understand.
3 Focus on key information and write down important facts.

Before second listening/watching:

1 Read the questions again.
2 Identify details you need to find out the second time you listen/watch..

During second listening/watching:

1 Complete any missing information.

4 Watch the video again and complete the sentences.

D ▸ More help, p. 153

1 In 1789, the United States became one of the first democracies in the world by adopting its …
2 Articles 1–3 deal with the three …
3 The system of … makes sure each branch limits the power of the other two.
4 The legislature is also called …
5 The job of Congress is to …
6 … has 100 members in total.
7 … is the head of the Executive.
8 The president can stay in office for a maximum of …
9 The president appoints members to his or her … to advise him on different areas of policy.
10 Article 3 of the US Constitution deals with the …

Speaking

5 Discuss with a partner. Do you think it's necessary for a country to limit the power of the Executive? Why? How does the US make sure that the president does not become too powerful?

Working with the text

21

S ▸ *Wörterbücher verwenden*, pp. 106–107

checks and balances ***pl*** *Kontrollmechanismen*

11 **military forces** ***pl*** *Streitkräfte*

12 to **approve sth** *etw genehmigen*

17 **veto power** *Vetorecht*

18 to **pass a law** *ein Gesetz verabschieden*

18 to **veto sth** *ein Veto gegen etw einlegen*

19 **federal offical** *Bundesbeamte/r*

22 **federal court** *Bundesgericht*

24 to **be to one's liking** *jdm zusagen, nach jds Geschmack sein*

38 **court case** *Gerichtsverfahren*

40 **the jury** *die Geschworenen (pl)*

6 Students have posted questions about the US elections on an online forum. Read the FAQs, then match the highlighted words with the German equivalents. Use a dictionary if necessary.

FAQ – Checks and balances in the US

The president of the US is sometimes called the most powerful person in the world. Does that mean he or she can spend money on projects and initiatives he or she likes (for example building a border wall)?
No, he or she can't. Congress has "the power of the purse". That means in order to get any funds the executive branch has to get approval from Congress, so the system of checks and balances makes sure that Congress controls the funding of the president's actions.

What about war and peace? Can the president start a war?
The president is the commander-in-chief of the military forces, but to declare war on another country, the president must first get military funds approved by Congress and must get their vote. But presidents sometimes take military action without asking Congress – and experts are still debating whether the president is allowed to do that. When it comes to signing a peace treaty, the president cannot do so without approval from the Senate.

How does the Executive branch check the Judiciary and the Legislative?
The president has veto power. That means the president doesn't have to sign a law that Congress has passed – he can veto it. In that case, Congress is only able to override such a veto if they get two-thirds of the votes in both houses. The president can nominate federal officials, but again, these need to be confirmed by the Senate. The president can also recommend legislation. And it is also within the powers of the president to check the judicial branch. The president can change the direction of federal courts and the Supreme Court by appointing members (judges) to it for life. The president would obviously appoint judges who are to his or her liking and in line with his or her own political beliefs, meaning more progressive or more conservative. These appointments may impact the law in the country for decades.

Do the federal courts and the Supreme Court have any powers to control the president?
Yes, they do. The judicial branch, including federal courts and the Supreme Court, can check the president and declare his or her actions or laws unconstitutional. This is called judicial review.

And who checks the Supreme Court?
Congress – by passing amendments to the Constitution.

What if the president does something illegal? Can he or she be removed from office, and if yes, by whom?
A president can be "impeached". The impeachment procedure is like a court case: the members of the House of Representatives gather evidence and vote to present their case to the Senate, which then acts as a jury and decides if the president may stay or has to step down.

(456 words)

1. Amtsenthebungsverfahren
2. ernennen
3. Finanzhoheit
4. Finanzierung
5. Friedensvertrag
6. gerichtliche Überprüfung
7. Oberbefehlshaber/in der Streitkräfte
8. überstimmen
9. verfassungswidrig
10. zurücktreten
11. Zusatzartikel zur Verfassung
12. Zustimmung

7 Based on what you learned in the video and online forum questions, match the terms with the correct arrow (1–6) in the diagram.

appoint judges | declare laws unconstitutional | declare presidential acts unconstitutional | impeach president | pass amendments to the Constitution | veto legislation

Checks and balances in the US government: Examples of how each branch is regulated by the other two branches

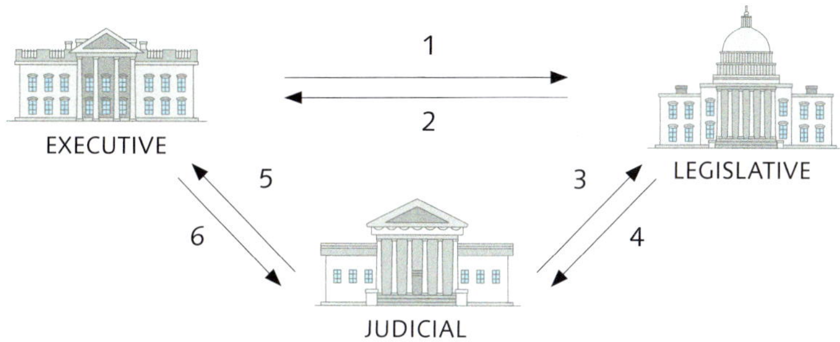

8 Look at the examples of modal verbs in the Remember box. Then find more examples in the FAQ text on page 92. Read the Remember box below, then sort them by type (1a–4).

G ▸ Modal auxiliary verbs, p. 166

Remember: Using modal verbs

Modal verbs can be sorted into categories based on their functions.

1a ability: *be able to*, *can*
The president ***can*** *veto bills.*

1b no ability: *not be able to*, *cannot/can't*
A politician ***cannot*** *please every voter.*

2a obligation: *have to*, *must*, *need to*
She ***has to*** *get a majority of votes to win.*

2b no obligation: *not have to*, *not need to*
They ***don't have to*** *get a majority to pass the law.*

3a permission: *be allowed to*, *can*, *may*
A senator ***may*** *run for president.*

3b no permission: *not be allowed to*, *cannot/can't*, *may not*, *mustn't*,
You ***mustn't*** *break the law.*

4 possibility: *can*, *could*, *may*, *might*, *would*
Either candidate ***could*** *win the election.*

Good to know

In English, *mustn't* is not the opposite of *must*! *Mustn't* means *not allowed to*. To express the idea of *nicht müssen*, you say *don't have to* or *don't need to*.

Writing

9 Together with a partner, write ten statements (some true, some false) about the US separation of powers. Use modal verbs in your statements. Then play a quiz with another group. Ask them whether your statements are true or false. When false, ask them to correct it by using the right modal verbs.

D ▸ More help, p. 153

Section D Houses of Parliament and the UK

Warm-up

1 Which UK political institutions do you associate with these buildings?

A

B

C

Crossover TV

Political Institutions in the UK

04

D ▸ More help, p. 153

Good to know

In order to decentralize the government in London, more power has been given to the local administrations in Scotland, Wales and Northern Ireland. This process is called "devolution" and the countries have "devolved parliaments".

Watching

2 Watch the video and answer the questions about the political institutions in the UK. You don't need to write full sentences.

1 Most countries have a written constitution – what about the UK?
2 What is the most powerful political institution in the UK?
3 How far does parliament go back?
4 What are the two chambers of parliament called?
5 Which of the two chambers is elected by the people?
6 How many countries does the UK consist of?
7 What areas are the regional parliaments responsible for? Name at least two.
8 Where did the 2014 referendum take place?

3 Watch the video again and complete the diagram with the words from the box.

British Electorate | House of Commons | House of Lords | Judicial | Legislative | Monarch | Prime Minister | Supreme Court

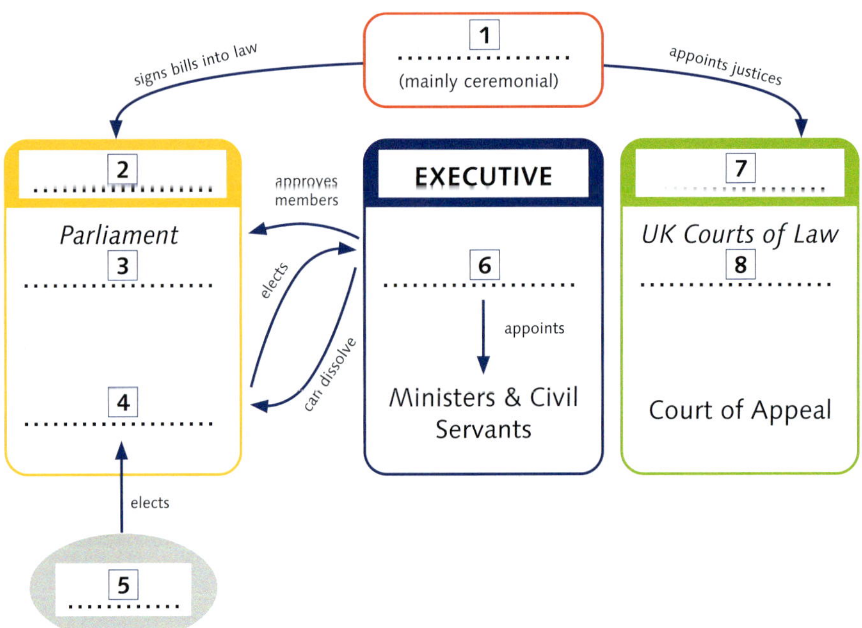

Speaking

4 In groups, describe the diagram of the separation of powers in the UK. Explain what each power does or can do.

S ▸ *Diagramme beschreiben u. analysieren*, pp. 70–71

5 Read the Good to Know box, then identify the numbered areas of the map.

British Isles | England | Great Britain | Ireland | Northern Ireland | Republic of Ireland | Scotland | United Kingdom | Wales

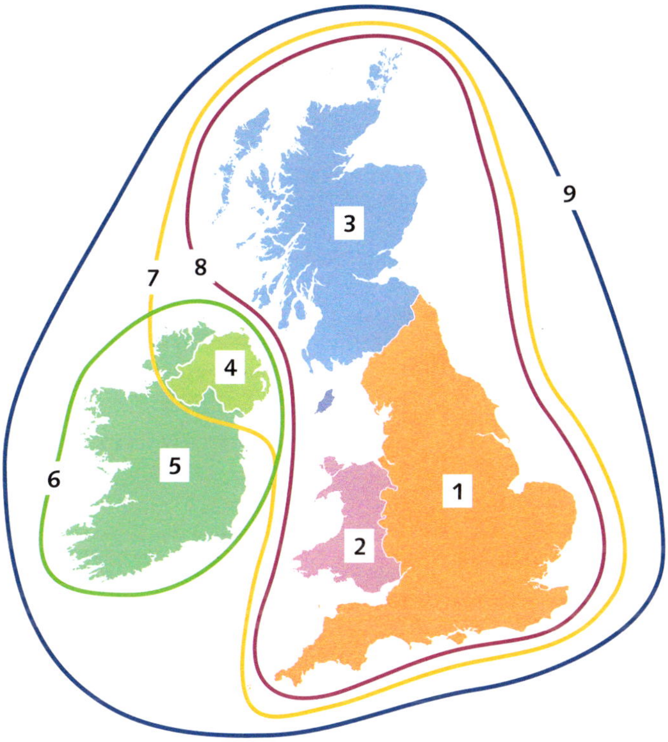

Good to know

The United Kingdom, Great Britain, the British Isles
The United Kingdom is a *political unit* which consists of England, Scotland, Wales and Northern Ireland. Great Britain is a *geographical unit* and is made up of England, Scotland and Wales. The British Isles are a *group of islands* including Great Britain, Ireland, the Isle of Man, the Hebrides and more than 6,000 smaller islands in the North Atlantic.

6 After Brexit, where on this map is the border between the EU and UK? Why could this border be problematic?

Speaking and writing

7 Make a short video explaining the political system in the UK. Work in four groups. Each group picks one of the questions below. Write a storyboard, shoot the video, and then present it to the class.

▸ Making a video, pp. 66–67

1. How have the powers of parliament and the monarch changed over the last few hundred years?
2. What are the main tasks of the House of Commons?
3. What function does the House of Lords have and how are its members elected?
4. What risks could devolution have for the UK?

Section E Political parties and voting system in the UK

Warm-up

1 Here's what people from different parts of the UK say about the voting rules. What's your opinion? Discuss with a partner.

"I really wish there was no voter registration deadline. In some countries, you can still register and vote on election day – no problem!"
Sandy – Inverness, Scotland

"In the UK, elections are on a weekday, and that's the best system, 'cause you can vote right after work." *Olivia – Cardiff, Wales*

"In Britain before 1948, business owners and university graduates were allowed to cast more than one vote. Sensible, if you ask me!"
Dylan – Manchester, England

"I think voting should be required by law. If you don't vote, you should pay a fine or do community service, like in Australia!"
Carla – Belfast, Northern Ireland

2 How much do you already know about the UK's parties and voting system? Do the following quiz and find out.

1 There are two main parties: the Conservative Party and …
a the Labour Party.
b the Liberal Party.
c the Social Democratic Party.

2 There is normally a general election every …
a three years.
b four years.
c five years.

3 Members of the Conservative Party are also called …
a Liberals.
b Tories.
c Whigs.

4 In the UK political system, the … is head of the government.
a president
b speaker
c prime minister

5 The voting areas in the UK are called …
a committees.
b constituencies.
c constitutions.

6 In the UK, voting always takes place on a …
a Thursday.
b Tuesday.
c Sunday.

7 The places where you can vote are called …
a election buildings.
b voting rooms.
c polling stations.

8 A party with no clear majority, tries to form a … with another party.
a a coalition
b an opposition
c an alliance

Working with the text

3 Read the questions and the info sheet on the UK voting system, then match the questions (1–8) to the paragraphs (A–H).

D ▸ More practice, p. 154

1 How often do we have a general election?
2 Who can vote in a general election?
3 Who elects the prime minister?
4 How does the voting system work?
5 Who do we actually vote for?
6 What can I expect to happen at the polling station?
7 "First past the post" is used in horse racing – what does it mean in elections?
8 What exactly is "tactical voting"?

The UK voting system explained: Here's what you should know when you go to the polling station

22

A You can vote in all elections if you hold British, Irish or qualifying Commonwealth citizenship. You must be over 18 years of age. EU citizens living in the UK can vote in all elections except those to the UK parliament.

B Usually every five years, and always on a Thursday. An early election can only be called if a vote of no confidence gets through either in the government or on a two-thirds majority of MPs.

C In person, by post or by proxy – but not online. Voting in person takes place at your local polling station. If you forgot to send your postal vote, you can still cast your vote at the polling station.

D After giving your name and address, the polling station staff will look for your name in the list of registered voters. Once they find it, you receive a ballot paper on which you mark the candidate of your choice and put it in a ballot box. At the end of polling day, all votes will be counted.

E The UK voting system makes it difficult for smaller parties to be successful. If you know your party cannot win the majority, you may want to vote for a candidate from another party who shares your political ideas or goals (for example, if they are for or against immigration).

F The UK is divided into 650 constituencies, each of which elects one MP to represent them in the House of Commons. MPs usually belong to a political party but may also stand as an independent.

G It means that the candidate with the most votes wins, the other votes are "lost". If there are 10 candidates for one seat with 9 of them getting 9.95% of the votes, and one getting just over 10%, then this candidate wins with a "relative majority" (called a "plurality" in American English). 10% is a very small majority, but the candidate will win the seat. In that case, 90% of the votes effectively do not count.

H In a general election, citizens vote for their local MP. The leader of the party which wins the majority of seats will become prime minister and be officially appointed by the monarch. (379 words)

polling station *Wahllokal*
[5] to **call an election** *eine Wahl ansetzen*
[5] **vote of no confidence** *Misstrauensabstimmung*
[7] **by proxy** *durch einen Bevollmächtigten*
[18] **constituency** *Wahlkreis*

Good to know

The British Commonwealth or **Commonwealth of Nations** is a political association of fifty-four states, which were part of the British Empire in the past. The member states are connected through their history but have no legal obligations towards each other.

Looking at language

Remember: Using the passive

Use the passive to stress results and processes (rather than who does something). If you mention the person, use *by*.

1 simple present
*The voters' interests **are represented** by their local MPs.*

2 simple past
*The cabinet minister **was appointed** by the prime minister last week.*

3 with modal verbs
*The ballot papers **must be counted**.*

G ▸ Using the passive, p. 170

4 Rewrite the sentences using the passive. Decide where to use *by + person*.

1 After a general election, the Queen officially appoints the prime minister.
2 The voter filled out the paper ballot incorrectly.
3 The UK holds general elections every five years.
4 The staff may count the votes only after the polling station closes.
5 People can send their votes by post, but they can't send them online.
6 You should leave dogs outside when you come to the polling station.

Listening

S ▸ *Richtig mit Hörverstehensaufgaben umgehen*, pp. 104–105
D ▸ More help, p. 154

23

5 Listen to an election special on the 2019 election in the UK. Fill in the missing information (1–14).

British political parties and the main issues of the 2019 general election

	Brexit	Immigration	Education	Economy
Conservatives	in favour	• reduce immigration	• spend £14bn on schools • **(6)** … of £30,000 for teachers	• reduce bureaucracy • reduce taxes **(12)** … (also for the wealthy)
Labour	call for **(2)** …	• **(4)** … where necessary, e.g. doctors & hospital staff	• abolish tuition fees for colleges and universities • cut **(7)** … to 30 students	• reduce taxes for 95% of people • **(13)** … for top 5%
Liberal Democrats	against	• **(5)** … within EU	• 35 hours a week **(8)** … for working parents • 20,000 **(9)** …	• boost economy by stopping Brexit
Green Party	**(1)** …	• free movement of people within EU	• **(10)** … for schools by £4bn a year	• boost economy by stopping Brexit • increase efforts to **(14)** … • fight climate change
Brexit Party	in favour	• limit immigration to **(3)** … per year	• give incentives to **(11)** … to take on apprentices	• no major polices announced • reduce foreign aid by 50%

Section F The British monarchy

Warm-up

1 Look at the photo and name the people you know. What is their position in the royal family? Draw a family tree of the royal family. Include family members not pictured here.

Working with the text

2 Read the text and write down the main duties members of the royal family have.

24

D ▸ More practice, p. 146

Meghan and Harry head to Hollywood

In 2020, Meghan Markle and Prince Harry announced they would be stepping down from their duties as senior members of the royal family because they wanted to earn their own living. They will also divide their time between the UK and the US.

Before we look at the "royal duties" of the family members, let's find out what the official website of the Palace says.

According to royal.uk: "Members of the royal family support the Queen in her many State and national duties, as well as carrying out important work in the areas of public and charitable service, and helping to strengthen national unity and stability."

That's why members of the royal family act as hosts or guests at garden parties, receptions or other meet-and-greet style events. In addition, they open buildings and bridges and of course they travel, both in the UK and internationally. Apart from representing the UK abroad, they often chair charities. Besides appearing at events, they give speeches, present awards, write letters and so on.

But what about the monarch as the most senior member of the royal family? What does the Queen have to do? Despite being the head of state, the Queen's political role is mostly symbolic and her executive powers limited. The monarch represents the country on state visits and official ceremonies, whereas politically, she must remain neutral. However, she has the right to be consulted by the government on important issues. One big event is the "State Opening of Parliament", which takes place at the beginning of each parliamentary session and includes the Queen's Speech.

to **head to sth** *sich auf den Weg zu etw machen*
[3] **senior** *hochrangig*
[4] to **earn one's (own) living** *seinen (eigenen) Lebensunterhalt verdienen*
[11] **public service** *Dienst an der Allgemeinheit*
[11] **charitable** *gemeinnützig, karitativ*
[11] **unity** *Einheit*
[16] to **chair sth** *den Vorsitz von etw innehaben, einer Sache vorstehen*
[17] to **present an award** *einen Preis überreichen*
[19] **head of state** *Staatsoberhaupt*
[22] to **consult sb** *jdn zu Rate ziehen, jdn konsultieren*
[24] **parliamentary session** *Legislaturperiode*

[29] **to raise a question** *eine Frage aufwerfen*
[32] **to bear sth** *etw (Kosten usw.) tragen, für etw aufkommen*
[34] **expense** *(finanzieller) Aufwand, Kosten*
[36] **figure** *Zahl, Ziffer*
[40] **to make up one's mind** *sich entscheiden*

But if the role of the monarch and the royal family is limited mostly to ceremonial duties, does the country still need them? And what benefits, if any, do they bring to the UK economy?

These questions were raised again when Harry and Meghan got married in 2018. Their wedding was very expensive, and although the cost of the wedding itself was paid by the royal family, the security costs, over £20 million, were borne by the taxpayer. The wedding resulted in another debate about wasting taxpayer money and whether the British still wanted to support the royals financially.

So, are the royals worth their expense? The truth is: it's complicated.

Although experts estimated the royal family contributed about £1.8 bn to the UK economy in 2017, the figure seems pretty small if you compare it to £543 bn the UK made in exports and the £22.5 bn international visitors spent that year. On the other hand, who knows how many tourists would visit the UK if it weren't for the royal family, the palaces, the traditions, the weddings, and the glamour.

Anyway, Meghan and Harry made up their minds to become financially independent, and after just signing a $100 million deal with Netflix, we shouldn't be worried about them. Best of luck, Meghan and Harry! (486 words)

Speaking

▸ Phrases for writing and discussion, inside front cover

3 With a partner, discuss what you think about the royal family and their duties.

How to say or write it

The monarchy should stay because …

I (don't) think the royal family are a great benefit to the UK as they …

I guess it must be hard to … all the time.

If I were a member of the royal family, I would/wouldn't …

In my opinion, the decision was the right one because …

Working with words

Skills training: Using connective words and phrases to write complex sentences

By using connective words and phrases, you can give more meaning and context to your statements and improve the flow of sentences.

1. **addition** – *also, as well as, in addition, additionally, besides, apart from*
2. **condition** – *if, when, provided*
3. **consequence or result** – *so, as a consequence, as a result*
4. **contrast or concession** – *but, although, whereas, while, on the one hand …, on the other hand, however, despite*
5. **reason or cause** – *because, because of, as, that's why, therefore*
6. **time** – *after, before, while*

4 Find the connectives in the article above and sort them under these headings.

addition **condition** **consequence** **contrast** **time**

D ▸ More help, p. 154

5 Rewrite the sentences using connectives.

1. The Sussexes stepped back from their royal duties. They will now spend most of their time in the US.
2. The royals have national duties. They carry out important work in public service.
3. Harry and Meghan paid for their wedding, they didn't pay for security.
4. A lot of people want to keep the monarchy. They think it's good for tourism.
5. The royals represent their country abroad. They chair charities.
6. The monarch's duties are mostly ceremonial. The country needs the royals?

Writing

6 Improve the highlighted passages with the help of the instructions on the right.

The British royal family has many duties. Not many people know how full their schedules are. They support about 3,000 charity organisations and often set up their own charities.	Combine the two sentences using *although*.
Prince William and Kate, for instance, established their own charity. Harry founded the Invictus Games, which are sports games for disabled veterans.	Combine the two sentences with the help of *while*.
The Queen has a mostly representative function, but she is also head of state and meets the prime minister regularly. The Queen, who is in her 90s, is very responsible about her duties.	Avoid *but* and use another connective instead.
She cannot handle all her engagements. Then she delegates some to other family members like her son and his wife.	Combine the two sentences using *if*.
Prince Charles and Camilla travel a lot internationally. They want to support and improve relationships with other countries.	Combine the two sentences using *in order to*.
Charles has introduced initiatives such as reducing food waste and growing organic food. He is very interested in environmental issues.	Combine the two sentences using *as* or *because*.

7 Comment on Harry and Meghan's decision to leave the royal family.

8 What do the newspaper headlines tell you about Harry and Meghan and their lives? Do some internet research to find out the background to these headlines and write a blog entry dealing with the question: Do you think Harry and Meghan made the right decision?

Exam preparation

S ▸ *Eine argumentierende/bewertende Schreibaufgabe bearbeiten*, pp. 35–40

S ▸ Operatoren, pp. 33–34

Harry claims wife bullied by media – just like his mother Diana!

Meghan in tears: "I never thought this would be easy, but I thought it would be fair!"

Invasion of privacy and phone hacking: The Sussexes begin legal action against tabloids.

Harry and Meghan sign mega Netflix deal to become producers!

Meghan in interview: "Glad to be back home!"

Meghan and Harry told to use Netflix money to pay back bills on their UK house!

Project Giving a speech

Read Emma González's speech, then answer the questions.

1. What sort of event do you think Emma is talking about in their speech?
2. What issues have led citizens to take to the streets?
3. Have you ever participated in a demonstration?
4. What issue would you feel inspired to make a speech about?

to **take to the streets** *auf die Straße gehen (um zu demonstrieren)*

Speech by Emma Gonzáles

March for Our Lives, 14 March 2018, Washington, DC

Six minutes and about twenty seconds.

In a little over six minutes, seventeen of our friends were taken from us, fifteen were injured, and everyone - absolutely everyone - in the Douglas community was forever altered.

Everyone who was there understands. Everyone who has been touched by the cold grip of gun violence understands. For us, long, tearful, chaotic hours in the scorching afternoon sun were spent not knowing. No one understood the extent of what had happened. No one could believe that there were bodies in that building waiting to be identified for over a day. No one knew that the people who were missing had stopped breathing long before any of us had even known that a code red had been called. No one could comprehend the devastating aftermath, or how far this would reach, or where this would go.

For those who still can't comprehend because they refuse to, I'll tell you where it went. Right into the ground. Six feet deep.

Six minutes and twenty seconds with an AR-15, and my friend Carmen would never complain to me about piano practice. Aaron Feis would never call Kiera "Miss Sunshine." Alex Schachter would never walk into school with his brother Ryan. Scott Beigel would never joke around with Cameron at camp. Helena Ramsay would never hang out after school with Max. Gina Montalto would never wave to her friend Liam at lunch. Joaquin Oliver would never play basketball with Sam or Dylan. Alaina Petty would never -; Cara Loughran would never -; Chris Hixon would never -; Luke Hoyer would never -; Martin Duque Anguiano would never -; Peter Wang would never -; Alyssa Alhadef would never -; Jaime Guttenberg would never -; Meadow Pollack would never -.

[Silence. Timer beeps.]

Since the time that I came out here, it has been six minutes and twenty seconds. The shooter has ceased shooting and will soon abandon his rifle, blend in with the students as they escape, and walk free for an hour before arrest. Fight for your lives before it's someone else's job.

[5] to be forever altered *nicht der der-/die-/dasselbe sein*
[8] **grip** *Griff, (zupackende) Hand*
[8] **gun violence** *(Schuss-)Waffengewalt*
[9] **tearful** *tränenreich, traurig*
[9] **scorching sun** *sengende Sonne*
[11] **extent** *Ausmaß*
[13] **(dead) body** *Leichnam, Leiche*
[15] to call a code red *den (höchsten) Alarmzustand ausrufen*
[15] to **comprehend sth** *etw begreifen, etw verstehen*
[15] devastating aftermath *verheerende Folgen*
[17] to **refuse to do sth** *sich weigern, etw zu tun*
[19] AR-15 *Modellname eines US-Sturmgewehrs*
[20] piano practice *Klavierstunde*
[23] to **wave to sb** *jdm zuwinken*
[29] **shooter** *Attentäter/in, Todesschütze/-in*
[30] to **cease doing sth** *aufhören, etw zu tun*
[30] to **abandon sth** *etw zurücklassen, etw stehen/liegen lassen*
[30] to **blend in with sb** *sich unter jdn mischen, in der Menge untertauchen*
[30] **rifle** *Gewehr*
[31] to **walk free** *frei herumlaufen*

Emma's speech is carefully composed and uses rhetorical techniques. Here are some speech-writing devices that are good to keep in mind when writing your own.

to **compose** *(Text) verfassen, schreiben*
device *Mittel, Methode, Kunstgriff*

Useful tools for speech writing

Repetition Repeating a phrase or word several times helps the audience remember, it creates a feeling of urgency, and it gives the speech focus, which is especially important when talking about complex issues.

Imagery Creating a picture in the audience's mind is a key to any successful speech. Use visual language that helps to evoke a physical sensation, and the speech will be much more memorable.

Direct address Using the word "you" in a speech can create a very powerful moment, but remember to be considerate when addressing the audience directly.

S ▸ *Stilmittel*, p. 108
urgency *Dringlichkeit, Eindringlichkeit*

to **evoke a sensation** *ein Gefühl hervorrufen*
memorable *einprägsam, anschaulich*

address *Ansprache, Anrede*
considerate *rücksichtsvoll, umsich*

You are going to write and deliver your own speech. First you will need to choose a topic. Now is the time to engage with an issue you feel passionate about!

Political issues
Public demonstrations and powerful speeches often touch on political issues such as the environment, global conflict, and individual liberties.

Local issues
Feelings can be just as strong – or stronger – when it comes to issues affecting the local community. Schools often have issues that spark debate.

Philosophy of life
Everyone has a "style of living", whether it's focused on money, pleasure, or public service. A speech can advocate for different approaches to life.

Your own topic
Think of what engages you most in life. To give a good speech it must be sincerely felt!

to **deliver a speech** *eine Rede halten*
to **engage with sth** *sich mit etw auseinandersetzen*
to **touch on sth** *etw ansprechen, etw berühren*
to **spark debate** *Diskussionen entfachen*
to **advocate sth** *für etw eintreten*
approach to life *Lebenseinstellung*
to **engage sb** *(Thema usw.:) jdn beschäftigen*
sincere(ly) *aufrichtig, ehrlich*

To help you write your own speech, here's a useful and clear structure to follow.

Paragraph 1: Introduction
What's the reason for this speech? What's your goal? Try to grab the audience's attention with a strong opening.

Paragraph 2: Make your first strong point
Give your audience a reason and motivation to listen by using different techniques: make them curious, tell them a personal story and give them useful information.

curious *neugierig*

Paragraph 3: Make your next point
Make sure your speech flows and it follows a logical sequence.

logical sequence *logische (Ab-)Folge*

Paragraph 4: Make your final and strongest point
Now present your strongest argument to convince the audience of your ideas.

Paragraph 5: Conclusion and call to action
Summarize the key points of your speech and tell the audience what you believe and how they can adopt these ideas and take action for change.

call to action *Aufruf zum Handeln*
to adopt sth *sich etw zu eigen machen*
to take action *handeln Maßnahmen ergreifen*

It's time to deliver your speech. After you have written, edited and rehearsed your text, present it in front of the class. Good luck!

Tips for public speaking

There's more to giving a speech than just reading. Follow these tips, and think of your speech as a performance rather than just a text.

Take a deep breath before you begin. There's nothing to be afraid of. Try to be calm, and you will do great.

Speak slowly. A common mistake is to race through your text. Take your time, and pause occasionally to allow the audience to absorb what you are saying.

Made a mistake? Ignore it! If you stumble over your words, or if something else unexpected happens, don't apologize – just keep reading and focus on your speech.

Don't forget to look up. Try to connect with your audience by occasionally looking around the room. Your goal is to connect with the audience!

Let the audience know when you've finished. The simplest way to do this is to pause after your last sentence, look up, and say "Thank you".

performance *Aufführung, Theaterstück*
to **race** *rasen, hetzen*
occasionally *ab und zu, gelegentlich*
to **absorb sth** *etw aufnehmen*
to **stumble** *stolpern*
to **connect with sb** *eine (emotionale) Verbindung zu jdm herstellen*

Richtig mit Hörverstehensaufgaben umgehen

Gut zu wissen

Das schriftliche **Abitur** beinhaltet eine Hörverstehensaufgabe (Dauer **30 min**).

Um Ihr Hörverstehen zu verbessern, hilft neben dem Englischunterricht vor allem eines, nämlich auch im privaten Bereich verstärkt gesprochenes Englisch zu hören. Neben Musik, Filmen und TV-Serien sind hier vor allem Podcasts sehr nützlich. Betrachten Sie das Hören nicht als Nebensache, während der Sie sich mit anderen Dingen beschäftigen können. Nehmen Sie sich lieber kürzere Hörphasen vor und konzentrieren Sie sich dafür aktiv auf das Gesprochene.

Textsorten

In Ihren Prüfungen kommen als Ausgangstexte z.B. **Radio-**, **Fernseh-**, **Internet-Mitschnitte von Nachrichtensendungen**, **Interviews**, **Reden**, **Gesprächen**, **Diskussionen** und **Hintergrundberichten** vor.

Beispielaufgabe

Sie hören ein **Radiointerview**, in dem es um das bevorstehende Interview von Oprah Winfrey mit Meghan Markle und Prince Harry über deren Beweggründe für das Verlassen des britischen Königshauses geht.

HINWEIS: *Zur besseren Veranschaulichung werden in der Übung auf der Folgeseite schrittweise die verschiedenen prüfungsrelevanten Aufgabenformate innerhalb eines Hörtextes demonstriert.*

Ablauf

Gut zu wissen

Im **Abitur** stehen Ihnen ein ein- und ein zweisprachiges **Wörterbuch** zur Verfügung.

Die Hörverstehensaufgabe in Ihrer Abiturprüfung beinhaltet drei bis maximal vier Hörtexte in Form verschiedener Aufgabenformate, für die Sie jeweils eine kurze Einlesezeit und Zeit für die nachträgliche Bearbeitung bekommen. Sie hören jeden Hörtext zweimal.

Strategien

Vor dem Hören

Das Wichtigste vorab: Damit Ihnen auf mentaler Ebene nichts im Wege steht, was Ihnen den Zugang zum Hörverstehen verbauen könnte, ist es wichtig, dass Sie sich auf ein entspanntes und gleichzeitig konzentriertes, aktives Zuhören einlassen. Befreien Sie sich von ablenkenden Gedanken!

- Lesen Sie sich die Aufgabenstellung aufmerksam durch.
- Aktivieren Sie bereits jetzt Ihr Vorwissen zum Thema, es wird Ihnen nützlich sein.
- Markieren Sie Schlüsselbegriffe.
- Wenn Ihnen Wörter unbekannt sind, schlagen Sie nur absolut wichtiges Schlüsselvokabular nach – Einlesezeit ist kostbare Zeit!

Während des Hörens

Geraten Sie nicht in Panik, wenn Sie beim ersten (und auch zweiten) Durchgang nicht alles verstehen – es gehört in der Oberstufe dazu, punktuell Unverstandenes zu tolerieren. Sie verpassen den Anschluss, wenn Sie sich damit während des Hörens aufhalten! Oft hilft Ihnen das Erfassen größerer Sinneinheiten, über kleine Probleme beim Verstehen von Einzelwörtern hinwegzukommen.

- Fertigen Sie bereits während des ersten Hörens Stichwortnotizen auf Englisch an.
- Vervollständigen Sie diese Notizen während des zweiten Durchlaufs.
- Verwenden Sie dabei Zeichen, Abkürzungen und Wortverkürzungen, um beim Notieren Zeit zu sparen.

Nach dem Hören

- Formulieren Sie stark verkürzte Stichpunkte zügig aus, damit Sie wichtige Inhalte später richtig deuten.
- Lassen Sie v.a. bei geschlossenen Aufgabenformaten keinen Aufgabenteil unbeantwortet. Sollten Sie die Antwort nicht wissen, stellen Sie sinnvolle Vermutungen an.

How to say or write it

Zeichen

= ≠	*(not) the same as*
→	*and so / therefore*
+	*and*

Abkürzungen

e.g.	*for example*
km	*kilometres*
w, w/o	*with, without*

Wortverkürzungen

govt	*government*
impt!	*important*
GB	*Great Britain*

Aufgabenformate

Übung

Wenden Sie die Hörstrategien bei den folgenden Aufgaben an.
You will hear a radio interview with Elisabeth Holmes, a journalist and longtime royal watcher about Oprah Winfrey's then upcoming interview with Meghan Markle and Prince Harry, who left the royal family.

upcoming *bevorstehend*

1 Mehrfachzuordnungen *(multiple matching)*

25

While listening, match the information A to E with the headings. There are two more options than you need.

A *Meghan's former place of residence*
B *wants to look into the matter*
C *said to be a bully*
D *published a story*
E *married to Prince William*

Duchess of Sussex ***Buckingham Palace*** ***Kensington Palace***

2 Mehrfachauswahlaufgaben *(multiple choice)*

26

While listening, find the correct answer (a, b, c, or d). There is only one correct answer.

The accusations …
a *included that Meghan fired two personal assistants.*
b *were first posted on Twitter.*
c *included that Meghan was an actress.*
d *refer to Meghan's time as a member of the royal family.*

3 Kurzantworten *(short answers)*

27

While listening, take notes on the following points. You need not write complete sentences.

1. *Two people speaking in the first teaser trailers*
2. *Another term describing the royal family*
3. *Role of a private letter in Meghan's relationship with the British press*

teaser trailer/clip *Filmausschnitt*

4 Satzergänzungen *(sentence completion)*

28

While listening, complete the sentences.

1. *Prince Harry's hatred of the media goes back to …*
2. *The stories that have been published about Meghan were often … and …*
3. *The … over The Mail on Sunday was important for Harry and Meghan because it affected their …*

Wörterbücher verwenden

Gut zu wissen

Im schriftlichen **Abitur** und in der Vorbereitungsphase der **Kommunikationsprüfung** (mündliches Abitur) haben Sie ein zweisprachiges und ein einsprachiges Wörterbuch zur Verfügung. Beide Versionen sind wichtig!

Ob online oder in Buchform – Wörterbücher sind enorm nützliche Werkzeuge. Der Umgang mit ihnen will jedoch gelernt sein. Denn unabhängig davon, ob Sie ein zwei- oder ein einsprachiges Wörterbuch nutzen, sollten Sie niemals automatisch die erstbeste Übersetzung bzw. Bedeutung wählen, sondern stets sorgfältig zwischen den verschiedenen gegebenen Möglichkeiten abwägen.

Wörterbücher kennenlernen

Verschaffen Sie sich zunächst einen Überblick über die zwei- und einsprachigen Wörterbücher, die an Ihrer Schule verwendet werden.

Übung 1

Beantworten Sie für das zweisprachige und einsprachige Wörterbuch folgende Fragen.

1 Gibt es eine Anleitung zur Benutzung? Wie ist diese aufgebaut?
2 Welche Abkürzungen und Symbole werden benutzt, und wo findet sich dazu eine Übersicht?
3 Wo befindet sich das Verzeichnis unregelmäßiger Verben?
4 Welche weiteren Verzeichnisse bietet das Wörterbuch?
5 Zu welchen Themen gibt es Illustrationen und Schaubilder?
6 Gibt es eine Übersicht zur Grammatik?
7 Bietet das Wörterbuch eine Übersicht zur Aussprache?

Wörterbücher nutzen

S ▸ Schwierige Texte lesen, S. 72–73

- **Arbeit mit Texten:** Schlagen Sie Wörter nach, wenn es nötig ist.
- **Erweitern Sie Ihr Vokabular:** Legen Sie sich gleich Übersichten mit Wortfamilien an.
- **Lernen Sie neue Redewendungen *(idioms)*:** Hierfür eignen sich vor allem einsprachige Wörterbücher.

Zweisprachige Wörterbücher

Das zweisprachige Wörterbuch führt in der Regel schnell zur gesuchten Bedeutung, wobei Sie im Umgang damit sehr genau sein müssen. Stellen Sie sich daher immer die folgenden Fragen:

1. Suche ich nach der richtigen Wortart? (Nomen, Verb, Adjektiv, Adverb usw.)
2. Habe ich die passende Übersetzung ausgewählt, nachdem ich den kompletten Wörterbucheintrag gründlich durchgesehen habe?

Übung 2

Schlagen Sie die englische Übersetzung für das Wort *verletzen* nach und übersetzen Sie folgende Sätze.

1 Das Recht auf freie Meinungsäußerung darf nicht verletzt werden.
2 Du verletzt meine Gefühle!
3 Er wurde bei dem Autounfall schwer verletzt.

Einsprachige Wörterbücher

Ein gutes einsprachiges Wörterbuch führt in jedem Eintrag die folgenden Merkmale bzw. Bestandteile auf:

- Wortart *(noun, verb, adjective, adverb …)*
- unregelmäßige Verbformen *(rise, rose, risen)*
- Aussprache und Sprachvarianten *(BE, AE, AusE)* der verschiedenen Bedeutungen
- Hinweise zur Grammatik
- Beispiele zur Verwendung im Kontext
- Präpositionen *(on the internet)*
- Redewendungen, in denen das Wort verwendet wird
- Häufigkeit des Auftretens in der Sprache

Gut zu wissen

Einsprachige Wörterbücher enthalten mehr Informationen als zweisprachige Wörterbücher und präsentieren Ihnen diese in leicht verständlicher Sprache mit dem Wortschatz, den Sie in der Unter- und Mittelstufe bereits gelernt haben.

Übung 3

Machen Sie in dem Wörterbucheintrag für *bill* die folgenden Angaben und Bestandteile ausfindig:

a) Kollokationen (häufig gemeinsames Auftreten von Wörtern)
b) Definitionen
c) Wortarten
d) Beispielsätze
e) Aussprache und Häufigkeit
f) Informationen zur Grammatik
g) Redewendungen
h) Verweis auf Bildmaterial
i) Redewendung
j) Präposition

Beantworten Sie die folgenden Fragen.

1 Welche Wortart ist *bill*?
2 Ist *bill* ein zählbares oder unzählbares Nomen?
3 Welche Bedeutung hat das Wort *bill* im folgenden Beispiel? *Leonardo DiCaprio always tops the bill in his movies.*
4 Wie häufig kommt das Wort in der gesprochenen und geschriebenen Sprache vor?
5 Wann wird im *BE* bzw. *AE* jeweils welche andere Bezeichnung statt *bill* benutzt?
6 Was bedeutet *bill and coo*?
7 Worin besteht der Bedeutungsunterschied zwischen *bill* und *law*?

bill[1] S1 W1 /bɪl/ n [C]

1 REQUEST FOR PAYMENT a written list showing how much you have to pay for services you have received, work that has been done etc: [+**for**] *The bill for the repairs came to $650.* | **phone/electricity/gas/water etc bill** *Have you **paid** the phone **bill**?*

2 RESTAURANT *especially BrE* a list showing how much you have to pay for food you have eaten in a restaurant; = **check** *AmE: Could we have the bill, please?*

3 LAW a written proposal for a new law, which is brought to a parliament so that it can be discussed: **approve/pass/veto a bill** *The House of Representatives passed a new gun-control bill.* | *The senator **introduced** a **bill** that would increase the minimum wage.*

4 MONEY *AmE* a piece of paper money; = **note** *BrE*; → **coin**: a five-dollar bill

5 fit/fill the bill to be exactly what you need: *This car fits the bill perfectly. It's cheap and gets good mileage.*

6 CONCERT/SHOW ETC a programme of entertainment at a theatre, concert, cinema etc, with details of who is performing, what is being shown etc: *Tricia **topped the bill*** (=was the most important performer) *at the Children's Variety Show.*

7 give sb/sth a clean bill of health to officially state that someone is in good health or that something is working correctly: *Maddox was given a clean bill of health.*

8 BIRD a bird's beak → *see picture at* BIRD OF PREY

9 ADVERTISEMENT a printed notice advertising an event

10 PART OF A HAT *AmE* the front part that sticks out on a hat such as a BASEBALL CAP

11 the (old) bill *BrE spoken* the police

bill[2] v [T] **1** to send someone a bill: *Clients will be billed monthly.* | **bill sb for sth** *I was billed for equipment that I didn't order.* **2 be billed to do sth** if someone is billed to appear, perform etc somewhere, it has been planned and advertised that they will do this: *Johnson was billed to speak at two conferences.* **3 bill and coo** *old-fashioned* if two lovers are billing and cooing, they are kissing and talking softly.

bill sth **as** sth *phr v* to advertise or describe something in a particular way: *The castle bills itself as the oldest in England.*

From *Longman Dictionary of Contemporary English*

Gut zu wissen

Als Teil der Textanalyse im schriftlichen Abitur müssen Sie Stilmittel im Text erkennen und bestimmen, welche Wirkung sie haben.

Stilmittel

Mit rhetorischen Mitteln oder literarischen Stilmitteln sind sprachliche Mittel gemeint, die verwendet werden, um einen mündlichen Vortrag oder einen Text besonders wirksam zu gestalten.

Begriff	Definition	Beispiel	Wirkung
alliteration Alliteration, Stabreim	Wiederholung der Anfangslaute in benachbarten Wörtern	*"Somewhere at this very moment a child is being born in America. Let it be our cause to give that child a happy home, a healthy family, and a hopeful future."* Bill Clinton, US-Präsident	durch rhythmische, klangliche Wiederholung wird das Gesagte betont, so dass es sich besser ins Gedächtnis einprägt
euphemism Euphemismus	beschönigende Umschreibung	*"alternative facts"* Kellyanne Conway, Seniorberaterin des US-Präsidenten Donald Trump mit ihrer Bezeichnung für Lügen, die von ihm verbreitet worden waren	Vermeidung von Begriffen, die einen negativen Eindruck erzeugen können
exaggeration Übertreibung	Behauptung, die über den Wahrheitsgehalt einer Aussage hinausgeht	*"I'm the least racist person you have ever interviewed."* Donald Trump, US-Präsident	Betonung einer Aussage durch Zuspitzung; kann ernst oder humorvoll sein
metaphor Metapher	Beschreibung eines Sachverhalts durch ein vergleichendes Bild	*"But there are many mountains yet to climb. We will not rest until every American enjoys the fullness of freedom, dignity, and opportunity as our birthright."* Ronald Reagan, US-Präsident	Veranschaulichung und Verdeutlichung abstrakter Ideen; wird oft verwendet, um die Einschätzung bzw. Position des Sprechers / der Sprecherin deutlich zu machen
parallelism Parallelismus	Verwendung ähnlicher Wörter oder Wendungen im selben Satz oder in benachbarten Sätzen	*"Let every nation know, whether it wishes us well or ill, that we shall pay any price, bear any burden, meet any hardship, support any friend, oppose any foe to assure the survival and the success of liberty."* John F. Kennedy, US-Präsident	betont einen Gedanken durch Wiederholung und macht ihn dadurch einprägsamer
repetition Wiederholung	mehrmaliges Benennen des gleichen Wortes oder einer Wortfolge	siehe die Wortfolge *"would never"* in Emma Gonzáles' Rede auf Seite 102	hebt eine Aussage besonders hervor und verleiht ihr Nachdruck
irony Ironie	Behauptung, die erkennen lässt, dass das Gegenteil gemeint ist	*"Does America really need to be the best at everything? You already dominate the world in economics, military power and obesity."* Trevor Noah, südafrikanischer Komiker	drückt auf versteckte oder indirekte Weise Kritik oder Spott gegenüber einer Sache oder Person aus
rhetorical question rhetorische Frage	Frage, auf die keine Antwort erwartet wird, weil die Antwort offensichtlich ist oder anschließend gegeben wird	*" I simply ache from smiling. Why are women expected to beam all the time? It's unfair. If a man looks solemn, it's automatically assumed he's a serious person, not a miserable one."* Queen Elizabeth II	durch das scheinbare Hinterfragen wird die Offensichtlichkeit oder Absurdität einer Aussage betont

altered *verändert;* **fullness** *Fülle;* **dignity** *Würde;* **birthright** *Geburtsrecht;* **to wish sb ill** *jdm übelwollen;* **to bear a burden** *eine Last tragen;* **to meet a hardship** *eine Not ertragen;* **to oppose a foe** *sich einem Feind widersetzen;* **to assure** *gewährleisten;* **to beam** *strahlen*

Review

1 Rank the Sections A–F in this Topic based on how interesting they were to you. Then, look back at your work on the overview of this Topic (pages 78–79) and how you ranked them there (page 78, exercise 2). Have your rankings changed? Share your results with a group, and tell them what you found most interesting.

2 Look back at your KWL list (page 79, exercise 5). Fill out the "Learnt" part of the list. Next, look at your "Want to know" list. What do you still want to know?

3 Make a list of ten words in the Topic that were new to you and you consider important to know. Then collect everyone's words and cluster them into groups. Finally, pick a word group and write a paragraph using all the words.

Evaluate

1 Do this task on your own. How much do you agree or disagree with the statements below? Rate each one on a scale of one to four. The references on the right show you what exercises you can review.

1 = totally disagree **2** = disagree **3** = agree **4** = totally agree

Section		Statement	
A	**1**	I can talk about some political opinions of the Democrats and Republicans as well as my own.	▸ pp. 80–82, exercises 3–9
B	**2**	I can talk and write about the election process in the US.	▸ p. 86, exercises 10–12
	3	I can use relative pronouns, present and past participles to improve flow.	▸ pp. 85–86, exercises 8–9
	4	I can actively take part in discussions, using appropriate phrases.	▸ p. 86, exercise 11
	5	I can make sentences stronger or more precise, using adverbs.	▸ p. 89, exercise 14
C	**6**	I understand the separation of powers in US government.	▸ pp. 90–93
	7	I know steps for dealing with listening/watching tasks.	▸ pp. 90–91, exercises 3–4
	8	I know the modal verbs and the functions of each one.	▸ p. 93, exercise 8
D	**9**	I can describe the separation of powers in the UK government and explain aspects of the political system.	▸ p. 95, exercises 4, 7
E	**10**	I understand the main features of the British voting system.	▸ pp. 96–97, exercises 1–3
	11	I can express results and processes using the passive.	▸ p. 98, exercise 4
	12	I understand the main issues of the British political parties.	▸ p. 98, exercise 5
F	**13**	I can talk about the main duties of the royal family.	▸ p. 100, exercise 3
	14	I can write complex sentences using connective words and phrases.	▸ p. 101, exercise 6
	15	I can research a current topic and express my opinion on it.	▸ p. 101, exercise 7
Skills	**16**	I can deal with the four typical listening comprehension tasks.	**S** ▸ pp. 104–105
	17	I know how to use dictionaries effectively..	**S** ▸ pp. 106–107
	18	I am familiar with the effects of common rhetorical devices.	**S** ▸ p. 108

Consolidate

You want to go deeper into US and UK politics and speed up your learning process? Scan this page with the PagePlayer app. There you'll find some suggestions for additional tasks.

Topic 4 The media

"We limit how much technology our kids use at home."
– Steve Jobs, co-founder of Apple

Section A
Screen time

digital media

information

communication

Fact: The average smartphone user touches their phone about 2,617 times a day (source: dscout.com).

expression

Section F
Instapoetry

Fact: Twenty-six-year-old Canadian poet Rupi Kaur has 3.4 million followers on Instagram, leads the bestsellers list and is responsible for almost £1m of sales of poetry books (source: The Guardian).

"I sometimes see Instagram poetry as a gateway drug, as it were, to poetry." – Atticus, instapoet

data protection

1 Read …

a the facts about the media.
Are these facts new to you?
b the quotations. What are your opinions about these statements?

2 The mind map shows you a preview of Topic 4. Copy it onto a piece of paper and add words and phrases from …

a the Word Bank on the opposite page.
b the facts and quotations.
c Sections A–F (skim them to find words you think are important).

Find information on each Section in the PagePlayer app!

Section B
The news

"The cure to eliminate fake news is that people stop reading 140-character tweets and start reading 600-page books."
– Piero Scaruffi, writer

Fact: 36% of US Americans believe that there is a "fair amount" of bias in news coverage, 20% a "great deal" of bias (sources: Statista, Gallup).

online community

Section C
Social media activism and finding your tribe online

Fact: 57% of all teens have made new friends online; 20% have met an online friend in person (source: Pew Research Center).

image pressure

"We go through all sorts of different emotions, and Instagram makes it look like everything's perfect, and that's rubbish." – Lily James, actress

Section D
How we portray ourselves online

Fact: 87% of women and 65% of men compare their bodies to images they consume on social and traditional media (source: FHE Health).

Section E
Online privacy

"Privacy is dead, and social media holds the smoking gun." – Pete Cashmore, CEO of Mashable

3 Rank Sections A–F on how interested you are in them.

4 Make a "KWL" (Know, Want to know, Learnt) list for the Topic.

5 With a partner, compare …

a your mind maps and say why you added words where you did.
b your rankings from exercise 3.
c what you want to find out about the media.

Then compare with another pair.

6 Save your work for reviewing when you've finished the Topic.

Word bank

audience *Publikum, Zielgruppe*
bias *Voreingenommenheit, Tendenz*
conspiracy theory Verschwörungstheorie
freedom of the press Pressefreiheit
freedom of speech *Recht auf freie Meinungsäußerung*
privacy *Privatsphäre*
quality press *seriöse Zeitungen/Zeitschriften*
stereotype *Klischee, Vorurteil*
tabloid *Boulevardzeitung, Massenblatt*

Section A Screen time

Warm-up

text message *SMS, Textnachricht*
caps *pl Großbuchstaben*
to **gossip about sb** *über jdn ablästern*
straight away *sofort*

1 Look at the list and decide what is acceptable smartphone etiquette.
In a group, choose your top three "smartphone sins", then compare in class.

1 Tell someone you're going to be late
2 End a relationship
3 Apologize for something you did wrong
4 Use ALL CAPS
5 Tell someone that you love them for the first time
6 Explain to someone why you're angry with them
7 Use lots ✨ ❤️ 🔥 of emojis 😂 😂 😂
8 Wait more than an hour to answer a message
9 Gossip about a classmate in a group chat
10 Send a voice message over three minutes long
11 Send an anonymous message
12 Write "???" if someone doesn't reply straight away

Exam preparation

Speaking

Skills training: Describing and analysing cartoons

Describe – talk about what you can see
The cartoon shows …
On the left/right, there's …
In the centre/corner/background/foreground, you can see …

Interpret – say what you think the message is
The cartoon shows … in an ironic / a humorous … way.
The caption reads …
In the speech bubble, the … says …
The cartoonist wants to express / show / encourage us to think about …

Comment – give your opinion
I think / don't think that the cartoonist gets his/her message across because …
I agree/disagree with the cartoonist's opinion because …

S ▸ *Bilder und Cartoons beschreiben und analysieren*, pp. 136–137

2 Work with a partner and each choose a cartoon. *Describe* it in detail. When your partner has finished, add any details you feel are important.

"I BET YOU KIDS ARE ALL LOSING YOUR MINDS WITHOUT A WI-FI SIGNAL."

3 Swap cartoons. *Interpret* what you think the cartoonist wishes to express. Add any extra information to your partner's interpretation.

4 Now *comment* on both cartoons. Say whether you think each cartoon gets its message across and if you agree with the cartoonist's views.

Working with the text

5 Read the text and decide which cartoon from exercise 2 best illustrates the article. Explain your decision.

29

This week, Mahmood tells us what gets on his nerves at home.

I'm a Gen Z teen, so OF COURSE I love my smartphone more than anything in the world ❤️ 🙄!!! It seems to me that adults – and especially my mom – spend all their time accusing us teenagers of being internet junkies. And yes, sometimes they're right, I do spend a lot of time messaging my buddies, watching videos and playing games on my smartphone when I could be doing something more productive. ... OK, I admit it, I *am* a bit of a screenager! But I'm not the only one: my little sister Salima is 9 and she loves watching TV. Mom is always telling her that she'll get square eyes from staring at a screen so much!

I'm annoyed because people only talk about screen addiction amongst kids and teens – never adults! I mean, yes, my family is a bunch of screen addicts: kids AND parents! But the people I worry about most are my grandparents: their screen time is getting out of hand! Let me explain. So, in our house, the rule is that everybody switches off their phone at least half an hour before they go to sleep. Or puts it into flight mode. But when I switch on my phone in the morning; who's been on her phone half the night and sent me videos of kittens or puppies? Grandma! Who sends me silly jokes and memes during the day? Grandma again! She's a real silver surfer!

Whenever my grandparents drop by our place, I have to put my phone away so we can all have "a proper chat". But guess whose phone keeps making noises because she doesn't know how to mute it? Grandma's of course! She's really addicted to her phone. Whenever we go around to my grandparents' house it's even worse. Not only does my grandma's phone bleep all the time, but my grandpa is glued to the TV, watching a series. I understand why: watching a TV series is addictive. Once one episode finishes, the next one starts right away! The sad thing is that Grandpa was very active until they bought their new TV, but since then, he's become a bit of a couch potato. I'm wondering whether we should get them a real-life puppy, so that they can go out for walks and chat to people on the way. But then Grandma would probably start filming the puppy and I'd get even more messages in the middle of the night! (422 words)

Good to know

Gen Z (or Generation Z) refers to people born between the mid-1990s and the early 2010s.

- 11 **annoyed** *genervt*
- 11 **addiction** *Sucht*
- 12 **a bunch of** *ein Haufen*
- 12 **addict** *Süchtige/r*
- 17 **kitten** *Kätzchen*
- 21 **proper** *richtig, ordentlich*
- 22 to **mute sth** *etw stummschalten*
- 26 to **be addictive** *süchtig machen*
- 26 **episode** *Folge (einer Serie)*
- 29 **puppy** *Welpe*

6 Work with a partner. Look at the ten highlighted words or phrases in the text and find the meaning from the context.

D ▸ More help, p. 155

Writing

7 Point out what gets on Mahmood's nerves at home.

8 Examine how the author presents his opinion and analyse the means used to convince the reader of his position.

Exam preparation

S ▸ *Eine Aufgabe zum integrierten Leseverstehen bearbeiten*, p. 76
S ▸ *Eine Textanalyse schreiben*, pp. 138–142
S ▸ *Operatoren*, pp. 33–34
S ▸ *Stilmittel*, p. 108

Section B The news

Warm-up

1 Answer the questions about yourself, then discuss with a partner. Share your answers with the class.

1. What sort of news are you interested in?
2. Where do you get your news from? Why do you trust certain news sources more than others?
3. Do you think journalists have a special responsibility to society?

Working with the text

S ▸ *Schwierige Texte lesen*, pp. 72–73

D ▸ More help, p. 155

2 Read the blog entry on page 115 and answer these questions with a partner.

1. Why is the press so important for democracy?
2. What responsibility do journalists and reporters have?
3. How is freedom of the press protected?
4. Why aren't privately funded broadcasters always trustworthy?
5. What is a disadvantage of checking the news on social media?
6. According to the author, what aspects should people consider when reading a news report?

Exam preparation

S ▸ *Eine Aufgabe zum integrierten Leseverstehen bearbeiten*, p. 76

S ▸ *Operatoren*, pp. 33–34

3 Summarize the main points of the blog entry.

Working with words

4 Which phrases in the blog entry can be used to replace the underlined phrases?

1. In general, people trust publications which reflect their political views. (l. 6)
2. A public service broadcaster has been accused of showing a strong preference towards the ruling political party. (l. 16)
3. The young journalism project is paid for by the EU. (l. 23)
4. It's extremely important that young people are equipped with a degree of media competence. (l. 41)
5. Different people have different ways of thinking about politics and society, and this influences which newspaper they choose to read. (l. 45)

S ▸ *Wörterbücher verwenden*, pp. 106–107

5 Copy and complete the table. Look at the blog entry for help, or use a dictionary.

Noun	Adverb	Adjective	Opposite
	accurately		
		biased	
	democratically		undemocratic

6 Use words from the table in exercise 5 to write three sentences about freedom of the press and the importance of independent journalism.

NO NEWS IS GOOD NEWS? NOT IN A FREE SOCIETY!

30

Hi everyone! My topic this week is the press – specifically news broadcasters and newspapers, both online and offline – and why it is so important!

I'd like to start by talking about the role of the press in society. Broadly speaking, the role of the press is to inform people about what is happening: internationally, nationally and regionally. This is of course significant on an individual level; people need to stay informed about issues that may affect their lives. But I think it's also essential that they follow what their government and other leaders are doing, so that if they don't like it, they can vote against them in the next election! That's why the press is paramount to democracy. And journalists and reporters play a vital role in society: to report and interpret events in a way that is factually correct and free from bias.

In fact, the freedom of the press is considered so important that some countries have made it a legal right for their citizens. For example, in the USA, the First Amendment of the Constitution protects the right to free speech and a free press. Furthermore, professional journalists around the world are bound by a code of ethics which prioritizes objective reporting.

That's why we have public service broadcasters (like the BBC in the UK), which are funded by governments and put the quality of their reporting over commercial interests (which can lead to bias in favour of big corporations, for example). This seems like an almost-impossible task, because, like all of us, journalists have their personal opinions and are not completely unbiased. However, the goal should be to remain as objective as possible. In general, public service broadcasters are accepted as a legitimate source of news reporting. Nevertheless, there is still a large amount of media bias.

Nowadays many people get their news from social media sites. This way you can kill two birds with one stone: find out what is happening in the world and what your friends are up to at the same time! The problem is that social media sites use algorithms to track which topics you are interested in and what you like – and from that they can also form a picture of your world view or political viewpoint. So you will probably only see news from sources which reflect your opinion. This is what they call an "echo chamber", and you can potentially miss out on crucial facts and other sides of the story.

Newspapers – whether print or online – are a very traditional way of reading the news. However, you should take what you read with a pinch of salt – even the so-called "quality press" (publications with a reputation for serious, accurate journalism) is not as neutral as it should be. And I believe it's imperative that people ask themselves questions like: Does this article have a more of a conservative (or right wing), liberal (left wing) or other kind of bias? Could the basic facts around the story I'm reading sound different if reported by a different source? Who are the main readers of this news source? Because the viewpoints represented in newspaper articles will most likely reflect the views of their readers.

(544 words)

specifically *insbesondere*
[2] **news broadcaster** *Nachrichtensender*
[9] to **be significant** *von Bedeutung sein*
[11] to **affect sb/sth** *jdn/etw betreffen*
[13] **leader** *führende/r Politiker/in*
[14] to be paramount for sth *Voraussetzung für etw sein*
[15] **to be factually correct** *den Tatsachen entsprechen*
[17] to **be considered sth** *als etw gelten, als etw erachtet werden*
[19] **free speech** *freie Meinungsäußerung*
[21] **code of ethics** *Verhaltenskodex*
[21] **reporting** *Berichterstattung*
[22] **public service broadcaster** *öffentlich-rechtlicher Sender*
[23] to **fund sth** *etw finanzieren*
[24] **in favour of sb/sth** *zugunsten von jdm/etw*
[24] **corporation** *Großunternehmen, Konzern*
[26] **unbiased** *unvoreingenommen, neutral*
[28] **legitimate** *vertrauenswürdig, legitim*
[31] to kill two birds with one stone *zwei Fliegen mit einer Klappe schlagen*
[33] to **track sth** *etw (nach) verfolgen*
[34] **viewpoint** *Blickwinkel, Perspektive*
[36] echo chamber *Hallraum (der nur die eigene Meinung verstärkt)*
[36] **sb misses out on sth** *jdm entgeht etw*
[39] to take sth with a pinch of salt *etw nicht wortwörtlich nehmen*
[41] **imperative** *zwingend erforderlich*

Working with the text

7 Copy the table. Then read the two newspaper excerpts and make notes on the main characteristics of each one.

	1. Tabloid press	2. "Quality press"
Language / Style of writing		
Punctuation		
Visual style		
Content		

1

"WE COULD'VE DIED IN THERE!!!"

Britain's poshest hotel burns!

One night at the exclusive Diamanté Hotel costs over a THOUSAND QUID. But Matt and Linda Davis were ready to pay any price for their DREAM HONEYMOON trip. But little did they know – the real price might have been THEIR LIVES!!! Last night, a panicked Matt called the hotel reception to tell them that there was a FIRE in their exclusive honeymoon suite.

THEY BARELY ESCAPED!

posh *nobel, vornehm*

quid *Pfund*

barely *gerade noch*

2

Guests evacuated from luxury hotel

Last night a small fire broke out in the honeymoon suite at the Diamanté Hotel in London. The couple in the room alerted the reception desk and the hotel was briefly evacuated; but nobody was injured. Investigators believe the fire was probably caused by an electrical fault in one of the rooms. According to statistics published by the London Fire Brigade, electrical faults account for around 15% of all indoor fires …

to **alert sb** *jdn alarmieren*
briefly *kurzzeitig*
investigator *Ermittler/in*
fault *Defekt, Störung*
to **account for sth** *etw ausmachen*

Writing

8 Work in small groups. Read the notes on three news items. For each story, write two headlines: one in tabloid and one in a "quality press" style.

1 litter problem | town centre | local mayor | start clean-up campaign
2 funding cuts | school meals in region | parents protesting
3 space probe | new planet | astronomers excited | surprising discovery

Exam preparation

9 Write an article about one of the stories in either tabloid or quality-press style.

Speaking

10 Working in groups of three, look at the partner files (Partner A, page 158; Partner B, page 160; Partner C, page 162). Match the texts from your file to the correct headlines and tell the others the main points of what you have read.

HOW *YOU* CAN SPOT FAKE NEWS

- Find out who the author is
- Check the date
- Locate the source
- Check what the article *actually* says
- Watch out for jokes!
- Check *your* biases

11 Which of these techniques do you use? How skilled do you think you are at detecting fake news? Can you add any tips of your own?

Working with words

Skills training: Getting meanings of words from affixes

If you don't know the meaning of a word, affixes may help. Affixes are added to the beginning of the word (prefix) or the end of a word (suffix).

Example of prefix: **mis-** (wrong or bad), e.g. ***mis****take* (done wrong), ***mis****behave* (behave in a bad way)
Example of suffix: **-able/-ible** (possible, able), e.g. *prevent****able*** (can be prevented), *believ****able*** (can be believed)

Here are some common affixes:

Prefixes
dis-: not, the opposite of: **dis**ability, **dis**gusting
pre-: before: **pre**fix, **pre**pare
re-: again, back: **re**turn, **re**peat
un-: not: **un**informed, **un**natural

Suffixes
-ful: full of: use**ful**, help**ful**, hope**ful**
-ist: a follower of: scient**ist**
-ive: the quality of sth: expens**ive**
-less: without: use**less**, point**less**

Good to know

Disinformation aims to manipulate people. It is deliberately misleading or false, and is usually produced by governments or political/social interest groups.

Misinformation is not intended to deceive. It can include rumours, exaggeration, satire or misinterpretation.

12 With a partner, make as many words as possible using prefixes and suffixes. You may have to change some letters to create a new word. Use a dictionary to check your words. Then share your words with the class.

dis-	use	believe	-able
mis-	confuse	important	-ful
re-	lead	mature	-less
pre-	return	understand	-ive
un-	view	bias	-ion
	create	inform	
	power	provoke	
	truth	verify	

Writing

13 Read one of the stories and write down the main facts. Check them using the tips from exercise 10. Then rewrite the story using the correct information.

31

crime *Straftat, Verbrechen*
astonished *erstaunt*
diner *Gast (in einem Restaurant)*
to **release sb** *jdn auf freien Fuß setzen*
warning *Verwarnung*

Ninety-year-old arrested in Georgia restaurant

Vita Dietrick was arrested in a fast-food restaurant whilst celebrating her birthday. Her crime: eating fried chicken with a knife and fork! A ridiculous Georgia law states that fried chicken must be eaten with the fingers. The restaurant owner called the cops and astonished diners watched as Ms Dietrick was driven away in a police car. She was later released with a warning.

parrot *Papagei*
to **insult sb** *jdn beleidigen, jdn beschimpfen*
to **swear at sb** *jdn anpöbeln, jdn beschimpfen*
bad language *Schimpfwörter*

Parrots insult visitors at wildlife park

Five beautiful African blue parrots at a wildlife park in eastern Scotland have been upsetting visitors by swearing at them. Even worse: whenever somebody appeared shocked or laughed at the parrots' behaviour, the birds tried to physically attack them. Zookeeper Steve Nichols says that the park has decided to separate the parrots and send them to different parks so that children don't hear them using bad language.

apparently *anscheinend*
to dispel a myth *mit einem Mythos aufräumen*
smelly *übelriechend*
public facilities *öffentliche Anlagen*

See-through public toilets built around Tokyo

Japanese artist Shigeru Ban has had the crazy idea of creating public toilets with transparent glass walls, so that potential visitors can easily see how clean they are from the outside! Apparently, Ban wants to dispel the myth that public toilets are dark and smelly. At night, however, the toilets are kept dark to prevent people from staring into the units. The idea is part of the Tokyo Toilet Project, which has asked seventeen different artists to redesign public facilities in the city.

incentive *Anreiz*
scheme *Programm*

People offered cash and incentives to move to Arkansas

A campaign has been set up to encourage people to move to underpopulated suburbs of Little Rock, the capital of Arkansas. Potential future residents are being offered $10,000 and a free car to relocate as part of the Life Works Here initiative, set up to promote the gentrification of areas which are "dying out" because they are not considered pleasant places to live. The scheme is funded by the Trump family, currently the richest family in the world.

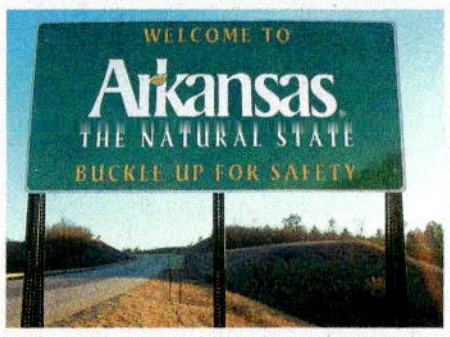

to **commission sth** *etw in Auftrag geben*
honouring sth *zu Ehren von etw*

Favourite family pet honoured in Turkmenistan

The president of Turkmenistan, Gurbanguly Berdimuhamedow, has commissioned a large multicoloured statue of the country's national dog, the Alabai. The statue will stand beside a motorway leading to the capital Ashgabat. Screens under the statue show the dogs doing special tricks at a parade honouring the birth of the nation. Berdimuhamedow has been known to give puppies as gifts to leaders of allied countries, such as Vladimir Putin.

Listening

14 **Before you listen to a news report, discuss the following questions in groups, then share your thoughts and ideas with the class.**

1 How would you define the term "conspiracy theorist"?
2 Why do you think people believe in conspiracy theories?
3 Do conspiracy theorists do any harm to society at large?

15 **Listen to the news report about a demonstration that occurred because of a conspiracy theory. While listening, choose the correct answers (a–d).**

Exam preparation

32

1 Matt was in the town centre because …
a it was on his route to work.
b he was part of a demonstration.
c he was reporting on a street protest.
d he wanted to see what was going on.

2 The protesters want politicians and other prominent figures to …
a listen to them.
b be sent to prison.
c support their cause.
d give them financial support.

3 Many protesters held signs with … on them.
a "QAnon"
b "Thank Q"
c "Q" and a pizza
d "Q" and the American flag

4 Followers of Q believe that he/she is a/an …
a investigative journalist.
b anti-government hacker.
c soldier in the US military.
d senior US army or government figure.

5 Anons believe that prominent Democrats and entertainment stars …
a will live forever.
b kidnap children.
c have alien blood.
d are fighting Satan.

16 **Copy and complete the table below. Listen to the radio show again if necessary.**

Exam preparation

1	Donald Trump's role during "the Storm":	
2	Two reasons for QAnon's success at the start of the pandemic:	
3	The intention behind the spread of the virus "hoax" (according to Q):	
4	Name one attempt to restrict the QAnon movement:	
5	In 2016, a man went to a pizzeria in Washington, DC, in order to …	

Speaking

17 **Reflect on the information from the radio show in groups. Then share your ideas with the class.**

- Did it make you change your mind about conspiracy theories? Why or why not?
- Do you think more should be done to combat their spread? If so, what?

Section C Social media activism and finding your tribe online

Warm-up

1 Match these activists to the causes below. Choose one activist and share with the class what you know about them.

1 Greta Thunberg

4 Harvey Milk

7 Malala Yousafzai

2 Nelson Mandela

5 Jane Goodall

8 Mahatma Gandhi

3 Emma Watson

6 Martin Luther King

a conservation, animal welfare
b education of women and girls
c independence from British rule (India)
d African-American civil rights
e anti-apartheid
f gender equality
g LGBTQ+ rights
h environment, fighting climate change

2 Work in groups. Research online. Have any of the activists used social media to support their cause? What other kinds of networks do or did they use to engage with their potential audience?

Listening

3 Read these short texts. What do you think "armchair activist" means? And what about you: are you more of an activist or a "slacktivist"?

Hi, I'm Ethan and I'm an activist. The only way to change things is to get out there and make your voice heard. So I join climate demonstrations, flash mobs, volunteer at beach clean-ups … whatever I can do to make our voices heard!

Hey, I'm Millie and I have to admit that I'm a slacktivist – or an armchair activist if you like! I sometimes sign online petitions that people send around, or share inspiring posts on social media; but to be honest, I don't go to demonstrations or write to politicians or anything like that.

4 Listen to the radio programme and match each speaker (1–5) with one of the opinions (a–f). There is one more opinion than you need.

Exam preparation

33

D ▸ More help, p. 155

1 Trisha
2 Lewis
3 Jay
4 Mia
5 Jacob

a is inspired by global youth activism.
b uses online media as a tool for activism.
c doesn't believe that activism achieves anything.
d believes that "slacktivism" will not bring about change.
e doesn't take part in street activism for personal reasons.
f thinks that "slacktivism" is mostly about personal image.

5 Listen again and make notes on the following for each speaker.

- the issue that is important to them
- the form/s of activism they engage in
- the kind/s of media used

Working with words

6 Complete the sentences with the correct prepositions from the box. Not all prepositions are needed, and some are needed more than once.

about | by | for | in | of | on | with

1 We all need to stand up … people living in poverty.
2 Politicians and big corporations don't care … small protests.
3 I'm a man who wants to fight … women's rights.
4 I've been encouraged … other people living with a disability.
5 I've been really inspired … the global Fridays for Future activism.
6 I took part … a few school strikes.
7 I'm strongly in favour … the Black Lives Matter movement.
8 The movement has made people from all walks of life conscious … the fight against racism.

7 Think about your own experiences and beliefs about activism and create three statements using the language from exercise 6. Compare your statements in small groups. What is the same/different?

Writing

8 Discuss the benefits and downsides of using social media for political activism.

Exam preparation

S ▸ *Eine argumentierende/ bewertende Schreibaufgabe bearbeiten*, pp. 35–40

S ▸ *Operatoren*, pp. 33–44

Working with the text

9 Before you read the article, share your experiences and opinions with the class. Have you ever made a friend online? Did you meet them in person later? Do you think online friendships are as valuable as IRL (in real life) friends? Explain.

10 Read the text. Did it make you change your mind or stick to your opinions?

34

lifeline *Rettungsanker*
10 **anti-social** *unsozial, asozial*
12 **tribe** *(Volks-)Stamm*
13 to **judge sb** *jdn beurteilen, jdn verurteilen*
14 to **rant** *losschimpfen*
17 to **come out to sb** *sich gegenüber jdm outen*
19 my life became a living hell *mein Leben wurde zur Hölle*
19 to **humiliate sb** *jdn demütigen*
21 to **bully sb** *jdn mobben*
23 to **reject sb** *jdn abweisen, jdn verstoßen*
28 **turning point** *Wendepunkt*
29 **counsellor** *Berater/in, Therapeut/in*
32 **confidence** *Selbstvertrauen*
32 **bully** *Mobber/in*
33 **victim** *Opfer*
42 **to educate sb** *jdn aufklären, jdn informieren*
43 **visible** *sichtbar*
47 **hidden** *verborgen*
48 to shine your light *(etwa:) ganz man selbst sein*

The internet was my lifeline By Lillian Campbell

… and I'm not the only one. There are millions of us who are able to carry on with our lives for one reason – because of the internet.

People can be very quick to criticize the fact that everyone seems to be staring at their smartphone instead of interacting with those around them. But what they don't think about is that most people are actually being *social* on their phone! They're either chatting and sharing experiences with others or posting funny memes to bring a smile to people's faces! How can you call that *anti*-social? At the end of the day, why do we call it SOCIAL media?

Even more importantly, there are people who find their "tribe" online. I'm one of them. I found friends who don't judge me, who laugh and cry with me, and who sometimes just let me rant. During my early teenage years, I didn't have a "tribe". In fact, I barely had any friends. Discovering that I was a lesbian in a small town with no LGBTQ+ community around was tough. I was different from the majority of kids at my school, I struggled with who I was and I didn't know who to turn to. I once came out to a girl called Emma who I thought was my friend but who went on to tell everybody at school. After that, my life became a living hell. People laughed at me, humiliated me or just ignored me and made me feel like a worthless freak. I wasn't even safe after the school day ended, because some kids also bullied me online and sent me horrible messages. I didn't dare tell my mum about it because I was afraid that she would find out about me and reject me.

It came to the point that I couldn't take it anymore. My marks at school were getting worse and worse and I was finding it a real struggle just to get out of bed in the morning. Then one day, I just happened to google "LGBTQ+ youth" and found an organization which offered support to people like me. I wrote them a short message: "Please help me. I can't take it anymore." That message was a turning point in my life. A counsellor wrote back straight away, and a day later we spoke on the phone. At last, I had someone to listen to me, support me and give me the courage to talk to my mum about how I was feeling. Soon after, I joined an online youth group and found friends who were just like me! This gave me strength and confidence, and the school bullies began to leave me alone because I wasn't an easy "victim" anymore. I made new friends and found my first girlfriend. My mum and I became really close. For what felt like the first time in my life, I was happy.

Now I've left school and decided that I wanted to help other young people in similar situations, so I'm volunteering as an online LGBTQ+ youth support worker. There are many young people with similar stories to mine and I want to help them through their struggles and show them that life *is* worth living, that they will get through the tough times. Our organization connects with similar groups in other countries, so it's been really exciting to connect with people from all around the world! We learn from each other and work together to find ways to educate the communities around us and become more visible. I'm hoping to get a permanent job here next year.

I don't understand why many people think that the connections we make online are any less valuable than in "real life". The internet and social media have made us more sociable, more knowledgeable and have given us the tools to educate and learn from others. Without the internet, I and many others would still be hidden in the shadows, lonely, bullied, not able to shine our light. Yet here we are, forming friendships, supporting each other, fighting for each other and changing the world a tiny bit each day.

(697 words)

11 Work with a partner. Answer the questions on the text using your own words wherever possible. Then compare your answers with another pair.

1 What advantages of social media does Lillian mention?
2 In what ways did the internet help Lillian?
3 What might Lillian's life have been like if she hadn't found help online?

12 Summarize the author's experience with the internet and illustrate your text with examples.

Exam preparation

S ▸ *Eine Aufgabe zum integrierten Leseverstehen bearbeiten*, p. 76
S ▸ *Operatoren*, pp. 33–34

Looking at language

Remember: Avoiding mistakes with conditionals

Don't use *will*, *would*, or *would have* in the conditional clause.

First conditional
*If you **see** the school counsellor, he **will give** you some advice.*

Second conditional
*If the organization did**n't help** LGBTQ+ youth, many of them **would feel** depressed.*

Third conditional
*If she **hadn't sent** her a message on social media, they **wouldn't have met**.*

13 Complete the conditional sentences. Make sure to use the correct verb form.

G ▸ Conditionals, p. 171

1 According to Lillian, people wouldn't judge others' smartphone behaviour if …
2 If Lillian hadn't come out to Emma, …
3 In Lillian's opinion, if she had told her mum about her feelings at the time, …
4 She might not have made friends with other LGBTQ+ youth if …
5 If the organization offers Lillian a permanent job, …
6 Many LGBTQ+ people would still feel if invisible if …

14 Continue the sentences with your own ideas. Use each conditional form at least once.

1 If I … (need) help, …
2 The world … (be) a better place if …
3 Discrimination … (not exist) if …
4 If I … (can change) one thing in the world, …
5 If the internet (not invent), …
6 I … (have) …

Speaking

15 Work in groups of four to perform this role-play. Decide on your roles. Partner A plays Alex, a teenager who has had a disagreement with his/her parents (turn to page 158); Partner B is Alex's best friend (turn to page 161); and Partners C and D are Alex's parents (turn to page 162).

16 Share your notes and prepare your arguments with the person on your "side" (the two parents or Alex and the friend).

17 Now role-play the discussion as a group and try to reach a conclusion together.

How to say or write it

I'm sorry but I disagree / don't agree.

I see what you're saying, but …

The problem with that is …

I don't think you've quite understood my point.

Have you considered the fact that …?

Section D How we portray ourselves online

Warm-up

Exam preparation

1 Describe the picture and the cartoon. Explain the message of each illustration and how they are linked. Do you agree with the messages? Do they relate to the life of the average young person?

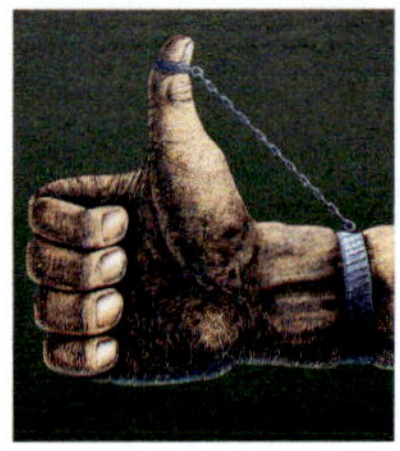

Working with the text

2 Skim the text and answer the following questions.

1 What can you guess about the person who wrote it?
2 What is the intention behind the text?
3 What is the main topic?

35

Wang Lee

I'm not perfect and nor are you – and that's fine!

This is a photo of me enjoying a well-deserved organic coffee after I'd got up at 5 a.m., gone for an energizing run, lifted weights to work out my perfectly toned muscles and spent time with other amazing individuals at college (BTW I also rescued a kitten ...).

Be somebody you're not on social media and people will love you!
The people who know me well are all LOL'ing right now cos they know that IRL most of this isn't true. For a start, I never get up that early and my muscles aren't exactly well-toned! Yes, I was enjoying a cup of coffee, which was indeed organic, but unfortunately, I'd forgotten to take my recyclable cup, so I was damaging the environment by guiltily drinking out of a disposable one.

My point is: social media puts us under so much pressure to pretend to live a healthy, perfect, caring and inspiring life 24/7. The message seems to be that to be loved you need to be successful, have cool friends, hang out at the right places, wear the latest fashion ... and do all that 10 times better than everyone else! So we waste precious time using filters to make photos look perfect and editing our social media profiles instead of enjoying life.

Seeming to be in perfect health all the time has consequences for ... our health!
We all have enough to deal with – college work, family, friends, thinking about our futures – without the added pressure of having to constantly project images of the perfect life that, TBH, none of us actually lives. And I admit that seeing all those images of perfect people living perfect lives can really get me down and make me feel like a loser.

For others, it creates even more serious issues. If someone is already struggling with depression and/or anxiety, how do you think it makes them feel when they look on social media and see that they are apparently the only ones who aren't 'living the dream'? Or people who struggle with their body image and are constantly being shown images of perfect, unrealistic bodies? The message to them seems to be that they are unlovable without the perfect weight, muscles, hair, or whatever it is.

So why are we doing this to ourselves? IMO we're addicted to all those likes and smilies – they make us feel loved and approved of. But it's all fake if people just love the image you project and not the real you. And it's our imperfections and mistakes that make us human and more interesting! So just be yourselves guys!

1 **well-deserved** *wohlverdient*
2 **energizing** *belebend*
2 **toned** *durchtrainiert*
10 to **pretend** *vorgeben; so tun, als ob*
11 **caring** *fürsorglich*
11 **24/7** *rund um die Uhr*
13 **precious** *wertvoll*
14 to **edit sth** *etw (Text usw.) bearbeiten*
21 **anxiety** *Angst, Ängste*
26 **to be addicted to sth** *nach etw süchtig sein, von etw abhängig sein*

Let's begin by getting this issue out into the open!
As you've probably guessed, this is something I feel really strongly about, so I've decided that I want to help end the social pressure young people feel on social media. I know I can't change the world through one little post, but I'd like to start a discussion. My first question to everyone reading this is: Do you also feel under pressure to present a perfect image of yourself on social media? LMK! Can't wait to hear from you!

Never really thought about it, TBH. I love making my mates laugh by posting stupid videos and stuff. And getting loads of likes really is a big dopamine hit!

Yes!!! I'm expected to become more responsible, cope with increasing amounts of schoolwork, think about my future and constantly post beautiful images of my perfect life?! How???

IMO there's far too much pressure to be perfect. I thought social media was supposed to connect people, but it just makes them constantly want to outdo each other.

(619 words)

[31] **sb feels strongly about sth** *jdm liegt etw sehr am Herzen*

[40] to **be supposed to do sth** *(eigentlich) etw tun sollen*

Good to know

Many abbreviations from texting and social media have become common in English. You might even hear someone say "LOL" instead of actually laughing! Here are some of the most common ones.
IRL – in real life
LOL – laugh out loud
IMO – in my opinion
BTW – by the way
LMK – let me know
OMG – oh my god!
TBH – to be honest

Working with words

3 Match the definitions with the words and phrases highlighted in the text.

1 what you say when you are feeling excited and impatient for sth to happen
2 having a perfect life
3 doing sth "bad" and simultaneously feeling ashamed
4 to display outwardly
5 to successfully deal with a difficult situation or struggle
6 to try to be better than sb else
7 faults or weaknesses
8 sth that makes you feel amazing
9 separate, unique human beings
10 to make sb to feel miserable

Working with the text

4 Examine how the author presents his opinion and analyse the means used to convince the reader of his position. Refer to the article and the picture and the cartoon above it.

5 Write your own comment in response to Wang's post.

Exam preparation

S ▸ *Eine Textanalyse schreiben*, pp. 138–143
S ▸ *Stilmittel*, p. 108
S ▸ *Operatoren*, pp. 33–34
S ▸ *Eine kreative Schreibaufgabe bearbeiten*, pp. 41–42

Speaking

6 Work in small groups. Re-read the comment thread and decide which comment you identify with most and why.

D ▸ More challenge, p. 156

7 Answer the following questions. Then compare in a group.

1 Who is your "audience" on social media? Who do you want to see what you post?
2 Do you use filters or other methods to enhance images of yourself in posts? Why (not)?
3 How do you want other people to perceive you on social media? Decide on three adjectives.
4 How close is your social media persona to your real self?
5 What do you think makes a "perfect" social media persona?

Section E Online privacy

Warm-up

D ▸ More help, p. 156

1 Do the quiz with a partner.

1 Which of the following are legally considered "personal information"?
- **a** Your name, address and telephone number and date of birth
- **b** Your fingerprints, medical records, height and weight
- **c** School/s and college/s attended, political allegiance
- **d** Credit card details, spending history and habits
- **e** All of the above

2 Which of the following personal information can be collected by websites?
- **a** Your personal preferences, e.g. the language you prefer to view the page in
- **b** The software you are using
- **c** Your approximate location
- **d** What you have clicked on, when and how often
- **e** All of the above

3 "Free games are great, they provide me with hours of fun and don't cost me anything!"
a True **b** False

4 "Privacy policies protect my personal information. If a website has one, the company won't share my data with anyone."
a True **b** False

5 "If the settings on my social media profile show that only 'friends' can see my profile then only people I allow to see my postings have access."
a True **b** False

6 What's the safest way to behave on social media?
- **a** Think before you post: will you still be OK with seeing what you posted in a few years' time?
- **b** Post everything you think will make people laugh – even if it's a bit embarrassing!
- **c** Delete all your accounts and write letters instead.

7 If someone you don't know wants to befriend or follow you on social media, should you accept?
- **a** Why not? The more the merrier on my profile!
- **b** It depends. If the person looks trustworthy, it's probably OK.
- **c** I would make sure I know who the person is first.

8 **There's going to be a big party this weekend and you and all of your friends are welcome! Is it OK to post the time, date and location details online so that everyone is informed?**
  a Yes, who cares where I'm going anyway unless they want to come along?
  b No, it's never a good idea to post details of where you will be at a certain time.
  c I think so: it's a convenient way to contact everyone at once, and there are no creepy strangers on my profile anyway.

Working with words

2 Before you listen to interviews with people about protecting their data, match the words and phrases to the correct definitions.

1 reject
2 party animal
3 mate
4 suited to
5 gutted
6 learn your lesson
7 privacy settings
8 trans
9 get in touch
10 big shot

a *(slang)* extremely disappointed
b sb with a lot of power or influence
c sb whose gender identity doesn't match their physical characteristics
d *(on a website)* where you control the visibility of your personal data
e *(slang)* friend
f not to accept sb/sth
g fits well together
h sb who loves to go out and have fun
i learn from your mistakes
j contact sb

Listening

Reesha

Alisha

Kay

Sam

3 Listen to three interviews about protecting personal data and answer the questions. 36

1 Why is Alisha so careful about what she posts on social media?
2 What has changed in her life?
3 What was the response to Kay's initial posts?
4 What did Kay do after speaking to a teacher?
5 What did Sam use his Instagram account to do?
6 How has Sam's social media experience changed his life?

4 Listen again and decide what you think Alisha, Kay and Sam would advise doing online.

5 Compare your answers with a partner. Can you add any other ideas to the list?

Looking at language

G ▸ Used to, p. 173

Remember: *Used to*

Used to follows the rules of the simple past:

Statements: *used to* + infinitive
Questions and negative statements: *did / didn't* + *use to* + infinitive

*She always **used to** enjoy going to parties.*
*Sam **didn't use to** post much on social media.*
***Did** he **use to** share a lot of memes?*
*What **did** she **use to** do on social media?*

Remember, don't use a time phrase (e.g. *last month*) together with *used to*.

6 Answer the questions about the interview using the correct form of *used to*.

1 What did Alisha use to enjoy doing when she was younger?
2 Why did she use to allow strangers access to her photos?
3 Why didn't Kay use to talk to people about being trans?
4 What did Sam use to do on Instagram?

7 Make up three questions using *used to*. Then work with a partner and interview each other about what you used to do when you were younger.

Mediation

S ▸ *Mediation*, pp. 134–135

Skills training: Mediation

1 Skim
- Skim the text to get an overview of the most important information.
- Ignore any irrelevant details.

2 Make notes
- Think about your target audience: what do they need to know?
- Read the text again and make notes on the most important points.

3 Mediate
- Formulate your text in short, clear sentences or bullet points, appropriate to your target audience.

Tips
- Don't translate! Try to use your own words in the target language.
- When you've finished, check the length of your mediation text. If it's longer than the original text, revise it and cut out any unnecessary information or long sentences.

Example
English: *Your personal data is your property. And, like any other property, it's worth money to companies and criminals alike – so look after it!*
German: *Schütze deine Daten – Firmen und Kriminelle wollen davon profitieren!*

8 You have a friend who doesn't speak much English and has asked for your help to understand the text on page 129. Summarize the important points in German.

Protect your personal data online!

37

Your personal data is *your* property. And, like any other property, it's worth money to companies and criminals alike – so look after it! Nobody has the right to save or use your data without your consent – with the exception of certain government authorities or the police. And respect the privacy of others: never share photos or videos in which another person can be recognized without their permission.

Social media
Set your profile settings to "private" and make sure you know your social media "friends" well enough to allow them access to your private data. And never give your address, phone number or email to someone you don't know!

Surfing the web
Don't access any sensitive information (e.g. your bank account) if you're connected to public wifi (e.g. in a café) because it is much easier for hackers to access your passwords.

Watch out for cookies (not the chocolate kind 😉)! A cookie is data saved on your device when you visit a website. It may help you use the website more easily, e.g. when filling out a booking form; but also tracks what you click on. This helps companies to build up a user profile so they can send you targeted advertising. Check your browser settings so you are alerted when a website wants to send a cookie, so that you can decide whether or not to allow it. Regularly delete any old cookies stored on your device.

General safety tips
- Always use strong passwords: a combination of numbers, letters and symbols.
- Install anti-virus software and a firewall and update them at regular intervals.
- Regularly update your operating system.
- Don't click on any links in emails if you don't know who they're from! Check the sender's address, and if it looks suspicious, delete it straight away.

(301 words)

[1] **property** *Eigentum*
[5] **consent** *Einwilligung*
[6] **government authority** *staatliche Stelle, Behörde*
[10] to **recognize sb** *jdn (wieder)erkennen*
[10] **permission** *Erlaubnis*
[13] **access (to sth)** *Zugriff (auf etw)*
[16] to **access sth** *auf etw zugreifen*
[16] **sensitive information** *vertrauliche Daten*
[22] **targeted advertising** *gezielte Werbung*
[23] to **alert sb** *jdn warnen*
[28] **at regular intervals** *in regelmäßigen Zeitabständen*
[31] to **look suspicious** *verdächtig aussehen*

Speaking

9 Work in groups. Create a video on online privacy and data protection. You can use information from the article on this page, internet research and your own ideas.

Consider the following:
- your target audience (adults/teenagers/children?)
- the most useful information for your audience and how you will convey it
- how to keep your audience's attention and help them to remember and follow your tips
- whether you would like to include any extra images, special effects or music
- the location of your video

Show your video to the class.

▸ Making an awareness campaign video, pp. 68–69

Section F Instapoetry

Warm-up

1 Work in small groups to complete the following tasks. Share your results with the class.

a Brainstorm how digital media can be expressive in an artistic way.
b Say if you already use digital media creatively and why (not).
c Describe any online art you have come across and if you liked it.

Speaking

38

Good to know

Instapoetry is a type of poetry written to be shared on social media such as Instagram and read in a smartphone format. It is usually short and written in an eye-catching font and accompanied by an image.

2 Close your eyes and listen to Jenny Bienemann read her poem. Then read it and discuss the questions with a partner.

1 Did you enjoy the poem more when reading it or when listening to the author?
2 How does the graphic design of the poem change its impact?
3 What is the poem about? Can you relate to it?

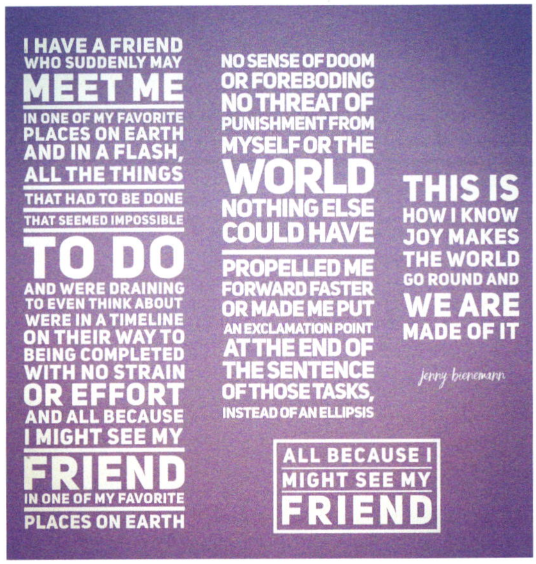

How to say or write it

The image emphasizes/ reflects …
The meaning of the words is expressed …
The image and the text work together to …
The poem and the image both have a … quality.

3 Work with a partner. Choose one instapoem each, read it aloud and explain how the image relates to the text.

4 Read the quote, and discuss with your partner whether or not you agree with it.

"Instapoetry isn't art. It's just a smartphone photo with a quote on top."

Working with words

5 Before you listen to an interview with Jenny Bienemann, read these phrases from the interview and match the underlined phrases with their synonyms.

D ▸ More practice, p. 156

access and use | amplify and illustrate | attack them viciously | briefly address | stop being aware of it | strengthening the effect

1 She gives creativity workshops, where she helps people to tap into their own personal creativity.
2 Her poems often touch on deep subjects, like love, and friendship.
3 The image and the words were working together, and one was deepening the impact of the other.
4 Friends are able to see the beauty in us when we lose track of it.
5 Part of my work is to shine a light on the ordinary in the everyday.
6 And then when we do hear something that disagrees with us, we get vicious, and we try to tear them limb from limb.

Watching/Listening

Exam preparation

Crossover TV

Interview with instapoet Jenny Bienemann

39 05

6 Complete the notes while listening to the interview and watching a slideshow.

1 Jenny's method of writing an instapoem: …
2 Typical themes in Jenny's poems: …
3 Two reasons Jenny chooses Instagram to publish her poems:
4 The syllable pattern of a haiku is …

7 Choose the correct answer (a–d).

1 What does Jenny say about friends?
   a They're like family.
   b They'll always love us.
   c They're people like ourselves.
   d They see our good side, even if we don't.

2 How does Instagram help Jenny's creative process?
   a People see her output daily.
   b Other artists' posts inspire her.
   c She needs the positive feedback.
   d She can post images without text.

8 Answer the following questions in note form.

1 What does Jenny feel society encourages people to do?
2 What do you do if you "throw shade" at yourself?
3 Why is it important to do something creative?
4 How does Jenny define an artist?

Writing

9 Follow the steps to create and present an instapoem. It should be in the form of a haiku and accompanied by an image.

1 Choose a theme that inspires you, e.g. a feeling, or "social justice".
2 Decide if you will begin the creative process with an image or your text.
3 Present your instapoem to the class and read the haiku aloud.

Project Creating a podcast

You are going to create a podcast on a particular aspect of media. The podcast will be judged and voted on by the rest of the class. It should be 3–5 minutes long and include either:

an in-depth interview with one or two people – in English

or

vox pops (one question, asked of a number of people) – in English or German (if in German then with English mediation).

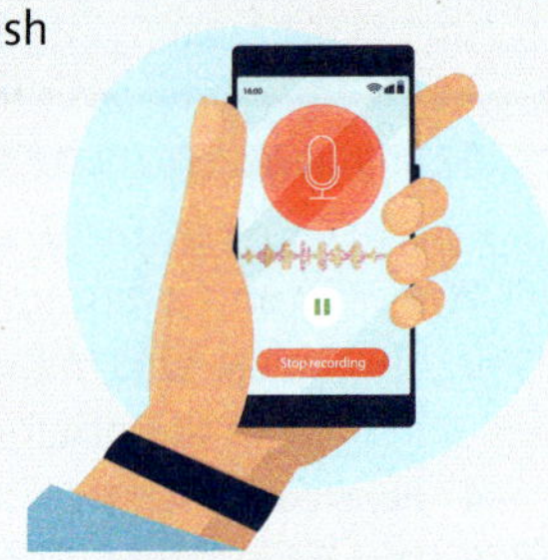

Good to know

Vox pops are short comments from members of the public on a particular topic, used as a reflection of popular opinion. The term comes from the Latin *vox populi* (voice of the people).

Work in groups. Choose the topic you would like to work on. Here are some ideas, but you are free to be as creative as you like!

- What role do screens play in your life?
- How dangerous is fake news?
- How real are you on social media?
- How careful are you with your data?
- How can the digital world be a good place for creative expression?

Tips

In your group, share knowledge that you already have about podcasts. Listen to a few minutes of other podcasts and make notes on which elements they include (e.g. music). Get ideas from successful podcasts about how to introduce and structure your topic and how to conclude the episode.

Steps

1 **Brainstorm:** which aspects of the topic you want to cover in your podcast and what you want to find out from your interview or vox pops.
2 Consider your **target audience**: Which age group are you aiming at? Why might they be interested in the topic?
3 Decide how will you **structure** your podcast.
4 **Assign roles** to each member of your group, e.g. presenter/s, interviewer/s, technical support, etc.
5 **Decide** what exactly you would like to find out in your interview or vox pops, then decide on the best question/s to ask to **obtain** the information you need.
6 **Carry out** your interviews or vox pops and decide what you would like to keep and what to cut.
7 **Write a script** for the rest of the podcast (introduction, main body, conclusion), **practise** reading it, then **record** it.
8 **Add** the interviews, jingles and any other necessary sound effects.
9 **Listen** to your podcast carefully, remove any mistakes and make any necessary improvements
10 **Write** a short statement introducing your podcast to the jury; **think about** questions the jury may ask and **make notes to** prepare your answers.

How to say or write it

Introduction
Hello and welcome to (this week's/month's episode of) …

I'm your host, … / This week's episode is presented by …

Today's topic is … / Today we're going to be discussing …

Main body
…, welcome to the show. / Thank you for speaking with us today.

Now let's join our reporter … who's interviewing people on the streets of …

Let's begin by …

Let's move on to …

Conclusion
What's your opinion? Please let us know by contacting us at …

That's all for this week/episode.

Thank you for listening and goodbye.

Tips for recording your podcast

Use a recording app and practise using it before you start interviewing!

Check the sound quality using headphones.

Record about ten seconds and play it back to test the sound quality and adjust the volume as necessary.

to **adjust sth** *etw regeln, etw einstellen*

Give your recording a title and save it in the appropriate format for editing.

editing *(Ton-, Video-) Schnitt, Schneiden*

While interviewing/recording speech: hold the phone about a fist-length away from the interviewee's face: close enough to hear them clearly, but not so close that you hit them in the face with the phone!

fist-length *Handbreit*

Tips for your interview or vox pops

- Always be polite and professional!
- Choose a suitable place to carry out your interview or vox pops: keep background noise to a minimum.
- Start by briefly introducing yourself: your name, organization and the topic of your project.
- Wait five seconds after your interviewee has finished answering to make sure you've captured the complete answer.
- Keep your questions short and the language simple.
- Ask all interviewees the same question(s) so that your results are truly representative of public opinion.
- Ask open-ended questions to elicit more interesting responses.

to **carry out sth** *etw durchführen*
background noise *Hintergrundgeräusche*
to **capture sth** *etw aufnehmen*
to **be representative of sth** *repräsentativ für etw sein*
open-ended *ergebnisoffen*
to **elicit a response** *eine Reaktion/Antwort hervorrufen*

Tips: using vox pops in another language

If people talk to you in German, you will need to **mediate** for your English-speaking audience: record a few seconds of their voice in German and then briefly convey the main point they made in English – don't translate!

S ▸ *Mediation*, pp. 134–135
to **convey sth** *etw vermitteln, etw umschreiben*

Permissions and rights

Create a form that participants can sign, showing that you have their consent to record and use their voice and opinion. Make sure the form states clearly how you will use the recording.

▸ Permissions and rights, p. 69
consent *Einverständnis(erklärung)*

Judging the podcasts

1 As a class, decide on the exact criteria for judging the podcasts, e.g. content, delivery, use of language (accuracy, varied vocabulary and phrases, etc.) and write them on the board.
2 Present and listen to the podcasts. After each podcast, the listeners ask questions of the creators.
3 Divide the class up into several panels of judges, ideally each with one member from each podcast team.
4 Each panel of judges chooses their winner according to the criteria on the board, and the team with the most wins wins!

Mediation

Mediation bedeutet „Vermittlung". Sie vermitteln dabei Inhalte von einer Sprache in eine andere. Dabei kann es sich um eine schriftliche oder mündliche Mediation handeln, manchmal auch um eine Sprachmittlung zwischen zwei verschiedensprachigen Gesprächspartnern.

BEISPIELAUFGABE

SITUATION: Eine Umfrage an Ihrer Schule hat ergeben, dass eine überwältigende Mehrheit der Schülerinnen und Schüler Nachrichten – wenn überhaupt – fast ausschließlich über Social-Media-Kanäle bezieht.

AUFGABE: Als Mitglied der Redaktion Ihrer Online-Schülerzeitung verfassen Sie für die nächste Ausgabe einen Podcast, in dem es um die Rolle der Presse in der Gesellschaft, die Pressefreiheit sowie um die Rolle von sozialen Medien und von traditionellen Zeitungen in der Nachrichtenwelt geht. Mit Ihrem Beitrag wollen Sie bei Ihren Mitschülerinnen und Mitschülern ein kritisches Bewusstsein für diese Fragen wecken und orientieren sich dabei an einem Blogeintrag, den Sie dazu gefunden haben: „No news is good news? Not in a free society!" von Seite 115.

Schritt 1: Analyse der Aufgabenstellung

1 Form

Die Form Ihrer Mediation hängt hauptsächlich von den folgenden drei Faktoren ab, die Sie durch sorgfältiges Lesen der Aufgabenstellung analysieren:

Adressat	Medium / Textsorte	Zweck
		Aufbereitung von ...
- Mitschüler/innen	- Infobroschüre, Aushang	- Informationen
- Kunden eines Unternehmens	- E-Mail, Brief	- Ratschlägen
- Familienmitglieder (z.B. Eltern)	- Podcast	- Argumenten
- Leser/innen einer Zeitung	- Zeitungsartikel	- ...
- ...	- ...	

Sprachebene/*register:*

Die oben genannten Faktoren bestimmen den situativen Kontext und somit auch, auf welcher Sprachebene Sie Ihre Mediation stilistisch ansiedeln: eher informell oder eher formell.

2 Inhalt

Grenzen Sie die relevanten Inhalte vorab ein; in der Regel werden die entsprechenden Aspekte in der Aufgabenstellung genannt.

Übung 1

1 **Bestimmen Sie Form und Inhalt in folgender Aufgabenstellung.**
An Ihrer Schule findet ein Projekttag zum Thema „Sicherer Umgang mit sozialen Netzwerken" statt. Sie sollen in Ihrer Klasse einen Vortrag über mögliche negative Folgen der Nutzung sozialer Medien und potenzielle Gegenmaßnahmen halten. Erstellen Sie hierfür ein begleitendes Infoblatt.

2 **Bestimmen Sie Form und Inhalt in der Aufgabenstellung zur Beispielaufgabe oben auf dieser Seite.**

Schritt 2: Bearbeitung des Ausgangstextes

Überfliegen Sie den Text zunächst, um einen ersten Überblick zu erhalten. Halten Sie sich dabei nicht mit Verständnisschwierigkeiten auf.

Danach erst gehen Sie den Text absatzweise durch und notieren diejenigen Inhalte, die Sie vorab bei der Analyse der Aufgabenstellung ausgemacht haben (s. Schritt 1).

Übung 2

Wenden Sie die beiden Lesestile *skimming* und *scanning* auf den Text auf S. 115 an.
Hinweis: Für Ihre Mediation ist ein kompletter Absatz *nicht* relevant!

Schritt 3: Verfassen der Mediation

Bevor Sie mit dem Schreiben beginnen, vergewissern Sie sich erneut, dass Sie die markierten Inhalte adressaten- und situationsgerecht wiedergeben, indem Sie die Aufgabenstellung nochmals durchlesen.

Beim Schreibprozess kommt es mitunter vor, dass Sie **paraphrasieren**, also umschreiben müssen. Dafür gibt es zwei Hauptgründe:

1 Redewendungen im Ausgangstext
Egal in welcher Ausgangssprache, Redewendungen können sehr knifflig in der Übertragung sein – die Bildsprache ist häufig von Sprache zu Sprache verschieden. Bei englischen Redewendungen ist ein einsprachiges Wörterbuch sehr hilfreich!

2 Vereinfachung / Verkürzung in der Wiedergabe
Eine Mediation ist grundsätzlich eine Zusammenfassung. Achten Sie darauf, dass Sie Wiederholungen, Beispiele, Anekdoten und Exkurse ausklammern und sich auf das Wesentliche konzentrieren. Zitate sollten einzeln bewertet werden und nur dann in Ihrer Wiedergabe verwendet werden, wenn sie eine Kernaussage beinhalten und nicht nur der Ausschmückung dienen.

Beispiele für Redewendungen *(idiomatic expressions)*
1. *The ball is in your court.* (Sie sind am Zug / dran.)
2. *to judge a book by its cover* (vorschnell nach dem äußeren Anschein urteilen)
3. Eselsbrücke *(method to make learning easier)*
4. sich aus dem Staub machen *(to leave)*

Beispiel für Vereinfachung / Verkürzung
Ausgangstext:
Article 19 of the Universal Declaration of Human Rights, adopted in 1948, states that everyone has the right to freedom of opinion and expression.
Wiedergabe in der Mediation:
Das Recht auf freie Meinungsäußerung ist gesetzlich verankert.

universal *allgemein(gültig)*
to **adopt (a law)** *(ein Gesetz) verabschieden*
to **state** *erklären, sagen*
freedom of opinion and expression *Meinungs- und Redefreiheit*

Übung 3

1 Finden Sie zwei englische Redewendungen im Ausgangstext der Beispielaufgabe und übertragen Sie diese sinngemäß in die deutsche Sprache.

2 Vereinfachen Sie folgende Aussage aus dem Ausgangstext in deutscher Sprache:
For example, in the USA, the First Amendment of the Constitution protects the right to free speech and a free press. (ll. 18–19)

3 Verfassen Sie nun den kurzen Podcast für Ihre Mitschülerinnen und Mitschüler.

amendment *Zusatzartikel*
constitution *Verfassung*
free speech *Meinungsfreiheit, Redefreiheit*

Bilder und Cartoons beschreiben und analysieren

Wenn Sie ein Bild oder einen Cartoon beschreiben, sollten Sie sich auf die Hauptaussage konzentrieren und sich nicht in Details verlieren. Vermeiden Sie, „um die Ecke zu denken", sondern bleiben Sie im Rahmen des Themas.

Beispielaufgabe:

Beschreiben Sie und analysieren Sie das Bild. Vergleichen Sie es mit dem Text.

Play time is screen time

According to a survey of parents and caregivers by Gallup, American children spend the largest share of their free time on screen-based activities. 2- to 10-year-olds spend 18.6 hours on screen-based play in a usual week. This is significantly more time than they spend on indoor screen-free play (14.6 hours) and outside play (10.6 hours).

according to *nach*
caregiver *Betreuer/in*
share *Anteil*

significantly *erheblich*

"Those are the basic necessities of life? Aren't you forgetting something?"

Schritt 1: Beschreibung

Beschreiben Sie das Bild: Schauen Sie sich alle Aspekte der Abbildung an, gehen Sie jedoch nur auf die Elemente ein, die für die Aussage wichtig sind.

chalkboard *Kreidetafel*

a classroom
a teacher and two children
a chalkboard
~~The desks are yellow and blue.~~

Geben Sie an, welches Objekt Sie beschreiben, indem Sie genau bestimmen, wo es sich im Bild befindet.

to **raise one's hand** *die Hand heben*

***On the left**, there's a chalkboard with the words "food, water, clothing, shelter" written on it.*

Verwenden Sie die Verlaufsform *present progressive*, um den Inhalt der Abbildung darzustellen.

Achtung: *be*, *seem*, *look* und *describe* werden i. d. R. nicht in der Verlaufsform verwendet.

One child is raising her hand.
*~~One child **raises** her hand.~~*
She seems very enthusiastic.
~~She seems very enthusiastic.~~

Schritt 2: Interpretation

Interpretieren Sie das Bild. Wenn Sie der Meinung sind, dass die Darstellung nicht viel aussagt, erwähnen Sie dies in Ihrer Interpretation. Bezeichnen Sie die Abbildung als mehrdeutig oder unklar.

*The **message** of the cartoon is **clearly** that children think electronic devices are as necessary as food, water, etc., and are therefore too dependent on them.*

Schritt 3: Wirkung auf Sie und Ihre Aussage

Stellen Sie dar, welche Auswirkung das Bild auf Sie hat: Fassen Sie die Hauptaussage zusammen und geben Sie Ihre eigene Meinung wieder.

***I (don't) agree** with the message that children depend on devices too much.*

***I (don't) find** the cartoon very funny/clever.*

Schritt 4: Bezug zum anderen Medium

Falls ein unabhängiger Text (s. oben) dazu einbezogen werden kann, vergleichen Sie die Abbildung mit dem Inhalt des Textes: Sagen Sie, ob das Bild die Aussage des Textes unterstützt oder ihr widerspricht.

***The cartoon supports the text**, which says that children spend many hours a week with screens.*

Describing the picture

- The cartoon shows …
- The comic/cartoon consists of four frames/parts.
- The picture seems to show …
- The scene depicts …
- The caption / speech bubble says …
- In the foreground/background/centre there is …
- On the left/right there is …
- The person seems to be (holding something / writing / walking away)
- It seems as if the person is (holding something / writing / walking away)

to **consist of** *bestehen aus*

to **depict** *darstellen*

Interpreting the picture

- The picture/cartoon deals with …
- The cartoon is intended to create …
- The (person in the centre) represents/shows/symbolizes …
- This shows/reveals/indicates …
- The impression of … is created.
- The point of the cartoon is / seems to be …
- The humour lies in the difference/misunderstanding/contrast between … and …

point *Zweck*

Commenting on the picture

- I think … / In my opinion …
- The cartoon makes a fair point.
- The cartoon convinces / doesn't convince me, because …
- I agree with the cartoonist, but …
- The cartoonist is partly right.
- The cartoonist exaggerates a little / a lot.
- It forces you to think about …
- It has the effect of …

to **exaggerate** *übertreiben*

to **force sb** *jdn zwingen*

Comparing the picture with the text

- Although the picture shows … , the text says …
- In the text we found out that …
- The cartoon/picture supports the information in the text in the following ways.
- The cartoon offers a completely different opinion of the information in the text.

to **support** *unterstützen*

Übung

Describe and analyse the cartoon. Compare it with the information from the survey.

The same Gallup survey described above found that children spend, on average, 9.6 hours a week doing screen-free things with a parent or adult.

"Your mother and I are concerned about how much time you spend online."

Eine Textanalyse schreiben

Gut zu wissen

Im **Abitur** verfassen Sie eine Textanalyse auf Grundlage eines nicht-literarischen Textes.

Bei dieser Schreibaufgabe analysieren Sie einen vorliegenden Text anhand einer bestimmten Aufgabenstellung. Meist verfolgt dieser Text eine bestimmte Intention. Auf dieser Grundlage verfassen Sie dann eine strukturierte und zusammenhängende Textanalyse, die je nach Aufgabenstellung sowohl inhaltliche als auch sprachliche Aspekte aus dem Text berücksichtigt.

▸ Topic 4, Section B, The news, S. 114–119

▸ Topic 3, Giving a speech, S. 102–103

In Ihren Prüfungen kommen als Ausgangstexte z. B. **Berichte und Artikel** verschiedenster Ausprägungen vor, die zumeist der seriösen Presse aus dem englischsprachigen Raum entstammen. Auch **Reden** können Ausgangstexte für eine inhaltliche und/oder sprachliche Textanalyse darstellen.

Nicht-literarische Textsorten und ihre Hauptmerkmale

Bericht/Zeitungsbericht *report/newspaper article*	**Leitartikel in der Zeitung** *leading article/leader/ editorial*	**Sonderbeitrag/Feature** (Zeitung/Magazin) *feature article*
meist informativ	**meist argumentativ**	**meist informativ**
• antwortet auf Fragen: *Who? What? Where? When? How? Why?* • behandelt aktuelle Themen • legt Fokus auf Fakten • meist objektive Berichterstattung • enthält oft Zitate	• drückt die Meinung eines Journalisten / einer Journalistin aus • behandelt aktuelle Themen • richtet sich eher an gebildete Leser	• oft länger als Zeitungsartikel • tiefere Auseinander-setzung mit einem Thema • legt Fokus auf Fakten und Unterhaltung • enthält oft Zitate

S ▸ Stilmittel, S. 108

Rede *speech*	**Leserbrief** *letter to the editor*	**Kommentar** *comment*
meist appellativ/persuasiv	**meist argumentativ**	**meist argumentativ**
• transportiert eine klare Meinung • versucht zu überzeugen • richtet sich direkt ans Publikum, nutzt häufig rhetorische Mittel	• stellt eine Reaktion zu einem Zeitungsbeitrag dar • drückt Zustimmung oder Widerspruch aus • enthält oft auch Fakten	• nimmt zu einem aktuellem Thema Stellung • enthält klare Schluss-folgerungen oder Forderungen • soll zum Nachdenken anregen

Weitere typische nicht-literarische Textsorten: formale Briefe, Biografien, Porträts, Reiseberichte, Rezensionen, technische/naturwissenschaftliche Texte etc.

Blogs

Ein Blog oder auch Weblog ist für sich genommen keine Textsorte, sondern ein von einem Blogger / einer Bloggerin genutztes Online-Medium, um verschiedenste Inhalte zu posten. Die inhaltliche Ausrichtung des Blogs definiert hier die Textsorte, z. B. Themenblog (Reise, Mode, Wirtschaft etc.), Fanblog (Musik, Sport, Film etc.), Meinungs-/Politikblog etc. Grundsätzlich fließt in einen Blog eine persönliche Note ein, er ist authentisch, transportiert meist eine Meinung und regt im Idealfall zu einer Diskussion an.

Die Analyse verfassen – Schritt für Schritt

Schritt 1: Vor der Textanalyse steht die Aufgabenanalyse

Die Aufgabenstellung kann beispielsweise das Herausarbeiten der **inhaltlichen Position** eines Autors bzw. einer Autorin, ggf. unter Verdeutlichung einer Auswahl an **sprachlichen Gestaltungsmitteln** beinhalten. Auch sogenannte **diskontinuierliche Texte**, also z. B. Grafiken, Bilder, Cartoons, können in den Analyseauftrag mit einbezogen werden.

S ▸ Stilmittel, S. 108

S ▸ Diagramme beschreiben und analysieren, S. 70–71

S ▸ Bilder und Cartoons beschreiben und analysieren, S. 136–137

Eine weitere Möglichkeit ist das Herausarbeiten der **sprachlichen Gestaltungsmittel**, die der Autor bzw. die Autorin einsetzt, um die Leserschaft von seinem bzw. ihrem **inhaltlichen Standpunkt** zu überzeugen. Auch hier sind zusätzliche **diskontinuierliche Texte** möglich, die es in Ihre Analyse einzubeziehen gilt.

Beispiele

Examine how the author presents his life and how this affects the reader. Refer to the article as well as to the documents he published with it.

Analyse the means used to convince the reader of the author's position. Refer to the article and the photo published with it.

Übung 1

Lesen Sie die folgende Aufgabenstellung zum Text *Dear Gavin Williamson, teenagers use mobile phones. Get with the times* von S. 142–143 und bestimmen Sie, welche Teile der Arbeitsanweisung jeweils inhaltliche, sprachliche und weitere Aspekte darstellen, die in Ihre Analyse einfließen müssen.

Examine how the author presents his opinion and analyse the means used to convince the reader of his position. Refer to the article and the cartoons on p. 112.

Schritt 2: *Text attack!* – was ist es für ein Text und worum geht es?

Sammeln Sie die Textstellen, die bei Ihrer Analyse als Belege dienen, indem Sie Notizen zu den folgenden Aspekten anfertigen oder diese direkt im Text verschiedenfarbig markieren, wenn Sie die Möglichkeit haben.

a) Textsorte *(text type)*
Bestimmen Sie die Textsorte.

b) Sprachebene *(register)*
Bei nicht-literarischen Texten treffen Sie auf folgende drei Hauptebenen:

excessive *übermäßig*
usage *Nutzung*
review *Überprüfung, Begutachtung*
to **conduct sth** *etw durchführen*
to **determine sth** *etw bestimmen, etw festlegen*
intervention *Maßnahme*
scientific evidence *wissenschaftliche Erkenntnisse*
radio frequency energy *Hochfrequenzenergie/-wellen*

Kontext	Merkmale	Beispiele
formell *formal*	• verwendet komplexe Satzstrukturen • Häufung von Fremdwörtern • oft wissenschaftlicher oder offizieller Kontext	*Excessive mobile device usage has led to a systematic review conducted to determine effective interventions to reduce it.*
neutral *neutral*	• orientiert sich am gebräuchlichen Wortschatz der modernen Alltagssprache • ist präzise, verständlich und eindeutig • wird von seriösen Zeitungen eingesetzt	*Current scientific evidence does not show a danger to any users of cell phones from radio frequency (RF) energy, including teenagers.*
informell *informal*	• verwendet einfache Satzstrukturen, Kurzformen • beinhaltet auch Umgangssprache und Slang • v.a. im persönlichen Gespräch mit Familie oder im Austausch unter Jugendlichen	*I'm a Gen Z teen, so OF COURSE I love my smartphone more than anything in the world!!! :-) OK, I admit it, I'm totally a screenager!*

c) Ton *(tone)*
Analysieren Sie den Ton des Textes. Dieser zeigt die Haltung des Autors bzw. der Autorin dem Thema gegenüber. Hier sind viele Färbungen möglich, z.B. ernst, humorvoll, ironisch, geistreich, sentimental, warmherzig, aggressiv oder sarkastisch. Oft lohnt es sich dabei, auch die Überschrift genauer unter die Lupe zu nehmen.

S ▸ Stilmittel, S. 108

d) Stilmittel *(stylistic devices)*
Finden Sie heraus, welche verschiedenen Stilmittel im Text Verwendung finden.

Strukturieren Sie Ihre Sammlung
Lassen Sie sich dabei von folgender zentraler Leitfrage lenken:

Welcher Effekt wird durch den Einsatz des jeweiligen Mittels bezweckt?
Folgen Sie dabei jedoch keineswegs dem Text chronologisch, sondern ordnen Sie die gefundenen Beispiele im Text (= Mittel) den verschiedenen Aspekten zu, die Sie analysieren sollen. Achten Sie darauf, dass die Beispiele auch aussagekräftig sind und Ihre Deutung jeweils sinnvoll untermauern.

Umgang mit Zitaten:

Zitate sind ein wichtiges Mittel als Beleg für die korrekte Verbindung zwischen dem Text und Ihrer Deutung.
Man unterscheidet zwischen **wörtlichen Zitaten**:
"extraordinary piece of ignorance" (l. 38)
und **sinngemäßen Zitaten**:
The author refers to a speech the Secretary of State for Education held about mobile phones. (l. 1)

Gut zu wissen

Vermeiden Sie Zitate, die länger sind für Ihren Beleg als unbedingt nötig. Sobald Sie Passagen oder Sätze aus dem vorliegenden Text übernehmen, müssen Sie diese als Zitat kennzeichnen.

Übung 2

Wenden Sie die oben erläuterten Schritte auf die Aufgabenstellung zum Text *Dear Gavin Williamson, teenagers use mobile phones. Get with the times* an.

Schritt 3: Die Analyse schreiben

Checkliste

a) Bevor Sie mit dem Schreiben loslegen, vergewissern Sie sich anhand der folgenden Checkliste, ob Sie alle wichtigen Aspekte untersucht und belegt haben:
Textsorte *(text type)* **Sprachebene** *(register)*
Stilmittel *(stylistic devices)* **Ton** *(tone)*

b) Welche(r) Effek(e) wird dadurch erzeugt?

S ▸ Stilmittel, S. 108

Einleitung
Schreiben Sie einen Einleitungssatz, in dem Sie die Quelle, den Autor bzw. die Autorin des Texts, die Textsorte, das Erscheinungsdatum, das Thema und die Intention des Textes nennen.

Einleitungssatz *(introductory sentence)*

In his [text type] "[title]" published in [name of newspaper/magazine] on [date] / in [year], [author's name] focuses on the topic of [general topic] and describes/stresses [positive/negative aspects/opportunities], using various means to convey his message.

to **stress sth** *etw betonen*
to **convey sth** *etw vermitteln*

Hauptteil
Präsentieren Sie Ihre Analyse, um Ihre zentrale Aussage (= Intention) im Einleitungssatz zu belegen. Denken Sie daran, Ihre Ausführungen in sinnvolle Absätze zu untergliedern, welche die Leser durch Ihren Text leiten. Listen Sie die Mittel und Belege nicht nur auf, sondern erläutern Sie ihre jeweilige Funktion und den Effekt auf den Leser bzw. die Leserin. Weisen Sie Ihre Textbelege durch Angabe detaillierter Zeilenbezüge bzw. durch wörtliche und sinngemäße Zitate nach.

Sprachebene und Wortwahl untersuchen *(examining register and choice of words)*

The author makes use of formal/neutral/informal language.
The author uses outdated/specialist terms / slang / colloquial elements.
This is indicated by l./ll. [line number(s)], where it is said that …
This can be demonstrated with l./ll. [line number(s)], where the author states …

outdated *veraltet*
slang *Umgangssprache*
colloquial *umgangsprachlich*
This is indicated by … *Dies zeigt sich / wird deutlich in …*

to **contain** *beinhalten*
harmonious *harmonisch, stimmig*
gloomy *düster*
mood *Stimmung*
marked *deutlich*

S ▸ Stilmittel, p. 108

to **employ sth** *etw anwenden*
to **apply sth** *etw anwenden*
rhetorical device *rhetorisches Mittel*
to **emphasize** *betonen*

Ton untersuchen *(examining the tone)*

The tone of the text is serious/humorous/sarcastic/ironic/comic/critical. It also contains … elements.
The author creates a harmonious/gloomy/depressing/optimistic mood/atmosphere.
The ironic tone of the passage is in marked contrast to …

Stilmittel untersuchen *(examining stylistic devices)*

The [stylistic device] has a(n) … effect.
We also find [stylistic device].
The author employs/uses/applies [stylistic device] to show …
This rhetorical device emphasizes/illustrates/suggests that … / symbolizes / attracts the reader's attention …
… is a symbol for … / The symbol/image chosen by the author refers to …

Schlussteil

Fassen Sie sich kurz, beziehen Sie sich auf Ihre Einleitung und formulieren Sie den dort verfassten Kern Ihrer Analyse mit anderen Worten in einem Satz neu. Fügen Sie keine neuen Aspekte, keine persönliche Meinung und keine Wertung in hinzu.

Übung 2

Schreiben Sie die Textanalyse zum Text *Dear Gavin Williamson, teenagers use mobile phones. Get with the times* gemäß Aufgabenstellung in Übung 1.

Gut zu wissen

Gavin Williamson is the Secretary of State for Education in the UK.

to get with the times *mit dem Zeitgeist Schritt halten*
to lure sb *jdn (an)locken*
matter *Thema*
to **distract from sth** *von etw ablenken*
good old-fashioned *gute/r alte/r*
to invoke sth *etw zitieren, etw ins Feld führen*
the olden days *die alten Zeiten*
to conjure sth up *etw heraufbeschwören*
impression *Imitation*
to **beat sb up** *jdn verprügeln*
invisible *unsichtbar*
breeding ground *Nährboden*
to **contribute to sth** *zu etw beitragen*

Dear Gavin Williamson, teenagers use mobile phones. Get with the times

[…] As with all great speeches, yours lured me back to your words, this time on the matter of mobile phones.

"Outside the classroom, the use of mobile phones distracts from healthy exercise and good old-fashioned play," you said.

As you've invoked the word "old-fashioned" here, perhaps I could take you back to the olden days of 1957–62 at my secondary school. You conjure up a picture of us exercising in a "healthy" way and having a "play". In my first year (aged 11 to 12) I did spend a lot of time playing a game we called "king-he", which involved us throwing a ball as hard as we could at each other, aiming to hit someone on the torso.

[…] For the next six years of school the nearest I got to exercise was when a group of us competed to see who could do the best impression of a man getting beaten up by the Invisible Man.

Then you suggested that the use of phones in school was a "breeding ground for cyberbullying". Of course this is a problem, but why the use of mobiles in school time contributes to this isn't clear. If you want to be a cyberbully, there are at least 12 hours away from school in which to do it.

Same goes for the other undesirables on your list: "inappropriate use of social media sites – such as anonymous Instagram accounts, where students are ranked on their appearance – can heighten insecurities, damage mental health and encourage harassment." This is all good crowd-pleasing stuff that fits into the usual pattern of people in authority blathering on about why teenagers are horrible.

Let me run this by you: in one of my least successful predictions ever, I came up with the theory 40 years ago that we were moving towards a non-literate world. The teens I was working with in London schools appeared not to need the written word for anything outside education. All their entertainment and information was coming to them via TV, radio, film and music, and if they wanted to communicate with others, they could do it face to face or on a landline.

Then the internet arrived, and after that, mobile phones. What's happened is an explosion of teenagers writing – in texts and posts. [...]

We are living in an incredible time: whole libraries, vast banks of knowledge and multimedia resources are available to us via an object that fits in our pockets. At the same time, it's a camera, a recording device, a film-maker and a means to talk in pairs or groups with people all over the world. Hadn't you noticed? You seem to despise an instrument that could play a wonderful part in learning. You're like someone in the 16th century despising teenagers for reading a ballad sold on the street because – heaven forbid – it had been produced on a printing press.

You closed this extraordinary piece of ignorance with this: "While it is for every school to make its own policy, I firmly believe that mobile phones should not be used or seen during the school day, and will be backing headteachers that implement such policies."

So rather than encouraging headteachers to come up with ways to harness the technology, you tried to recruit them to a regime of blocking it. I make notes, write poems and blogs, read newspapers and academic articles, Google for facts and biographies, talk and write to friends, family and colleagues, take photos, and make videos on my phone. Some of my children make films on theirs. Are you seriously saying that right now we haven't got a fantastic opportunity to do similar things – and more – with the thing you want to ban?

What an old fuddy-duddy you are.

Yours, Michael Rosen

(639 words) From: *The Guardian*, 24 April 2021

undesirable *unerwünscht*
inappropriate *unangemessen*
appearance *Aussehen*
to **heighten sth** *etw verstärken*
insecurities pl *Verunsicherung*
to **encourage sth** *etw begünstigen*
harassment *Schikane, Mobbing*
crowd-pleasing *populär, beifallheischend*
to **fit into a pattern** *in ein Muster passen*
person in authority *maßgebliche Person*
to blather on *(herum) schwafeln*
to run sth by sb *jdm etw erzählen*
non-literate *schriftlos*
via *über, mittels*
vast *riesig*
bank of knowledge *Wissenschatz*
to **despise sb/sth** *jdn/etw verachten*
ballad *Ballade*
heaven forbid *Gott bewahre*
printing press *Druckerpresse*
extraordinary *außergewöhnlich*
to **back sb** jdn *unterstützen*
headteacher *Schulleiter/in*
to **implement sth** *etw umsetzen*
to **come up with sth** *sich etw ausdenken*
to **harness sth** *etw nutzen*
to **recruit sb to sth** *jdn für etw gewinnen/rekrutieren*
regime *Regelung, System*
to **ban sth** *etw verbieten*
fuddy duddy *altmodischer Mensch, Kauz, Spießer*

Review

1 Rank the Sections A–F in this Topic based on how interesting they were to you. Then, look back at your work on the Overview of this Topic (pages 110–111) and how you ranked them there (page 111, exercise 3). Have your rankings changed? Share your results with a group, and tell them what you found most interesting.

2 Look back at your KWL list (page 111, exercise 4). Fill out the "Learnt" part of the list. Next, look at your "Want to know" list. What do you still want to know?

3 Make a list of ten words in the Topic that were new to you and you consider important to know. Then collect everyone's words and cluster them into groups. Finally, pick a word group and write a paragraph using all the words.

Evaluate

1 Do this task on your own. How much do you agree or disagree with the statements below? Rate each one on a scale of one to four. The references on the right show you what exercises you can review.

1 = totally disagree **2** = disagree **3** = agree **4** = totally agree

Review	Section		Statement
▸ p. 112, exercises 2–4	**A**	**1**	I can describe and analyse the cartoons.
▸ p. 114, exercises 2, 3, 5	**B**	**2**	I understand the importance of press freedom for democracy.
▸ p. 116, exercises 7–9		**3**	I know the main differences between tabloid and "quality" press.
▸ pp. 117–118, exs. 10, 11, 13		**4**	I know what to check when judging the truthfulness of a news article.
▸ p. 117, exercise 12		**5**	I can understand and create new words with affixes.
▸ p. 119, exercises 15–16		**6**	I can understand a news report about conspiracy theories.
▸ p. 121, exercise 8	**C**	**7**	I can write an argumentative text on social media activism.
▸ p. 123, exercises 13–14		**8**	I can avoid typical mistakes when making conditional sentences.
▸ p. 123, exercises 15–17		**9**	I can participate in a discussion about social media.
▸ p. 125, exercises 6–7	**D**	**10**	I can talk about image pressure and social media personas.
▸ p. 127, exercises 3–5	**E**	**11**	I understand people talking about their internet use and personal data.
▸ p. 128, exercises 6–7		**12**	I understand when and how to use the different forms of *used to*.
▸ p. 128, exercise 8		**13**	I can express the most important points of an English-language text in German (mediation).
▸ p. 129, exercise 9		**14**	I can explain and give practical tips on online privacy and data protection in a video tutorial.
▸ p. 130, exercises 2–4	**F**	**15**	I can describe and discuss the genre of instapoetry.
▸ p. 131, exercise 9		**16**	I can create an instapoem in the form of a haiku.
S ▸ pp. 134–135	**Skills**	**17**	See 13 above.
S ▸ pp. 136–137		**18**	I can describe and analyse cartoons orally.
S ▸ pp. 138–143		**19**	I can deal with text analysis tasks.

Consolidate

You want to go deeper into media topics and speed up your learning process? Scan this page with the PagePlayer app. There you'll find some suggestions for additional tasks.

Differentiation files

10 More challenge: Looking at language

▸ Topic 1, Section A, p. 11

Translate the following sentences into English.

1 Ich bin ein Mensch, der an die Redefreiheit glaubt.
2 Kim Kardashian ist eine Berühmtheit, der ich früher online gefolgt bin.
3 Eine Person, mit der ich identifiziere, ist Greta Thunberg.
4 Er ist ein Mensch, dessen Werte ich nicht teile.
5 Ich würde keinem Online-Profil folgen, das oberflächliche Sachen postet.
6 Instagram ist eine Plattform, auf der ich glaube, ich selbst sein zu können.
7 „Migrant" ist eine Identität, die viele Deutsche haben.
8 Attraktiv sein zu wollen ist ein Wert, den ich viel in sozialen Netzwerken beobachte.

6 More help: Working with the text

▸ Topic 1, Section B, p. 12

Which of these are suitable headings for the paragraphs?

Ambitions | Body image | Depression | Disagreements | Disease | Eat healthy | Exercise | Family issues | Fear of failure | Global events | Meditate | Pet a cat | Romance and friendship | School life | Sleep | Social pressure | Talk about your problems | Think positive and laugh

7 More practice: Working with words

▸ Topic 1, Section B, p. 13

Complete the paragraph using the phrases. Each phrase is a common collocation related to wellness and stress.

deal with coursework | dealing with deadlines | feel calm | feel desperate | reduce stress | stress level | worry about other people's expectations | worry about the environment

During exam time, the **(1)** ... at school gets really high. When I walk down the hallway, I see a lot of people who look tired. When students are **(2)**..., sometimes we don't sleep enough, and that only makes us **(3)** .... Normally, I **(4)** ... about schoolwork, but the exams are really important, and I **(5)** .... So I have a trick to **(6)** ...: whenever there is a big exam coming up, I stop reading the news. I can't **(7)** ... and **(8)** ... at the same time. That would be too much for anyone!

▸ Topic 1, Section B, p. 14

11 More practice: Looking at language

The pictures show a young woman named Rhoda. As you can see, she has some good habits that help mitigate stress, but she has some bad habits too. Make a sentence for each picture. There are many correct sentences you can make, but you must use the adverbial phrases in the correct place in the sentence.

Adverbial phrases

Time
last/next weekend
at bedtime

Place
at the gym / in the bathtub / in the forest

Frequency
every evening/day/week
every other day
always/often/sometimes/occasionally/rarely/never

Example:

1 *Rhoda looks at her phone every evening at bedtime.*

▸ Topic 1, Section B, p. 15

Good to know

In psychology, the "Big Five" personality traits are: agreeableness, conscientiousness, extroversion, neuroticism and openness to experience.

13 More challenge: Working with words

Write definitions for these personality traits.

1 neurotic
2 agreeable
3 extroverted
4 conscientious
5 open to experience

Where do you place yourself on each of the "Big Five" scales, i.e. how extroverted/neurotic/etc. are you?

1 = not at all 9 = extremely

Then make sentences explaining your answers.

Example:
I almost never go to parties because I'm not an extroverted person.

16 More help: Listening

▸ Topic 1, Section B, p. 16

In Part 3 of the interview, Lori Mann talks about dealing with academic pressure and she gives the tips listed below. Before you listen, sort them into one of the three categories.

a general stress relief
b looking at grades from a healthy point of view
c practical help for better grades

1 using calming techniques
2 exercising
3 seeing a tutor outside of school
4 practicing yoga and mindfulness
5 not overreacting to "bad" grades
6 taking control of grades through work and good study skills
7 using breathing techniques
8 picking just one intention for the day

18 More challenge: Speaking

▸ Topic 1, Section B, p. 16

Read the Skills Training box below. Then, with a partner, evaluate the trustworthiness of the diagram on page 15.

Skills training: Evaluating sources of information

Evaluate the source. What do you know, if anything, about the reputation of the source? Could they be attempting to sell you something, to get you to vote a certain way, or just trying to get you to look at advertisements? Does the content seem serious or does it seem like clickbait?

The Pew Research Center has a good reputation.
I don't know the Pew Research Center, but …
This is in a schoolbook, so I trust the information is true.
The content seems serious / like clickbait.

Evaluate the method of research. Can you trust it? Do you need any more information to make a judgement?

The method of research is a survey/questionnaire.
Some of the respondents may not have told the truth, because …
Unfortunately, we don't know how many respondents there were.
We also don't know …

▸ Topic 1, Section C, p. 20

8 More practice: Working with words

The words in bold in the table are from the task you just did on page 20. Copy and complete the table by filling in the missing parts of speech (nouns, adjectives, etc.). A dictionary can help you. The first row (*accessible*) has been done for you.

	noun	adjective	verb	present participle of verb	past participle of verb
	access	**accessible**	to access sth	accessing	accessed
1	…	…	to … sb	**energizing**	…
2			to … sb	…	**exhausting**
3		**familiar**	to … oneself with sth	…	…
4	**friend**	…	to … sb	…	…
5	…		to … sth	…	**known**
6	…	**occasional**			
7	**pain**	…		…	…
8	**pleasure**	…	to … sb	…	…
9	**punishment**	…	to … sb	…	…
10	**reward**		to … sb	…	…

▸ Topic 1, Section C, p. 21

10 More practice: Looking at language

Use the present progressive and words in the box to describe the things people are saying. Use each word once.

complain | explain | get passionate about | nag | open up | respond | scream/yell | vent

Example:
1 *The parent is **responding** to a question.*

1 Parent to child: "The answer to your question is no."
2 Adolescent to parent: "The reason I can't sleep is that my teenage brain doesn't get tired until very late."
3 Teenagers: "You never let us go anywhere, Mum."
4 Kids: "Oh my God, I love this song so much!" – "Me too! Let's listen to it a hundred times!"
5 Friend to friend: "Can I tell you about a problem I've been having? I really hate it when people …"
6 Children: "AAAAAARGH!!!"
7 Son to father: "I feel really stressed out at school. I always feel like I'm not good enough."
8 Mother to son, ten times a day: "Do your homework!"

Use the same words (in their *-ing* forms) to complete the following sentences. Which of your sentences use the present progressive and which use only the present participle?

1 I'm not …
2 Am … ?
3 We're not …
4 Are … ?
5 Please stop …
6 Thank you for not …
7 … won't help things.
8 They're always …

4 More help: Working with the text

▸ Topic 1, Section E, p. 27

Here are some phrases to help you.

If I was/were Jenny, I would …

tell my father …
demand that …
change my …
speak to …
quit …

2 More help: Watching/Listening

▸ Topic 2, Section A, p. 47

These are the sections from the dialogue that relate to the multiple-choice questions. Read them, and then try again to answer the questions.

"She's actually well-known in the London art scene and one of my all-time favourite artists. Very rich colours and of course you can't miss the religious and political message."

"When you walk through Shoreditch, there's often a smell of spray paint in the air. And it's possible to see artists drawing, painting or spraying graffiti on walls, doors or shutters – that is, if you're lucky."

"You know, standing right in front of it, it's pretty scary … it feels as if it will fly off the wall and come at you!"

"After that, I'll show you some pieces of street art I find particularly fascinating. And at the end, we'll come to my personal highlight of today's tour."

"I'm glad to see so many of you here! I'm going to take you around to see street art in Shoreditch and show you some of the best graffiti here in London."

"True, your favourite piece may not be there any longer, but on the other hand, that's part of the charm of street art!"

11 More help: Working with words

▸ Topic 2, Section B, p. 52

Match the words (1–8) with their synonyms (a–h) from the text on page 51.

1 inhabitants
2 companies or firms
3 unusual, strange or weird
4 wealthy
5 established
6 number of inhabitants
7 money a person earns
8 place to live

a accommodation
b affluent
c businesses/corporations
d founded
e income/salary/wage
f quirky
g residents
h population

▸ Topic 2, Section C, p. 55

3 More challenge: Looking at language

Correct the errors in the following sentences.

1 She usually rides a taxi to the airport.
2 I love to drive by car to work.
3 She never drives her bike to school.
4 They always walk on foot.
5 Did he drive here by train?
6 I drive the bus to school.

▸ Topic 2, Section C, p. 58

11 More help: Working with the text

Use the words from this box to complete exercise 11 on page 58.

attention | homemade | pothole | protect | separate | temporary

▸ Topic 2, Section C, p. 60

17 More help: Writing

Use the below format to help you create your letter to the mayor.

Subject: …

Dear Mr/Ms …

The reason why I am writing to you is that …

As a cyclist, I have experienced some issues with …. One problem is that …. Let me give you an example of how …

To sum up, I think there are a number of things which need to be done. To improve the situation, you could …. And I think it would also be a good idea to …

Thank you for …

I look forward to your reply.

Yours …

▸ Topic 2, Section D, p. 62

4 More challenge: Speaking

Do some online research about New Zealand and discover another exciting aspect of the country that might be appealing to tourists. Then tell a partner about this "must-do experience" in New Zealand.

▸ Topic 2, Section D, p. 63

6 More help: Working with words

There are many of these typical expressions in the text. You can find examples on lines 2, 5–6, 9, 20, 23, 27–28, 29, 31, 33, 44, 48, 50, 54 and 56.

8 More help: Writing

▸ Topic 2, Section D, p. 63

Use these phrases to describe a place you like (or where you live) in your brochure.

... lies in ...
... has an interesting landscape including....
... the weather...
... the best time to travel is...
... is/isn't dangerous because...
... is an absolute must.
This is a place you shouldn't miss if...
There's everything from ... to...
... is the place to go.
Take a guided tour of...

4 More help: Listening

▸ Topic 2, Section E, p. 64

Helen likes living in the city, and Tim likes living in the country. But why? Here are some of the reasons. Match each reason with either Helen or Tim.

likes having restaurants nearby
likes having a garden
likes living in a diverse place
likes driving
likes peace and quiet
likes privacy
likes community

7 More challenge: Looking at language

▸ Topic 2, Section E, p. 65

Express comparisons between city and country while using the following adverbs.

almost
definitely
even
far
much
possibly
slightly
surprisingly

5 More help: Speaking

▸ Topic 2, Section F, p. 67

To answer the questions in this exercise, consider using the following words and phrases.

1 respectful of – attached to – conflicted
2 gambling – uneducated – not wealthy
3 stars – mountains – beautiful view
4 expressive – repetition – long lines
5 proud – ashamed – bored by – excited by – mixed feelings

6 More practice: Working with the text

▸ Topic 3, Section A, p. 81

Find words in the VOTE-O-MAT that correspond to the following German words.

1 Klimaveränderung
2 Grenze
3 durchsetzen
4 erhöhen
5 Darlehen
6 Waffen tragen
7 abbremsen
8 zugelassen

Then write eight sentences, each using one of the above words.

▸ Topic 3, Section B, p. 84

3 More help: Listening

Below is a transcription from Part 1 of the podcast. However, some of the words have been taken out. Read this while you are listening to the podcast and match the words (1–5) with the gaps (a–e). Then try again to complete exercise 3 on p. 84.

1 Electoral College
2 General Election
3 National Conventions
4 primaries
5 takes office

(a) … take place in all 50 states between February and August. The next step is the parties' **(b)** …, which take place in August. After that, we have the main event: the **(c)** … in November. Following that, the **(d)** … places their votes in December, and finally the race to the White House is finished when the President **(e)** … in January.

▸ Topic 3, Section B, p. 86

9 More practice: Looking at language

Complete the sentences with the correct participle (present or past).

ask | campaign | give | have | nominate | result | take part

1 … the presidential candidate is an important event in each party's election schedule.
2 … the right to vote is one of the most fundamental civic rights defined in the US Constitution.
3 Before … throughout the country, the candidates must raise funds.
4 … the Republican's strict views on immigration, many Latino voters won't vote for him.
5 Many young voters were unhappy with their state's handling of LGBTQ+ rights … in young people … in demonstrations.
6 … about her political vision, she told the interviewer she wanted to reform gun laws in the US.

▸ Topic 3, Section B, p. 86

10 More help: Looking at language

Use the phrases to complete the description of the US presidential election process.

After counting and confirming | based on the results | Voting | when | where each party nominates | which are state-level elections | which consists of | which take place in August | who will form

The first step in the US voting process are the state primaries, **(1)** … held between February and August in an election year. The second step are the National Conventions, **(2)** …. This is **(3)** … their presidential candidate. **(4)** … their parties' nominations, the candidates continue to campaign across the country until the general election in November. On election day, American voters cast their ballots. **(5)** … in the general election also means making decisions about who goes to Congress. Selecting the electors **(6)** … the Electoral College is the next important step in the voting process. The Electoral College, **(7)** … 538 electors, chooses the President and Vice-President **(8)** … of the general election. The process is complete **(9)** … the President takes office in January at the inauguration ceremony.

4 More help: Watching

▸ Topic 3, Section C, p. 91

Use the words and phrases to complete exercise 4 on page 91.

cabinet | checks and balances | Congress | Constitution | eight years | make laws | president | the judiciary | the Senate | the three branches of federal government

9 More help: Writing

▸ Topic 3, Section C, p. 93

Use the phrases to help you complete exercise 9 on page 93.

The President can veto / pass / nominate …
The Supreme Court declares …
Congress approves / passes / can impeach …
… has the power to declare war.
… can pass amendments to the constitution.
… can declare laws unconstitutional.
… has the "power of the purse".
… can sign a peace treaty.
… can nominate a judge.
… acts as a jury in an Impeachment trial.

2 More help: Watching

▸ Topic 3, Section D, p. 94

Match the questions with the correct answer.

1 Most countries have a written constitution – what about the UK?
2 What is the most powerful political institution in the UK?
3 How far does parliament go back?
4 What are the two chambers of parliament called?
5 Which of the two chambers is elected by the people?
6 How many countries does the UK consist of?
7 What areas are the regional parliaments responsible for? Name at least two.
8 Where did the 2014 referendum take place?

a four countries
b health, economic development, agriculture, education, tourism
c House of Commons
d House of Commons, House of Lords
e in Scotland
f to the 13th century
g Parliament
h It does not

▸ Topic 3, Section E, p. 97

3 More practice: Working with a text

Complete the sentences with the correct verbs. Make sure to use the correct verb form.

appoint | belong | cast | get | hold | hold | mark | represent | share | take

1 My friend … Irish and British citizenship.
2 Elections normally … place every five years.
3 Members of Parliament usually … to a political party.
4 The next election won't … in two years, but in four.
5 No confidence votes only … through on a two-thirds majority.
6 Please … the name of the candidate you want to vote for on the ballot paper.
7 People vote for candidates who … their political ideas.
8 Voting by proxy means you ask somebody else to … your vote for you.
9 I don't know this candidate and I'm not sure which party she ….
10 The PM always gets … by the Queen.

▸ Topic 3, Section E, p. 98

5 More help: Listening

Use the words and phrases to complete exercise 5 on page 98.

50,000 people
a new referendum
against
business owners
childcare
class sizes
extra teachers
for everyone
free movement of people
increase spending
increase taxes
protect the environment
starting salary
wants to keep immigration

▸ Topic 3, Section F, p. 99

2 More practice: Working with the text

Match the words and phrases to complete collocations used to describe royal duties.

1 act as
2 carry out
3 give
4 present
5 represent the
6 support the

a awards
b charitable work
c country
d hosts or guests at events
e Queen
f speeches

▸ Topic 3, Section F, p. 100

5 More help: Working with words

Use the following connectives to complete exercise 5 on page 100.

1 after
2 as well as
3 while
4 because
5 in addition to
6 if

6 More help: Working with the text

▸ Topic 4, Section A, p. 113

Match the words and phrases with their meanings.

1 to get on sb's nerves
2 internet junkie
3 screenager
4 square eyes
5 to get out of hand
6 silver surfer
7 to drop by
8 to bleep
9 to be glued to sth
10 couch potato

a a teenager who is addicted to electronic devices
b to be unable to stop watching sth
c poor eyesight from watching too much TV
d a lazy person, who spends most of their time watching TV
e to get out of control
f an older person who loves surfing the web/spending time online
g to make buzzing sounds typical of a mobile phone when you get a message
h to visit someone spontaneously
i sb who is addicted to the internet
j to annoy sb about the person/people they live with

2 More help: Working with the text

▸ Topic 4, Section B, p. 114

Use the line numbers to help you complete exercise 2 on page 114.

1 lines 11–13
2 lines 14–16
3 lines 17–18
4 line 24
5 lines 32–34
6 line 42–45

4 More help: Listening

▸ Topic 4, Section C, p. 121

Here are five transcribed excerpts from the radio programme. Read them carefully, and then listen again. These excerpts will help you complete exercise 4 on page 121.

"It's not enough to sit at home and do nothing or share online posts – if you don't show that you really care, then politicians and big corporations won't care about your opinion either and nothing will change!"

"You know, I think online activism – like, just sharing and liking political posts – is a lazy way people for to look like they care without having to do anything!"

"Who would've thought that a teenager in Sweden could've started a global movement? Well done Greta!"

"My activism happens online: I sign petitions and share posts on social media."

"I make videos on YouTube and stuff like that. I was born with a physical disability so I don't look like everybody else and can't walk without crutches."

▸ Topic 4, Section D, p. 125

6 More challenge: Speaking

Find someone in your group whose position on social media presentation is slightly (or a lot) different than yours. You are are going to have a short debate with this person, and the other members of your group will judge the debate. Follow the steps as outlined below.

- Write down a statement about social media that one of you agrees with and one of you does not. This statement is called the debate *resolution*.
- Prepare for the debate by making some notes: 3–5 bullet points that support (or oppose) the resolution.
- Set a timer for two minutes. You will each have two minutes to speak. The person agreeing with the resolution goes first.
- Set a timer for one minute. You now each have one minute to respond to the other person.
- Ask the other members of the group to decide who offered the strongest arguments in the debate. The entire group should now offer suggestions for making better arguments on both sides.

▸ Topic 4, Section E, p. 126

1 More help: Warm-up

Here are hints to help you answer complete exercise 1 on page 126.

1. Personal information is anything which makes you an "identifiable individual".
2. Many websites use "cookies", small files which may make the site easier to navigate, but which are also able to collect and store a variety of information about you.
3. Many online games are designed to collect information about your habits, interests and things you like to buy, and then sell this data to advertisers. Your data is valuable!
4. Privacy policies are often written in a way that can be confusing or difficult to understand.
5. Bear in mind that the app or website itself will still be collecting and saving everything you post.
6. Well, you probably want to maintain a social life! But always think about whether you'd feel ok with seeing your posts – it could be your teacher, parent, neighbour or future employer!
7. Always exercise caution! If the person has no apparent connection to you or your friends, it's probably safer to ignore it because it could be a fake profile
8. If someone hacks into your profile, or happens to see the post in some other way, your information is no longer safe.

▸ Topic 4, Section F, p. 131

5 More practice: Working with words

The following verbs (1–6) are from the interview with Jenny Bienemann. Match them with their synonyms (a–f).

1 to come upon	**a** to fail to pay attention to
2 to get sth across	**b** to communicate
3 to lose track of	**c** to misunderstand
4 to reach out	**d** to discover
5 to take it the wrong way	**e** to repress oneself
6 to keep oneself down	**f** to make contact

Partner files

18 Speaking – Partner A

▸ Topic 1, Section B, p. 16

Describe the pie chart to your partner so that they can draw it.

How often are you stressed?
Answers from teens in the USA

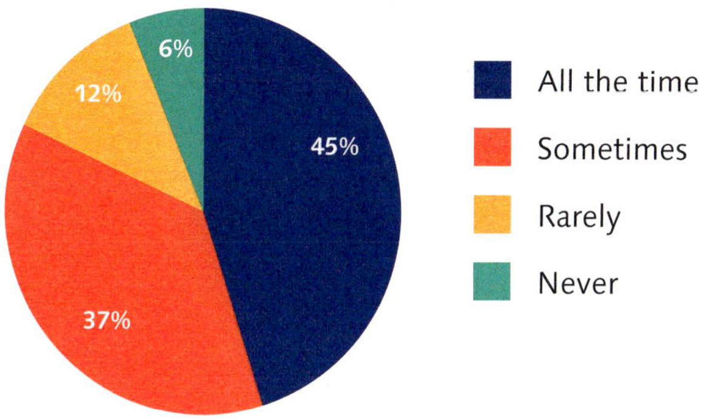

(Source: afterschoolapp.com)

When you have finished, discuss with your partner whether you think a survey of German teenagers would get similar results.

15 Speaking – Partner A

▸ Topic 1, Section E, p. 31

Dear British time traveller,

Welcome to twenty-first-century Germany. Your German classes start tomorrow (good luck!). Today, some English speakers are going to help you decide how to finish your education.

Prepare some questions to ask them. For example, you may want to ask …

How long does the programme last?

What does it qualify me for? What will my options be when I'm finished?

Do I get paid?

What is an "Abitur"?

Girls: What professions are open to me as a female? Can I become a … ?

Boys: Will I have to compete with women? Will people disapprove if I choose a "woman's profession"?

▸ Topic 1, Section E, p. 31

to **convince sb** *jdn überzeugen*
field *Bereich*
salary *Gehalt*
employment *Anstellung*
challenging *anspruchsvoll*

15 Speaking – Partner B

Your goal is to convince the time traveller that they should do an apprenticeship. There are apprenticeships in many fields, but not in every field.

The time traveller can apply for an apprenticeship if they want to learn a profession. If a company accepts them, they get paid a nice monthly salary. They'll also go to a vocational school part time. Germans call this the "dual system".

Apprentices also have excellent chances for employment after finishing the programme.

The advantage of an apprenticeship over an internship is that apprentices get challenging tasks, while interns generally do unimportant things like making coffee.

What other arguments for the dual system can you think of? What else makes this option better than the other ones?

▸ Topic 4, Section B, p. 117

unless *es sei denn*
to **be in on sth** *über etw Bescheid wissen, etw verstehen*
credible *glaubwürdig*
to **discredit sb/sth** *jdn/etw diskreditieren*

10 Speaking – Partner A

Headline: ...
Make sure the article you're referencing isn't a work of satire! Comedic journalism can be funny – unless you're not in on the joke. However, sexist, homophobic or racist jokes are not acceptable.

Headline: ...
Is the person who wrote this article credible? Do they appear elsewhere in the media? Is this even a real person? A quick search for their name may quickly discredit the writer's arguments.

▸ Topic 4, Section C, p. 123

15 Speaking – Partner A

You are Alex, a teenager living with your parents.

You have made a friend online and really want to meet the person in real life. However, your parents have said "no" and you are really upset. You want to talk to them again and have asked your best friend to come around and support you.

Think about:
- who you want to meet and how you came into contact with them;
- why is it important for you to meet them in person;
- where you want to meet them and when;
- the arguments your parents may have against this and how you could respond to them.

18 Speaking – Partner B

▸ Topic 1, Section B, p. 16

Describe the pie chart to your partner so that they can draw it.

What stresses you out the most?

Answers from teens in the USA

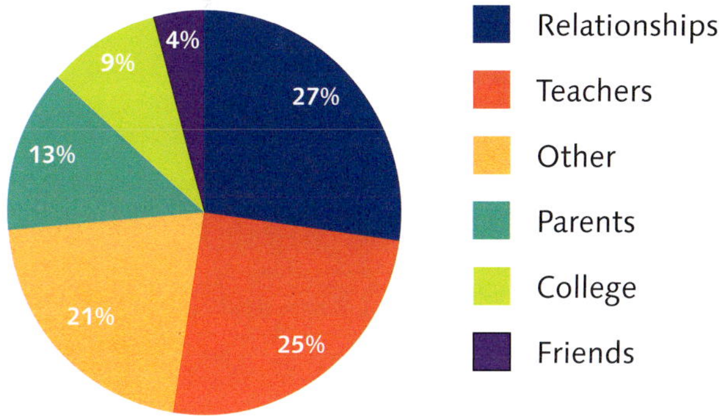

(Source: afterschoolapp.com)

When you have finished, discuss with your partner what you think might fall under the category "other".

15 Speaking – Partner C

▸ Topic 1, Section E, p. 31

Your goal is to convince the time traveller that they should go to a college or technical college. It can be in any practical field.

Colleges generally have specializations, e.g. applied sciences, arts, business, childcare, etc., and so they are great for people who know they want to go into a specific field. You can say that college prepares you better for the workforce than university, where people sometimes spend many years and then have a hard time finding a job in the field they studied.

You need good grades to get into a college, but they are easier to get into than university. What other arguments for colleges can you think of? What else makes this option better than the other ones?

to **convince sb** *jdn überzeugen*
field *Bereich*
applied *angewandt*

▸ Topic 1, Section E, p. 31

to **convince sb** *jdn überzeugen*
field *Bereich*
work environment *Arbeitsumfeld*
to **commit oneself to sth** *sich zu etw verpflichten, sich auf etw festlegen*

15 Speaking – Partner D

Your goal is to convince the time traveller that they should do an internship. It can be in any field. Interns work and gain experience for little or no pay.

Internships are a very good idea for people who have no idea what they want to do after school and need to try out a work environment, e.g. an office, a hotel or a factory. They are also good for people who know exactly what they want to do and can find an internship in that environment. For example, if you know you want to be a lawyer, you might find an internship as an assistant to one.

It is rather easy to get an internship, and it is rather easy to quit one too. You don't have to commit to a long programme.

What else makes this option better than the other ones?

▸ Topic 4, Section B, p. 117

invalid *gegenstandslos, hinfällig*
valid *stichhaltig, berechtigt, gültig*
legitimate *vertrauenswürdig, legitim*

10 Speaking – Partner B

Headline: ...
The "news" article you're reading might actually be from years ago. Old facts and opinions may become invalid when replaced by new information. Remember, all legitimate news items will provide the date of publication.

Headline: ...
If sources are provided, click on them and see if they're reliable. Journalists should offer sources for quotes and statistics. If the article you're reading is full of surprising "facts", they may not be accurate; do more research and check for yourself.

15 Speaking – Partner B

▸ Topic 4, Section C, p. 123

You are a teenager and Alex is your best friend.

Alex has told you about someone he/she has met online and wants to meet in real life. Alex's parents have said no, and Alex is really upset about this. Alex has asked you to come around and help in another discussion with his/her parents.

Think about:
- what you would like to ask Alex about the person;
- how you feel about Alex meeting up with a stranger;
- why Alex's parents might not think that this is a good idea;
- how you can help everybody involved to reach a compromise.

15 Speaking – Partner E

▸ Topic 1, Section E, p. 31

Your goal is to convince the time traveller that they should go to university, where they can choose any academic field that interests them.

To get into a university, they will need an *Abitur*. Universities offer a wide range of academic subjects, but some are only for students with excellent grades. Most lead to a bachelor's degree. From there they can get a master's and then a PhD.

University graduates tend to earn the most money, depending on what they study. What else makes this option better than the other ones?

to **convince sb** *jdn überzeugen*
field *Bereich*
graduate *Absolvent/in*
to **tend to do sth** *etw tendenziell tun*

▸ Topic 1, Section E, p. 31

to **convince sb** *jdn überzeugen*
field *Bereich*
pocket money *Taschengeld*
nursery school *Kindergarten*
the elderly *Senioren*
the disabled *Behinderte*

15 Speaking – Partner F

Your goal is to convince the time traveller that they should do a voluntary social service year.

This is a good option for people who don't know what they would choose to study or what job they would do after school, or for people who know they want to work in a social-services field.

As a social service volunteer, you work for a bit of pocket money in a social-services field. In this way you help people directly, and you help society. Common workplaces are nursery schools, care homes for the elderly, workshops for the disabled, hospitals and rehabilitation clinics. The people you work with will be very happy you're there. And because you'll be there a long time, you'll be well-integrated into the staff.

It's also possible to do your social service year in a foreign country.

What else makes this option better than the other ones?

▸ Topic 4, Section B, p. 117

10 Speaking – Partner C

Headline: ...
We all have our own beliefs. But we should look past them when collecting information – that's the only way to get closer to the truth. Just because you disagree with an opinion, doesn't mean it isn't valid.

Headline: ...
Headlines are designed to attract readers. But they don't always tell the whole story and can even be misleading. Read the full article before you form an opinion.

▸ Topic 4, Section C, p. 123

solely *ausschließlich, nur*
to **insist on sth** *auf etw bestehen*

15 Speaking – Partners C and D

You and your partner are the parents of a teenager, Alex.

Alex would like to meet an online friend. You said no, but Alex is very upset and still wants to meet the person. Now Alex's best friend is coming around and you will all discuss the issue later.

Think about:
- the concerns you have about Alex meeting the person;
- how you could convince Alex to continue the friendship solely online;
- the arguments Alex may have and how you will respond to them;
- how you will react if Alex insists on meeting the person: under what conditions you might allow it.

GRAMMAR TOPICS

The simple present

▸ Übung S. 21

1 I **go** to the disco most weeks, but **I don't go** every week.
2 Mr Brown **teaches** us English every day.
3 We **live** in Bavaria. Where **does** Mathew live?

Man verwendet das **simple present** für regelmäßige, sich wiederholende Ereignisse oder Handlungen (1, 2) und für Dauerzustände (3).

Das **simple present** wird häufig mit den folgenden Zeitangaben verwendet:
- *always, never, often, rarely, seldom, sometimes*
- *generally, mostly, normally, regularly, usually*
- *every day/week/month ..., every morning/afternoon ...*
- *on Mondays/Tuesdays ..., on weekdays*
- *in (the) summer/winter ...*
- *at Christmas/Easter, at weekends*

The present progressive

▸ Übung S. 21

1 **I'm calling** to say that Ben's ill. He **isn't feeling** well.
2 He**'s staying** in bed today.

Man verwendet das **present progressive** (auch **present continuous** genannt) für Vorgänge oder Handlungen, die im Moment des Sprechens oder Schreibens vor sich gehen und noch nicht abgeschlossen sind (1).

Es wird auch für vorübergehende Situationen gebraucht (2).

Das **present progressive** wird oft mit den folgenden **Zeitangaben** verwendet:
at the moment, at present, now, this week/month

⚠ Diese Verben bilden normalerweise keine **progressive**-Form:
be, believe, doubt, feel (meinen), *hate, hear, imagine, know, like/dislike, love, mean, notice, prefer, realize, recognize, remember, see* (begreifen), *seem, suppose, think* (meinen), *understand, want, wish*

▸ Übung S. 52

The simple past

1 We **wanted** to go to the USA last year, but in the end we **didn't go**.
2 Jasmin **went** on that school trip to London in March. **Did** you **go** too?

Man verwendet das **simple past**, um über Vergangenes zu berichten, insbesondere wenn im Vordergrund steht, **wann** etwas geschehen ist (1, 2).

Das **simple past** wird häufig mit den folgenden **Zeitangaben** verwendet:
- *yesterday, the day before yesterday, the week/month ... before last*
- *last night/week/month/summer/December/Easter ...*
- *two/three ... hours/days/years ... ago*
- *in 2015 / in the 20th century ...*
- *at that time, in those days*

The past progressive

1 The teacher **was talking** to Heather **during the break**.
2 I **wasn't doing** anything particular when Pete **came** round.

Wenn man ausdrücken möchte, dass eine Handlung zu einem bestimmten Zeitpunkt oder während eines bestimmten Zeitraums in der Vergangenheit **im Gange** war, verwendet man das **past progressive** (auch **past continuous** genannt) (1).

Das **past progressive** wird auch verwendet um auszudrücken, dass eine Handlung im Gange war, als ein neues Ereignis (plötzlich) eintrat (2).

⚠ Einige Verben haben **keine progressive-Form** (siehe die Liste unter **present progressive**).

▸ Übung S. 52

The present perfect

1 I**'ve bought** a new car. I **haven't driven** many kilometres yet.
2 **How long has** it **been** warm with you? We**'ve had** sunshine **for** two weeks.
3 She**'s had** a cold **since** December.

Wenn man ausdrücken will, dass etwas geschehen ist, ohne dass der genaue Zeitpunkt des Ereignisses im Vordergrund steht, wird das **present perfect** verwendet (1).

Man verwendet das **present perfect** auch um mitzuteilen, seit wann oder wie lange ein Zustand oder eine Handlung bereits andauert (2, 3). Dafür wird in Fragen sehr oft *how long*, in Aussagen *for* bzw. *since* verwendet. (Im Deutschen steht dafür „seit" plus Gegenwart.)

Das **present perfect** wird oft mit den folgenden Zeitangaben verwendet:
- *already, still (not), (not) yet*
- *(not) ever, just, lately, never, recently*
- *so far this week/month ..., till/until now*

The present perfect progressive

1 I**'ve been learning** English since I was 10.
2 They**'ve not been speaking** to each other lately.

Das **present perfect progressive** (auch **present perfect continuous** genannt) verwendet man für Handlungen und Vorgänge, die in der Vergangenheit begonnen haben und zum Zeitpunkt des Sprechens bzw. Schreibens noch andauern (1).

Es wird auch für vorübergehende Situationen gebraucht, die noch nicht beendet sind (2).

⚠ Einige Verben haben normalerweise **keine progressive-Form** (siehe die Liste unter **present progressive**).

The past perfect

1 Nina **had** already **left** the coffee bar by the time I arrived.
2 When I visited John in hospital, he **had been** there for ten days.

Mit Hilfe des **past perfect** wird ausgedrückt, dass zwei Handlungen oder Vorgänge in der Vergangenheit aufeinanderfolgten (1). Die Handlung, die zeitlich voranging, steht im **past perfect**.

Das **past perfect** wird auch verwendet um auszudrücken, dass ein Zustand vor einem Zeitpunkt in der Vergangenheit begonnen hatte und zu diesem Zeitpunkt noch andauerte (2).

Wenn zwei oder mehrere kurze Handlungen in der Vergangenheit direkt aufeinanderfolgten, wird für alle Handlungen das **simple past** verwendet: *The cat **ran** out when Joanne **opened** the door.*

The past perfect progressive

1 Rod **had been travelling** for three months when he ran out of money.
2 When I found Mary, I could see that she **had been crying**.

Das **past perfect progressive** wird verwendet, wenn man ausdrücken möchte, dass eine Handlung oder ein Vorgang vor einem Zeitpunkt in der Vergangenheit begonnen hatte und bis (oder fast bis) zu diesem Zeitpunkt andauerte.

▸ Übung S. 29

The future (will)

1 In the future people **will use** public transport more. There **won't be** so many private cars.
2 We can only hope that everyone **will accept** this shift in attitudes.
3 You've forgotten your purse? Don't worry. I**'ll lend** you some money.

Das **will-future** wird verwendet, um Vorhersagen zu treffen (1) oder Hoffnungen bzw. Vermutungen über die Zukunft zu äußern (2).

Man verwendet es auch, wenn man sich spontan zu etwas entschließt, etwas anbietet oder etwas verspricht (3).

Das **will-future** kommt häufig mit den folgenden einleitenden Verben und Ausdrücken vor:
- *believe, expect, forecast, hope, imagine, suppose, think*
- *It's clear/obvious that ..., There's no doubt that ...*

▸ Übung S. 29

The future (going to)

1 Look at these clouds. It**'s going to rain** soon.
2 This time I**'m going to get** good marks in the class test.

Das **going-to future** verwendet man für Ereignisse und Situationen, die nach Meinung der/des Sprechenden bald eintreten werden (weil es bereits Anzeichen dafür gibt) (1).

Es wird auch für Pläne und Absichten verwendet (2).

▸ Übung S. 93

Modal auxiliary verbs

1 He **can speak** several languages.
2 You **must accept** your new situation.
3 We **needn't go** to work today.
4 **May** I **interrupt** you?

Um auszudrücken, was geschehen kann, muss, darf, soll usw., verwendet man ein modales Hilfsverb in Verbindung mit einem Vollverb (1–4).
Im Englischen steht ein Hilfsverb – anders als im Deutschen – **nie ohne** Vollverb:
Lena kann Spanisch. ⚠ *Lena can speak Spanish.* NICHT: ~~*can Spanish*~~

Abgesehen von *could* (wenn es für eine Fähigkeit gebraucht wird) kann man modale Hilfsverben nur im Präsens und – mit einer geeigneten Zeitangabe – mit zukünftiger Bedeutung verwenden, zum Beispiel:
- *You **can go** home now.* (Präsens)
- *You **can go** home an hour early tomorrow.* (Futur)
- *I **must write** these letters now.* (Präsens)
- *I **must write** a long report next week.* (Futur)

⚠ Um ein modales Hilfsverb in der Vergangenheit zu verwenden, muss ein geeignetes Ersatzverb verwendet werden:

must *The provider **had to** block access to the internet last December.*
can *I **couldn't** start the car yesterday.* (Fähigkeit)
*We **weren't allowed to** go home early last Friday.* (Erlaubnis)

Übersicht der modalen Hilfsverben nach Funktion

Funktion	Modale(s) Hilfsverb(en)	
Fähigkeit	*He **can** speak several languages.* *The first satellites **could** only transmit sound.*	
Möglichkeit	*With your qualifications you **could** work abroad.* *The boss **may** come in at any moment.* *He **might** ask you what you are doing.*	
Bitte	***Can** I have a word with Ms Sims, please?* ***Could** I speak to Ms Sims, please?* ***May** I interrupt you?* ***Might** I ask you a personal question?*	(neutral) (höflich) (betont höflich) (äußerst höflich)
Erlaubnis	*You **can** go in now.* *The boss is free. You **may** go in now.*	(neutral) (freundlich)
Verbot	*We **mustn't** be late for work tomorrow.*	
Vorschrift	*You **must** wear a hard hat in the factory.*	
freie Wahl	*Good food **needn't** be expensive.*	
Empfehlung	*You **should** get better qualifications.* *You **ought to** get better qualifications.* *You **must** get better qualifications.*	(neutral) (betont) (streng)

The definite article

1 **Sociologists** say that **violence** is increasing.
2 **Most** of us aren't interested, **half** of us have never heard of the place.
3 I came to **school** today **by car**. I parked in **George Street.**
4 I love **winter** weekends. Often I don't get up or have **breakfast** before 12.

Hat ein Substantiv eine allgemeine, uneingeschränkte Bedeutung – also „alle ohne Ausnahme" – dann steht es ohne Artikel (1).

Ferner wird der Artikel in den folgenden Fällen und Wendungen im Englischen – z. T. anders als im Deutschen – **nicht** verwendet:
- bei *most* in der Bedeutung „die meisten" und bei *half* (2),
- bei öffentlichen Gebäuden im allgemeinen Sinne, Straßennamen und Verkehrsmitteln (3)
- bei Tageszeiten, Mahlzeiten, Wochentagen, Monaten und Jahreszeiten im allgemeinen Sinne (4).

Reported speech (Aussagesätze)

1 "There are some jobs robots can't do."
The speaker **said** that there **were** some jobs robots **couldn't do**.

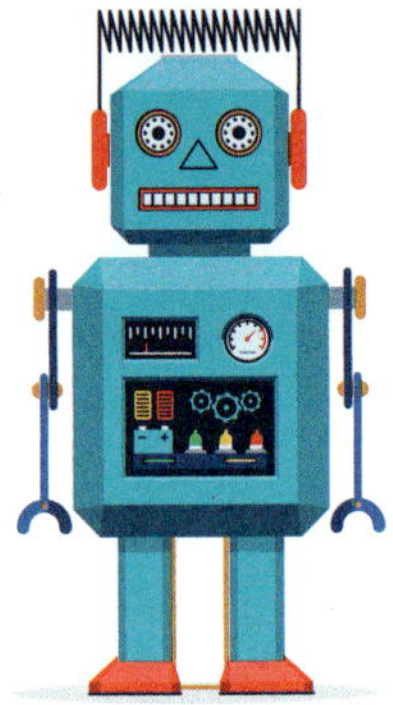

Wenn man einem Dritten berichten möchte, was jemand gesagt hat, verwendet man die **indirekte Rede**.

Bei Verwendung der indirekten Rede verwendet man ein einleitendes Verb wie *say, claim, remind, answer, think, mention* usw.

Steht das einleitende Verb in der Vergangenheit – also *said, answered, mentioned* usw. –, dann verschieben sich die Zeiten wie folgt:

direkte Rede		indirekte Rede
simple present *she works hard*	⟹	simple past *she worked hard*
present progressive *she is working hard*	⟹	past progressive *she was working hard*
simple past *she worked hard*	⟹	past perfect *she had worked hard*
past progressive *she was working hard*	⟹	past perfect progressive *she had been working hard*
present perfect *she has worked hard*	⟹	past perfect *she had worked hard*
present perfect progressive *she has been working hard*	⟹	past perfect progressive *she had been working hard*
past perfect *she had worked hard*	⟹	(keine Verschiebung)
past perfect progressive *she had been working hard*	⟹	(keine Verschiebung)
will *she will work hard*	⟹	*would* *she would work hard*
am/is/are going to *she is going to work hard*	⟹	*was/were going to* *she was going to work hard*
would/might, etc. *she would work hard*	⟹	(keine Verschiebung)
would have / might have, etc. *she would have worked hard*	⟹	(keine Verschiebung)

Die modalen Hilfsverben werden folgendermaßen verschoben:

Modalverb	Bedeutung	indirekte Rede
can	Fähigkeit	*could, was/were able to*
can	Erlaubnis	*was/were allowed to*
may	Möglichkeit	*might*
may	Erlaubnis	*was/were allowed to*
must	Pflicht	*had to*
mustn't	Verbot	*was/were not allowed to*
needn't	freie Wahl	*did not/didn't have to*

Außer wenn man über ein Gespräch berichtet, das am selben Tag stattgefunden hat, müssen fast alle **Zeit-** und einige **Ortsangaben** entsprechend der folgenden Tabelle verändert werden. (Angaben, die nicht aufgeführt sind, bleiben unverändert.)

direkte Rede	indirekte Rede
today	*(on) that day*
tomorrow	*the next day*
yesterday	*the day before*
the day after tomorrow	*two days later*
the day before yesterday	*two days before*
next day/Friday/week/Christmas …	*the following day/Friday/week/Christmas …*
last Friday/week/summer …	*the Friday/week/summer … before*
two years/months/weeks … ago	*two years/months/weeks … before*
now, at present	*then*
at the moment	*at that moment*
at this time	*at that time*
here	*there*
in this place	*at that place*
this	*that*
these	*those*

Reported speech (Fragesätze)

1 "What led to the widespread use of robots?"
A member of the audience **asked what had led** to the widespread use of robots.
2 "Is my job endangered?"
She **wanted to know if/whether** her job **was endangered**.

Bei Fragen **mit Fragewort** wird das Fragewort übernommen (1).

Bei Fragen **ohne Fragewort** verwendet man *if* bzw. *whether* (= ob) (2).

Alle anderen Änderungen erfolgen wie bei den Aussagesätzen (siehe **Aussagesätze** oben).

Reported speech (Bitten, Aufforderungen und Befehle)

1 "Show me the robot."
Lucy **asked the engineer to show her** the robot.
2 "Don't go too close to it."
He **told her not to go** too close to it.

Bei **Bitten** verwendet man meist *asked* (= bitten) + Person + Infinitiv (1).

Für **Aufforderungen** und **Befehle** verwendet man *told* (= sagen) + Person + Infinitiv (2).

Bei **negativen Sätzen** setzen wir *not* unmittelbar vor *to* (2).

Die Wörter *tell* und *ask* stehen immer mit einem Objekt:
"Don't enter the studio when the red light is on."
Ben ***told people / everybody / visitors*** *not to enter the studio when the red light was on.*

▸ Übung S. 98

The passive

1 Measures **are being introduced** to reduce traffic pollution.
2 Pollution **is caused by** some thoughtless people.

Ist der Urheber einer Handlung unbekannt oder zweitrangig, verwendet man das Passiv. Man verwendet eine Zeitform von *be* + dritte Form des Verbs. Im Vordergrund steht also das Ergebnis des Vorgangs (1).

Möchte man den Urheber doch angeben, verwendet man *by* und den Namen auf keinen Fall *from* (2)!

Zeit	Zeitform von *be*	3. Form
simple present	*am/is/are*	*caused*
present progressive	*am/is/are being*	*introduced*
simple past	*was/were*	*buried*
past progressive	*was/were being*	*built*
present perfect	*has/have been*	*installed*
will-future	*will be*	*blocked*
going to-future	*am/is/are going to be*	*sacked*

Beim Verwendung von modalen Hilfsverben wird nach folgendem Muster verfahren:

bei Aussagen	Hilfsverb + *be* + 3. Form	*must be displayed*
bei Fragen	Hilfsverb + Subjekt + *be* + 3. Form	*Can ... be persuaded?*

The impersonal passive

1 **It is said that** petrol should cost more.
2 **The man is thought to** have gone to hospital. **He is believed to** be not very badly injured.

Das **impersonal passive** wird vor allem dann verwendet, wenn man sich objektiv bzw. unbeteiligt ausdrücken möchte. Daher kommt diese Struktur oft in Polizeiberichten, seriösen Zeitungsartikeln usw. vor.

Dabei wird häufig folgendes Satzmuster verwendet: *It is/was* ... + 3. Form des einleitenden Verbs + *that*-Satz (1).

Bei Verben des Berichtens, Vermutens usw. kann man eine Person (*the man, he* usw.) zum Subjekt des Satzes machen. Hinter dem Verb steht dann ein *to*-Infinitiv (2).

Conditionals

▸ Übung S. 123

1 If we **invest** in new technology, a lot of people **will lose** their jobs.
2 If more people **retrained**, they **wouldn't have to worry** about finding a new job.
3 We **won't have** political censorship if we **don't start** to censor the internet.

Ein **Konditionalsatz** besteht aus zwei Teilen: dem ***if*-Teil** und dem **Hauptteil**. Der ***if*-Teil** drückt eine **Bedingung** aus, der Hauptteil deren **Folge**.

Je nach Sinn können *if*-Teil, Hauptteil oder Satzteile **verneint** werden (2, 3).

Bei **Konditionalsätzen** kommen folgende **Zeitmuster** am häufigsten vor:

Typ I *If + simple present*	+	*will*-future
Typ II *If + simple past*	+	*would* + Infinitiv
Typ III *If + past perfect*	+	*would have* + 3. Form des Verbs

if-Sätze werden gemäß der **Wahrscheinlichkeit** der zu erwartenden Folge eingesetzt:

– **Typ I:** Folge (fast) sicher:
If we ***invest in*** *new technology, a lot of people* ***will lose*** *their jobs.*
D. h. viele Leute werden (vermutlich) ihre Stellen verlieren, da wir (sehr wahrscheinlich) in die neue Technologie investieren werden.

– **Typ II:** Folge theoretisch möglich, aber kaum wahrscheinlich.
If we ***invested in*** *new technology, a lot of people* ***would lose*** *their jobs.*
D. h. es ist kaum zu erwarten, dass viele Leute ihre Stellen verlieren werden, da wir (wahrscheinlich) nicht in die neue Technologie investieren werden.

– **Typ III:** Folge unmöglich, da die Bedingung nicht erfüllt wurde und bereits in der Vergangenheit liegt.
If we ***had invested in*** *new technology, a lot of people* ***would have lost*** *their jobs.*
D. h. der Sprecher weiß bereits, dass niemand seinen Job verloren hat, da wir nicht in die neue Technologie investiert haben.

Gerund/Infinitive

1 Max **enjoys playing** football.
2 Can you **afford to buy** that DVD collection?
3 Cem and Julie **continued to meet / continued meeting** even though they had spilt up.
4 Alison **normally likes to go / likes going** to parties, but **today** she **would prefer to stay** at home.

Nach bestimmten Verben folgt stets die *-ing*-Form (**gerund**) (1). Am wichtigsten sind: *admit, avoid, consider, deny, enjoy, finish, imagine, mention, mind* (etwas dagegen haben), *miss, practise, risk, suggest*

Nach bestimmten Verben folgt stets der Infinitiv (**infinitive**) (2). Die wichtigsten Verben dieser Gruppe sind:
afford, choose, decide, expect, hope, mean, promise, refuse, want

Nach den Verben *begin, continue, intend, start, like, love, hate, prefer* können sowohl der **Infinitiv** als auch die ***-ing*-Form beliebig verwendet werden**. Nach *would like, would love, would hate, would prefer* steht jedoch stets der **Infinitiv** (3, 4).

forget/remember

***forget/remember* + *-ing*-Form** bezieht sich auf etwas, das in der Vergangenheit geschehen ist.
– *I still **remember getting** my first bicycle.*
– *I'll never **forget going** to the Rock Against Hunger concert last year.*

***forget/remember* + Infinitiv** dagegen bezieht sich auf etwas Zukünfiges.
– *Dad, please **remember / don't forget to pick me up** from the station.*
– *Oh dear. I **forgot / didn't remember to pick Sally up** from the station.*
In diesem letzten Satz drückt jemand aus, dass er vergessen hat, etwas zu tun, das damals in der Zukunft lag.

regret

***regret* + *-ing*-Form** drückt Bedauern über eine vergangene Situation bzw. einen vergangenen Vorfall aus. Häufig geht es dabei um verpasste Chancen.
– *I really **regret leaving** school without qualifications.*
– *I know they will **regret buying** such a big, expensive car.*

***regret* + Infinitiv** – fast immer mit einem Verb des Mitteilens wie *inform, say, tell* – wird zur Verkündung schlechter Nachrichten verwendet.
– *I **regret to say** that I can't attend the meeting tomorrow.*
– *We **regret to inform** you that the vacancy has now been filled.*

stop

Bedeutet *stop* „aufhören, etwas zu tun", steht das nachfolgende Verb in der ***-ing*-Form**. Bedeutet aber *stop* „kurz anhalten, um etwas anderes zu tun", folgt ein Verb im **Infinitiv**.
- *For heaven's sake* ***stop shouting*** *at me.*
- *I'm a little late because I* ***stopped to give*** *somebody a lift.*

try

Bedeutet *try* „etwas ausprobieren", steht das nachfolgende Verb in der ***-ing*-Form**. Bedeutet aber *try* „sich anstrengen, etwas zu tun", folgt ein Verb im **Infinitiv**.
- *I* ***tried phoning*** *Ellie, but she wasn't at home.*
- *We****'ll try to repair*** *your computer by the weekend.*

Used to

▸ Übung S. 128

1 I **used to do** a lot of sport, but I haven't got time now.
2 I **didn't use to drink** coffee, but I do now because I enjoy it.
3 **Didn't** you **use to live** in London? – Yes, I did. But now I live in Stuttgart.

Used to + infinitive wird verwendet, um Handlungen, Zustände oder Gewohnheiten, die in der Vergangenheit bestanden haben, zu beschreiben. (1– 3) Im Deutschen werden dafür oft Sätze mit *früher* oder *damals* verwendet.

Adjectives and adverbs

▸ Übung S. 89

1 John has a **new** DVD player. It wasn't **expensive**.
2 That CD sounds **terrible**.
3 We can make printouts **quickly** and **cheaply**.

Um **Personen** oder **Sachen** näher zu beschreiben, verwendet man **Adjektive** (1, 2).

Adjektive stehen **unmittelbar vor** Substantiven oder **unmittelbar nach** einer Form von *be* (bzw. *become* oder *seem*, die *be* ersetzen können) (1).

Adjektive können mit Verben wie *feel, look* (aussehen), *sound, smell* und *taste* eine **sinnliche Wahrnehmung** ausdrücken (2).

Um ein **Tätigkeitsverb** näher zu beschreiben, setzt man ein Adverb **unmittelbar hinter das Verb** bzw. Verb + Objekt (3).
⚠ Im Englischen können ein Verb und sein Objekt – anders als im Deutschen – nicht durch ein Adverb getrennt werden. Also NICHT: ~~We can make quickly printouts~~.

Die meisten Adverbien werden durch Anhängen von *-ly* an das entsprechende Adjektiv gebildet (3). Eine kleine Anzahl von Adverbien hat jedoch dieselbe Form wie die zugehörigen Adjektive; die häufigsten sind *fast, hard, early, late, long, daily*.

Adverbien werden auch verwendet, um **Adjektive**, **andere Adverbien** und **ganze Sätze** näher zu bestimmen:
- *MP3 players have become* ***surprisingly cheap***. (Adverb + Adjektiv)
- *You can buy them* ***surprisingly cheaply***. (Adverb + Adverb)
- ***Luckily*** *Gerd left a message on my mailbox.* (Satzadverb)

Comparison of adjectives and adverbs

1 A hundred years ago life was **slower** and people may have been **happier**.
2 Which technological innovation is the **most/least important**?
3 Today you can copy data **more easily than** ever before.

Einsilbige und **zweisilbige Adjektive**, die auf *-y* enden – zum Beispiel *easy, happy* und *lucky* –, werden mit *-(i)er* und *-(i)es* gesteigert (1).

Mehrsilbige Adjektive und **Adverbien**, die auf *-ly* enden, werden mit *more/most* gesteigert (2, 3).

Adverbien, die dieselbe Form wie das entsprechende Adjektiv haben (*fast, hard, early* usw.) werden mit *-er/-est* gesteigert.

Um Personen oder Sachen im Satz miteinander zu vergleichen, gibt es folgende Möglichkeiten:

– kein Unterschied	***as** good **as***	genau so gut wie
– Unterschied	***not as** good **as***	nicht so gut wie
– Unterschied	*better **than***	besser als

▸ Übung S. 14

Word order – positions of adverbs of time, place and frequency

1 She goes shopping **every week**. She goes to the mall **in Wexham.**
2 **Last year** we went to India for our holidays.
3 Paul and Emily went to **the USA last year**.
4 Rob **is never** at home on Saturday afternoon. He **always goes** swimming.
5 I like to stay at home **now and then**.
6 Gina acted **strangely at the party last night**.

Zeitangaben (Wann?) und Ortsangaben (Wo?, Wohin?) stehen in der Regel am Satzende (1).

Um die Zeit eines bestimmten Ereignisses hervorzuheben, kann man die Zeitangabe an die erste Stelle setzen (2).

Stehen eine Zeitangabe und eine Ortsangabe zusammen am Satzende, dann gilt die Reihenfolge Ort vor Zeit (alphabetisch merken: O vor Z!) (3).

Besteht eine Häufigkeitsangabe aus einem Wort, z. B. *always, often, sometimes*, steht sie hinter dem Verb *be*, sonst vor dem Vollverb (4). ⚠ Sie darf nicht zwischen Vollverb und Objekt stehen, also NICHT: ~~*He goes always swimming*~~.

Besteht die Häufigkeitsangabe aus mehreren Wörtern, z. B. *every day, now and then*, steht sie wie eine Zeitangabe am Satzende (5).

Adverbien der Art und Weise stehen in der Regel am Satzende. Kommen noch Zeit- oder Ortsadverbien hinzu, lautet die Reihenfolge: Art und Weise – Ort – Zeit (AOZ) (6).

Relative clauses and contact clauses

▸ Übung S. 11

1 Car manufacturers are designing cars **which/that** can use hydrogen fuel cells.
2 Wildernesses are being spoiled by tourists **who/that** want to go to "unspoiled" places.
3 Tony filled in a questionnaire **(which/that)** he found on the Internet.
4 Fred Foley is a photojournalist **whose** pictures sell for huge sums.
5 Call centre employees, most of **whom** come from India, work long hours.
6 Some non-GM crops are attacked by pests **against which** they have no resistance.

Relativsätze werden verwendet, um den Hauptsatz durch zusätzliche Informationen genauer zu bestimmen.

Für **Sachen** verwendet man das Relativpronomen *which* bzw. *that* (1) und für Personen *who* bzw. *that* (2).

Bezieht sich das Relativpronomen auf das **Objekt des Hauptsatzes**, dann kann man es weglassen (3). Solche Relativsätze heißen **contact clauses**.

Um **Besitz** bzw. **Zugehörigkeit** anzuzeigen, verwendet man *whose* unmittelbar vor dem **Substantiv** bei Personen und Sachen (4).

Steht eine **Präposition** vor dem **Relativpronomen**, wird *whom* für Personen und *which* für Sachen verwendet (5, 6). In solchen Fällen ist die Verwendung von *that* nicht möglich.

Defining and non-defining relative clauses

1 The first Europeans **who** settled in Australia came from Britain.
2 Sydney, **which** is famous for its unusually designed opera house, is situated on the south-eastern coast of Australia.

Im **ersten Beispielsatz** ist der Sinn des Hauptsatzes *The first Europeans came from Britain* ohne den Relativsatz *who settled in Australia* offensichtlich nicht zu verstehen. Solche Relativsätze sind also wesentlich notwendig für das Verständnis des gesamten Satzes – sie nennt man **defining relative clauses** (notwendige oder bestimmende Relativsätze).
⚠ Notwendige Relativsätze erhalten kein **trennendes Komma**.
Dies signalisiert, dass sie fester Bestandteil der Hauptaussage sind.

Im **zweiten Beispielsatz** ist die Aussage des Hauptsatzes *Sydney is situated on the south-eastern coast of Australia* auch ohne den Relativsatz völlig verständlich, weil der Relativsatz *which is famous for its unusually designed opera house* eine zusätzliche, also nebensächliche, Information enthält. Daher werden solche Relativsätze ***non-defining relative clauses*** (nicht notwendige oder nicht bestimmende Relativsätze) genannt.

Participle constructions

1 Malaria, preventable with treatment **costing** less than one pound per bed, is endemic.
2 Many men believe that any work **involved** with cooking is a woman's chore.
3 **Losing** more and more people to AIDS, Africa now needs effective help more urgently than ever before.
4 **Burdened** with declining life-expectancy, large parts of Africa are caught in a poverty trap.
5 **Having fetched** water from a river for many years, some women in developing countries are now happy to have modern systems.
6 Although **facing** extreme destitution, many residents haven't given up hope.
7 Donors should invest in projects that help local inhabitants become self-supporting, thereby **making** sure that the money isn't wasted.
8 Poor infrastructure is a key barrier to economic growth in Nepal, thus **causing** huge additional costs to the transport of commercial goods.
9 Life is becoming hard in the developing countries, **with** many small farmers **going** out of business.
10 AIDS represents a major challenge to sub-Saharan Africa, currently **killing** more than two million people every year.

Die englische Sprache ist geprägt durch die häufige Verwendung von Partizipialkonstruktionen. Diese ermöglichen einen eleganteren Sprachfluss. Partizipialkonstruktionen verkürzen:
- Relativsätze; dabei kann entweder das **present participle** (1) oder das **past participle** (2) verwendet werden.
- Adverbiale Nebensätze (3–9).

Wie bei der Verkürzung von Relativsätzen kommen auch bei der Verkürzung von adverbialen Nebensätzen das **present participle** (3, 6–9) und das **past participle** (4) zur Anwendung. Darüber hinaus wird hier auch noch das **perfect participle** verwendet (5), und zwar um die Vorzeitigkeit der Handlung im Nebensatz auszudrücken. *(Nachdem sie jahrelang Wasser aus dem Fluss geholt hatten, ...)*

Schließlich verknüpft man mit einer Partizipialkonstruktion zwei Hauptsätze zu einem einzigen Satz, und zwar ausnahmslos mittels **present participle** (10).

Countable and uncountable nouns, nouns that are only plural

1 Visit our website for more **information** on our firm. NICHT ~~informations~~
2 Have you read the paper today? The political **news** is interesting. NICHT ~~news are~~
3 Who can give me a piece of / some **advice**? NICHT ~~an advice~~

Einige wichtige **Substantive** sind **zählbar im Deutschen**, **nicht jedoch im Englischen**. Diese Substantive können also nicht direkt mit dem unbestimmten Artikel *a/an* oder mit einem Zahlwort verwendet werden. Hier ist eine Liste solcher Wörter, die Sie auswendig lernen sollten:
advice, baggage, damage, data, equipment, evidence, furniture, garbage *(Abfall)*, information, knowledge, luck, luggage, machinery, news, progress, research, rubbish, work (housework, homework)

Um diese Substantive zählbar zu machen, verwendet man Ausdrücke wie *a bit of, a piece of, some* (3).

⚠ Einige Substantive gibt es im Englischen nur im Singular oder nur im Plural.

4 Economics **is** a popular subject. Politics **doesn't interest** me.
5 The media **have** a lot of influence.
6 The police **are looking** for the murderer.
7 The scissors **need** sharpening.

Auf *economics, politics, physics* folgt ein Verb im Singular, trotz End-*s* (4).

Auf *media, police, scissors, trousers* etc. folgt immer ein Verb im Plural (5–7).

Unit word list

Dieses Wörterverzeichnis enthält alle Wörter in der Reihenfolge ihres Erscheinens (Seitenzahlen sind angegeben). Nicht aufgeführt sind Wörter, die nicht unbedingt zum aktiven Wortschatz gehören müssen. Daher eignet sich diese Liste hervorragend für die Vorbereitung auf Klausuren, sowie auf die Abiturprüfung.

Wörter aus Hörverständnisübungen sind gelb, aus Partner Files grün, aus Videos blau markiert.

Abkürzungen: AE = amerikanisches Englisch, BE = britisches Englisch, etw = etwas, jdm = jemandem, jdn = jemanden, jds = jemandes, pl = plural, sb = somebody, sth = something, <> Gegenteil

Topic 1 We are Gen Z

▸ page 8/9

value ['vælju:]	e.g. honesty, education, ethics	*Wert, Wertvorstellung*
background ['bækgraʊnd]	sb's family, education, social setting	*Hintergrund, Herkunft, Verhältnisse*
gender ['dʒendə]	e.g. male, female, etc	*Geschlecht*
prominent ['prɒmɪnənt]	noticeable, standing out	*auffällig, deutlich*
marker ['mɑ:kə]	sth that shows a place or position	*Kennzeichen*
overlap ['əʊvəlæp]	area of common interest	*Überschneidung(en), Gemeinsamkeit(en)*
multi-layered [ˌmʌlti 'leɪəd]	having many levels	*vielschichtig*
well-being [ˌwel 'bi:ɪŋ]	being comfortable, healthy, happy	*Wohl, Wohlbefinden*
challenge ['tʃælɪndʒ]	a difficult task	*(schwere) Aufgabe, Herausforderung*
behaviour [bɪ'heɪvjə]	the way sb acts around other people	*Verhalten*
lack (of sth) [læk]	when sth is missing	*Mangel (an etw), Fehlen (von etw)*
inadequate [ɪn'ædɪkwət]	not enough, not good enough	*unzulänglich*
nutrition [nju:'trɪʃn]	food needed for health	*Ernährung*
obesity [əʊ'bi:səti]	problematic fat, weight	*Fettleibigkeit*
generational conflict [dʒenəˌreɪʃənl 'kɒnflɪkt]	e.g. children fighting with parents	*Generationenkonflikt*
not necessarily [ˌnɒt nesə'serəli]	perhaps, maybe	*nicht unbedingt*
authority figure [ɔ:'θɒrəti fɪgə]	e.g. police officer, teacher, parent	*Autorität(sperson)*
ironically [aɪ'rɒnɪkli]	not seriously	*ironischerweise*
to **be terrified of sth** [bɪ 'terəfaɪd əv]	to be afraid/scared of sth	*(fürchterliche) Angst vor etw haben*
to **fail** [feɪl]	to be unsuccessful in a test or exam	*scheitern, versagen*
adolescence [ˌædə'lesns]	the time when a child becomes an adult	*Pubertät*
to **confirm sth** [kən'fɜ:m]	to make sure sth is true or correct	*etw bestätigen*
to **skim** [skɪm]	to read sth quickly	(Text) *überfliegen*
to **review sth** [rɪ'vju:]	to check sth, to look at sth carefully	*etw überprüfen, etw überarbeiten*

Section A Identity and values

▸ page 10

authentic [ɔ:'θentɪk]	real, true	*echt, authentisch*
confident ['kɒnfɪdənt]	feeling certain, being sure of oneself	*selbstbewusst*
shy [ʃaɪ]	feeling nervous around other people	*schüchtern*
cause [kɔ:z]	an important topic or issue	*Anliegen, Sache (für die man eintritt)*
dishonest [dɪ'sɒnɪst]	<> honest	*unehrlich, unaufrichtig*
obnoxious [əb'nɒkʃəs]	horrible, awful	*unausstehlich, eklig*
progressive [prə'gresɪv]	when sth brings change and improvement	*fortschrittlich*
politics *pl* ['pɒlətɪks]	government and decision making	*Politik, politische Einstellung(en)*
nurse [nɜ:s]	sb who looks after people in hospital	*Krankenpfleger/-schwester*
cute [kju:t]	sweet, adorable	*niedlich, süß*
to **mind** [maɪnd]	to have a problem with sth	*etw dagegen haben*

silly ['sɪli]	<> serious	*albern, doof*	
to be honest with you [tə ˌbi 'ɒnɪst wɪð ju]	to be frank, to tell the truth	*ehrlich gesagt*	
lie [laɪ]	<> truth	*Lüge*	
to **appear** [ə'pɪə]	to look or seem a special way	*scheinen*	
professional [prə'feʃənl]	concerning sb's work	*beruflich*	
You wish! [ˌju 'wɪʃ]	This is sth you would like but won't get!	*Das hättste wohl gerne!*	
to **identify as sb/sth** [aɪ'dentɪfaɪ əz]	to say sb/sth belongs to a group or category	*sich als jd/etw bezeichnen, sich als zu jdm/etw zugehörig erklären*	
to **identify with sb/sth** [aɪ'dentɪfaɪ wɪð]	to feel the same as sb/sth	*sich mit jdm/etw identifizieren*	
affinity [ə'fɪnəti]	liking and understanding sb/sth	*Neigung, Vorliebe*	
likeable ['laɪkəbl]	nice, friendly, pleasant	*sympathisch, nett*	▸ page 11
to **rate sth** [reɪt]	to say/think sb/sth has a certain rank or value	*etw einstufen, etw bewerten*	
popularity [ˌpɒpju'lærəti]	how much people like sb/sth	*Beliebtheit*	
to **value sth** ['vælju:]	to think sth is important or valuable	*etw schätzen, etw wertschätzen*	
to **refer to sth** [rɪ'fɜ: tə]	what it is sb is talking about	*sich auf etw beziehen*	
kindness ['kaɪndnəs]	friendliness, loveliness	*Freundlichkeit, Liebenswürdigkeit, Güte*	
to **crumple sth up** [ˌkrʌmpl 'ʌp]	to crush sth in your hand	*etw zusammenknüllen*	
snowball fight ['snəʊbɔ:l faɪt]	throwing snow at other people	*Schneeballschlacht*	

Section B Well-being

level ['levl]	how high or low sth is	*Niveau, Grad*	▸ page 12
breath [breθ]	the air going in and out of lungs	*Atem, Atemzug*	
to **take a deep breath** [teɪk ə ˌdi:p 'breθ]	to take a lot of air into your lungs	*tief einatmen, durchatmen*	
mind [maɪnd]	spirit, thoughts	*Geist, Bewusstsein*	
to **give sb/sth a break** [ˌgɪv ə 'breɪk]	to give sb/sth the chance to pause	*jdm/etw eine Pause gönnen*	
to **let go of sth** [ˌlet 'gəʊ əv]	<> hold on to sth	*etw lösen, etw loslassen*	
tension ['tenʃn]	<> relaxation	*Spannung(en), Angespanntheit*	
calf, calves [kɑ:f, kɑ:vz]	the muscles on the back of the lower leg	*Unterschenkel*	
thigh [θaɪ]	the upper part of the leg	*Oberschenkel*	
rear end [ˌrɪər 'end]	buttocks	*Hinterteil*	
belly ['beli]	abdomen, stomach	*Bauch*	
chest [tʃest]	upper part of the torso	*Brust, Brustkorb*	
jaw [dʒɔ:]	lower part of the face	*Unterkiefer*	
forehead ['fɔrhɛd]	upper part of the face, above the eyes	*Stirn*	
evenly distributed [ˌi:vnli dɪ'strɪbju:tɪd]	in equal amounts	*gleichmäßig verteilt*	
to **rest sth on sth** ['rest ɒn]	e.g. rest your head on the table	*etw auf etw ablegen, etw auf etw ruhen lassen*	
lap [læp]	e.g. As a child, I used to sit on my mother's lap.	*Schoß*	
emotional state [ɪˌməʊʃənl 'steɪt]	how sb feels at the moment	*Gefühlszustand*	
to **be upset about sth** [bi ʌp'set əbaʊt]	to feel sad and angry about sth	*sich über etw ärgern, sich über etw aufregen*	
progressive [prə'gresɪv]	more and more	*schrittweise, stufenweise*	
to **relax sth** [rɪ'læks]	to let go of tension	*etw entspannen*	
muscle ['mʌsl]	e.g. bicep, quadricep	*Muskel*	
relaxation [ˌri:læk'seɪʃn]	<> tension, excitement	*Entspannung, Lockerheit*	
huge [hju:dʒ]	very big	*enorm, (riesig) groß*	

impact ['ɪmpækt]	the effect sth has on sth else	*Einfluss, Auswirkung(en), Folge(n)*
to **have an impact on sth** [həv ən 'ɪmpækt ɒn]	to make a difference to sth	*sich auf etw auswirken*
mental ['mentl]	in the mind	*geistig, psychisch*
physical ['fɪzɪkl]	in the body	*körperlich, physisch*
cause [kɔːz]	the reason for sth	*Ursache*
to **do sth about sth** ['duː əbaʊt]	to try to solve a problem	*etw gegen etw unternehmen*
visual ['vɪʒuəl]	relating to things one can see	*visuell, bildorientiert*
society [sə'saɪəti]	a group of people who live together	*Gesellschaft*
to **compete with sth** [kəm'piːt wɪð]	to try to be better than sb/sth	*sich mit etw messen, mit etw mithalten*
to **be on a diet** [bi ˌɒn ə 'daɪət]	to eat less in order to lose weight	*eine Diät machen*
eating disorder [ˌiːtɪŋ dɪs'ɔːdə]	problems with food and eating	*Ess-Störung*
to **be on the rise** [bi ɒn ðə 'raɪz]	to become bigger/more	*(ständig) zunehmen, auf dem Vormarsch sein*
to **be desperate to do sth** [bi 'despərət tə duː]	to need or want to do sth very much	*etw unbedingt (aus Verzweiflung) tun wollen*
stress levels *pl* ['stres levlz]	amounts of stress and tension	*Stressniveau*
present moment [ˌpreznt 'məʊmənt]	now	*gegenwärtiger Zeitpunkt*
suffering ['sʌfərɪŋ]	pain, bad feelings	*Leiden, Leid*
▸ page 13 to **be painful** [bi 'peɪnfl]	to hurt	*wehtun*
natural disaster [ˌnætʃrəl dɪ'zɑːstə]	e.g. fire, flood, earthquake	*Naturkatastrophe*
threat (to sth) [θret]	sth bad that might happen to sth	*Bedrohung (von etw)*
to **fight sth** [faɪt]	to take action against sth	*etw bekämpfen*
to **calm sb/sth** [kɑːm]	to make sb/sth relax	*etw/jdn beruhigen*
to **exercise** ['eksəsaɪz]	to do sport, to work out	*trainieren*
laughter ['lɑːftə]	e.g. Ha ha ha!	*Lachen*
outlook on life [ˌaʊtlʊk ɒn 'laɪf]	the way sb looks at the world	*Lebensperspektive*
the bright side [ðə ˌbraɪt 'saɪd]	the positive things	*die positiven Aspekte*
to **place high value on sth** [pleɪs ˌhaɪ 'væljuː ɒn]	to think sth is important or a good idea	*großen Wert auf etw legen*
to **fit into sth** ['fɪt ɪntə]	to feel comfortable in a place or situation	*sich in etw einfügen*
anxiety [æŋ'zaɪəti]	fear, bad feelings, tension	*Ängste, Angst*
peer pressure ['pɪə preʃə]	feeling forced to do sth by people your own age	*sozialer Druck (unter Gleichaltrigen)*
additional [ə'dɪʃənl]	extra, more	*zusätzlich*
wholly ['həʊli]	100%	*völlig, hundertprozentig*
to **feel run down** [fiːl ˌrʌn 'daʊn]	to have no energy	*sich schlapp fühlen*
defences *pl* [dɪ'fensɪz]	the ability of the body to protect itself against illnesses, stress, etc	*Abwehrkräfte*
varied diet [ˌveərɪd 'daɪət]	different types of food	*abwechslungsreiche Ernährung*
to **boost sth** [buːst]	to make sth bigger, to make sth work better	*etw ankurbeln, etw auf Touren bringen*
to **deal with sth** ['diːl wɪð]	to handle sth e.g. a problem	*mit etw umgehen, etw bewältigen, mit etw zurechtkommen*
bullying ['bʊliɪŋ]	sb being cruel and hurtful to sb else	*Mobbing*
to **meet a deadline** [ˌmiːt ə 'dedlaɪn]	to finish work on time	*eine (Abgabe-)Frist einhalten*

to **live up to sb's expectations** [lɪv ˌʌp tu ekspek'teɪʃnz]	to do as well as sb expects	*jds Erwartungen erfüllen*	
sth suffers ['sʌfəz]	sth shows negative effects	*etw wird in Mitleidenschaft gezogen*	
essential [ɪ'senʃl]	very important	*unverzichtbar, wesentlich*	
independence [ˌɪndɪ'pendəns]	e.g. when sb can look after themselves	*Unabhängigkeit*	
to **behave** [bɪ'heɪv]	to act in a particular way	*sich verhalten*	
to **cause sth** [kɔːz]	to make sth happen	*etw verursachen*	
to **trigger sth** ['trɪgə]	to bring up a bad feeling or memory	*etw auslösen*	
fixed [fɪkst]	not moving	*fest, feststehend*	
ranking ['ræŋkɪŋ]	e.g. from 1 to 10	*Einstufung, Bewertung*	▸ page 14
frequency ['friːkwənsi]	how often sth happens	*Häufigkeit*	
occasionally [ə'keɪʒənəli]	sometimes	*gelegentlich*	
habit ['hæbɪt]	sth sb does often, e.g. every day	*Gewohnheit*	
to **worsen sth** ['wɜːsn]	<> to better sth	*etw verschlimmern*	
easy-going [ˌiːzi 'gəʊɪŋ]	calm, relaxed	*unkompliziert, locker*	▸ page 15
moody ['muːdi]	having feelings that change quickly	*launisch*	
outgoing ['aʊtgəʊɪŋ]	extroverted	*kontaktfreudig, kommunikativ*	
selfish ['selfɪʃ]	thinking only of oneself	*egoistisch*	
sensible ['sensəbl]	to do the right thing at the right time	*vernünftig*	
stubborn ['stʌbən]	not likely to change their opinion	*stur, dickköpfig*	
bull [bʊl]	<> cow	*Stier*	
to **change sb's mind** [ˌtʃeɪndʒ 'maɪnd]	to make sb change their opinion	*jds Meinung ändern*	
to **be prone to sth** [bi 'prəʊn tə]	to be likely to suffer from sth	*anfällig für etw sein, zu etw neigen*	
to **consider sth sth** [kən'sɪdə]	to think about sth in a particular way	*etw für etw halten, etw als etw ansehen*	
to **attend school** [əˌtend 'skuːl]	to go to school	*die Schule besuchen*	
suburbs *pl* ['sʌbɜːbz]	a place between city and countryside	*Stadtrand, Randbezirke*	
regardless of sth [rɪ'gɑːdləs əv]	not caring about sth	*unabhängig von etw, ungeachtet einer Sache*	
academic performance [ækəˌdemɪk pə'fɔːməns]	grades, marks	*schulische Leistung(en)*	
workforce ['wɜːkfɔːs]	people who work	*Arbeitnehmerschaft*	
professional [prə'feʃənl]	what sb does for work	*professionell, hauptberuflich*	
guidance counsellor ['gaɪdəns kaʊnsələ]	sb who talks to students about their problems	*Vertrauenslehrer/in, Berater/in*	
to **take care of sth** [ˌteɪk 'keər əv]	to look after sth	*sich um etw kümmern*	
suburban [sə'bɜːbən]	at the edge of a city	*außerhalb (des Stadtzentrums), am Stadtrand*	
currently ['kʌrəntli]	at the moment	*momentan, aktuell*	
flavour ['fleɪvə]	atmosphere, feeling	*Note, Atmosphäre, Touch*	
scheduling ['ʃedjuːlɪŋ]	time planning	*Terminplanung, Zeitplan*	
campus ['kæmpəs]	the place where a school/university is	*Schul-/Universitätsgelände*	
trade school ['treɪd skuːl]	a school which trains students for particular jobs e.g. nurse, mechanic, etc	*Berufsschule*	
findings *pl* ['faɪndɪŋz]	results	*Ergebnisse*	
to **fit in socially** [fɪt ˌɪn 'səʊʃəli]	to be part of a group, to have friends	*sich anpassen, dazugehören*	
to **be involved in sth** [bi ɪn'vɒlvd ɪn]	to take part in sth	*bei etw mitmachen/mitwirken*	
extracurricular [ekstrəkə'rɪkjʊlə]	activities outside of school	*außerschulische Aktivität, AG*	

to **participate in sth** [pɑː'tɪsɪpeɪt ɪn]	to be part of sth	*an etw teilnehmen, bei etw mitwirken*
to **experience sth** [ɪk'spɪəriəns]	to find out what sth is like	*etw durchmachen, etw erleben, etw erfahren*
to **be stressed out** [bi ˌstrest 'aʊt]	to have too much stress, pressure	*(völlig) gestresst sein*
peer [pɪə]	sb the same age or in the same group	*Gleichaltrige/r, Mitschüler/in*
discord ['dɪskɔːd]	conflict, problems	*Konflikt(e), Zwist, Streitigkeiten*
stressor ['stresə]	the thing that brings stress, conflict	*Stressfaktor*
sb encounters sth [ɪn'kaʊntəz]	sb sees/finds/learns about sth	*etw begegnet jdm*
to **deal with sth** ['diːl wɪð]	to handle e.g. a problem	*sich mit etw befassen, mit etw zu tun haben*

▸ page 16

to **mitigate sth** ['mɪtɪgeɪt]	to make sth easier, smaller	*etw lindern, etw mildern*
calming technique ['kɑːmɪŋ tekniːk]	a way to relax	*Beruhigungs-/Entspannungstechnik*
to **stress sb out** [ˌstres 'aʊt]	<> to calm sb down	*jdn stressen*
to **relieve sth** [rɪ'liːv]	to make sth feel better, easier	*etw abbauen, etw lindern*
mindfulness ['maɪndflnəs]	relaxed way of paying attention	*Achtsamkeit*
point of view [ˌpɔɪnt əv 'vjuː]	a way of seeing sth	*Perspektive, Blickwinkel*
to **be in control of sth** [bi ɪn kən'trəʊl əv]	to be calm and able to think	*etw in der Hand haben*
inhalation [ˌɪnhə'leɪʃn]	breathing in	*Einatmen*
exhalation [ˌekshə'leɪʃn]	breathing out	*Ausatmen*
to **clear one's mind** [ˌklɪə wʌnz 'maɪnd]	to think about nothing, to stop worrying	*den Kopf freibekommen/freimachen*
intention [ɪn'tenʃn]	purpose, reason to do sth	*Absicht, Vorhaben*
to **break sth down to sth** [ˌbreɪk 'daʊn tə]	to reduce sth to sth smaller	*etw auf etw reduzieren*
instead of [ɪn'sted əv]	e.g. I would like tea instead of coffee.	*anstatt, anstelle von*
bite [baɪt]	piece of sth	*Stück, Bissen*
to **shove sth** [ʃʌv]	to push sth hard	*etw schieben, etw stecken*
to **get some perspective** [ˌget sʌm pə'spektɪv]	to see things in a different way	*etw relativieren*
to **tend to do sth** ['tend tə]	to usually do sth in a particular way	*dazu neigen, etw zu tun*
to **illustrate sth** ['ɪləstreɪt]	to give an example for sth	*etw veranschaulichen*
to **benefit from sth** ['benɪfɪt frəm]	to profit from sth	*von etw profitieren*
to **draw a conclusion** [drɔː ə kən'kluːʒn]	to state a logical consequence	*eine Schlussfolgerung ziehen*
pie chart ['paɪ tʃɑːt]	circle-shaped diagram	*Tortendiagramm*
to **draw** [drɔː]	to make a picture with a pencil or pen	*zeichnen*
rarely ['reəli]	<> often	*(nur) selten*
whether ['weðə]	e.g. Tell me whether this is true or not!	*ob*
argument ['ɑːgjumənt]	a (verbal) fight	*(verbale) Auseinandersetzung, Streit*
episode ['epɪsəʊd]	one part of a TV series, podcast, etc	*Folge* (einer TV-Serie etc.)

Section C Generational conflict

▸ page 17

criticism (of sth) ['krɪtɪsɪzəm]	saying what is wrong with sth	*Kritik (an etw)*
poor(ly) [pʊə]	bad(ly)	*schlecht*
overly dramatic [ˌəʊvəli drə'mætɪk]	<> with understatement	*übertrieben dramatisch*
row [raʊ]	fight, argument	*Streit, Auseinandersetzung*
to **distract sb from sth** [dɪ'strækt frəm]	to take sb's attention away from sth	*jdn von etw ablenken*

to **fight** [faɪt]	to argue	*sich streiten*	
to **pay off** [ˌpeɪ 'ɒf]	to bring good results, to be worth the effort	*sich bezahlt machen*	
meaningful ['miːnɪŋfl]	carrying relevant information	*aussagekräftig*	
to **tidy sth** ['taɪdi]	<> to mess sth up	*etw aufräumen*	▸ page 18
to **argue with sb** ['ɑːgjuː wɪð]	to (verbally) fight with sb	*sich mit jdm streiten*	
demand [dɪ'mɑːnd]	sth that is asked for, needed	*Anspruch, Forderung*	
to **occur** [ə'kɜː]	to happen	*stattfinden, geschehen*	
to **rely on sb/sth** [rɪ'laɪ ɒn]	to be able to count on sb/sth	*sich auf jdn/etw verlassen*	
no matter what [nəʊ ˌmætə 'wɒt]	In every situation, this is the truth.	*was auch (immer) passiert*	
to **be down to sth** [bi 'daʊn tə]	to be the reason sth happens	*an etw liegen*	
specifically [spə'sɪfɪkli]	especially, exactly	*insbesondere, genauer gesagt*	
rigid ['rɪdʒɪd]	strict, unmoving	*starr*	
sb finds sth a struggle [ˌfaɪndz ə 'strʌgl]	e.g. Teenagers find waking up a struggle.	*jdm fällt etw (sehr) schwer*	
to **approve of sth** [ə'pruːv əv]	to think sth is a good idea	*etw gutheißen*	
to **accuse sb of sth** [ə'kjuːz əv]	to say, 'You did this!'	*jdn einer Sache beschuldigen, jdm etw vorwerfen*	
laziness ['leɪzinəs]	<> productivity	*Faulheit*	
lazy ['leɪzi]	not wanting to do anything at all	*faul*	
to **undergo sth** [ˌʌndə'gəʊ]	to experience sth	*etw durchmachen*	
to **play havoc with sth** [ˌpleɪ 'hævək wɪð]	e.g. Curry plays havoc with my stomach!	*etw komplett durcheinanderbringen*	
sleeping pattern(s) ['sliːpɪŋ pætn]	when the body sleeps and wakes	*Schlafrhythmus*	
to **suggest sth** [sə'dʒest]	to put forward an idea, to indicate sth	*etw nahelegen, auf etw schließen lassen*	
sadly ['sædli]	<> happily	*leider, bedauerlicherweise*	
opportunity [ˌɒpə'tjuːnəti]	possibility, chance	*Möglichkeit, Gelegenheit*	
to **sleep in** [ˌsliːp 'ɪn]	to stay in bed for longer than normal	*ausschlafen, länger schlafen*	
restricted [rɪ'strɪktɪd]	limited	*beschränkt*	
to **emphasize** ['emfəsaɪz]	to show that sth is important, to stress	*betonen, hervorheben, herausstellen*	
insufficient [ˌɪnsə'fɪʃnt]	not enough	*unzureichend*	
to **affect sth** [ə'fekt]	to have negative consequences for sth	*sich negativ auf etw auswirken*	
to **obstruct sth** [əb'strʌkt]	to stop sth happening	*etw behindern, etw hemmen*	
lie-in ['laɪ ɪn]	sleeping for longer than normal	*langes Schlafen, Ausschlafen*	
stimulating ['stɪmjuleɪtɪŋ]	bringing excitement	*aufputschend*	
to **mature** [mə'tʃʊə]	to become older, more grown up	*reifen, sich entwickeln*	
rate [reɪt]	speed	*Tempo*	
response [rɪ'spɒns]	answer	*Reaktion*	
to **operate** ['ɒpəreɪt]	to work, to function	*laufen, funktionieren*	
peak performance [ˌpiːk pə'fɔːməns]	the best sb/sth can be	*Höchstleistung, Hochtouren*	
outburst ['aʊtbɜːst]	sth said in an angry way	*Ausbruch, Anfall*	▸ page 19
to **get passionate about sth** [ˌget 'pæʃənət əbaʊt]	to become very interested in sth	*sich (leidenschaftlich) für etw begeistern/einsetzen*	
to **baffle sb** [bæfl]	to confuse sb	*jdn vor ein Rätsel stellen*	
racket ['rækɪt]	a lot of noise	*Lärm, Krach*	
to **upset sb** [ˌʌp'set]	to make sb feel sad and angry	*jdn verstören, jdn aufregen, jdm an die Nieren gehen*	
to **put sth off** [ˌpʊt 'ɒf]	to decide to do sth at a later time	*etw (auf später) verschieben*	
to **bottle sth up** [ˌbɒtl 'ʌp]	to shut down emotions	*etw unterdrücken*	
to **revolve around sth** [rɪ'vɒlv əraʊnd]	e.g. The earth revolves around the sun.	*sich um etw drehen*	
blazing row [ˌbleɪzɪŋ 'raʊ]	a very bad argument	*erbitterter/wilder Streit*	

messy ['mesi]	untidy, not in order	*unordentlich, unaufgeräumt*
to **insist** [ɪn'sɪst]	e.g. I insist you do exactly what I say!	*darauf bestehen*
familiar [fə'mɪliə]	well-known	*bekannt*
reward [rɪ'wɔːd]	sth given to sb who did sth good	*Belohnung*
pleasure ['pleʒə]	good feelings	*Vergnügen, Annehmlichkeit*
to **overhaul sth** [əʊvə'hɔːl]	to do sth in a completely different way	*etw überholen, etw neu instandsetzen*
simultaneously [ˌsɪml'teɪniəsli]	at the same time as sth else	*gleichzeitig, zur selben Zeit*
to **crave sth** [kreɪv]	to really want sth	*sich nach etw sehnen*
novelty ['nɒvlti]	sth new and fun	*Neuartigkeit, Abwechslung*
on sb's terms [ɒn 'tɜːmz]	in sb's own way	*zu jds Bedingungen, nach jds Vorstellungen*
decade ['dekeɪd]	ten years	*Jahrzehnt*
to **provide for sb** [prə'vaɪd fə]	to look after sb	*für jdn sorgen*
closed off [ˌkləʊzd 'ɒf]	not wanting to communicate	*abgeschottet*
to **be reluctant to do sth** [bi rɪ'lʌktənt tə]	to not want to do sth	*sich dagegen sträuben, etw zu tun; etw nur widerwillig tun*
to **absorb sth** [əb'sɔːb]	e.g. My brain doesn't absorb information in the morning.	*etw* (Lernstoff usw.) *aufnehmen*
constantly ['kɒnstəntli]	all the time	*die ganze Zeit, andauernd*
sb isn't bothered about sth [ɪznt 'bɒðəd əbaʊt]	sb doesn't worry about sth	*jdm ist etw (völlig) egal*
to **be sensitive to sth** [bi 'sensətɪv tə]	e.g. I'm very sensitive to noise.	*auf etw empfindlich reagieren, empfänglich für etw sein*
approval [ə'pruːvl]	positive feedback	*Anerkennung*
nagging ['nægɪŋ]	always asking sb to do sth	*Genörgel, Gemeckere*
to **take the edge off** [ˌteɪk ði 'edʒ ɒf]	to make things a little easier	*die Schärfe nehmen*
to **demand** [dɪ'mɑːnd]	to ask forcefully	*fordern, verlangen*
▸ page 20 **punishment** ['pʌnɪʃmənt]	what sb gets when they do sth bad	*Strafe, Bestrafung*
partially ['pɑːʃəli]	a little bit, in part	*teilweise*
accessible [ək'sesəbl]	easy to get	*zugänglich*
▸ page 21 **permanent** ['pɜːmənənt]	always there	*dauerhaft, beständig*
temporary ['temprəri]	there for a short time only	*vorübergehend*

Section D Gap years

▸ page 22 **volunteer work** [vɒlənˌtɪə 'wɜːk]	unpaid work, often for a charity	*ehrenamtliche Tätigkeit(en)*
to **overwhelm sb** [ˌəʊvə'welm]	to be too much for sb to handle	*jdn überwältigen*
option ['ɒpʃn]	choice	*Möglichkeit*
range [reɪndʒ]	different things to choose from	*Angebot, Auswahl, (Produkt-)Palette*
to **fancy sth** ['fænsi]	to want to do/have sth	*auf etw Lust haben*
to **look into sth** [ˌlʊk 'ɪntə]	to get information about sth	*sich über etw informieren, sich um etw kümmern*
crucial ['kruːʃl]	the most important	*entscheidend, äußerst wichtig*
animal care [ˌænɪml 'keə]	e.g. Zookeepers specialize in animal care.	*Tierpflege*
(animal) shelter ['ʃeltə]	a place for abandoned animals	*Tierheim*
surgery ['sɜːdʒəri]	a place where doctors work	*Arztpraxis*
vet [vet]	animal doctor	*Tierarzt/-ärztin*
to **rescue sb** ['reskjuː]	to bring sb to safety	*jdn retten*
resident ['rezɪdənt]	local	*ortsansässig, vor Ort*
professional [prə'feʃənl]	sb who is skilled in their job	*Fachmann/-frau*
to **volunteer** [ˌvɒlən'tɪə]	to work for no money	*ehrenamtlich arbeiten*
orphanage ['ɔːfənɪdʒ]	a place for children who have no parents	*Waisenhaus, Kinderheim*

to **cover sth** ['kʌvə]	to include sth	*etw abdecken, sich über etw erstrecken*	
to **dig a well** [ˌdɪg ə 'wel]	to find a water source in the earth	*einen Brunnen bohren/graben*	
village ['vɪlɪdʒ]	a very small town	*Dorf*	
to **make a difference** [ˌmeɪk ə 'dɪfrəns]	to do sth good for sb else	*etwas bewirken*	
pride [praɪd]	a good feeling sb has about themselves	*Stolz*	
self-sufficiency [ˌself sə'fɪʃənsi]	the ability to look after yourself	*Eigenständigkeit*	
conservation [ˌkɒnsə'veɪʃn]	saving the environment	*Naturschutz, Umweltschutz*	▸ page 23
endangered wildlife [ɪnˌdeɪndʒəd 'waɪldlaɪf]	animals which might die out soon	*bedrohte Tier- und Pflanzenarten*	
to **protect sb/sth** [prə'tekt]	to keep sb/sth safe	*jdn/etw schützen*	
to **conserve sth** [kən'sɜːv]	to save sth, to protect sth	*etw erhalten, etw schützen*	
particularly [pə'tɪkjələli]	especially, exactly	*insbesondere*	
pursuit [pə'sjuːt]	activity, sth to do	*Aktivität, Beschäftigung*	
arts and crafts *pl* [ˌɑːts ənd 'krɑːfts]	e.g. painting, ceramics, weaving	*Kunsthandwerk*	
underprivileged [ˌʌndə'prɪvəlɪdʒd]	not having much, coming from a poor background	*benachteiligt, unterprivilegiert*	
thrill [θrɪl]	excitement	*Nervenkitzel*	
commitment [kə'mɪtmənt]	a promise to do sth	*Leistungsbereitschaft, Einsatz*	
to **advertise sth** ['ædvətaɪz]	to let other people know about sth	*Werbung für etw machen*	
service ['sɜːvɪs]	helpful activity	*Dienstleistung*	
spontaneous(ly) [spɒn'teɪniəs]	sudden(ly), without planning	*spontan*	
proposal [prə'pəʊzl]	offer	*Vorschlag, Angebot*	
to **be relevant to sb/sth** [bi 'reləvənt tə]	to be important to sb/sth	*für jdn/etw wichtig / von Bedeutung sein*	
wildlife ['waɪldlaɪf]	e.g. plants, animals, nature	*Pflanzen- und Tierwelt, Natur*	
destination [ˌdestɪ'neɪʃn]	the end place of a journey	*Zielort*	
to **caution sb against sth** ['kɔːʃn əgenst]	to tell sb that sth is a bad idea	*jdn vor etw warnen*	
common ['kɒmən]	normal, usual	*verbreitet, üblich*	▸ page 24
fortune ['fɔːtʃuːn]	a lot of money	*Vermögen*	
inexpensive [ˌɪnɪk'spensɪv]	cheap	*billig*	
accommodation [əˌkɒmə'deɪʃn]	a place to stay e.g. a hotel	*Unterkunft, Bleibe*	
free board and lodging(s) [friː ˌbɔːd ənd 'lɒdʒɪŋ]	a place to stay for no money	*freie Kost und Logis*	
tight [taɪt]	not much money to spend	*(Geld:) knapp*	
to **be committed to sth** [bi kə'mɪtɪd tə]	to really want to do sth, to believe in sth	*von etw überzeugt sein*	
concern [kən'sɜːn]	worry	*Befürchtung, Bedenken, Sorge*	
approximately [ə'prɒksɪmətli]	e.g. Maybe 9, maybe 11, so approximately 10.	*ungefähr, circa*	
to **defer sth** [dɪ'fɜː]	to do sth later	*etw verschieben, etw aussetzen*	
to **incorporate sth into sth** [ɪn'kɔːpəreɪt ɪntə]	to combine two things	*etw in etw einbinden, etw in etw aufnehmen*	
to **disapprove of sth** [ˌdɪsə'pruːv əv]	to think sth is a bad idea	*etw missbilligen, etw ablehnen*	
persistent [pə'sɪstənt]	not giving up	*beharrlich, hartnäckig*	
vineyard ['vɪnjəd]	a place where grapes are grown for wine	*Weingut*	
to **treat sb/sth** [triːt]	to handle sb/sth	*jdn/etw behandeln*	
to **pursue a profession** [pəˌsjuː ə prə'feʃn]	to try and do a job	*einen Beruf ergreifen*	▸ page 25
asset ['æset]	a plus point, advantage	*Pluspunkt, Vorteil*	

	sb has a hard time doing sth [həz ə ˌhɑːd 'taɪm]	sb finds it difficult to do sth	*jdm fällt es schwer, etw zu tun*
	to **consider sth** [kən'sɪdə]	to think about sth	*über etw nachdenken, sich Gedanken über etw machen*
	to **work one's ass/arse off** [ˌwɜːk wʌnz 'ɑːs ɒf]	to work very hard	*sich abrackern, sich kaputtarbeiten*
	to **pick grapes** [ˌpɪk 'greɪps]	to collect grapes from the vine	*Trauben ernten*
	rewarding [rɪ'wɔːdɪŋ]	satisfying, pleasing	*befriedigend, lohnend*
	to **sympathize with sb** ['sɪmpəθaɪz wɪð]	to understand how sb feels	*für jdn Verständnis haben, mit jdm mitfühlen*
	to **keep an eye on sb** [ˌkiːp ən 'aɪ ɒn]	to take care of sb	*auf jdn aufpassen, jdn im Auge behalten*
	to **tease sb** [tiːz]	to laugh at, make jokes about sb	*jdn aufziehen, jdn necken*
	hometown ['həʊmtaʊn]	the place sb comes from	*Heimatstadt*
	food for thought [ˌfʊd fə 'θɔːt]	sth to think about	*Denkanstöße*

Section E Educational possibilities

▸ page 26	to **relate to sth** [rɪ'leɪt tə]	to find a connection with sth	*einen Zugang zu etw finden, etw mit etw anfangen können*
	to **educate** ['edʒukeɪt]	to teach, to instruct	*schulen, (aus)bilden, unterrichten*
	screenplay ['skriːnpleɪ]	the script of a film	*Drehbuch*
	sweat [swet]	water that comes out of sb's skin	*Schweiß*
	to **drip** [drɪp]	to fall like water	*tropfen*
	textbook ['tekstbʊk]	school book	*Schulbuch*
▸ page 27	**interview** ['ɪntəvjuː]	= job interview	*Vorstellungsgespräch*
	to **join in** [ˌdʒɔɪn 'ɪn]	to participate	*(bei etw) mitmachen,* (Verein usw.) *beitreten*
	rebel ['rebl]	sb who opposes authority, teachers, etc	*Rebell/in*
	to **miss sth** [mɪs]	to not get/understand sth	*etw nicht mitbekommen*
	sarcasm ['sɑːkæzəm]	irony, often used to criticize sb/sth	*Sarkasmus*
	headmistress [ˌhed'mɪstrəs]	female head teacher	*Direktorin*
	advanced [əd'vɑːnst]	far on, ahead	*fortgeschritten*
	ridiculous [rɪ'dɪkjələs]	crazy, silly	*lächerlich*
	to **stare at sb** ['steər ət]	to look at sb for a long time	*jdn anstarren*
	intimidated [ɪn'tɪmɪdeɪtɪd]	feeling held back because of fear	*eingeschüchtert*
▸ page 28	**excuse** [ɪk'skjuːs]	a reason not to do sth	*Ausrede, Entschuldigung*
	to **be in need of sth** [bi ɪn 'niːd əv]	to require sth	*etw benötigen*
	to **rehearse sth** [rɪ'hɜːs]	to practise sth	*etw proben, etw einstudieren*
	point [pɔɪnt]	reason	*Sinn, Zweck*
	one day [wʌn 'deɪ]	sometime in the future	*eines Tages*
▸ page 29	**armed services** *pl* [ˌɑːmd 'sɜːvɪsɪz]	i.e. army, navy, airforce	*Streitkräfte, Armee*
	prediction [prɪ'dɪkʃn]	a prognosis for the future	*Vorhersage, Voraussage*
	to **predict sth** [prɪ'dɪkt]	to guess sth that might happen in the future	*etw vorhersagen, etw voraussagen*
	to **hire sb** ['haɪə]	to give work/a job to sb	*jdn einstellen, jdn anstellen*
	citizen ['sɪtɪzn]	a member of a city/state/country	*(Staats-)Bürger/in*
	to **apply** [ə'plaɪ]	to formally ask for sth e.g. a job	*sich bewerben*
▸ page 30	to **vary** ['veəri]	to be different	*variieren, unterschiedlich sein*
	majority [mə'dʒɒrəti]	<> minority	*Mehrheit*
	to **be comparable to sth** [bi 'kɒmpərəbl tə]	to be similar to sth, not very different	*mit etw vergleichbar sein*
	to **postpone sth** [pə'spəʊn]	to do sth later	*etw vertagen, etw verschieben*
	specific [spə'sɪfɪk]	exact	*bestimmte/r/s*
	breadth [bredθ]	how wide sth is	*Breite*

depth [depθ]	how deep sth is	*Tiefe*
variety [vəˈraɪəti]	different things to choose from	*Abwechslung, Vielfalt*
fairness [ˈfeənəs]	being equal	*Gerechtigkeit*
similarly [ˈsɪmələli]	<> differently	*ebenso, in gleicher Weise*
marking [ˈmɑːkɪŋ]	grading e.g. exam papers	*Benotung*
harsh [hɑːʃ]	very hard, difficult	*streng, rigoros*
bright [braɪt]	intelligent, clever	*gescheit, intelligent*

▸ page 31

in depth [ɪn ˈdepθ]	<> superficially	*gründlich, eingehend*
academic [ˌækəˈdemɪk]	in university, in science	*akademisch, wissenschaftlich*
to **rule sth out** [ˌruːl ˈaʊt]	to decide against sth	*etw ausschließen, etw unmöglich machen*
time traveller [ˈtaɪm trævələ]	sb who can travel between the past and the future	*Zeitreisende/r*
to **figure sth out** [ˌfɪgər ˈaʊt]	to find the answer to sth	*etw herausfinden*
apprenticeship [əˈprentɪʃɪp]	a training programme for a job	*Lehre, Ausbildung*
internship [ˈɪntɜːnʃɪp]	work experience	*Praktikum*
voluntary [ˈvɒləntri]	working without payment	*freiwillig*
century [ˈsentʃəri]	one hundred years	*Jahrhundert*
to **convince sb** [kənˈvɪns]	to persuade sb	*jdn überzeugen*
employment [ɪmˈplɔɪmənt]	paid work	*Anstellung, Beschäftigung*
challenging [ˈtʃælɪndʒɪŋ]	difficult (in a good way)	*anspruchsvoll*
intern [ˈɪntɜːn]	sb who is getting work experience	*Praktikant/in*
applied sciences *pl* [əˌplaɪd ˈsaɪənsɪz]	e.g. engineering, health care, IT	*angewandte Wissenschaften*
childcare [ˈtʃaɪldkeə]	looking after children	*Kinderbetreuung*
work environment [ˈwɜːk ɪnvaɪrənmənt]	the place, people, atmosphere at a workplace	*Arbeitsumfeld*
lawyer [ˈlɔːjə]	sb who works with the law and legal rights	*Anwalt/Anwältin*
to **quit sth** [kwɪt]	to stop doing sth e.g. a job	*etw beenden, etw kündigen*
depending on [dɪˈpendɪŋ ɒn]	determined or decided by sth	*je nachdem*
volunteer [ˌvɒlənˈtɪə]	sb who works for no money	*Freiwillige/r, ehrenamtlich Tätige/r*
nursery school [ˈnɜːsəri skuːl]	an informal school for very young children	*Kindergarten*
care home [ˈkeə həʊm]	a place where old or ill people live	*Pflegeheim*
the elderly [ði ˈeldəli]	very old people	*Senioren*
the disabled [ðə dɪsˈeɪbld]	people who are physically or mentally limited	*Behinderte*

Topic 2 Cities and regions in anglophone countries

▸ page 44/45

property [ˈprɒpəti]	building(s) and land	*Immobilie(n)*
exhibition [ˌeksɪˈbɪʃn]	display of art, paintings, etc	*Ausstellung*
gentrification [ˌdʒentrɪfɪˈkeɪʃn]	the process of improving an area	*Gentrifizierung*
neighbourhood [ˈneɪbəhʊd]	district, community	*Stadtviertel, Gegend*
affordability [əˌfɔːdəˈbɪləti]	the cost or price of sth	*Erschwinglichkeit*
urban transport [ˌɜːbən ˈtrænspɔːt]	e.g. buses, trams, metro, etc	*Stadtverkehr*
ridable [ˈraɪdəbl]	can be travelled	*fahrbar*
just about [ˌdʒʌst əˈbaʊt]	almost	*fast, so ziemlich*
congested [kənˈdʒestɪd]	blocked, full	*verkehrsreich, (Straßen:) verstopft*
inhabitant [ɪnˈhæbɪtənt]	sb who lives in a place	*Einwohner/in*
indigenous people [ɪnˌdɪdʒənəs ˈpiːpl]	people who are native to a place	*Ureinwohner*
countryside [ˈkʌntrisaɪd]	<> city, town	*ländliche Gegend(en), Land*
in the middle of nowhere [ɪn ðə ˌmɪdl əv ˈnəʊweə]	far away from people, cities, houses	*am Ende der Welt, mitten in der Pampa*

	director [də'rektə]	sb who tells actors (in a film) what to do	*Regisseur/in*
	poetry ['pəʊɪtri]	e.g. sonnets by William Shakespeare	*Dichtung, Gedichte*
	rural ['rʊərəl]	from/in the countryside	*ländlich*
	root [ruːt]	where sb/sth comes from	*Wurzel*
	poet ['pəʊɪt]	e.g. Goethe, Schiller, etc	*Dichter/in*

Section A London street art

▸ page 46	**lively** ['laɪvli]	full of energy	*lebendig, lebhaft, quirlig*
	guided tour [ˌgaɪdɪd 'tʊə]	a visit to a place with sb who gives information about the place	*Führung, Rundgang*
	wall painting ['wɔːl peɪntɪŋ]	a picture painted on a wall	*Wandgemälde*
	to **take a stand against sth** [ˌteɪk ə 'stænd əgenst]	to reject or be opposed to sth	*ein Zeichen gegen etw setzen*
	impressive [ɪm'presɪv]	amazing, astonishing	*beeindruckend*
	diverse [daɪ'vɜːs]	very different, varied	*vielfältig, breit gefächert, divers*
	to **grab sb's attention** [ˌgræb ə'tenʃn]	to make sb notice sth	*jmds Aufmerksamkeit erregen*
	mural ['mjʊərəl]	a large wall painting	*Wandbild*
	against a background [əˌgenst ə 'bækgraʊnd]	scenery behind sth	*vor einem Hintergrund*
	masterpiece ['mɑːstəpiːs]	e.g. the Mona Lisa	*Meisterwerk*
	evil ['iːvl]	very bad	*böse*
	large-scale ['lɑːdʒskeɪl]	very big	*großformatig*
	bright [braɪt]	<> dark, dull	(Farbe:) *hell, leuchtend*
	colourful ['kʌləfl]	e.g. red, blue, green, yellow, all together	*bunt, farbenfroh*
	to **remind sb of sth** [rɪ'maɪnd əv]	to make sb remember/think about sth	*jdn an etw erinnern*
	dot [dɒt]	point	*Punkt, Tupfen*
	block [blɒk]	area of only one colour	*(Farb-)Fläche*
	creature ['kriːtʃə]	animal, monster	*Gestalt, Wesen*
	real eye-opener [ˌrɪəl 'aɪ əʊpnə]	aha effect	*echtes Aha-Erlebnis*
	to **be packed with sth** [bi 'pækt wɪð]	to be full of sth	*voll von etw sein, voller … sein*
▸ page 47	**walking tour** ['wɔːkɪŋ tʊə]	a visit to a place on foot	*Rundgang*
	to **hesitate** ['hezɪteɪt]	to pause before doing sth	*zögern*
	to **interrupt sb** [ˌɪntə'rʌpt]	to break what sb is saying	*jdn unterbrechen, jdm ins Wort fallen*
	particularly [pə'tɪkjələli]	especially	*besonders*
	temporary ['temprəri]	<> permanent	*vorläufig, provisorisch*
	nature ['neɪtʃə]	the way sth is	*Wesen, Art*
	to **whitewash sth** ['waɪtwɒʃ]	to paint over sth	*etw übertünchen*
	to **vandalize sth** ['vændəlaɪz]	to damage sth on purpose	*etw mutwillig beschädigen, etw verwüsten*
	charm [tʃɑːm]	delight, fascination	*Charme*
	rich [rɪtʃ]	(colours:) strong, bright	(Farbe:) *satt*
	sb misses sth ['mɪsɪz]	sb doesn't catch sth	*jdm entgeht etw*
	covered ['kʌvəd]	having sth on top of it	*überdeckt*
	to **appear** [ə'pɪə]	to be present	*vorkommen*
	scary ['skeəri]	frightening	*unheimlich, furchteinflößend*
	to **be a shame** [ˌbi ə 'ʃeɪm]	e.g. I've lost £20! – What a shame!	*schade sein, eine Schande sein*
	(sense of) humour ['hjuːmə]	ability to find things funny	*Humor*
	superb [suː'pɜːb]	excellent, wonderful	*erstklassig, hervorragend*
	brick [brɪk]	a block used in buildings	*Ziegelstein*
	inspirational [ˌɪnspɪ'reɪʃnəl]	stimulating, exciting	*inspirierend*
	by chance [baɪ 'tʃɑːns]	<> planned	*zufällig*

to **come across sb** [ˌkʌm əˈkrɒs]	to meet sb without planning to	*jdm (zufällig) begegnen, auf jdn stoßen*	
to **check** [tʃek]	to have a look	*nachsehen*	
smell [smel]	sth recognized by your nose	*Geruch*	
spray paint [ˈspreɪ peɪnt]	paint from an aerosol can	*Sprühfarbe*	
shutter [ˈʃʌtə]	a solid cover on a window	*Fensterladen, Rollladen*	
acrylic screen [əˌkrɪlɪk ˈskriːn]	solid, transparent plastic cover	*Plexiglaswand*	
fluffy [ˈflʌfi]	<> rough, flat	*flauschig*	
poodle [ˈpuːdl]	a type of dog with curly hair	*Pudel*	
designated area [ˌdezɪgneɪtɪd ˈeəriə]	a place that has been especially selected	*ausgewiesener Bereich*	
litter [ˈlɪtə]	rubbish, trash	*Abfall, Müll*	
to **join sb** [dʒɔɪn]	to go together with sb, to be with sb	*bei jdm sein*	
guide [gaɪd]	sb who leads a tour	*Führer/in*	
connotations *pl* [ˌkɒnəˈteɪʃnz]	ideas, feelings, associations about sth	*Assoziationen, Anklänge, Konnotationen*	
frightening [ˈfraɪtnɪŋ]	scary	*beängstigend*	
can [kæn]	small metal container	*(Blech-)Dose*	
to **conclude** [kənˈkluːd]	to finish, to end	*schließen, zum Schluss kommen*	▸ page 48
audience [ˈɔːdiəns]	people who are watching sth	*Publikum, Zuschauer/innen, Zuhörer/innen*	
to **focus on sth** [ˈfəʊkəs ɒn]	to look closely at sth	*sich auf etw konzentrieren*	
signposting [ˈsaɪnpəʊstɪŋ]	words and phrases which direct sb's presentation	orientierende Hinweise für die Zuhörer/innen in einem Vortrag	
to **guide sb** [gaɪd]	to lead/guide sb	*jdn führen, jdn leiten*	
to **turn sb's attention to(wards) sth** [ˌtɜːn əˈtenʃn tə]	to make sb look at/listen to sth	*jds Aufmerksamkeit auf etw lenken*	
on a positive note [ɒn ə ˈpɒzətɪv nəʊt]	in a good, happy way	*positiv*	

Section B Gentrification case study: Seattle

sense of community [ˌsens əf kəˈmjuːnəti]	a feeling of belonging	*Gemeinschaftsgefühl, -sinn*	▸ page 49
hangout [ˈhæŋgaʊt]	a place to meet other people	*Stammlokal, Laden*	
to **disappear** [ˌdɪsəˈpɪə]	to go away	*verschwinden*	
bicycle lane [ˈbaɪsɪkl leɪn]	part of a street only for bicycles	*Fahrradspur*	
beneficial [ˌbenɪˈfɪʃl]	positive, good	*vorteilhaft, positiv*	
unaffordable [ˌʌnəˈfɔːdəbl]	too expensive	*unerschwinglich, zu teuer*	
housing [ˈhaʊzɪŋ]	places to live	*Wohnungen, Wohnraum*	
rent [rent]	money paid for a house, flat, etc	*Miete*	
working class [ˌwɜːkɪŋ ˈklɑːs]	social group who do low-paid work	*aus der Arbeiterklasse, Arbeiter-*	
run-down [ˌrʌn ˈdaʊn]	not cared for, shabby	*heruntergekommen, verwahrlost*	
to **transform sth** [trænsˈfɔːm]	to change sth in a better way	*etw verwandeln, etw umwandeln, etw (grundlegend) verändern*	
food stall [ˈfuːd stɔːl]	a kiosk that sells food	*Imbissstand*	
organic [ɔːˈgænɪk]	grown without chemical fertilizers	*Bio-*	
eatery [ˈiːtəri]	restaurant, bistro, café	*Restaurant, Lokal*	
wealthy [ˈwelθi]	having lots of money	*wohlhabend*	
economy [ɪˈkɒnəmi]	system of money, trade, consumption	*Wirtschaft*	
rental [ˈrentl]	money paid for a house, flat, etc	*Miete, Miet-*	
the big picture [ðə ˌbɪg ˈpɪktʃə]	<> the small details	*das große Ganze*	▸ page 50
to **memorize sth** [ˈmeməraɪz]	to learn sth so that you can remember it perfectly	*sich etw einprägen*	
to **branch off** [ˌbrɑːntʃ ˈɒf]	to go in a different direction	*abzweigen*	

	pay [peɪ]	money, wages, salary	*Bezahlung, Gehalt*
	rise (in sth) [raɪz]	growth, sth becoming bigger	*Anstieg (von etw)*
▸ page 51	**unrecognizable** [ʌn'rekəgnaɪzəbl]	cannot be identified	*nicht wiederzuerkennen*
	past [pɑːst]	<> future	*vergangen*
	rise [raɪz]	reaching a higher level	*Aufstieg*
	resident ['rezɪdənt]	sb who lives in a particular place	*Einwohner/in*
	to **long for sth** ['lɒŋ fə]	to really want sth	*sich nach etw sehnen*
	vibrant ['vaɪbrənt]	dynamic, exciting	*dynamisch, pulsierend, spannend*
	unlike [ˌʌn'laɪk]	different from	*anders als*
	corporation [ˌkɔːpə'reɪʃn]	big business, large company	*Großunternehmen, Konzern*
	to **operate** ['ɒpəreɪt]	to work	*geschäftlich tätig sein, arbeiten, operieren*
	to crowd oneself into sth ['kraʊd ɪntə]	to move into a small space	*sich in etw hineinzwängen*
	paradoxically [ˌpærə'dɒksɪkli]	absurd, contradictory	*paradoxerweise*
	to **attract sb** [ə'trækt]	to make sb move towards sth	*jdn anlocken, jdn anziehen*
	to **destroy sth** [dɪ'strɔɪ]	<> to create sth	*etw zerstören*
	in the first place [ɪn ðə 'fɜːst pleɪs]	to begin with	*überhaupt (erst), in erster Linie*
	industry ['ɪndəstri]	group of businesses	*Branche, Sparte*
	above all [əˌbʌv 'ɔːl]	most importantly	*vor allen Dingen, allen voran*
	key driver [ˌkiː 'draɪvə]	main motivating factor	*treibende Kraft, Hauptmotor*
	to **found sth** [faʊnd]	to start sth e.g. a business	*etw gründen*
	inequality [ɪnɪ'kwɒləti]	unfairness	*Ungleichheit, Unterschied(e)*
	to **afford sth** [ə'fɔːd]	to have enough money for sth	*sich etw leisten*
	available [ə'veɪləbl]	able to be used	*verfügbar, erhältlich*
	to **surge** [sɜːdʒ]	to rise quickly	*sprunghaft ansteigen*
	incredible(-ly) [ɪn'kredəbl]	unbelievable(-ly)	*unglaublich*
	to **be forced to do sth** [bi 'fɔːst tə duː]	<> to be free to do sth	*sich gezwungen sehen, etw zu tun; etw (notgedrungen) tun müssen*
	to **end up living on the streets** [end ˌʌp ˌlɪvɪŋ ɑn ðə 'striːts]	to have lost one's home and have nowhere to go	*auf der Straße landen*
	tent camp ['tent kæmp]	a place where people live in tents	*Zeltlager*
	homeless ['həʊmləs]	having no place to live or stay	*obdachlos*
	permanent home [ˌpɜːmənənt 'həʊm]	<> temporary accommodation	*fester Wohnsitz*
▸ page 52	to **set up business** [ˌset ʌp 'bɪznəs]	to start a new enterprise	*sich (geschäftlich) niederlassen*
▸ page 53	**expressive** [ɪk'spresɪv]	showing an idea or meaning	*aussagekräftig, prägnant*
	to **slump** [slʌmp]	to fall down	*absacken, stark zurückgehen*
	to **plummet** ['plʌmɪt]	to fall down suddenly	*abstürzen, stark fallen*

Section C Urban transport and activism

▸ page 54	**journey** ['dʒɜːni]	going from one place to another	*Fahrt*
	rating ['reɪtɪŋ]	saying how good or bad sth is	*Bewertung, Einstufung*
	taxi rank ['tæksi ræŋk]	a place where taxis wait for customers	*Taxistand*
	hire scheme ['haɪə skiːm]	a system of renting sth	*Verleihsystem*
	electric vehicle [ɪˌlektrɪk 'viːəkl]	a car/bus/bike that uses electricity, not gasoline or other fuel	*Elektrofahrzeug*
	charging point ['tʃɑːdʒɪŋ pɔɪnt]	a place to charge a battery	*Ladestation*
▸ page 56	**congestion charge** [kən'dʒestʃən tʃɑːdʒ]	money paid to drive a car through a city	*Innenstadtmaut, Citymaut*
	to **introduce sth** [ˌɪntrə'djuːs]	to start sth new	*etw einführen*
	purpose ['pɜːpəs]	intention	*Zweck, Absicht*

penalty ['penlti]	money paid if you do the wrong thing	*Strafe, Bußgeld*
truth [tru:θ]	<> lies	*Wahrheit*
transit ['trænzɪt]	traffic, public transport	*(öffentlicher) Verkehr, Stadtverkehr*
to **take measures** [ˌteɪk 'meʒəz]	to do sth to get certain results	*Maßnahmen ergreifen*
bold [bəʊld]	brave, strong	*mutig, gewagt*
traffic control ['træfɪk kəntrəʊl]	the flow of traffic in a city	*Verkehrssteuerung*
exhaust [ɪg'zɔ:st]	emissions from cars	*Abgase*
literally ['lɪtərəli]	with the original meaning of a word or phrase	*buchstäblich, tatsächlich*
air pollution [ˌeə pə'lu:ʃn]	toxic chemicals in the air	*Luftverschmutzung*
congestion [kən'dʒestʃən]	overcrowding, blockage	*(starke) Verkehrsbelastung, Verstopfung*
to **generate money** [ˌdʒenəreɪt 'mʌni]	to make money	*Geld einnehmen*
to **invest** [ɪn'vest]	to put money into a project, scheme	*investieren*
charge [tʃɑ:dʒ]	money paid for goods, services	*Gebühr*
charging zone ['tʃɑ:dʒɪŋ zəʊn]	an area in which people have to pay for a service	*Gebührenzone*
to **cover an area** [ˌkʌvər ən 'eəriə]	e.g. Charging zone covers most of London's inner city.	*sich über einen Bereich erstrecken*
on top of sth [ɒn 'tɒp əv]	additionally, extra	*zusätzlich zu etw*
to **meet emission standards** [ˌmi:t ɪ'mɪʃn stændədz]	to produce an accepted amount of pollution	*Emissionsgrenzwerte einhalten*
number plate ['nʌmbə pleɪt]	registration signs on a car	*Nummernschild*
recognition [ˌrekəg'nɪʃn]	identification	*Erkennung*
in advance [ɪn əd'vɑ:ns]	beforehand	*im Voraus*
automated ['ɔ:təmeɪtɪd]	run by machines	*automatisch*
debit card ['debɪt kɑ:d]	a card used to get money from a machine	*Geldkarte*
direct debit [dəˌrekt 'debɪt]	a transfer of money from sb's account	*Lastschrift, Bankeinzug*
penalty charge notice ['penəlti tʃɑ:dʒ nəʊtɪs]	a letter informing sb to pay a fine	*Bußgeldbescheid*
capital ['kæpɪtl]	the main city of a state or country	*Hauptstadt*
harmful ['hɑ:mfl]	damaging	*schädlich*
badge [bædʒ]	a small sign	*Plakette*
windscreen ['wɪndskri:n]	glass screen at the front of a vehicle	*Windschutzscheibe*
driving ban ['draɪvɪŋ bæn]	when sb is not allowed to drive	*Fahrverbot*
garage ['gærɑ:ʒ]	repair shop for cars	*Kfz-Werkstatt*
car registration office ['kɑ: redʒɪstreɪʃn ɒfɪs]	a place to register a car/vehicle	*Kfz-Zulassungsstelle*
fine [faɪn]	money paid as a punishment	*Bußgeld*
cyclist ['saɪklɪst]	sb who rides a bicycle	*Fahrradfahrer/in*
concerned [kən'sɜ:nd]	worried about sth	*besorgt, beunruhigt*
to **take sb/sth seriously** [teɪk 'sɪəriəsli]	to think sth is very important	*jdn/etw ernst nehmen*
as a consequence [æz ə 'kɒnsɪkwəns]	because of this	*infolgedessen*
proper ['prɒpə]	correct, right, decent	*richtig, echt, anständig*
to **result in sth** [rɪ'zʌlt ɪn]	to cause sth to happen	*etw zur Folge haben*
department of transportation [dɪˌpɑ:tmənt əf trænspɔ:'teɪʃn]	government office for vehicles and roads	*Verkehrsbehörde*
to **lead to sth** ['li:d tə]	to go towards sth	*zu etw führen*
death [deθ]	<> life	*Tod, Todesfall*
to **collide with sth** [kə'laɪd wɪð]	to crash into sth	*mit etw kollidieren*
unsafe [ˌʌn'seɪf]	dangerous	*gefährlich*

▸ page 57

	unseparated lane [ʌnˌsepəreɪtɪd 'leɪn]	a lane on a street for all vehicles	*nicht abgetrennte Fahrspur*
	motorist ['məʊtərɪst]	sb who drives a car	*Autofahrer/in*
	to **mind sb/sth** [maɪnd]	to be careful of sb/sth	*auf jdn/etw achten*
	Caution! ['kɔːʃn]	Careful!	*Achtung!*
	to **pass** [pɑːs]	to overtake	*überholen*
	icon ['aɪkɒn]	symbol	*Symbol*
	to **campaign for sth** [kæm'peɪn fə]	to fight for sth	*sich für etw engagieren, für etw kämpfen*
	road surface ['rəʊd sɜːfɪs]	e.g. asphalt	*Straßenbelag*
	pothole ['pɒthəʊl]	a hole in the road	*Schlagloch*
	anonymous [ə'nɒnɪməs]	not named, not identified	*anonym*
	to **sense sth** [sens]	to feel sth	*etw fühlen, etw spüren*
	bump [bʌmp]	a hit, a strike; an uneven part of a road's surface	*Schlag, Stoß; Unebenheit, Hubbel*
	council ['kaʊnsl]	a city's government	*Stadtverwaltung*
	a string of events [ə ˌstrɪŋ əv ɪ'vents]	things that happen in a sequence	*eine Reihe von Ereignissen*
	traffic cone ['træfɪk kəʊn]	marker placed on a road	*Leitkegel, Pylon*
	equally ['iːkwəli]	the same as	*ebenso, gleichermaßen*
	inventive [ɪn'ventɪv]	original	*originell, einfallsreich*
	annoyed [ə'nɔɪd]	irritated, angry	*verärgert*
	barrier ['bæriə]	sth that blocks sb's way	*Absperrung*
	to **draw attention to sth** [ˌdrɔː ə'tenʃn tə]	to make sb notice sth	*die Aufmerksamkeit auf etw lenken*
	soldier ['səʊldʒə]	member of an army	*Soldat/in*
	secretly ['siːkrətli]	hidden	*im Verborgenen*
	authority [ɔː'θɒrəti]	official power to do sth	*Befugnis, Legitimation*
▸ page 58	**pedestrian** [pɪ'destriən]	a person on the street	*Fußgänger/in*
	speeding ['spiːdɪŋ]	going too fast	*Geschwindigkeitsüberschreitung, zu schnelles Fahren*
	in the distance [ɪn ðə 'dɪstəns]	far away	*in der Ferne*
	to **approach** [ə'prəʊtʃ]	to get closer	*näherkommen*
	traffic calming ['træfɪk kɑːmɪŋ]	slowing down cars, traffic	*Verkehrsberuhigung*
	nevertheless [ˌnevəðə'les]	all the same	*nichtsdestotrotz, trotzdem*
	to **fine sb** [faɪn]	to make sb pay for a mistake	*ein Bußgeld gegen jdn verhängen*
▸ page 59	**structure** ['strʌktʃə]	format	*Aufbau*
	to **consist of sth** [kən'sɪst əv]	to be made up of sth	*aus etw bestehen*
	introduction [ˌɪntrə'dʌkʃn]	the beginning	*Einleitung*
	main body [ˌmeɪn 'bɒdi]	the central portion of a text	*Haupttext*
	conclusion [kən'kluːʒn]	ending, logical consequence	*Schluss*
	brief(ly) [briːf]	short	*kurz (gefasst)*
	to **provide sth** [prə'vaɪd]	to give sth	*etw bereitstellen, für etw sorgen*
	in conclusion [ɪn kən'kluːʒn]	summarizing (at the end of a speech, etc)	*abschließend, zum Schluss*
	to **take immediate action** [teɪk ɪˌmiːdiət 'ækʃn]	to do sth right away	*unverzüglich tätig werden*
	to **suggest sth** [sə'dʒest]	to put an idea forward	*etw vorschlagen*
	to **solve sth** [sɒlv]	to find a solution for sth	*etw lösen*
▸ page 60	**mayor** [meə]	leader of a city's government	*Bürgermeister/in*

Section D Geography, culture and history down under

▸ page 61	**to associate sb/sth with sth** [ə'səʊʃieɪt wɪð]	to connect sb/sth with sth in one's mind	*jdn/etw mit etw in Verbindung bringen, jdn/etw mit etw assoziieren*

to **share** sth [ʃeə]	to tell other people about sth	*sich über etw austauschen, über etw sprechen*
to **depict** sth [dɪ'pɪkt]	to describe/draw a picture of sth	*etw abbilden*
adrenaline rush [ə'drenlɪn rʌʃ]	a strong feeling of excitement	*Adrenalinrausch*
present ['preznt]	existing now	*gegenwärtig*
varied ['veərid]	different from one another	*vielfältig, vielgestaltig*
mountain range ['maʊntən reɪndʒ]	e.g. the Alps, the Andes	*Gebirge, Gebirgszug*
glacier ['glæsiə]	slow moving frozen river	*Gletscher*
to **shift** [ʃɪft]	to move	*sich bewegen, sich verschieben*
earthquake ['ɜːθkweɪk]	sudden, violent movement of the earth	*Erdbeben*
unpredictable [ˌʌnprɪ'dɪktəbl]	uncertain, changeable	*unberechenbar*
to **vary wildly** [ˌveəri 'waɪldli]	to be very different from other things	*sehr unterschiedlich sein*
experience [ɪk'spɪəriəns]	an event that leaves a strong impression	*Unternehmung, Erlebnis*
to **feature** sth ['fiːtʃə]	to have sth, to include sth	*etw aufweisen, etw haben*
stunning ['stʌnɪŋ]	very beautiful	*atemberaubend*
to **explore** sth [ɪk'splɔː]	to travel in or through	*etw erkunden*
to **keep** sth **handy** [ˌkiːp 'hændi]	to have sth in case you need it	*etw griffbereit haben*
parrot ['pærət]	colourful exotic bird	*Papagei*
to **originate in** sth [ə'rɪdʒɪneɪt ɪn]	to start in sth	*von etw (her)kommen*
to **take the plunge** [ˌteɪk ðə 'plʌndʒ]	to jump into sth	*den Sprung wagen, springen*
to **establish** sth [ɪ'stæblɪʃ]	to start sth, to define sth	*etw schaffen, etw definieren*
unique [ju'niːk]	one of a kind	*eigen, spezifisch*
to **claim** sth [kleɪm]	to take sth for oneself	*etw (für sich) beanspruchen*
chief [tʃiːf]	the leader of a tribe	*Häuptling*
constitutional [ˌkɒnstɪ'tjuːʃənl]	official, governmental	*Verfassungs-*
national holiday [ˌnæʃnəl 'hɒlədeɪ]	a day of holiday for a country	*Nationalfeiertag*
to **struggle to do** sth ['strʌgl tə duː]	to find it difficult to do sth	*etw nur mit Mühe tun können; es schwer haben, etw zu tun*
to **maintain** sth [meɪn'teɪn]	to keep sth going	*etw (aufrecht)erhalten*
custom ['kʌstəm]	tradition	*Brauch*
marine life [mə'riːn laɪf]	animals and plants in the ocean	*Tier- und Pflanzenwelt des Meeres*
whale [weɪl]	e.g. in literature, Moby Dick	*Wal*
close-up ['kləʊs ʌp]	from very near	*aus der Nähe, von Nahem*
cruise [kruːz]	journey by ship	*Seereise, Kreuzfahrt*
sea creature ['siː kriːtʃə]	animal that lives in the ocean	*Meerestier*
memorable ['memərəbl]	<> forgettable	*unvergesslich, beeindruckend*
backdrop ['bækdrɒp]	<> foreground	*Kulisse, Hintergrund*
scenery ['siːnəri]	natural landscape	*Landschaft*

▸ page 62

Section E Big city vs countryside in the UK

▸ page 64

to **resemble** sb/sth [rɪ'zembl]	to look like sb/sth	*jdm/etw ähneln*
carefree ['keəfriː]	having no worries	*unbeschwert, sorglos*
on sb's doorstep [ɒn 'dɔːstep]	near where sb lives	*vor der Haustür*
within walking distance [wɪðɪn 'wɔːkɪŋ dɪstəns]	so close one can walk there	*in Laufweite, fußläufig erreichbar*

	patience ['peɪʃns]	being able to accept problems without getting angry	*Geduld*
	to **get along with sb** [ˌget ə'lɒŋ wɪð]	to have a good relationship with sb	*mit jdm auskommen, mit jdm zurechtkommen*
	background ['bækgraʊnd]	sb's parents and culture	*Herkunft, Vorgeschichte*
	to **commute** [kə'mjuːt]	to travel to and from work	*zur Arbeit fahren, pendeln*
	rare [reə]	unusual, seldom seen	*selten*
	to **raise animals** [ˌreɪz 'ænɪmlz]	to take care of animals	*Tiere züchten, Tiere halten*
	privacy ['prɪvəsi]	not seen or disturbed by other people	*Privatsphäre*
	to **stand sb/sth** [stænd]	to be able to deal with sb/sth	*jdn/etw ertragen*
	to **lend sb a hand** [ˌlend ə 'hænd]	to be helpful to sb	*jdm helfen, jdm zur Hand gehen*
	convenient [kən'viːniənt]	practical, easy	*praktisch*
▸ page 65	**bothersome** ['bɒðəsəm]	problematic	*lästig*

Section F Modern poetry in rural America

▸ page 66	to **be true to sth** [bi 'truː tə]	e.g. to be true to the facts	*einer Sache entsprechen*
	to **be suspicious of sb** [bi sə'spɪʃəs əv]	to not trust sb	*jdm misstrauen, jdm mit Argwohn begegnen*
	to **value sth over sth** ['væljuː əʊvə]	to think that sth is more important than sth else	*etw höher schätzen als etw, etw über etw stellen*
	as though [əz 'ðəʊ]	like, as if	*als ob*
	to **support your family** [səˌpɔːt jɔː 'fæmli]	to look after and feed your family	*die eigene Familie ernähren*
	to **be ashamed of sth** [bi ə'ʃeɪmd əv]	to feel bad about sth	*sich für etw schämen*
	to **feed sb** [fiːd]	to give sb food	*jdn ernähren*
	to **be unimpressed by sth** [bi ˌʌnɪm'prest baɪ]	to think sth is not very interesting or important	*sich von etw unbeeindruckt zeigen*
▸ page 67	**decent person** [ˌdiːsnt 'pɜːsn]	a good person	*anständiger Mensch*
	backyard [ˌbæk'jɑːd]	garden behind a house	*Garten (hinter dem Haus), Hof*
	to **shame sb** [ʃeɪm]	to make sb feel bad about themselves in public	*jdn an den Pranger stellen, jdn der Lächerlichkeit preisgeben*
	attitude (towards sth) ['ætɪtjuːd]	feeling or opinion about sth	*Einstellung (zu etw)*
	to **contribute to sth** [kən'trɪbjuːt tə]	to give sth to make sth else successful	*zu etw beitragen*
	to **be conflicted** [bi kən'flɪktɪd]	to have mixed feelings	*hin- und hergerissen sein, widersprüchliche Gefühle haben*
	author ['ɔːθə]	writer	*Autor/in, Verfasser/in*
	vivid ['vɪvɪd]	lively, captivating	*anschaulich, lebendig*
	tone [təʊn]	sound	*Tonfall, Ton*
	mood [muːd]	feeling, atmosphere	*Stimmung*
	humorous ['hjuːmərəs]	funny	*humorvoll, witzig*
	repetition [ˌrepə'tɪʃn]	when sth is said again and again	*Wiederholung*
	rhyme scheme ['raɪm skiːm]	pattern of words which sound the same	*Reimschema*
	stylistic device [staɪˌlɪstɪk dɪ'vaɪs]	way of writing	*Stilmittel*
	to **contain sth** [kən'teɪn]	to have sth inside	*etw enthalten*
	touching ['tʌtʃɪŋ]	emotional	*rührend, bewegend*

Topic 3 American and British political systems

▸ page 78/79

to **argue one's position fervently** [ˌɑːgjuː wʌnz pəˌzɪʃn ˈfɜːvntli]	to say one's opinion with passion	*den eigenen Standpunkt leidenschaftlich vertreten*
voter [ˈvəʊtə]	sb who states which political candidate they choose	*Wähler/in*
swing voter [ˈswɪŋ vəʊtə]	sb who has not yet decided who they will vote for	*Wechselwähler/in*
electoral system [ɪˈlektərəl sɪstəm]	system of rules for an election	*Wahlsystem*
election [ɪˈlekʃn]	choosing sb for a political office	*(Parlaments-, Präsidentschafts-)Wahl*
participation [pɑːˌtɪsɪˈpeɪʃn]	taking part in sth	*Teilnahme, Beteiligung*
presidential election [prezɪˌdenʃl ɪˈlekʃn]	choosing sb for president	*Präsidentschaftswahl*
share [ʃeə]	a part of sth	*Anteil*
eligible [ˈelɪdʒəbl]	having the right to vote	*wahlberechtigt*
to **cast a ballot** [ˌkɑːst ə ˈbælət]	to vote in an election	*die/seine (Wahl-)Stimme abgeben*
by contrast [baɪ ˈkɒntrɑːst]	compared to	*dagegen, im Gegensatz dazu*
turnout [ˈtɜːnaʊt]	the number of people who come to vote	*Wahlbeteiligung*
separation of powers [sepəˌreɪʃn əf ˈpaʊəz]	three branches of government	*Gewaltenteilung*
checks and balances *pl* [ˌtʃeks ənd ˈbælənsɪz]	control mechanism	*Kontrollmechanismen*
to **oblige sb to do sth** [əˈblaɪdʒ]	to force sb to do sth (by law)	*jdn (dazu) verpflichten, etw zu tun*
parliament [ˈpɑːləmənt]	group of elected politicians	*Parlament*
electorate [ɪˈlektərət]	the people who can vote in an election	*Wahlberechtigte pl, Wahlvolk*
referendum [ˌrefəˈrendəm]	a nationwide vote on a single question e.g. Brexit	*Volksabstimmung*
to **vote** [vəʊt]	to choose a political candidate or action	*abstimmen, stimmen, wählen, wählen gehen*
to **remain** [rɪˈmeɪn]	to stay	*bleiben*
contemporary issues *pl* [kənˌtemprəri ˈɪʃuːz]	current topics	*aktuelle Themen*
to **maintain sb/sth** [meɪnˈteɪn]	to support sb/sth financially	*jdn/etw (finanziell) unterhalten*
taxpayer [ˈtækspeɪə]	sb who pays money to the government	*Steuerzahler/in*
funding [ˈfʌndɪŋ]	money for a project	*Finanzierung, (finanzielle) Mittel*
to **generate money** [ˌdʒenəreɪt ˈmʌni]	to make/receive money	*Geld erwirtschaften*
annual(ly) [ˈænjuəl]	every year	*jährlich, pro Jahr*

Section A Political parties in the US

▸ page 80

to **be considered sth** [bi kənˈsɪdəd]	to be thought to be sth	*als etw gelten, als etw erachtet werden*
to **align with sth** [əˈlaɪn wɪð]	to agree with the ideas of sth	*mit etw übereinstimmen, sich hinter etw stellen*
to **stick to sth** [ˈstɪk tə]	to stay with sth	*an etw festhalten, bei etw bleiben*
belief [bɪˈliːf]	accepting that sth is true	*Überzeugung, Glaube*
to **deserve sth** [dɪˈzɜːv]	to earn sth, to have the right to sth	*etw verdienen*
health care [ˈhelθ keə]	medical services	*Gesundheitsfürsorge, Gesundheitswesen*

▸ page 81

to **imagine** [ɪˈmædʒɪn]	to picture sth in one's mind	*sich (etw) vorstellen*
foreigner [ˈfɒrənə]	sb from a different country	*Ausländer/in*
right to vote [ˌraɪt tə ˈvəʊt]	legal possibility to choose government officials	*Wahlrecht*

	minimum voting age [ˌmɪnɪməm ˈvəʊtɪŋ eɪdʒ]	e.g. 18 years old	*Mindestwahlalter*
	general election [ˌdʒenrəl ɪˈlekʃn]	choosing the government	*Parlamentswahl*
	to **lower sth** [ˈləʊə]	to reduce sth	*etw senken*
	loan [ləʊn]	money borrowed, e.g. from a bank	*Kredit, Darlehen*
	to **raise sth** [reɪz]	to increase sth	*etw* (Steuern usw.) *anheben*
	wall [wɔːl]	e.g. the Berlin Wall	*Mauer*
	along [əˈlɒŋ]	e.g. the cars drove along the street	*entlang*
	border [ˈbɔːdə]	e.g. the border between Germany and Poland	*Grenze*
	to **be required to do sth** [bi rɪˌkwaɪəd tə ˈduː]	to have to do sth	*etw* (aufgrund von Vorschriften) *tun müssen*
	measles *pl* [ˈmiːzlz]	dangerous childhood illness	*Masern*
	to **be pro-choice** [bi ˌprəʊ ˈtʃɔɪs]	to have the opinion that abortion is OK	*Abtreibungsbefürworter/in sein*
	to **implement sth** [ˈɪmplɪmənt]	to put sth in place, e.g. a new law	*etw* (Gesetz usw.) *einführen, etw umsetzen*
	to **slow sth down** [ˌsləʊ ˈdaʊn]	to make sth go slower	*etw bremsen, etw verlangsamen*
	to **limit sth** [ˈlɪmɪt]	to restrict sth	*etw beschränken, etw einschränken*
	offshore [ˌɒfˈʃɔː]	away from the coast, in the sea	*vor der Küste, auf dem Meer*
	oil drilling [ˈɔɪl drɪlɪŋ]	getting oil from under the earth's surface	*Ölbohrungen, Ölförderung*
	to **not be allowed to do sth** [nɒt bi əˈlaʊd tə duː]	to be forbidden to do sth	*etw nicht tun dürfen*
▸ page 82	**party affiliation** [ˈpɑːti əfɪlieɪʃn]	connection with a political party	*Parteizugehörigkeit*
	to **side with sb/sth** [ˈsaɪd wɪð]	to have the same opinion or beliefs as sb/sth	*sich hinter jdn/etw stellen, für jdn/etw Partei ergreifen*
	to **believe in sth** [bɪˈliːv ɪn]	to be sure about sth	*an etw glauben, von etw überzeugt sein*
	to **tackle sth** [ˈtækl]	to deal with sth, to fight sth	*etw bekämpfen*
	social inequality [ˌsəʊʃl ɪnɪˈkwɒləti]	unfairness in society	*soziale Ungerechtigkeit*
	social welfare [ˌsəʊʃl ˈwelfeə]	government services that help old/ill people	*Sozialhilfe*
	in need [ɪn ˈniːd]	needing help	*bedürftig*
	with regard to [wɪð rɪˈɡɑːd tə]	looking at, thinking about	*hinsichtlich, in puncto*
	abortion [əˈbɔːʃn]	ending a pregnancy	*Abtreibung*
	likely [ˈlaɪkli]	probably	*wahrscheinlich*
	marriage [ˈmærɪdʒ]	legal relationship between two adults	*Ehe*
	to **favour sth** [ˈfeɪvə]	to prefer sth	*etw favorisieren, für etw sein*
	to **interfere with sth** [ˌɪntəˈfɪə wɪð]	<> to leave sth alone	*sich in etw einmischen*
	bureaucracy [bjʊəˈrɒkrəsi]	official paperwork	*Bürokratie*
	inefficiency [ɪnɪˈfɪʃnsi]	doing sth slowly and expensively	*Ineffizienz, Schlendrian*
	law and order [ˌlɔː ənd ˈɔːdə]	e.g. the police maintain law and order	*Recht und Ordnung*
	to **take a tough stance towards sth** [teɪk ə ˌtʌf ˈstɑːns əgenst]	to take strong action against sth	*eine harte Haltung gegenüber etw einnehmen*

Section B The US electoral system

▸ page 83	to **boo** [buː]	to make a noise to show dislike	*buhen*
	citizenship [ˈsɪtɪznʃɪp]	e.g. German, Austrian, British, etc	*Staatsbürgerschaft*
	natural-born US citizen [nætʃərəl ˌbɔːn ˌjuː es ˈsɪtɪzn]	sb born in the USA	*US-Staatsbürger/in von Geburt*
	extensive [ɪkˈstensɪv]	far-reaching	*umfangreich*

ceremony ['serəməni]	special event	*Feier, Feierlichkeit(en), Zeremonie*
office ['ɒfɪs]	formal position in government	*Amt*
to **take office** [ˌteɪk 'ɒfɪs]	to begin an official job	*sein/ihr Amt antreten*
inauguration [ɪˌnɔːgjə'reɪʃn]	the formal beginning	*Einweihung, Amtseinführung*
party convention ['pɑːti kənvenʃn]	meeting of a political party	*Parteitag*
representative [ˌreprɪ'zentətɪv]	sb who officially speaks on behalf of a group of people, e.g. in parliament	*(Parlaments-)Abgeordnete/r*
cabinet ['kæbɪnət]	senior government ministers	*Kabinett*
Senate *AE* ['senət]	one of two chambers of the US parliament	*Senat*
House of Commons *BE* [ˌhaʊs əf 'kɒmənz]	one of two chambers of the British parliament	*Unterhaus*
first-time voter [ˌfɜːst taɪm 'vəʊtə]	sb who is over 18 and voting in their first election	*Erstwähler/in*
election process [ɪ'lekʃn prəʊses]	system of choosing persons for the government	*Wahlverfahren*
refresher [rɪ'freʃə]	reminder	*Auffrischung*
voting system ['vəʊtɪŋ sɪstəm]	process to choose the government	*Wahlsystem*
timeline ['taɪmlaɪn]	schedule	*Zeitplan*
primary ['praɪməri]	election to determine the presidential candidate	*Vorwahl*
National Convention *AE* [ˌnæʃnəl kən'venʃn]	event to nominate candidates for president and vice president	*Nominierungsparteitag*
event [ɪ'vent]	planned social occasion	*Ereignis, Veranstaltung*
Electoral College *AE* [ɪˌlektərəl 'kɒlɪdʒ]	group of people who represent the US states in the final presidential vote	*Wahlmännergremium*
swing state *AE* ['swɪŋ steɪt]	US state that has about the same number of supporters for both parties	US-Bundesstaat mit hohem Wechselwähleranteil
elector *AE* [ɪ'lektə]	sb who has the right to vote	*Wahlmann*
to **cast one's vote** [ˌkɑːst wʌnz 'vəʊt]	to vote in an election	*seine Stimme abgeben*
upcoming ['ʌpkʌmɪŋ]	soon to happen	*bevorstehend*
ambitious [æm'bɪʃəs]	wanting to succeed	*ehrgeizig*
to **campaign** [kæm'peɪn]	to try to win the election	*Wahlkampf machen*
funds *pl* [fʌndz]	money	*Gelder, (Geld-)Mittel*
to **raise funds** [ˌreɪz 'fʌndz]	to get money	*Geld sammeln, Mittel beschaffen*
campaign [kæm'peɪn]	an organized attempt to win an election	*Wahlkampf*
supporter [sə'pɔːtə]	sb who favours a political party	*Anhänger/in, Unterstützer/in*
to **select sb/sth** [sɪ'lekt]	to choose sb/sth	*jdn/etw auswählen*
presidential candidate [prezɪˌdenʃl 'kændɪdət]	sb who is campaigning to be president	*Präsidentschaftskandidat/in*
vice president [ˌvaɪs 'prezɪdənt]	the president's second-in-command	*Vizepräsident/in*
ballot (paper) ['bælət]	piece of paper for sb's vote	*Stimmzettel, Wahlzettel*
senator ['senətə]	member of the senate	*Senator/in*
election result [ɪ'lekʃn rɪzʌlt]	outcome of the election process	*Wahlergebnis*
to **depend on sth** [dɪ'pend ɒn]	e.g. What you can buy depends on the amount of money you have.	*von etw abhängen*
population [ˌpɒpju'leɪʃn]	number of people living in one place	*Bevölkerung*
populated ['pɒpjuleɪtɪd]	occupied, inhabited	*bevölkert*
to **lean (towards sth)** [liːn]	to have a tendency towards sth	*(zu etw) tendieren*
in order to [ɪn 'ɔːdə tə]	so that …	*um … zu*
nomination [ˌnɒmɪ'neɪʃn]	suggesting sb for a job	*Nominierung*
outcome ['aʊtkʌm]	the end result	*(Wahl-)Ergebnis, Resultat*

▸ page 84

	uncertain [ʌn'sɜːtn]	unclear	*unsicher*
▸ page 85	**nominee** [ˌnɒmɪ'niː]	sb who is put forward for a job	*Kandidat/in*
	ballot ['bælət]	voting secretly	*Wahl, Abstimmung*
	convincing(ly) [kən'vɪnsɪŋ]	believable(-ly)	*überzeugend*
▸ page 86	**delegate** ['delɪgət]	sb who represents others, e.g. in parliament	*Delegierte/r*
	to **learn sth** [lɜːn]	being told sth	*etw erfahren*
	to **form sth** [fɔːm]	to create sth	*etw bilden*
	to **appoint sb** [ə'pɔɪnt]	to give sb a job	*jdn ernennen*
	to **outline sth** ['aʊtlaɪn]	to summarize the main points	*etw darstellen, etw skizzieren*
▸ page 87	**despite** [dɪ'spaɪt]	e.g. I like him despite his shortcomings.	*trotz*
	it/that depends [ɪt/ðət dɪ'pendz]	e.g. Is the system fair? That depends on who you ask.	*es/das kommt darauf an*
	outdated [ˌaʊt'deɪtɪd]	old-fashioned	*antiquiert, veraltet*
	on a national level [ɒn ə ˌnæʃnəl 'levl]	regarding the country as a whole	*auf Landesebene, landesweit*
	national popular vote [ˌnæʃnəl ˌpɒpjələ 'vəʊt]	referendum	*landesweite Volksabstimmung*
	to **abolish sth** [ə'bɒlɪʃ]	to formally end sth	*etw abschaffen*
	to **run for president** [ˌrʌn fə 'prezɪdənt]	e.g. In 2008, Barack Obama ran for President and was elected.	*sich um die Präsidentschaft bewerben*
	confusing [kən'fjuːzɪŋ]	unclear	*verwirrend*
	to **end up empty-handed** [end ˌʌp ˌempti 'hændɪd]	to have nothing in the end	*am Ende mit leeren Händen dastehen*
	to **be on sb's mind** [bi ɒn 'maɪnd]	to think about sth	(Thema, Problem:) *jdn beschäftigen*
▸ page 88	**competitor** [kəm'petɪtə]	sb who takes part in a competition	*Mitbewerber/in*
	to **elect sb (sth)** [ɪ'lekt]	to choose sb for the government	*jdn (zu etw) wählen*
	voter registration ['vəʊtə redʒɪstreɪʃn]	citizens registering to be able to vote	*Wählerregistrierung*
	to **question sth** ['kwestʃən]	to doubt sth, to feel uncertain about sth	*etw in Frage stellen*
	to **serve a purpose** [ˌsɜːv ə 'pɜːpəs]	to exist for a reason	*einen Zweck erfüllen, zweckdienlich sein*
	legitimate [lɪ'dʒɪtɪmət]	right, acceptable, authorized	*legitim*
	binary choice [ˌbaɪnəri 'tʃɔɪs]	choosing between two possibilities	*Wahl zwischen zwei Möglichkeiten*
	appropriate (to sb) [ə'prəʊpriət]	correct (for sb)	*(jdm) angemessen, geeignet (für jdn)*

Section C Separation of powers in the US

▸ page 90	**executive branch** [ɪg'zekjətɪv brɑːntʃ]	branch of government that deals with law	*Exekutive*
	judicial branch [dʒu'dɪʃl brɑːntʃ]	branch of government that deals with justice	*Judikative*
	judiciary [dʒu'dɪʃəri]	system of law courts	*Judikative*
	legislative branch ['ledʒɪslətɪv brɑːntʃ]	branch of government that makes new laws	*Legislative*
	Supreme Court *AE* [suˌpriːm 'kɔːt]	the highest law court in the US	*Oberster Gerichtshof*
	branches *pl* **of government** [ˌbrɑːntɪz əv 'gʌvənmənt]	divisions of the government	*die (drei) Gewalten, staatliche Organe*
	as opposed to [əz ə'pəʊzd tə]	rather than, instead of	*im Gegensatz zu*
	constitution [ˌkɒnstɪ'tjuːʃn]	central legal document of a country	*Verfassung*
▸ page 91	to **adopt sth** [ə'dɒpt]	to take sth on	*etw annehmen, etw verabschieden*
	power ['paʊə]	influence	*Macht, Einfluss*
	to **declare sth** [dɪ'kleə]	to make sth known	*etw erklären*

to **be in force** [bi ɪn 'fɔːs]	to be used, to be effective	*in Kraft sein*	
legislature ['ledʒɪsleɪtʃə]	group of people or institutions who make and change laws	*Legislative*	
to **be supposed to do sth** [bi sə'pəʊzd tə du]	to be intended/expected to do sth	*etw (eigentlich) tun sollen*	
to **approve sth** [ə'pruːv]	to accept or allow sth	*etw genehmigen*	
federal ['fedərəl]	e.g. Federal Republic of Germany	*Bundes-*	
judge [dʒʌdʒ]	e.g. sb has to appear in court before a judge	*Richter/in*	
to **exercise a right** [ˌeksəsaɪz ə 'raɪt]	e.g. I exercised my democratic rights by voting in the election.	*von einem Recht Gebrauch machen*	
to **refuse** [rɪ'fjuːz]	<> to accept sth	*sich weigern*	
to **veto sth** ['viːtəʊ]	to reject sth	*ein Veto gegen etw einlegen*	
to **advise sb on sth** [əd'vaɪz ɒn]	to recommend what to do	*jdm bei etw beraten*	
area of policy [ˌeəriə əf 'pɒləsi]	e.g. economy, foreign relations, defence, finance	*Politikfeld, Politikbereich*	
commander-in-chief [kəˌmaːndər ɪn 'tʃiːf]	sb responsible for all the armed forces	*Oberbefehlshaber/in*	
armed forces *pl* [ˌɑːmd 'fɔːsɪz]	e.g. army, navy, airforce	*Streitkräfte*	
declaration of war [dekləˌreɪʃn əv 'wɔː]	a formal statement saying that one country is at war with another	*Kriegserklärung*	
to **order sth** ['ɔːdə]	to say that sth must happen	*etw befehlen, etw anordnen*	
unconstitutional [ˌʌnˌkɒnstɪ'tjuːʃənl]	not allowed by a country's laws	*nicht verfassungsgemäß*	
to **forbid** [fə'bɪd]	<> to permit, allow	*verbieten, untersagen*	
in a nutshell [ɪn ə 'nʌtʃel]	in summary	*kurz gesagt, kurz zusammengefasst*	
powerful ['paʊəfl]	having great influence	*mächtig, einflussreich*	
military forces *pl* [ˌmɪlətri' fɔːsɪz]	e.g. army, navy, airforce	*Streitkräfte*	▸ page 92
to **check sb/sth** [tʃek]	to inspect sb/sth, to examine sb/sth	*jdn/etw kontrollieren, jdn/etw in Schach halten*	
veto power ['viːtəʊ paʊə]	the possibility to refuse sth e.g. a law	*Vetorecht*	
to **pass a law** [ˌpɑːs ə 'lɔː]	e.g. the government passed a law that made texting while driving illegal	*ein Gesetz verabschieden*	
to **nominate sb** ['nɒmɪneɪt]	to suggest sb for election	*jdn nominieren*	
federal official [ˌfedərəl ə'fɪʃl]	national-level civil servant	*Bundesbeamte/r*	
legislation [ˌledʒɪs'leɪʃn]	law-making	*Gesetze, Gesetzgebung*	
federal court [ˌfedərəl 'kɔːt]	law court dealing with state law	*Bundesgericht*	
obviously ['ɒbviəsli]	naturally, of course	*natürlich*	
to **be to one's liking** [bi tu wʌnz 'laɪkɪŋ]	to think sth is good, to fit to one's taste	*jdm zusagen, nach jds Geschmack sein*	
to **be in line with sth** [bɪ ˌɪn 'laɪn wɪð]	to have the same opinion about sth	*mit etw übereinstimmen*	
to **impact sth** [ɪm'pækt]	to have an influence on sth	*Auswirkungen auf etw haben*	
to **remove sb from office** [rɪˌmuːv frəm 'ɒfɪs]	to force sb to leave an official position	*jdn des Amtes entheben, jdn absetzen*	
court case ['kɔːt keɪs]	legal action	*Gerichtsverfahren*	
to **gather evidence** [ˌgæðər 'evɪdəns]	to collect proof	*Beweismaterial sammeln*	
the jury [ðə 'dʒʊəri]	twelve people who decide the outcome of a legal action	*die Geschworenen*	
to **regulate** ['regjuleɪt]	to bring under control	*regulieren, steuern*	▸ page 93
to **express sth** [ɪk'spres]	to tell sb what one thinks	*etw ausdrücken*	
obligation [ˌɒblɪ'geɪʃn]	sth that sb must do	*Verpflichtung*	
permission [pə'mɪʃn]	being allowed to do sth	*Erlaubnis*	
either ['aɪðə]	one and the other of two things	*jede/r (von beiden)*	

Section D Houses of Parliament and the UK

▸ page 94

authority [ɔː'θɒrəti]	institution or person having the power to make commands, decisions, etc	*Instanz*
monarch ['mɒnək]	e.g. Queen Elizabeth II of England, King Harald V of Norway	*Monarch/in*
the commons *pl BE* [ðə 'kɒmənz]	<> peers	*der dritte Stand (freie Bauern und Bürger)*
to **call a meeting** [ˌkɔːl ə 'miːtɪŋ]	to organize a meeting, gathering	*eine Versammlung einberufen*
to **collect taxes** [kəˌlekt 'tæksɪz]	to get money from citizens to pay for public services	*Steuern eintreiben*
in return [ɪn rɪ'tɜːn]	as an exchange	*als Gegenleistung, im Gegenzug*
ceremonial [ˌserɪ'məʊniəl]	<> informal, unofficial	*zeremoniell*
duty ['djuːti]	responsibility, sth one must do	*Aufgabe, Pflicht*
House of Lords *BE* [ˌhaʊs əv 'lɔːdz]	unelected members of the British government	*Oberhaus*
to **delay sth** [dɪ'leɪ]	to do sth at a later time	*etw aufschieben, etw aufhalten*
bishop ['bɪʃəp]	senior member of the church	*Bischof/Bischöfin*
peer *BE* [pɪə]	British nobility	Angehörige/r des brit. Hochadels
hereditary [hə'redɪtri]	given by parent to child	*erblich*
to **inherit sth** [ɪn'herɪt]	to get sth after the owner of it has died	*etw erben*
constituency [kən'stɪtjuənsi]	voting area	*Wahlkreis*
nuclear weapons *pl* [ˌnjuːkliə 'wepənz]	atomic bombs, missiles, etc	*Kernwaffen*
federal country [ˌfedərəl 'kʌntri]	a nation made of separate states with their own political control	*Bundesstaat*
Time will tell. [ˌtaɪm wɪl 'tel]	We will know the results after some time has passed.	*Die Zeit wird es zeigen.*
chamber (of parliament) ['tʃeɪmbə]	e.g. House of Commons, House of Lords, Bundestag, Bundesrat	*Kammer, Haus (des Parlaments)*
administration [ədˌmɪnɪ'streɪʃn]	government, management of public affairs	*Regierung, Verwaltung*
devolution [ˌdiːvə'luːʃn]	decentralizing political power	*Dezentralisierung, Übertragung von Amtsgewalt*
to **devolve** [dɪ'vɒlv]	to transfer power to a lower level	(Amtsgewalt) *übertragen*
civil servant *BE* [ˌsɪvl 'sɜːvənt]	government official	*Beamte/-in*
Court of Appeal *BE* [ˌkɔːt əv ə'piːl]	a court that reviews past decisions about legal cases	*Berufungsgericht*

▸ page 95

the Hebrides *pl* [ðə 'hebrɪdiːz]	group of Islands on the coast of Scotland	*die Hebriden*

Section E Political parties and voting system in the UK

▸ page 96

to **register** ['redʒɪstə]	to put one's name on an official list	*sich anmelden, sich registrieren lassen*
required by law [rɪˌkwaɪəd baɪ 'lɔː]	e.g. if sb drives a car, that person is required by law to have a driver's license	*gesetzlich vorgeschrieben*
fine [faɪn]	money paid as a punishment	*Geldstrafe*
to **do community service** [du ˌkə'mjuːnəti sɜːvɪs]	unpaid work that helps a community, often as punishment	*Sozialstunden leisten*
prime minister [ˌpraɪm 'mɪnɪstə]	British head of government	*Premierminister/in*
committee [kə'mɪti]	official group of people who do particular work	*Gremium, Komitee*

polling station *BE* ['pəʊlɪŋ steɪʃn]	place to vote on election day	*Wahllokal*	
to **call an election** [ˌkɔːl ən ɪ'lekʃn]	to set a date for an election	*eine Wahl ansetzen*	▸ page 97
vote of no confidence [ˌvəʊt əv ˌnəu 'kɒnfɪdəns]	vote that shows the majority of people do not support the leader	*Misstrauensvotum*	
MP (Member of Parliament) *BE* [ˌem 'piː]	politician elected for a certain area	*(Parlaments-)Abgeordnete/r*	
by proxy [baɪ 'prɒksi]	permission given to sb to do sth e.g. vote for sb else	*durch einen Bevollmächtigten*	
to **represent sb** [ˌreprɪ'zent]	to be the deputy for sb	*jdn vertreten, jdn repräsentieren*	
association [əˌsəʊsi'eɪʃn]	group of people with the same purpose	*Vereinigung, Bund*	
to **shift away from sth** [ˌʃɪft ə'weɪ frəm]	to move/go away from sth slowly	*von etw abrücken*	▸ page 98
free movement [ˌfriː 'muːvmənt]	being able to move around without borders	*Freizügigkeit*	
tuition fees *pl* [tju'ɪʃn fiːz]	money paid for education	*Studiengebühren*	
free of charge [ˌfriː əf 'tʃɑːdʒ]	at no cost	*kostenlos*	
to **call for sth** ['kɔːl fə]	to demand that sth happens	*etw fordern*	
foreign aid [ˌfɒrən 'eɪd]	money paid to other countries for development	*Entwicklungshilfe*	
incentive [ɪn'sentɪv]	sth that encourages sb to do sth	*Anreiz*	

Section F The British monarchy

monarchy ['mɒnəki]	e.g. queens, kings, etc	*Monarchie*	▸ page 99
royal ['rɔɪəl]	being a king or queen	*königlich, Königs-*	
family tree [ˌfæməli 'triː]	diagram showing the members of a family	*Stammbaum*	
to **picture sb/sth** ['pɪktʃə]	to draw/illustrate sb/sth	*jdn/etw abbilden*	
to **head to sth** ['hed tə]	to go towards a destination	*sich auf den Weg zu etw machen*	
to **step down** [ˌstep 'daʊn]	to resign	*zurücktreten*	
senior ['siːniə]	high level	*hochrangig*	
to **earn one's (own) living** [ˌɜːn wʌnz 'lɪvɪŋ]	to make money to support oneself	*seinen (eigenen) Lebensunterhalt verdienen*	
public service [ˌpʌblɪk 'sɜːvɪs]	doing things for the benefit of all	*Dienst an der Allgemeinheit*	
charitable ['tʃærətəbl]	assisting people in need	*gemeinnützig, karitativ*	
to **strengthen sth** ['streŋθn]	to make sth stronger	*etw stärken*	
unity ['juːnəti]	<> divided	*Einheit*	
host [həʊst]	<> guest	*Gastgeber/in*	
reception [rɪ'sepʃn]	formal occasion	*Empfang*	
to **chair sth** [tʃeə]	to be the head of a meeting, etc	*den Vorsitz von etw innehaben, einer Sache vorstehen*	
to **appear** [ə'pɪə]	to be seen somewhere	*auftreten, erscheinen*	
to **give a speech** [ˌgɪv ə 'spiːtʃ]	to speak in front of an audience	*eine Rede halten*	
to **present an award** [prɪˌzent ən ə'wɔːd]	to hand over a prize	*einen Preis überreichen*	
head of state [ˌhed əf 'steɪt]	e.g. Queen, President, etc	*Staatsoberhaupt*	
whereas [ˌweər'æz]	compared to, although	*während*	
to **consult sb** [kən'sʌlt]	to turn to sb for advice	*jdn zu Rate ziehen, jdn konsultieren*	
parliamentary session [pɑːləˌmentri 'seʃn]	when the government meets to make laws	*Legislaturperiode*	
to **be limited to sth** [bi 'lɪmɪtɪd tə]	<> to have total freedom	*auf etw beschränkt sein*	▸ page 100

	to **raise a question** [ˌreɪz ə 'kwestʃən]	to bring up a point of discussion	*eine Frage aufwerfen*
	to **bear sth** [beə]	to carry sth	*etw* (Kosten usw.) *tragen, für etw aufkommen*
	expense [ɪk'spens]	cost(s)	*(finanzieller) Aufwand, Kosten*
	to **estimate** ['estɪmeɪt]	to guess or calculate costs, etc	*schätzen*
	figure ['fɪgə]	number	*Zahl, Ziffer*
	to **make up one's mind** [meɪk ˌʌp wʌnz 'maɪnd]	to come to a decision	*sich entscheiden*
	provided [prə'vaɪdɪd]	under certain conditions	*unter der Voraussetzung, dass*
	as a consequence [əz ə 'kɒnsɪkwəns]	following on, therefore	*folglich, demzufolge*
	concession [kən'seʃn]	sth given in response to demands	*Zugeständnis*
	to **guess** [ges]	to form an opinion	*vermuten*
▸ page 101	**schedule** ['ʃedjuːl]	time plan	*Terminkalender*
	to **delegate sth** ['delɪgeɪt]	to give work to sb else	*etw delegieren*
	blog entry ['blɒg entri]	sth posted online	*Blog-Eintrag, -Beitrag*
	to **claim sth** [kleɪm]	to say that sth is true	*etw behaupten*
	to **bully sb** ['bʊli]	to be a tyrant to sb	*jdn mobben, jdn tyrannisieren*
	tear [tɪə]	water from sb's eye	*Träne*
	invasion of privacy [ɪnˌveɪʒn əf 'prɪvəsi]	failure to respect sb's personal information	*Verletzung der Privatsphäre*
	tabloid ['tæblɔɪd]	yellow press	*Boulevardzeitung, Massenblatt*
	the tabloids *pl* [ðə 'tæblɔɪdz]	e.g. The Sun, News of the World	*die Boulevardpresse*

Topic 4 The media

▸ page 110/111	**cure (for sth)** [kjʊə]	e.g. vaccination, medicine, etc	*Heilmittel (für etw), Rezept (gegen etw)*
	to **eliminate sth** [ɪ'lɪmɪneɪt]	to kill sth, to delete sth	*etw beseitigen, etw eliminieren*
	character ['kærəktə]	letter or number	*Buchstabe, Zeichen*
	a fair amount [ə ˌfeər ə'maʊnt]	quite a lot	*ziemlich viel …, nicht unerhebliche Menge*
	bias ['baɪəs]	tendency towards sth	*Voreingenommenheit, Tendenz*
	coverage ['kʌvərɪdʒ]	how much the media deals with a topic	*Berichterstattung*
	tribe [traɪb]	sb's people	*(Volks-)Stamm*
	rubbish ['rʌbɪʃ]	garbage, nonsense	*Unsinn, Quatsch*
	data protection ['deɪtə prətekʃn]	safety of personal information online	*Datenschutz*
	gateway drug ['geɪtweɪ drʌg]	sth that leads to sth else that is far more dangerous	*Einstiegsdroge*
	as it were [əz ɪt 'wɜː]	so to speak	*sozusagen, wenn man so will*
	expression [ɪk'spreʃn]	a way of saying sth	*Ausdruck*

Section A Screen time

▸ page 112	**sin** [sɪn]	doing sth very bad	*Sünde*
	caps *pl* [kæps]	e.g. A B C D	*Großbuchstaben*
	to **gossip about sb** ['gɒsɪp əbaʊt]	to talk about sb when they are not there	*über jdn ablästern*
	straight away [ˌstreɪt ə'weɪ]	immediately	*sofort*
	caption ['kæpʃn]	writing under a picture that explains it	*Bildunterschrift*
	to **read** [riːd]	e.g. the sign reads 'No smoking'	*lauten*
▸ page 113	to **admit sth** [əd'mɪt]	to tell sth about oneself	*etw zugeben, etw eingestehen*
	annoyed [ə'nɔɪd]	irritated	*genervt*
	addiction [ə'dɪkʃn]	e.g. an addiction to alcohol, heroin, etc	*Sucht*
	a bunch of [ə 'bʌntʃ əv]	a lot of	*ein Haufen*
	addict ['ædɪkt]	e.g. a smoker, meth user	*Süchtige/r*

kitten ['kɪtn]	baby cat	*Kätzchen*	
puppy ['pʌpi]	baby dog	*Welpe*	
proper ['prɒpə]	correct, right	*richtig, ordentlich*	
to **mute sth** [mjuːt]	to shut off sth's sound	*etw stummschalten*	
to **be addicted to sth** [bi ə'dɪktɪd tə]	to be unable to stop using sth e.g. drugs	*nach etw süchtig sein, von etw abhängig sein*	
to **be addictive** [bi ə'dɪktɪv]	to make sb unable to stop using it	*süchtig machen*	

Section B The news

to **trust sb/sth** [trʌst]	to believe sb/sth is truthful and accurate	*jdm/einer Sache vertrauen*	▸ page 114
responsibility to(wards) sb/sth [rɪˌspɒnsə'bɪləti tə]	having a duty to deal with sb/sth	*Verantwortung jdm/einer Sache gegenüber*	
freedom of the press [ˌfriːdəm əv ðə 'pres]	the right to publish information	*Pressefreiheit*	
broadcaster ['brɔːdkɑːstə]	radio or TV station	*(Radio-/TV-)Sender*	
to **consider sth** [kən'sɪdə]	to think about sth	*etw berücksichtigen, auf etw achten*	
accurate(ly) ['ækjərət]	correct(ly)	*(genau) zutreffend*	
news broadcaster ['njuːz brɔːdkɑːstə]	radio or TV station that brings news to the public	*Nachrichtensender*	
broadly speaking ['brɔːdli spiːkɪŋ]	generally	*grob gesagt, vereinfacht gesagt*	▸ page 115
to **be significant** [bi sɪg'nɪfɪkənt]	to be important, to be relevant	*von Bedeutung sein*	
to **affect sb/sth** [ə'fekt]	to make a difference to sb/sth	*jdn/etw betreffen*	
leader ['liːdə]	important politician	*führende/r Politiker/in*	
to **be factually correct** [bi ˌfæktʃuəli kə'rekt]	to be true and accurate	*den Tatsachen entsprechen*	
free speech [ˌfriː 'spiːtʃ]	the right to express opinions without censorship	*freie Meinungsäußerung*	
furthermore [ˌfɜːðə'mɔː]	additionally, as well	*außerdem, darüber hinaus*	
code of ethics [ˌkəʊd əv 'eθɪks]	rules on how to behave professionally	*Verhaltenskodex*	
reporting [rɪ'pɔːtɪŋ]	writing or speaking about sth one has seen or heard	*Bereichterstattung*	
public service broadcaster [ˌpʌblɪk sɜːvɪs 'brɔːdkɑːstə]	information service that is funded by the state, e.g. BBC, ARD	*öffentlich-rechtlicher Sender*	
to **fund sth** [fʌnd]	to finance sth	*etw finanzieren*	
in favour of sb/sth [ɪn 'feɪvər əv]	to prefer sb/sth	*zugunsten von jdm/etw*	
unbiased [ˌʌn'baɪəst]	neutral, fair	*unvoreingenommen, neutral*	
to **be up to sth** [bi 'ʌp tə]	to do sth, to intend to do sth	*etw anstellen, etw machen, etw vorhaben*	
to **track sth** [træk]	to follow sth	*etw (nach)verfolgen*	
viewpoint ['vjuːpɔɪnt]	perspective	*Blickwinkel, Perspektive*	
sb misses out on sth [ˌmɪsɪz 'aʊt ɒn]	sb doesn't get sth	*jdm entgeht etw*	
quality press ['kwɒləti pres]	serious newspapers or newsfeeds	*seriöse Zeitungen/Zeitschriften*	
imperative [ɪm'perətɪv]	extremely important	*zwingend erforderlich*	
posh [pɒʃ]	high-class	*nobel, vornehm*	▸ page 116
barely ['beəli]	only just	*gerade so, gerade noch*	
to **alert sb** [ə'lɜːt]	to make sb aware of sth	*jdn alarmieren*	
briefly ['briːfli]	for/in a short time	*kurzzeitig*	
investigator [ɪn'vestɪgeɪtə]	inspector, examiner, detective	*Ermittler/in*	
fault [fɔːlt]	defect, problem	*Defekt, Störung*	
to **account for sth** [ə'kaʊnt fə]	to make up (a certain proportion of) sth	*etw* (Anteil usw.) *ausmachen*	

	funding cuts *pl* ['fʌndɪŋ kʌts]	less money for a company or government to spend	*Mittelkürzungen*
	space probe ['speɪs prəʊb]	unmanned spacecraft which gets information about space	*Weltraumsonde*
	discovery [dɪ'skʌvəri]	sth new that has been found	*Entdeckung*
▸ page 117	to **spot sth** [spɒt]	to discover or recognize sth	*etw erkennen, etw entdecken*
	to **locate sb/sth** [ləʊ'keɪt]	to find the exact place/position of sb/sth	*etw/jdn ausfindig machen*
	to **reference sth** ['refərəns]	to mention sth, to cite sth	*auf etw verweisen, etw zitieren*
	unless [ən'les]	on the condition that sth does not happen	*außer wenn*
	to **be in on sth** [bi 'ɪn ɒn]	to know about a secret	*über etw Bescheid wissen*
	credible ['kredəbl]	<> incredible, unbelievable	*glaubwürdig*
	to **discredit sb/sth** [dɪs'kredɪt]	to show that sb/sth is not legitimate	*jdn/etw diskreditieren*
	invalid [ɪn'vælɪd]	<> valid	*gegenstandslos, hinfällig*
	valid ['vælɪd]	correct, authentic	*gültig, stichhaltig, berechtigt*
	publication [ˌpʌblɪ'keɪʃn]	making information known	*Veröffentlichung*
	to **look past sth** [ˌlʊk 'pɑːst]	to ignore sth, to not consider sth	*über etw hinwegsehen*
	misleading [ˌmɪs'liːdɪŋ]	confusing, false	*irreführend*
	to **detect sth** [dɪ'tekt]	to find sth out, to spot sth	*etw aufspüren, etw erkennen*
	disinformation [ˌdɪsɪnfə'meɪʃn]	lies, dishonesty	*Desinformation*
	deliberate(ly) [dɪ'lɪbərət]	on purpose	*absichtlich, vorsätzlich*
	misinformation [ˌmɪsɪnfə'meɪʃn]	misleading facts	*Fehlinformation*
	to **be intended to do sth** [bi ɪn'tendɪd tə duː]	to have plans to do sth	*dazu/dafür gedacht sein, etw zu tun*
	rumour ['ruːmə]	unconfirmed information	*Gerücht*
	exaggeration [ɪɡˌzædʒə'reɪʃn]	over the top description	*Übertreibung*
	misinterpretation [ˌmɪsɪntɜːprɪ'teɪʃn]	misunderstanding	*Fehlinterpretation*
	to **provoke sb** [prə'vəʊk]	to make sb have a feeling or do sth	*jdn provozieren*
	to **verify** ['verɪfaɪ]	to find out if sth is true	*etw überprüfen, etw verifizieren*
▸ page 118	to **arrest sb** [ə'rest]	(for the police) to stop sb	*jdn verhaften*
	crime [kraɪm]	e.g. murder, stealing, etc	*Straftat, Verbrechen*
	astonished [ə'stɒnɪʃt]	shocked, amazed	*erstaunt*
	diner ['daɪnə]	restaurant guest	*Gast (in einem Restaurant)*
	to **release sb** [rɪ'liːs]	to let sb go free	*jdn auf freien Fuß setzen*
	warning ['wɔːnɪŋ]	official statement telling sb they did sth wrong	*Verwarnung*
	to **insult sb** [ɪn'sʌlt]	to say bad things to sb	*jdn beleidigen, jdn beschimpfen*
	to **swear at sb** ['sweər ət]	to curse at sb	*jdn anpöbeln, jdn beschimpfen*
	to **separate sb/sth** ['sepəreɪt]	to move sb/sth apart	*jdn/etw (voneinander) trennen*
	bad language [ˌbæd 'læŋɡwɪdʒ]	<> polite language	*Schimpfwörter*
	see-through ['siːθruː]	transparent	*durchsichtig*
	apparently [ə'pærəntli]	so it seems	*anscheinend*
	to **prevent sb/sth from doing sth** [prɪ'vent frəm]	to stop sb/sth from doing sth	*jdn/etw daran hindern, etw zu tun*
	public facilities *pl* [ˌpʌblɪk fə'sɪlətiz]	public toilet	*öffentliche Toiletten*
	to **relocate** [riːləʊ'keɪt]	to move to a different place to live	*umziehen*
	scheme [skiːm]	programme	*Programm*
	to **commission sth** [kə'mɪʃn]	to pay money for a project	*etw in Auftrag geben*

conspiracy theorist [kən'spɪrəsi θɪərɪst]	sb who believes in conspiracies	*Verschwörungstheoretiker/in*	► page 119
conspiracy theory [kən'spɪrəsi θɪəri]	e.g. the government controls our minds with radio waves	*Verschwörungstheorie*	
to **do harm to sb/sth** [ˌduː 'hɑːm tə]	to hurt sb/sth	*jdm/einer Sache Schaden zufügen*	
to **block sth off** [ˌblɒk 'ɒf]	to cover or close sth so nothing can move through	*etw absperren*	
unannounced [ˌʌnə'naʊnst]	<> expected	*unangekündigt*	
to **get caught up in sth** [get ˌkɔːt 'ʌp ɪn]	to be in the middle of sth	*in etw geraten*	
to **kidnap sb** ['kɪdnæp]	to steal a person	*jdn entführen*	
to **abuse sb** [ə'bjuːz]	to handle sb in a cruel way	*jdn misshandeln*	
jail [dʒeɪl]	prison	*Gefängnis*	
to **cover sth up** [ˌkʌvər 'ʌp]	to make it look like sth bad didn't happen	*etw vertuschen*	
Shame on you! [ˌʃeɪm ɒn 'juː]	That was a very bad thing to do!	*Schämen Sie sich! Schäm dich!*	
to **approach sth** [ə'prəʊtʃ]	to go closer to sth	*sich einer Sache nähern*	
demonstrator ['demənstreɪtə]	e.g. sb participating in Fridays for Future	*Demonstrant/in*	
mass arrest [ˌmæs ə'rest]	many people caught by the police	*Massenverhaftung*	
plot [plɒt]	secret plan	*Komplott*	
key figure [ˌkiː 'fɪgə]	the most important person	*Schlüsselfigur*	
alleged(ly) [ə'ledʒd]	maybe this happened …	*angeblich*	
celebrity [sə'lebrəti]	famous person	*Prominente/r*	
to **shut sth down** [ˌʃʌt 'daʊn]	to stop sth happening	*etw stillegen*	
to **spread** [spred]	to cover a wider area	*sich verbreiten*	
pandemic [pæn'demɪk]	e.g. Covid-19	*Pandemie*	
hoax [həʊks]	joke, swindle	*Täuschung, Schwindel*	
to **spread sth** [spred]	to put sth everywhere	*etw verbreiten*	
evidence ['evɪdəns]	facts or information that show if sth is true or not	*Beleg(e), Beweis(e)*	
owner ['əʊnə]	sb who has property, things	*Inhaber/in, Besitzer/in*	
death threat ['deθ θret]	a promise to kill sb	*Morddrohung*	
to **commit a crime** [kəˌmɪt ə 'kraɪm]	e.g. to murder sb, to steal sth	*ein Verbrechen / eine Straftat begehen*	
financial support [faɪˌnænʃl sə'pɔːt]	help in the form of money	*finanzielle Unterstützung*	
spread [spred]	how far sth has grown or increased	*Ausbreitung, Verbreitung*	
to **combat sth** ['kɒmbæt]	to fight sth	*etw bekämpfen*	
if so ['ɪf səʊ]	in this case	*falls ja*	

Section C Social media activism and finding your tribe online

animal welfare [ˌænɪml 'welfeə]	animal rights and protection	*Tierwohl*	► page 120
rule [ruːl]	control over an area or people	*Herrschaft*	
civil rights *pl* [ˌsɪvl 'raɪts]	social freedom and equality	*Bürgerrechte*	
equality [ɪ'kwɒləti]	each person having the same rights and freedom	*Gleichstellung, Gleichberechtigung*	
to **engage with sb** [ɪn'geɪdʒ wɪð]	to talk to and try to understand sb	*mit jdm ins Gespräch kommen, auf jdn zugehen*	
audience ['ɔːdiəns]	people who watch or listen	*Zielgruppe, Publikum*	
armchair ['ɑːmtʃeə]	comfortable chair	*Sessel*	
to praise sb/sth [preɪz]	e.g. Congratulations – well done!	*jdn/etw loben*	► page 121
to **speak up for sb** [ˌspiːk 'ʌp fə]	to show support for sb	*für jdn eintreten, sich für jdn stark machen*	

	poverty ['pɒvəti]	being extremely poor	*Armut*
	food bank ['fu:d bæŋk]	a place where food is given out for free	*Lebensmitteltafel*
	to **take action** [ˌteɪk 'ækʃn]	to do sth about a problem	*Maßnahmen ergreifen*
	to **progress** [prə'gres]	to move forward	*vorankommen, Fortschritte machen*
	to **be critical of sth** [bi 'krɪtɪkl əv]	to question sth, to say sth is not OK	*etw kritisch sehen*
	to **turn violent** [ˌtɜ:n 'vaɪələnt]	to become damaging and forceful	*in Gewalt umschlagen*
	disability [ˌdɪsə'bɪləti]	physical or mental handicap	*Behinderung, Beeinträchtigung*
	crutches *pl* ['krʌtʃɪz]	sticks to help sb walk	*Krücken*
	humanity [hju:'mænəti]	compassion, kindness	*(die) Menschheit*
	dignity ['dɪgnəti]	worthy of honour or respect	*Würde*
	from all walks of life [frəm ˌɔ:l wɔ:ks əv 'laɪf]	from every part of society	*aus allen Gesellschaftsschichten*
	to **engage in sth** [ɪn'geɪdʒ ɪn]	to be involved in sth	*sich für etw engagieren*
	to **be conscious of sth** [bi 'kɒnʃəs əv]	to think about sth	*sich einer Sache bewusst sein*
	downside ['daʊnsaɪd]	negative aspect	*Nachteil*
▸ page 122	**lifeline** ['laɪflaɪn]	escape from a difficult situation	*Rettungsanker*
	to **criticize sb/sth** ['krɪtɪsaɪz]	to say sb/sth has done the wrong thing	*jdn/etw kritisieren*
	anti-social [ˌæntɪ'səʊʃl]	acting in a way that causes anger in others	*unsozial, asozial*
	to **judge sb** [dʒʌdʒ]	to form an opinion about sb, usually negative	*jdn beurteilen, jdn verurteilen*
	to **rant** [rænt]	to speak/write in an uncontrolled, angry way	*losschimpfen*
	barely ['beəli]	almost not	*kaum*
	to **struggle with sth** ['stʌgl wɪð]	to have a problem with sth	*mit etw zu kämpfen haben*
	to **turn to sb** ['tɜ:n tə]	to ask sb for help	*sich an jdn wenden*
	to **come out to sb** [ˌkʌm 'aʊt tə]	to tell sb that one is LGBTQ	*sich gegenüber jdm outen*
	to **humiliate sb** [hju:'mɪlieɪt]	to make sb feel ashamed and foolish	*jdn demütigen*
	to **reject sb** [rɪ'dʒekt]	<> to accept sb	*jdn abweisen, jdn verstoßen*
	turning point ['tɜ:nɪŋ pɔɪnt]	moment when sth changes	*Wendepunkt*
	counsellor ['kaʊnsələ]	therapist, adviser	*Berater/in, Therapeut/in*
	courage ['kʌrɪdʒ]	having strength in a difficult time	*Mut*
	confidence ['kɒnfɪdəns]	feeling sure of oneself	*Selbstvertrauen*
	bully ['bʊli]	sb who hurts or intimidates others	*Mobber/in*
	victim ['vɪktɪm]	sb who is hurt or injured by others	*Opfer*
	to **educate sb** ['edʒukeɪt]	to teach sb, to inform sb	*jdn aufklären, jdn informieren*
	visible ['vɪzəbl]	can be seen	*sichtbar*
	permanent ['pɜ:mənənt]	definite, lasting	*unbefristet, fest*
	hidden ['hɪdn]	unseen	*verborgen*
▸ page 123	to **perform sth** [pə'fɔ:m]	to present sth	*etw aufführen, etw spielen*
	solely ['səʊlli]	only, singularly	*ausschließlich, nur*
	to **insist on sth** [ɪn'sɪst ɒn]	to not take no for an answer	*auf etw bestehen*

Section D How we portray ourselves online

▸ page 124	to **portray sb** [pɔ:'treɪ]	to show/describe sb in a particular way	*jdn darstellen, jdn porträtieren*
	well-deserved [ˌwel dɪ'zɜ:vd]	e.g. her reputation was well-deserved	*wohlverdient*
	energizing ['enədʒaɪzɪŋ]	bringing liveliness	*belebend*
	to **lift weights** [ˌlɪft 'weɪts]	to raise heavy objects for sport	*Gewichte heben*
	toned [təʊnd]	well-trained, with defined muscles	*durchtrainiert*
	disposable [dɪ'spəʊzəbl]	sth that can be thrown away	*Einweg-*
	to **pretend** [prɪ'tend]	to act as if sth is real when it is not	*vorgeben; so tun, als ob*

caring ['keərɪŋ]	kind, nice	*fürsorglich*	
24/7 [twenti,fɔː 'sevn]	day and night	*rund um die Uhr*	
precious ['preʃəs]	valuable	*wertvoll*	
to **edit sth** ['edɪt]	to cut out text	*etw* (Text usw.) *bearbeiten*	
unlovable [ʌn'lʌvəbl]	<> lovable	*nicht liebenswert*	
to **approve of sb/sth** [ə'pruːv əv]	to think sb/sth is good, worthwhile	*jdn/etw akzeptieren*	
sb feels strongly about sth [ˌfiːlz 'strɒŋgli əbaʊt]	to have extreme feelings about sth	*jdm liegt etw sehr am Herzen*	▸ page 125
to **outdo sb** [ˌaʊt'duː]	to do sth better than sb else	*jdn überbieten, jdn ausstechen*	
impatient [ɪm'peɪʃnt]	to get angry, frustrated easily	*ungeduldig*	
to **feel ashamed** [ˌfiːl ə'ʃeɪmd]	to feel embarrassed or guilty	*sich schämen*	
to **display sth** [dɪ'spleɪ]	to show sth	*etw zur Schau stellen*	
outwardly ['aʊtwədli]	<> inwardly	*nach außen, äußerlich*	
fault [fɔːlt]	mistake	*Fehler*	
unique [ju'niːk]	one of a kind	*einzigartig*	
to **feel miserable** [ˌfiːl 'mɪzrəbl]	to have a really bad feeling	*sich schlecht/elend fühlen*	

Section E Online privacy

fingerprints *pl* ['fɪŋgəprɪnts]	a one-of-a-kind mark left behind by sb	*Fingerabdrücke*	▸ page 126
medical records *pl* [ˌmedɪkl 'rekɔːdz]	information about sb's medical care	*Krankenakten*	
spending history ['spendɪŋ hɪstri]	a record of what you have bought	*Kaufhistorie*	
the more the merrier [ðə ˌmɔː ðə 'meriə]	sth will be more fun if more people join in	*je mehr, desto besser*	
trustworthy ['trʌstwɜːði]	honest and truthful	*vertrauenswürdig*	
Who cares? [ˌhuː 'keəz]	What does it matter?	*Wen kümmert's?*	▸ page 127
creepy ['kriːpi]	scary, freaky	*unheimlich, gruselig*	
characteristic [ˌkærəktə'rɪstɪk]	a feature or quality about sb	*Merkmal*	
visibility [ˌvɪzə'bɪləti]	being seen	*Sichtbarkeit*	
at the time [ət ðə 'taɪm]	in that moment	*seinerzeit*	
rejection [rɪ'dʒekʃn]	<> acceptance	*Ablehnung*	
recruitment [rɪ'kruːtmənt]	finding people for jobs	*(Personal-)Anwerbung, Rekrutierung*	
to **interview sb** ['ɪntəvjuː]	to ask sb questions about their work, life, etc	*mit jdm ein Vorstellungsgespräch führen*	
responsible [rɪ'spɒnsəbl]	caring for or controlling sth in your work	*verantwortungsbewusst*	
upset [ˌʌp'set]	sad and angry	*mitgenommen, aufgebracht*	
to **be gutted** [bi 'gʌtɪd]	to be very disappointed	*am Boden zerstört sein*	
to **learn one's lesson** [ˌlɜːn wʌnz 'lesn]	to know better for the future	*seine Lektion lernen*	
embarrassing [ɪm'bærəsɪŋ]	shameful	*peinlich*	
Things turned out well. [θɪŋz ˌtɜːnd aʊt 'wel]	Everything was OK in the end.	*Die Sache ging gut aus.*	
to **connect with sb** [kə'nekt wɪð]	to get closer to sb	*mit jdm in Verbindung treten, zu jdm ein inniges Verhältnis aufbauen*	
understanding [ˌʌndə'stændɪŋ]	sympathetic, tolerant	*verständnisvoll*	
nasty ['nɑːsti]	horrible, awful	*gemein, ekelhaft*	
connection [kə'nekʃn]	relationship	*Verbindung, Beziehung*	
not quite [nɒt 'kwaɪt]	not one hundred per cent	*nicht ganz, nicht direkt*	
afterwards ['ɑːftəwədz]	at a later time	*hinterher*	
initial [ɪ'nɪʃl]	the first thing	*erste/r/s*	
bullet point ['bʊlɪt pɔɪnt]	a marker for each point of a list	*Stichpunkt*	▸ page 128

▸ page 129	**property** ['prɒpəti]	sth that you own	*Eigentum*
	consent [kən'sent]	agreeing to sth	*Einwilligung*
	exception [ɪk'sepʃn]	a special case	*Ausnahme*
	government authority [ˌgʌvənmənt ɔː'θɒrəti]	e.g. the police, the tax office, etc	*staatliche Stelle, Behörde*
	to **recognize sb** ['rekəgnaɪz]	e.g. When I had my hair cut, people didn't recognize me.	*jdn (wieder)erkennen*
	access (to sth) ['ækses]	<> exclusion (from sth)	*Zugriff (auf etw)*
	to **access sth** ['ækses]	to get (into) sth	*auf etw zugreifen*
	sensitive information [ˌsensətɪv ɪnfə'meɪʃn]	private data	*vertrauliche Daten*
	targeted advertising [ˌtɑːgɪtɪd 'ædvətaɪzɪŋ]	advertising directed at a particular person	*gezielte Werbung*
	to **alert sb** [ə'lɜːt]	to warn sb	*jdn warnen*
	at regular intervals [ət ˌregjələ 'ɪntəvlz]	at times that are equally separated	*in regelmäßigen Zeitabständen*
	to **look suspicious** [ˌlʊk sə'spɪʃəs]	to seem dishonest, fishy, strange	*verdächtig aussehen*
	to **convey sth** [kən'veɪ]	to give an impression of sth	*etw vermitteln*

Section F Instapoetry

▸ page 130	**artistic** [ɑː'tɪstɪk]	creative skill	*künstlerisch, kreativ*
	eye-catching ['aɪkætʃɪŋ]	attractive, noticeable	*auffällig*
	font [fɒnt]	design of letter and numbers	*Zeichensatz, Schrift*
	to **drain sb** [dreɪn]	to take sb's energy	*jdn auslaugen, jdn erschöpfen*
	strain [streɪn]	pressure	*Druck, Strapaze(n)*
	doom [duːm]	fate, destiny (negative feeling)	*Verhängnis*
	foreboding [fɔː'bəʊdɪŋ]	a feeling that sth bad will happen	*(düstere) Vorahnung*
	threat of punishment [ˌθret əf 'pʌnɪʃmənt]	promise that there will be negative consequences	*Strafandrohung*
	to **propel sb** [prə'pel]	to push sth forward	*jdn antreiben, jdn vorwärtstreiben*
	exclamation point [ˌekskləˈmeɪʃn pɔɪnt]	!	*Ausrufezeichen*
	ellipsis [i'lɪpsɪs]	...	*Auslassungspünktchen*
	joy [dʒɔɪ]	happiness	*Freude*
▸ page 131	to **amplify sth** ['æmplɪfaɪ]	to make sth stronger or louder	*etw verstärken*
	vicious(ly) ['vɪʃəs]	brutal(ly)	*gewalttätig, brutal*
	to **address sth** [ə'dres]	to think about and deal with a problem	*etw ansprechen*
	to **be aware of sth** [bi ə'weər əv]	to know about sth	*etw wissen, sich einer Sache bewusst sein*
	to **tap into sth** [ˌtæp 'ɪntə]	to find a way into sth	*einen Zugang zu etw finden, sich etw erschließen*
	to **touch on sth** ['tʌtʃ ɒn]	to mention sth	*etw (Thema usw.) berühren, etw streifen*
	superficial [ˌsuːpə'fɪʃl]	on the surface	*oberflächlich*
	to **show sth off** [ˌʃəʊ 'ɒf]	to display sth	*etw zur Schau stellen*
	deep [diːp]	<> superficial	*tiefgründig*
	impression [ɪm'preʃn]	an idea or feeling about sb/sth	*Eindruck*
	syllable ['sɪləbl]	e.g. dog has 1 syllable, apple has 2 syllables, impression has 3 syllables	*Silbe*
	to **do the heavy lifting** [duː ðə ˌhevi 'lɪftɪŋ]	to do hard/difficult work	*die schwere Arbeit erledigen*
	to **deepen the impact** [ˌdiːpn ði 'ɪmpækt]	to make an effect stronger	*die Wirkung / den Effekt verstärken*
	impact ['ɪmpækt]	effect	*Wirkung*
	sunset ['sʌnset]	<> sunrise	*Sonnenuntergang*
	ancient ['eɪnʃənt]	very old	*alt*
	interplay ['ɪntəpleɪ]	the effect things have on each other	*Wechselspiel*

to **relate to sth** [rɪ'leɪt tə]	to connect to sth else	*in Beziehung zu etw stehen*
to **lose track of sth** [ˌluːz 'træk əv]	to no longer know what is happening	*etw aus den Augen verlieren*
to **engage oneself in sth** [ɪn'geɪdʒ wʌnself ɪn]	to involve oneself in sth	*sich auf etw einlassen*
meaningful ['miːnɪŋfl]	important, significant	*bedeutsam, wichtig*
to **reach out (to sb)** [ˌriːtʃ 'aʊt]	to contact sb, to ask sb for help	*sich an jdn wenden*
tiny ['taɪni]	very small	*klein, winzig*
dispossession [ˌdɪspə'zeʃn]	taking possessions, property away from sb	*Enteignung, Entzug (von etw)*
to **shine a light on sth** [ˌʃaɪn ə 'laɪt ɒn]	to highlight sth	*etw beleuchten*
ordinary ['ɔːdnri]	normal, usual	*gewöhnlich, normal*
checkout counter ['tʃekaʊt kaʊntə]	the place to pay for sth at a shop	*Kasse*
to **incentivize sb to do sth** [ɪn'sentɪvaɪz]	to give sb a reason to do sth	*jdm einen Anreiz bieten, etw zu tun*
to **make sense** [ˌmeɪk 'sens]	to have a reason	*einen Sinn ergeben*
mean [miːn]	<> nice, generous	*böse, gemein*
conscious(ly) ['kɒnʃəs]	knowing(ly)	*bewusst*
to **tear sb limb from limb** [teə ˌlɪm frəm 'lɪm]	to destroy sb	*jdn in Stücke reißen*
to **disbelieve sth** [ˌdɪsbɪ'liːv]	to think sth isn't true	*etw bezweifeln, etw anzweifeln*
shade [ʃeɪd]	shadows, out of the light	*Schatten*
to **raise sb** [reɪz]	e.g. to raise children	*jdn großziehen*
arena [ə'riːnə]	stage area	*Bühne, Bereich*
to **constitute sb/sth** ['kɒnstɪtjuːt]	to be made up of sb/sth	*jdn/etw ausmachen*
output ['aʊtpʊt]	<> input	*Produktion, Werke*
to **accompany sb/sth** [ə'kʌmpəni]	to go with sb/sth	*jdn/etw begleiten*

A–Z word list

Dieses Worterverzeichnis enthält alle in Crossover 1 – 6th edition eingeführten in den Texten angegebenen Vokabeln in alphabetischer Reihenfolge.

Abkürzungen: AE = amerikanisches Englisch, BE = britisches Englisch, etw = etwas, jdm = jemandem, jdn = jemanden, jds = jemandes, pl = plural, sb = somebody, sth = something, P = Partner files, T = Audio transcript, V = Video transcript

24/7 124 *rund um die Uhr*

A

to **abolish sth** 87 *etw abschaffen*

abortion 82 *Abtreibung*

about, to **do sth ~ sth** 12 *etw gegen etw unternehmen;* **just ~** 45 *fast, so ziemlich*

above all 51 *vor allen Dingen, allen voran*

to **absorb sth** 19 *etw* (Lernstoff usw.) *aufnehmen*

to **abuse sb** 119T *jdn misshandeln*

academic 31 *akademisch, wissenschaftlich;* **~ performance** 15 *schulische Leistung(en)*

access (to sth) 129 *Zugriff (auf etw)*

to **access sth** 129 *auf etw zugreifen*

accessible 20 *zugänglich*

accommodation 24 *Unterkunft, Bleibe*

to **accompany sb/sth** 131 *jdn/etw begleiten*

to **account for sth** 116 *etw* (Anteil usw.) *ausmachen*

accurate(ly) 114 *(genau) zutreffend*

to **accuse sb of sth** 10 *jdn einer Sache beschuldigen, jdm etw vorwerfen*

acrylic screen 47T *Plexiglaswand*

action, *to* **take ~** 121T *Maßnahmen ergreifen;* to **take immediate ~** 59 *unverzüglich tätig werden*

addict 113 *Süchtige/r*

addicted, *to* **be ~ to sth** 113 *nach etw süchtig sein, von etw abhängig sein*

addiction 113 *Sucht*

addictive, *to* **be ~** 113 *süchtig machen*

additional 13 *zusätzlich*

to **address sth** 131 *etw ansprechen*

administration 94 *Regierung, Verwaltung*

to **admit sth** 113 *etw zugeben, etw eingestehen*

adolescence 8 *Pubertät*

to **adopt sth** 91 *etw annehmen, etw verabschieden*

adrenaline rush 61 *Adrenalinrausch*

advance, in ~ 56T *im Voraus*

advanced 27 *fortgeschritten*

to **advertise sth** 23 *Werbung für etw machen*

advertising, targeted ~ 129 *gezielte Werbung*

to **advise sb on sth** 91V *jdm bei etw beraten*

to **affect: ~ sb/sth** 115 *jdn/etw betreffen;* **~ sth** 18 *sich negativ auf etw auswirken*

affiliation, party ~ 82 *Parteizugehörigkeit*

affinity 10 *Neigung, Vorliebe*

to **afford sth** 51 *sich etw leisten*

affordability 45 *Erschwinglichkeit*

afterwards 127T *hinterher*

aid, foreign ~ 98T *Entwicklungshilfe*

air pollution 56T *Luftverschmutzung*

to **alert sb** 116 *jdn alarmieren;* 129 *jdn warnen*

to **align with sth** 80 *mit etw übereinstimmen, sich hinter etw stellen*

alleged(ly) 119T *angeblich*

along 81 *entlang*

allowed, *to* **not be ~ to do sth** 81 *etw nicht tun dürfen*

ambitious 84T *ehrgeizig*

amount, a fair ~ 111 *ziemlich viel …, nicht unerhebliche Menge*

to **amplify sth** 131 *etw verstärken*

ancient 131T *alt*

animal: ~ care 22 *Tierpflege;* **~ shelter** 22 *Tierheim;* **~ welfare** 120 *Tierwohl;* to **raise ~s** 64T *Tiere züchten, Tiere halten*

annoyed 57 *verärgert;* 113 *genervt*

annual(ly) 78 *jährlich, pro Jahr*

anonymous 57 *anonym*

anti-social 122 *unsozial, asozial*

anxiety 13 *Ängste, Angst*

apparently 118 *anscheinend*

appeal, Court of A~ *BE* 94 *Berufungsgericht*

to **appear** 10T *scheinen;* 47T *vorkommen;* 99 *auftreten, erscheinen*

applied sciences pl 31P *angewandte Wissenschaften*

to **apply** 29 *sich bewerben*

to **appoint sb** 86 *jdn ernennen*

apprenticeship 31 *Lehre, Ausbildung*

to **approach** 58 *näherkommen;* **~ sth** 119T *sich einer Sache nähern*

appropriate (to sb) 88 *(jdm) angemessen, geeignet (für jdn)*

approval 19 *Anerkennung*

to **approve: ~ sth** 91V *etw genehmigen;* **~ of sth** 18 *etw gutheißen;* **~ of sb/sth** 121 *jdn/etw akzeptieren*

approximately 24 *ungefähr, circa*

area, designated ~ 47T *ausgewiesener Bereich;* **~ of policy** 91V *Politikfeld, Politikbereich;* to **cover an ~** 56T *sich über einen Bereich erstrecken*

arena 131T *Bühne, Bereich*

to **argue: ~ with sb** 18 *sich mit jdm streiten;* **~ one's position fervently** 78 *den eigenen Standpunkt leidenschaftlich vertreten*

argument 16 *(verbale) Auseinandersetzung, Streit*

armchair 120 *Sessel*

armed forces/services pl 29 *Streitkräfte*
arrest, mass ~ 119T *Massenverhaftung*
to **arrest sb** 118 *jdn verhaften*
arse, *to* **work one's ~ off** 25T *sich abrackern, sich kaputtarbeiten*
artistic 130 *künstlerisch, kreativ*
arts and crafts pl 23 *Kunsthandwerk*
as: ~ though 66 *als ob;* **~ it were** 110 *sozusagen, wenn man so will;* **~ a consequence** 57 *infolgedessen;* 100 *folglich, demzufolge*
ashamed, *to* **be ~ of sth** 66 *sich für etw schämen;* to **feel ~** 125 *sich schämen*
ass, *to* **work one's ~ off** 25T *sich abrackern, sich kaputtarbeiten*
asset 25 *Pluspunkt, Vorteil*
to **associate sb/sth with sth** 61 *jdn/etw mit etw in Verbindung bringen, jdn/etw mit etw assoziieren*
association 97 *Vereinigung, Bund*
astonished 118 *erstaunt*
to **attend school** 15 *die Schule besuchen*
attention, *to* **draw ~ to sth** 57 *die Aufmerksamkeit auf etw lenken;* to **grab sb's ~** 46 *jmds Aufmerksamkeit erregen;* to **turn sb's ~ to(wards) sth** 48 *jds Aufmerksamkeit auf etw lenken*
attitude (towards sth) 67 *Einstellung (zu etw)*
to **attract sb** 51 *jdn anlocken, jdn anziehen*
audience 48 *Publikum, Zuschauer/innen, Zuhörer/innen;* 120 *Zielgruppe*
authentic 10 *echt, authentisch*
author 67 *Autor/in, Verfasser/in*
authority 57 *Befugnis, Legitimation;* 94V *Instanz;* **government ~** 129 *staatliche Stelle, Behörde;* **~ figure** 9 *Autorität(sperson)*
automated 56T *automatisch*
available 51 *verfügbar, erhältlich*
award, *to* **present an ~** 99 *einen Preis überreichen*
aware, *to* **be ~ of sth** 131 *etw wissen, sich einer Sache bewusst sein*

B

backdrop 62 *Kulisse, Hintergrund*
background 8 *Hintergrund, Herkunft, Verhältnisse;* 64T *Vorgeschichte;* **against a ~** 46 *vor einem HIntergrund*
backyard 67 *Garten (hinter dem Haus), Hof*
bad language 118 *Schimpfwörter*
badge 56T *Plakette*
to **baffle sb** 19 *jdn vor ein Rätsel stellen*
balance, checks and ~es pl 79 *Kontrollmechanismen*
ballot 85 *Wahl, Abstimmung;* 84T *Stimmzettel, Wahlzettel;* to **cast a ~** 79 *die/seine (Wahl-)Stimme abgeben*
ban, driving ~ 56T *Fahrverbot*
bank, food ~ 121T *Lebensmitteltafel*
barely 116 *gerade so, gerade noch;* 122 *kaum*
barrier 57 *Absperrung*
to **be: ~ down to sth** 18 *an etw liegen;* **~ in on sth** 117P *über etw Bescheid wissen;* **~ up to sth** 115 *etw anstellen, etw machen, etw vorhaben;* **~ to one's liking** 92 *jdm zusagen, nach jds Geschmack sein;* **as it were** 110 *sozusagen, wenn man so will*
to **bear sth** 100 *etw* (Kosten usw.) *tragen, für etw aufkommen*
to **behave** 13 *sich verhalten*
behaviour 9 *Verhalten*
being, well-~ 9 *Wohl, Wohlbefinden*
belief 80 *Überzeugung, Glaube*
to **believe in sth** 82 *an etw glauben, von etw überzeugt sein*
belly 12 *Bauch*
beneficial 49T *vorteilhaft, positiv*
to **benefit from sth** 16 *von etw profitieren*
bias 111 *Voreingenommenheit, Tendenz*
bicycle lane 49T *Fahrradspur*
the big picture 50 *das große Ganze*
binary choice 88 *Wahl zwischen zwei Möglichkeiten*
bishop 94V *Bischof/Bischöfin*
bite 16T *Stück, Bissen*
blazing row 19 *erbitterter/wilder Streit*
block 46 *(Farb-)Fläche*
to **block sth off** 119T *etw absperren*
blog entry 101 *Blog-Eintrag, -Beitrag*
board, free ~ and lodging(s) 24 *freie Kost und Logis*
body, main ~ 59 *Haupttext*
bold 56T *mutig, gewagt*
to **boo** 83 *buhen*
to **boost sth** 13 *etw ankurbeln, etw auf Touren bringen*
border 81 *Grenze*
bothered, sb isn't ~ about sth 19 *jdm ist etw (völlig) egal*
bothersome 65 *lästig*
to **bottle sth up** 19 *etw unterdrücken*
to **branch off** 50 *abzweigen*
branch, executive ~ 90 *Exekutive;* **judicial ~** 90 *Judikative;* **legislative ~** 90 *Legislative;* **~es** pl **of government** 90 *die (drei) Gewalten, staatliche Organe*
breadth 30 *Breite*
to **break sth down to sth** 16T *etw auf etw reduzieren*
break, *to* **give sb/sth a ~** 12 *jdm/etw eine Pause gönnen*
breath 12 *Atem, Atemzug;* to **take a deep ~** 12 *tief einatmen, durchatmen*
brick 47T *Ziegelstein*
brief(ly) 59 *kurz (gefasst);* 116 *kurzzeitig*
bright 30 *gescheit, intelligent;* 46 (Farbe:) *hell, leuchtend;* **the ~ side** 13 *die positiven Aspekte*
broadcaster 114 *(Radio-/TV-) Sender;* **news ~** 115 *Nachrichtensender;* **public service ~** 115 *öffentlich-rechtlicher Sender*
broadly speaking 115 *grob gesagt, vereinfacht gesagt*
bull 15 *Stier*
bullet point 128 *Stichpunkt*
bully 122 *Mobber/in*
to **bully sb** 101 *jdn mobben, jdn tyrannisieren*
bullying 13 *Mobbing*
bump 57 *Schlag, Stoß; Unebenheit, Hubbel*
bunch, a ~ of 113 *ein Haufen*
bureaucracy 82 *Bürokratie*
business, *to* **set up ~** 52 *sich (geschäftlich) niederlassen*

C

cabinet 83 *Kabinett*

calf, calves 12 *Unterschenkel*

to **call: ~ for sth** 98T *etw fordern;* **~ a meeting** 94V *eine Versammlung einberufen;* **~ an election** 97 *eine Wahl ansetzen*

to **calm sb/sth** 13 *etw/jdn beruhigen*

calming, traffic ~ 58 *Verkehrsberuhigung;* **~ technique** 16T *Beruhigungs-/Entspannungstechnik*

campaign 84T *Wahlkampf*

to **campaign** 84T *Wahlkampf machen;* **~ for sth** 57 *sich für etw engagieren, für etw kämpfen*

campus 15T *Schul-/Universitätsgelände*

can 47 *(Blech-)Dose*

candidate, presidential ~ 84T *Präsidentschaftskandidat/in*

capital 56T *Hauptstadt*

caps pl 112 *Großbuchstaben*

caption 112 *Bildunterschrift*

car registration office 56T *Kfz-Zulassungsstelle*

care, *to* **take ~ of sth** 15 *sich um etw kümmern;* **animal ~** 22 *Tierpflege;* **health ~** 80 *Gesundheitsfürsorge, Gesundheitswesen;* **~ home** 31P *Pflegeheim*

to **care: Who ~es?** 127 *Wen kümmert's?*

carefree 64 *unbeschwert, sorglos*

caring 124 *fürsorglich*

case, court ~ 92 *Gerichtsverfahren*

to **cast: ~ a ballot** 79 *die/seine (Wahl-)Stimme abgeben;* **~ one's vote** 84T *seine Stimme abgeben*

caught up, *to* **get ~ in sth** 119T *in etw geraten*

cause 10 *Anliegen, Sache (für die man eintritt);* 12 *Ursache*

to **cause sth** 13 *etw verursachen*

Caution! 57 *Achtung!*

to **caution sb against sth** 23 *jdn vor etw warnen*

celebrity 119T *Prominente/r*

century 31P *Jahrhundert*

ceremonial 94V *zeremoniell*

ceremony 83 *Feier, Feierlichkeit(en), Zeremonie*

to **chair sth** 99 *den Vorsitz von etw innehaben, einer Sache vorstehen*

challenge 9 *(schwere) Aufgabe, Herausforderung*

challenging 31P *anspruchsvoll*

chamber (of parliament) 94 *Kammer, Haus (des Parlaments)*

chance, by ~ 47T *zufällig*

to **change sb's mind** 15 *jds Meinung ändern*

character 111 *Buchstabe, Zeichen*

characteristic 127 *Merkmal*

charge 56T *Gebühr;* **congestion ~** 56 *Innenstadtmaut, Citymaut;* **free of ~** 98T *kostenlos;* **penalty ~ notice** 56T *Bußgeldbescheid*

charging: ~ point 54 *Ladestation;* **~ zone** 56T *Gebührenzone*

charitable 99 *gemeinnützig, karitativ*

charm 47T *Charme*

chart, pie ~ 16P *Tortendiagramm*

to **check** 47T *nachsehen;* **~ sb/sth** 92 *jdn/etw kontrollieren, jdn/etw in Schach halten*

checkout counter 131T *Kasse*

checks and balances pl 79 *Kontrollmechanismen*

chest 12 *Brust, Brustkorb*

chief 62 *Häuptling*

childcare 31P *Kinderbetreuung*

choice, binary ~ 88 *Wahl zwischen zwei Möglichkeiten*

citizen 29 *(Staats-)Bürger/in;* **natural-born US ~** 83 *US-Staatsbürger/in von Geburt*

citizenship 81 *Staatsbürgerschaft*

civil: ~ rights pl 120 *Bürgerrechte;* **~ servant** *BE* 94 *Beamte/-in*

to **claim sth** 62 *etw (für sich) beanspruchen;* 101 *etw behaupten*

to **clear one's mind** 16T *den Kopf freibekommen/freimachen*

closed off 19 *abgeschottet*

close-up 62 *aus der Nähe, von Nahem*

code of ethics 115 *Verhaltenskodex*

to **collect taxes** 94V *Steuern eintreiben*

college, Electoral C~ *AE* 84T *Wahlmännergremium*

to **collide with sth** 57 *mit etw kollidieren*

colourful 46 *bunt, farbenfroh*

to **combat sth** 119 *etw bekämpfen*

to **come: ~ across sb** 47T *jdm (zufällig) begegnen, auf jdn stoßen;* **~ out to sb** 122 *sich gegenüber jdm outen*

commander-in-chief 91V *Oberbefehlshaber/in*

to **commission sth** 118 *etw in Auftrag geben*

to **commit a crime** 119T *ein Verbrechen / eine Straftat begehen*

commitment 23 *Leistungsbereitschaft, Einsatz*

committed, *to* **be ~ to sth** 24 *von etw überzeugt sein*

committee 96 *Gremium, Komitee*

common 24 *verbreitet, üblich*

commons pl: **the ~** 94V *der dritte Stand (freie Bauern und Bürger);* **House of C~** *BE* 83 *Unterhaus*

community, sense of ~ 49T *Gemeinschaftsgefühl, -sinn;* to **do ~ service** 96 *Sozialstunden leisten*

to **commute** 64T *zur Arbeit fahren, pendeln*

comparable, *to* **be ~ to sth** 30 *mit etw vergleichbar sein*

to **compete with sth** 12 *sich mit etw messen, mit etw mithalten*

competitor 88 *Mitbewerber/in*

concern 24 *Befürchtung, Bedenken, Sorge*

concerned 57 *besorgt, beunruhigt*

concession 100 *Zugeständnis*

to **conclude** 48 *schließen, zum Schluss kommen*

conclusion 59 *Schluss;* **in ~** 59 *abschließend, zum Schluss;* to **draw a ~** 16 *eine Schlussfolgerung ziehen*

to **conduct sth** 140 *etw durchführen*

cone, traffic ~ 57 *Leitkegel, Pylon*

confidence 122 *Selbstvertrauen;* **vote of no ~** 97 *Misstrauensvotum*

confident 10 *selbstbewusst*

to **confirm sth** 8 *etw bestätigen*

conflict, generational ~ 9 *Generationenkonflikt*

conflicted, *to* **be ~** 67 *hin- und hergerissen sein, widersprüchliche Gefühle haben*

confusing 87 *verwirrend*

congested 45 *verkehrsreich, (Straßen:) verstopft*

congestion 56T *(starke) Verkehrsbelastung, Verstopfung;* **~ charge** 56 *Innenstadtmaut, Citymaut*

to **connect with sb** 127T *mit jdm in Verbindung treten, zu jdm ein inniges Verhältnis aufbauen*

connection 127T *Verbindung, Beziehung*

connotations pl **47** *Assoziationen, Anklänge, Konnotationen*
conscious(ly) 131T *bewusst;* to **be ~ of sth 121** *sich einer Sache bewusst sein*
consent 129 *Einwilligung*
consequence, as a ~ 57 *infolgedessen;* **100** *folglich, demzufolge*
conservation 23 *Naturschutz, Umweltschutz*
to **conserve sth 23** *etw erhalten, etw schützen*
to **consider: ~ sth 25T** *über etw nachdenken, sich Gedanken über etw machen;* **114** *etw berücksichtigen, auf etw achten;* **~ sth sth 15** *etw für etw halten, etw als etw ansehen*
considered, *to* **be ~ed sth 80** *als etw gelten, als etw erachtet werden*
to **consist of sth 59** *aus etw bestehen*
conspiracy:
~ theorist 119 *Verschwörungstheoretiker/in;* **~ theory 119** *Verschwörungstheorie*
constantly 19 *die ganze Zeit, andauernd*
constituency 94V *Wahlkreis*
to **constitute sb/sth 131T** *jdn/etw ausmachen*
constitution 90 *Verfassung*
constitutional 62 *Verfassungs-*
to **consult sb 99** *jdn zu Rate ziehen, jdn konsultieren*
to **contain sth 67** *etw enthalten*
contemporary issues pl **79** *aktuelle Themen*
contrast, by ~ 79 *dagegen, im Gegensatz dazu*
to **contribute to sth 67** *zu etw beitragen*
control, *to* **be in ~ of sth 16T** *etw in der Hand haben;* **traffic ~ 56T** *Verkehrssteuerung*
convenient 64T *praktisch*
convention, National C~ AE **84T** *Nominierungsparteitag;* **party ~ 83** *Parteitag*
to **convey sth 129** *etw vermitteln*
to **convince sb 31P** *jdn überzeugen*
convincing(ly) 85 *überzeugend*
corporation 51 *Großunternehmen, Konzern*
correct, *to* **be factually ~ 115** *den Tatsachen entsprechen*
council 57 *Stadtverwaltung*
counsellor 122 *Berater/in, Therapeut/in;* **guidance ~ 15** *Vertrauenslehrer/in, Berater/in*
counter, checkout ~ 131T *Kasse*
country, federal ~ 94V *Bundesstaat*
countryside 45 *ländliche Gegend(en), Land*
courage 122 *Mut*
court, federal ~ 90 *Bundesgericht;* **Supreme C~** *AE* **90** *Oberster Gerichtshof;* **~ case 92** *Gerichtsverfahren*
Court of Appeal *BE* **94** *Berufungsgericht*
to **cover: ~ sth 22** *etw abdecken, sich über etw erstrecken;* **~ sth up 119T** *etw vertuschen;* **~ an area 56T** *sich über einen Bereich erstrecken*
coverage 111 *Berichterstattung*
covered 47T *überdeckt*
craft, arts and ~s pl **23** *Kunsthandwerk*
to **crave sth 19** *sich nach etw sehnen*
creature 46 *Gestalt, Wesen;* **sea ~ 62** *Meerestier*
credible 117P *glaubwürdig*
creepy 127 *unheimlich, gruselig*
crime 118 *Straftat, Verbrechen;* to **commit a ~ 119T** *ein Verbrechen / eine Straftat begehen*
critical, *to* **be ~ of sth 121T** *etw kritisch sehen*
criticism (of sth) 17 *Kritik (an etw)*
to **criticize sb/sth 122** *jdn/etw kritisieren*
to **crowd oneself into sth 51** *sich in etw hineinzwängen*
crucial 22 *entscheidend, äußerst wichtig*
cruise 62 *Seereise, Kreuzfahrt*
to **crumple sth up 11** *etw zusammenknüllen*
crutches pl **121T** *Krücken*
cure (for sth) 111 *Heilmittel (für etw), Rezept (gegen etw)*
currently 15T *momentan, aktuell*
custom 62 *Brauch*
cuts pl, **funding ~ 116** *Mittelkürzungen*
cute 10T *niedlich, süß*
cyclist 56 *Fahrradfahrer/in*

D

data protection 110 *Datenschutz*
day, one ~ 28 *eines Tages*
deadline, *to* **meet a ~ 13** *eine (Abgabe-)Frist einhalten*
to **deal with sth 13** *mit etw umgehen, etw bewältigen, mit etw zurechtkommen;* **15T** *sich mit etw befassen, mit etw zu tun haben*
death 57 *Tod, Todesfall;* **~ threat 119T** *Morddrohung*
debit, direct ~ 56T *Lastschrift, Bankeinzug;* **~ card 56T** *Geldkarte*
decade 19 *Jahrzehnt*
decent person 67 *anständiger Mensch*
declaration of war 91V *Kriegserklärung*
to **declare sth 91V** *etw erklären*
deep 131T *tiefgründig*
to **deepen the impact 131T** *die Wirkung / den Effekt verstärken*
defences pl **13** *Abwehrkräfte*
to **defer sth 24** *etw verschieben, etw aussetzen*
to **delay sth 94V** *etw aufschieben, etw aufhalten*
delegate 86 *Delegierte/r*
to **delegate sth 101** *etw delegieren*
deliberate(ly) 117 *absichtlich, vorsätzlich*
demand 18 *Anspruch, Forderung*
to **demand 19** *fordern, verlangen*
demonstrator 119T *Demonstrant/in*
department of transportation 57 *Verkehrsbehörde*
to **depend: ~ on sth 84T** *von etw abhängen;* **it/that ~s 87** *es/das kommt darauf an*
depending on 31P *je nachdem*
to **depict sth 61** *etw abbilden*
depth 30 *Tiefe;* **in ~ 31** *gründlich, eingehend*
to **deserve sth 80** *etw verdienen*
deserved, well-~ 124 *wohlverdient*
designated area 47T *ausgewiesener Bereich*
desperate, *to* **be ~ to do sth 12** *etw was unbedingt (aus Verzweiflung) tun wollen*
despite 87 *trotz*
destination 23 *Zielort*
to **destroy sth 51** *etw zerstören*
to **detect sth 117** *etw aufspüren, etw erkennen*
device, stylistic ~ 67 *Stilmittel*
devolution 94 *Dezentralisierung, Übertragung von Amtsgewalt*
to **devolve 94** (Amtsgewalt) *übertragen*

diet, varied ~ 13 *abwechslungsreiche Ernährung*; to **be on a ~ 12** *eine Diät machen*
difference, *to* **make a ~ 22** *etwas bewirken*
to **dig a well 22** *einen Brunnen bohren/graben*
dignity 121T *Würde*
diner 118 *Gast (in einem Restaurant)*
direct debit 56T *Lastschrift, Einzug*
director 45 *Regisseur/in*
the disabled 31P *Behinderte*
disability 121T *Behinderung, Beeinträchtigung*
to **disappear 49T** *verschwinden*
to **disapprove of sth 24** *etw missbilligen, etw ablehnen*
disaster, natural ~ 13 *Naturkatastrophe*
to **disbelieve sth 131T** *etw bezweifeln, etw anzweifeln*
discord 15T *Konflikt(e), Zwist, Streitigkeiten*
discovery 116 *Entdeckung*
to **discredit sb/sth 117P** *jdn/etw diskreditieren*
dishonest 10 *unehrlich, unaufrichtig*
disinformation 117 *Desinformation*
disorder, eating ~ 12 *Ess-Störung*
to **display sth 125** *etw zur Schau stellen*
disposable 124 *Einweg-*
dispossession 131T *Enteignung, Entzug (von etw)*
distance, in the ~ 58 *in der Ferne*; **within walking ~ 64T** *in Laufweite, fußläufig erreichbar*
to **distract sb from sth 17** *jdn von etw ablenken*
distributed, evenly ~ 12 *gleichmäßig verteillt*
diverse 46 *vielfältig, breit gefächert, divers*
to **do sth about sth 12** *etw gegen etw unternehmen*
doom 130 *Verhängnis*
doorstep, on sb's ~ 64T *vor der Haustür*
dot 46 *Punkt, Tupfen*
down, *to* **be ~ to sth 18** *an etw liegen*
downside 121 *Nachteil*
to **drain sb 130** *jdn auslaugen, jdn erschöpfen*
dramatic, overly ~ 17 *übertrieben dramatisch*
to **draw 16P** *zeichnen*; **~ a conclusion 16** *eine Schlussfolgerung ziehen*; **~ attention to sth 57** *die Aufmerksamkeit auf etw lenken*
drilling, oil ~ 81 *Ölbohrungen, Ölförderung*
to **drip 26** *tropfen*
driver, key ~ 51 *treibende Kraft, Hauptmotor*
driving ban 56T *Fahrverbot*
drug, gateway ~ 110 *Einstiegsdroge*
duty 94V *Aufgabe, Pflicht*

E

to **earn one's (own) living 99** *seinen (eigenen) Lebensunterhalt verdienen*
earthquake 61 *Erdbeben*
easy-going 15 *unkompliziert, locker*
eatery 49T *Restaurant, Lokal*
eating disorder 12 *Ess-Störung*
economy 49 *Wirtschaft*
to **edit sth 124** *etw* (Text usw.) *bearbeiten*
edge, *to* **take the ~ off 19** *die Schärfe nehmen*
to **educate 26** *schulen, (aus)bilden, unterrichten*; **~ sb 122** *jdn aufklären, jdn informieren*
either 93 *jede/r (von beiden)*
the elderly 31P *Senioren*
to **elect sb (sth) 88** *jdn (zu etw) wählen*
election 79 *(Parlaments-, Präsidentschafts-)Wahl*; **general ~ 81** *Parlamentswahl*; **presidential ~ 79** *Präsidentschaftswahl*; to **call an ~ 97** *eine Wahl ansetzen*; **~ process 84** *Wahlverfahren*; **~ result 84T** *Wahlergebnis*
elector *AE* **84T** *Wahlmann*
electoral: E~ College *AE* **84T** *Wahlmännergremium*; **~ system 79** *Wahlsystem*
electorate 79 *Wahlberechtigte* pl, *Wahlvolk*
electric vehicle 54 *Elektrofahrzeug*
eligible 79 *wahlberechtigt*
to **eliminate sth 111** *etw beseitigen, etw eliminieren*
ellipsis 130 *Auslassungspünktchen*
embarrassing 127T *peinlich*
emotional state 12T *Gefühlszustand*
to **emphasize 18** *betonen, hervorheben, herausstellen*
employment 31P *Anstellung, Beschäftigung*
empty-handed, *to* **end up ~ 87** *am Ende mit leeren Händen dastehen*
to **encounter: sb ~s sth 15T** *etw begegnet jdm*
end, rear ~ 12 *Hinterteil*
to **end up: ~ empty-handed 87** *am Ende mit leeren Händen dastehen*; **~ living on the streets 51** *auf der Straße landen*
endangered wildlife 23 *bedrohte Tier- und Pflanzenarten*
energizing 124 *belebend*
to **engage: ~ in sth 121** *sich für etw engagieren*; **~ oneself in sth 131T** *sich auf etw einlassen*; **~ with sb 120** *mit jdm ins Gespräch kommen, auf jdn zugehen*
entry, blog ~ 101 *Blog-Eintrag, -Beitrag*
episode 16 *Folge* (einer TV-Serie etc.)
equality 120 *Gleichstellung, Gleichberechtigung*
equally 57 *ebenso, gleichermaßen*
essential 13 *unverzichtbar, wesentlich*
to **establish sth 62** *etw schaffen, etw definieren*
to **estimate 100** *schätzen*
ethics, code of ~ 115 *Verhaltenskodex*
evenly distributed 12 *gleichmäßig verteillt*
event 84T *Ereignis, Veranstaltung*; **a string of ~s 57** *eine Reihe von Ereignissen*
evidence 119T *Beleg(e), Beweis(e)*; to **gather ~ 92** *Beweismaterial sammeln*
evil 46 *böse*
exaggeration 117 *Übertreibung*
exception 129 *Ausnahme*
exclamation point 130 *Ausrufezeichen*
excuse 28 *Ausrede, Entschuldigung*
executive branch 90 *Exekutive*
to **exercise 13** *trainieren*; **~ a right 91V** *von einem Recht Gebrauch machen*
exhalation 16T *Ausatmen*
exhaust 56T *Abgase*
exhibition 45 *Ausstellung*
expectation, *to* **live up to sb's ~s 13** *jds Erwartungen erfüllen*
expense 100 *(finanzieller) Aufwand, Kosten*

experience 62 *Unternehmung, Erlebnis*
to **experience sth** 15T *etw durchmachen, etw erleben, etw erfahren*
to **explore sth** 62 *etw erkunden*
to **express sth** 93 *etw ausdrücken*
expression 110 *Ausdruck*
expressive 53 *aussagekräftig, prägnant*
extensive 83 *umfangreich*
extracurricular 15 *außerschulische Aktivität, AG*
eye, *to* **keep an ~ on sb** 25T *auf jdn aufpassen, jdn im Auge behalten*
eye-catching 130 *auffällig*
eye-opener, real ~ 46 *echtes Aha-Erlebnis*

F

facilities pl**, public ~** 118 *öffentliche Toiletten*
factually, *to* **be ~ correct** 115 *den Tatsachen entsprechen*
to **fail** 8 *scheitern, versagen*
fair, a ~ amount 111 *ziemlich viel ..., nicht unerhebliche Menge*
fairness 30 *Gerechtigkeit*
familiar 19 *bekannt*
family tree 99 *Stammbaum*
to **fancy sth** 22 *auf etw Lust haben*
fault 116 *Defekt, Störung;* 125 *Fehler*
favour, in ~ of sb/sth 115 *zugunsten von jdm/etw*
to **favour sth** 82 *etw favorisieren, für etw sein*
to **feature sth** 62 *etw aufweisen, etw haben*
federal 91V *Bundes-;* **~ country** 94V *Bundesstaat;* **~ court** 92 *Bundesgericht;* **~ official** 92 *Bundesbeamte/r;*
to **feed sb** 66 *jdn ernähren*
to **feel: ~ ashamed** 125 *sich schämen;* **~ miserable** 125 *sich schlecht/elend fühlen;* **~ run down** 13 *sich schlapp fühlen;* **sb ~s strongly about sth** 125 *jdm liegt etw sehr am Herzen*
fees pl**, tuition ~** 98T *Studiengebühren*
fervently, *to* **argue one's position ~** 78 *den eigenen Standpunkt leidenschaftlich vertreten*
to **fight** 17 *sich streiten;* **~ sth** 13 *etw bekämpfen*
fight, snowball ~ 11 *Schneeballschlacht*
figure 100 *Zahl, Ziffer;* **authority ~** 9 *Autorität(sperson);* **key ~** 119T *Schlüsselfigur*
to **figure sth out** 31 *etw herausfinden*
financial support 119 *finanzielle Unterstützung*
findings pl 15 *Ergebnisse*
fine 56T *Bußgeld;* 96 *Geldstrafe*
to **fine sb** 58 *ein Bußgeld gegen jdn verhängen*
fingerprints pl 126 *Fingerabdrücke*
first, in the ~ place 51 *überhaupt (erst), in erster Linie;* **~-time voter** 84 *Erstwähler/in*
to **fit: ~ into sth** 13 *sich in etw einfügen;* **~ in socially** 15 *sich anpassen, dazugehören*
fixed 13 *fest, feststehend*
flavour 15T *Note, Atmosphäre, Touch*
fluffy 47T *flauschig*
to **focus on sth** 48 *sich auf etw konzentrieren*
font 130 *Zeichensatz, Schrift*
food: ~ for thought 25T *Denkanstöße;* **~ bank** 121T *Lebensmitteltafel;* **~ stall** 49T *Imbissstand*
to **forbid** 91V *verbieten, untersagen*
force, *to* **be in ~** 91V *in Kraft sein;* **armed ~es** pl 91V *Streitkräfte* **military ~es** pl 92 *Streitkräfte*
to **force:** to **be ~ed to do sth** 51 *sich gezwungen sehen, etw zu tun; etw (notgedrungen) tun müssen*
foreboding 130 *(düstere) Vorahnung*
forehead 12 *Stirn*
foreign aid 98T *Entwicklungshilfe*
foreigner 81 *Ausländer/in*
to **form sth** 86 *etw bilden*
fortune 24 *Vermögen*
to **found sth** 51 *etw gründen*
free: ~ of charge 98T *kostenlos;* **~ board and lodging(s)** 24 *freie Kost und Logis;* **~ movement** 98T *Freizügigkeit;* **~ speech** 115 *freie Meinungsäußerung*
freedom of the press 114 *Pressefreiheit*
frequency 14 *Häufigkeit*
frightening 47 *beängstigend*
to **fund sth** 115 *etw finanzieren*
funding 78 *Finanzierung, (finanzielle) Mittel;* **~ cuts** pl 116 *Mittelkürzungen*
funds pl 84T *Gelder, (Geld-)Mittel;* to **raise ~** 84T *Geld sammeln, Mittel beschaffen*
furthermore 115 *außerdem, darüber hinaus*

G

garage 56T *Kfz-Werkstatt*
gateway drug 110 *Einstiegsdroge*
to **gather evidence** 92 *Beweismaterial sammeln*
gender 8 *Geschlecht*
general election 81 *Parlamentswahl*
to **generate money** 56T *Geld einnehmen;* 78 *Geld erwirtschaften*
generational conflict 9 *Generationenkonflikt*
gentrification 45 *Gentrifizierung*
to **get: ~ along with sb** 64T *mit jdm auskommen, mit jdm zurechtkommen;* **~ caught up in sth** 119T *in etw geraten*
to **give: ~ sb/sth a break** 12 *jdm/etw eine Pause gönnen;* **~ a speech** 99 *eine Rede halten*
glacier 61 *Gletscher*
to **gossip about sb** 112 *über jdn ablästern*
government, branches pl **of ~** 90 *die (drei) Gewalten, staatliche Organe;* **~ authority** 129 *staatliche Stelle, Behörde*
to **grab sb's attention** 46 *jmds Aufmerksamkeit erregen*
grape, *to* **pick ~s** 25T *Trauben ernten*
to **guess** 100 *vermuten*
guidance counsellor 15 *Vertrauenslehrer/in, Berater/in*
guide 47 *Führer/in*
to **guide sb** 48 *jdn führen, jdn leiten*
guided tour 46 *Führung, Rundgang*
gutted, *to* **be ~** 127T *am Boden zerstört sein*

H

habit 14 *Gewohnheit*
hand, *to* **lend sb a ~** 64T *jdm helfen, jdm zur Hand gehen*
handy, *to* **keep sth ~** 62 *etw griffbereit haben*
hangout 49T *Stammlokal, Laden*

hard, sb has a ~ time doing sth 25T *jdm fällt es schwer, etw zu tun*
harm, *to* **do ~ to sb/sth** 119 *jdm/einer Sache Schaden zufügen*
harmful 56T *schädlich*
harsh 30 *streng, rigoros*
havoc, *to* **play ~ with sth** 18 *etw komplett durcheinanderbringen*
to **head to sth** 99 *sich auf den Weg zu etw machen*
head of state 99 *Staatsoberhaupt*
headmistress 27 *Direktorin*
health care 80 *Gesundheitsfürsorge, Gesundheitswesen*
heavy, *to* **do the ~ lifting** 131T *die schwere Arbeit erledigen*
the Hebrides pl 95 *die Hebriden*
hereditary 94V *erblich*
to **hesitate** 47T *zögern*
hidden 122 *verborgen*
to **hire sb** 29 *jdn einstellen, jdn anstellen*
hire scheme 54 *Verleihsystem*
history, spending ~ 126 *Kaufhistorie*
hoax 119T *Täuschung, Schwindel*
holiday, national ~ 62 *Nationalfeiertag*
home, permanent ~ 51 *fester Wohnsitz;* **care ~** 31P *Pflegeheim*
homeless 51 *obdachlos*
hometown 25T *Heimatstadt*
honest, to be ~ with you 10T *ehrlich gesagt*
host 99 *Gastgeber/in*
house, H~ of Commons *BE* 83 *Unterhaus;* **H~ of Lords** *BE* 94V *Oberhaus*
housing 49T *Wohnungen, Wohnraum*
huge 12 *enorm, (riesig) groß*
humanity 121T *(die) Menschheit*
to **humiliate sb** 122 *jdn demütigen*
humorous 67 *humorvoll, witzig*
humour 47T *Humor*

I

icon 57 *Symbol*
to **identify: ~ as sb/sth** 10 *sich als jd/etw bezeichnen, sich als zu jdm/etw zugehörig erklären;* **~ with sb/sth** 10 *sich mit jdm/etw identifizieren*
if so 119 *falls ja*
to **illustrate sth** 16 *etw veranschaulichen*
to **imagine** 81 *sich (etw) vorstellen*
immediate, *to* **take ~ action** 59 *unverzüglich tätig werden*
impact 12 *Einfluss, Auswirkung(en), Folge(n);* 131T *Wirkung;* to **deepen the ~** to **have an ~ on sth** 12 *sich auf etw auswirken;* 131T *die Wirkung / den Effekt verstärken*
to **impact sth** 92 *Auswirkungen auf etw haben*
impatient 125 *ungeduldig*
imperative 115 *zwingend erforderlich*
to **implement sth** 81 *etw* (Gesetz usw.) *einführen, etw umsetzen*
impression 131T *Eindruck*
impressive 46 *beeindruckend*
in, *to* **be ~ on sth** 117P *über etw Bescheid wissen*
inadequate 9 *unzulänglich*
inauguration 83 *Einweihung, Amtseinführung*
incentive 98 *Anreiz*
to **incentivize sb to do sth** 131T *jdm einen Anreiz bieten, etw zu tun*
to **incorporate sth into sth** 24 *etw in etw einbinden, etw in etw aufnehmen*
incredible(-ly) 51 *unglaublich*
independence 13 *Unabhängigkeit*
indigenous people 45 *Ureinwohner*
industry 51 *Branche, Sparte*
inefficiency 82 *Ineffizienz, Schlendrian*
inequality 51 *Ungleichheit, Unterschied(e);* **social ~** 82 *soziale Ungerechtigkeit*
inexpensive 24 *billig*
information, sensitive ~ 129 *vertrauliche Daten*
inhabitant 45 *Einwohner/in*
inhalation 16T *Einatmen*
to **inherit sth** 94V *etw erben*
initial 127 *erste/r/s*
to **insist** 19 *darauf bestehen;* **~ on sth** 123P *auf etw bestehen*
inspirational 47T *inspirierend*
instead of 16T *anstatt, anstelle von*
insufficient 18 *unzureichend*
to **insult sb** 118 *jdn beleidigen, jdn beschimpfen*
intended, *to* **be ~ to do sth** 117 *dazu/dafür gedacht sein, etw zu tun*
intention 16T *Absicht, Vorhaben*
to **interfere with sth** 82 *sich in etw einmischen*
intern 31P *Praktikant/in*
internship 31 *Praktikum*
interplay 131T *Wechselspiel*
to **interrupt sb** 47T *jdn unterbrechen, jdm ins Wort fallen*
interval, at regular ~s 129 *in regelmäßigen Zeitabständen*
interview 27 *Vorstellungsgespräch*
to **interview sb** 127T *mit jdm ein Vorstellungsgespräch führen*
intimidated 27 *eingeschüchtert*
to **introduce sth** 56 *etw einführen*
introduction 59 *Einleitung*
invalid 117P *gegenstandslos, hinfällig*
invasion of privacy 101 *Verletzung der Privatsphäre*
inventive 57 *originell, einfallsreich*
to **invest** 56T *investieren*
investigator 116 *Ermittler/in*
involved, *to* **be ~ in sth** 15 *bei etw mitmachen/mitwirken*
ironically 9 *ironischerweise*
issue, contemporary ~s pl 79 *aktuelle Themen*

J

jail 119T *Gefängnis*
jaw 12 *Unterkiefer*
to **join: ~ sb** 47T *bei jdm sein;* **~ in** 27 *(bei etw) mitmachen,* (Verein usw.) *beitreten*
journey 54 *Fahrt*
joy 130 *Freude*
judge 91V *Richter/in*
to **judge sb** 122 *jdn beurteilen, jdn verurteilen*
judicial branch 90 *Judikative*
judiciary 90 *Judikative*
the jury 92 *die Geschworenen*
just about 45 *fast, so ziemlich*

K

to **keep: ~ an eye on sb** 25T *auf jdn aufpassen, jdn im Auge behalten;* **~ sth handy** 62 *etw griffbereit haben*
key: ~ driver 51 *treibende Kraft, Hauptmotor;* **~ figure** 119T *Schlüsselfigur*
to **kidnap sb** 119T *jdn entführen*
kindness 11 *Freundlichkeit, Liebenswürdigkeit, Güte*
kitten 113 *Kätzchen*

L

lack (of sth) 9 *Mangel (an etw), Fehlen (von etw)*
lane, bicycle ~ 49T *Fahrradspur;* **unseparated ~** 57 *nicht abgetrennte Fahrspur*
language, bad ~ 118 *Schimpfwörter*
lap 12 *Schoß*
large-scale 46 *großformatig*
laughter 13 *Lachen*
law, *to* **pass a ~** 92 *ein Gesetz verabschieden;* **~ and order** 82 *Recht und Ordnung;* **required by ~** 96 *gesetzlich vorgeschrieben*
lawyer 31P *Anwalt/Anwältin*
laziness 18 *Faulheit*
lazy 18 *faul*
to **lead to sth** 57 *zu etw führen*
leader 115 *führende/r Politiker/in*
to **lean (towards sth)** 84T *(zu etw) tendieren*
to **learn: ~ sth** 86 *etw erfahren;* **~ one's lesson** 127T *seine Lektion lernen*
legislation 92 *Gesetze, Gesetzgebung*
legislative branch 90 *Legislative*
legislature 91V *Legislative*
legitimate 88 *legitim*
to **lend sb a hand** 64T *jdm helfen, jdm zur Hand gehen*
lesson, *to* **learn one's ~** 127T *seine Lektion lernen*
to **let go of sth** 12 *etw lösen, etw loslassen*
level 12 *Niveau, Grad;* **income ~** 50 *Einkommensniveau;* **stress ~s** pl 12 *Stressniveau;* **on a national ~** 87 *auf Landesebene, landesweit*
lie 10T *Lüge*
lie-in 18 *langes Schlafen, Ausschlafen*
life, outlook on ~ 13 *Lebensperspektive;* **from all walks of ~** 121T *aus allen Gesellschaftsschichten*
lifeline 122 *Rettungsanker*
to **lift weights** 124 *Gewichte heben*
lifting, *to* **do the heavy ~** 131T *die schwere Arbeit erledigen*
likeable 11 *sympathisch, nett*
likely 82 *wahrscheinlich*
liking, *to* **be to one's ~** 92 *jdm zusagen, nach jds Geschmack sein*
limb, *to* **tear sb ~ from ~** 131T *jdn in Stücke reißen*
to **limit sth** 81 *etw beschränken, etw einschränken*
limited, *to* **be ~ to sth** 100 *auf etw beschränkt sein*
line, *to* **be in ~ with sth** 92 *mit etw übereinstimmen*
literally 56T *buchstäblich, tatsächlich*
litter 47T *Abfall, Müll*
to **live up to sb's expectations** 13 *jds Erwartungen erfüllen*
lively 46 *lebendig, lebhaft, quirlig*
living, *to* **earn one's (own) ~** 99 *seinen (eigenen) Lebensunterhalt verdienen*
loan 81 *Kredit, Darlehen*
to **locate sb/sth** 117 *etw/jdn ausfindig machen*
lodging, free board and ~(s) 24 *freie Kost und Logis*
to **long for sth** 51 *sich nach etw sehnen*
to **look: ~ into sth** 22 *sich über etw informieren, sich um etw kümmern;* **~ past sth** 117P *über etw hinwegsehen*
lord, House of L~s *BE* 94V *Oberhaus*
to **lose track of sth** 131T *etw aus den Augen verlieren*
to **lower sth** 81 *etw senken*

M

main body 59 *Haupttext*
to **maintain: ~ sth** 62 *etw (aufrecht)erhalten;* **~ sb/sth** 78 *jdn/etw (finanziell) unterhalten*
majority 30 *Mehrheit*
to **make: ~ up one's mind** 100 *sich entscheiden;* **~ a difference** 22 *etwas bewirken;* **~ sense** 131T *einen Sinn ergeben*
marine life 62 *Tier- und Pflanzenwelt des Meeres*
marker 8 *Kennzeichen*
marking 30 *Benotung*
marriage 82 *Ehe*
mass arrest 119T *Massenverhaftung*
masterpiece 46 *Meisterwerk*
matter, no ~ what 18 *was auch (immer) passiert*
to **mature** 18 *reifen, sich entwickeln*
mayor 60 *Bürgermeister/in*
mean 131T *böse, gemein*
meaningful 17 *aussagekräftig;* 131T *bedeutsam, wichtig*
measles pl 81 *Masern*
measure, *to* **take ~s** 56T *Maßnahmen ergreifen*
medical records pl 126 *Krankenakten*
to **meet: ~ a deadline** 13 *eine (Abgabe-)Frist einhalten;* **~ emission standards** 56T *Emissionsgrenzwerte einhalten*
meeting, *to* **call a ~** 94V *eine Versammlung einberufen*
memorable 62 *unvergesslich, beeindruckend*
to **memorize sth** 50 *sich etw einprägen*
mental 12 *geistig, psychisch*
merry, the more the ~ier 126 *je mehr, desto besser*
messy 19 *unordentlich, unaufgeräumt*
middle, in the ~ of nowhere 45 *am Ende der Welt, mitten in der Pampa*
military forces pl 92 *Streitkräfte*
mind 12 *Geist, Bewusstsein;* to **be on sb's ~** 87 (Thema, Problem:) *jdn beschäftigen;* to **clear one's ~** 16T *den Kopf freibekommen/ freimachen;* to **make up one's ~** 100 *sich entscheiden*
to **mind** 10T *etw dagegen haben;* **~ sb/sth** 57 *auf jdn/etw achten*
mindfulness 16T *Achtsamkeit*
minimum voting age 81 *Mindestwahlalter*
miserable, *to* **feel ~** 125 *sich schlecht/elend fühlen*
misinformation 117 *Fehl-information*
misinterpretation 117 *Fehl-interpretation*
misleading 117P *irreführend*
to **miss: ~ sth** 27 *etw nicht mitbekommen;* **sb ~es sth** 47T *jdm entgeht etw;* **sb ~es out on sth** 115 *jdm entgeht etw*
to **mitigate sth** 16T *etw lindern, etw mildern*
moment, present ~ 12 *gegenwärtiger Zeitpunkt*
monarch 94V *Monarch/in*
monarchy 99 *Monarchie*
mood 67 *Stimmung*
moody 15 *launisch*
the more the merrier 126 *je mehr, desto besser*
motorist 57 *Autofahrer/in*
mountain range 61 *Gebirge, Gebirgszug*

movement, free ~ 98T *Freizügigkeit*
MP (Member of Parliament) *BE* 97 *(Parlaments-)Abgeordnete/r*
multi-layered 8 *vielschichtig*
mural 46 *Wandbild*
muscle 12T *Muskel*
to **mute sth** 113 *etw stummschalten*

N

nagging 19 *Genörgel, Gemeckere*
nasty 127T *gemein, ekelhaft*
national: N~ Convention *AE* 84T *Nominierungsparteitag;* **~ holiday** 62 *Nationalfeiertag;* **~ popular vote** 87 *landesweite Volksabstimmung;* **on a ~ level** 87 *auf Landesebene, landesweit*
natural: ~ disaster 13 *Naturkatastrophe;* **~-born US citizen** 83 *US-Staatsbürger/in von Geburt*
nature 47T *Wesen, Art*
necessarily, not ~ 9 *nicht unbedingt*
need, in ~ 82 *bedürftig;* to **be in ~ of sth** 28 *etw benötigen*
neighbourhood 45 *Stadtviertel, Gegend*
nevertheless 58 *nichtsdestotrotz, trotzdem*
news broadcaster 115 *Nachrichtensender*
to **nominate sb** 92 *jdn nominieren*
nomination 84 *Nominierung*
nominee 85 *Kandidat/in*
note, on a positive ~ 48 *positiv*
notice, penalty charge ~ 56T *Bußgeldbescheid*
novelty 19 *Neuartigkeit, Abwechslung*
nowhere, in the middle of ~ 45 *am Ende der Welt, mitten in der Pampa*
nuclear weapons pl 94V *Kernwaffen*
number plate 56T *Nummernschild*
nurse 10 *Krankenpfleger/-schwester*
nursery school 31P *Kindergarten*
nutrition 9 *Ernährung*
nutshell, in a ~ 91V *kurz gesagt, kurz zusammengefasst*

O

obesity 9 *Fettleibigkeit*
obligation 93 *Verpflichtung*
to **oblige sb to do sth** 79 *jdn (dazu) verpflichten, etw zu tun*
obnoxious 10 *unausstehlich, eklig*
to **obstruct sth** 18 *etw behindern, etw hemmen*
obviously 92 *natürlich*
occasionally 14 *gelegentlich*
to **occur** 18 *stattfinden, geschehen*
office 83 *Amt;* to **take ~** 83 *sein/ihr Amt antreten;* to **remove sb from ~** 92 *jdn des Amtes entheben, jdn absetzen*
official, federal ~ 92 *Bundesbeamte/r*
offshore 81 *vor der Küste, auf dem Meer*
oil drilling 81 *Ölbohrungen, Ölförderung*
one day 28 *eines Tages*
to **operate** 18 *laufen, funktionieren;* 51 *geschäftlich tätig sein, arbeiten, operieren*
opportunity 18 *Möglichkeit, Gelegenheit*
opposed, as ~ to 90 *im Gegensatz zu*
option 22 *Möglichkeit*
to **order sth** 91V *etw befehlen, etw anordnen*
order, in ~ to 84T *um … zu;* **law and ~** 82 *Recht und Ordnung*
ordinary 131T *gewöhnlich, normal*
organic 49T *Bio-*
to **originate in sth** 62 *von etw (her)kommen*
orphanage 22 *Waisenhaus, Kinderheim*
outburst 19 *Ausbruch, Anfall*
outcome 84 *(Wahl-)Ergebnis, Resultat*
outdated 87 *antiquiert, veraltet*
to **outdo sb** 125 *jdn überbieten, jdn ausstechen*
outgoing 15 *kontaktfreudig, kommunikativ*
to **outline sth** 86 *etw darstellen, etw skizzieren*
outlook on life 13 *Lebensperspektive*
output 131 *Produktion, Werke*
outwardly 125 *nach außen, äußerlich*
to **overhaul sth** 19 *etw überholen, etw neu instandsetzen*
overlap 8 *Überschneidung(en), Gemeinsamkeit(en)*
overly dramatic 17 *übertrieben dramatisch*
to **overwhelm sb** 22 *jdn überwältigen*
owner 119T *Inhaber/in, Besitzer/in*

P

packed, *to* **be ~ with sth** 46 *voll von etw sein, voller … sein*
painful, *to* **be ~** 13 *wehtun*
paint, spray ~ 47T *Sprühfarbe*
painting, wall ~ 46 *Wandgemälde*
pandemic 119T *Pandemie*
paradoxically 51 *paradoxerweise*
parliament 79 *Parlament;* **chamber of ~** 94 *Kammer, Haus (des Parlaments);* **MP (Member of P~)** *BE* 97 *(Parlaments-) Abgeordnete/r*
parliamentary session 99 *Legislaturperiode*
parrot 62 *Papagei*
partially 20 *teilweise*
to **participate in sth** 15 *an etw teilnehmen, bei etw mitwirken*
participation 79 *Teilnahme, Beteiligung*
particularly 23 *insbesondere;* 47T *besonders*
party: ~ affiliation 82 *Parteizugehörigkeit;* **~ convention** 83 *Parteitag*
to **pass** 57 *überholen;* **~ a law** 92 *ein Gesetz verabschieden*
passionate, *to* **get ~ about sth** 19 *sich (leidenschaftlich) für etw begeistern/einsetzen*
past 51 *vergangen;* to **look ~ sth** 117P *über etw hinwegsehen*
patience 64T *Geduld*
pattern, sleeping ~(s) 18 *Schlafrhythmus*
pay 50 *Bezahlung, Gehalt*
to **pay off** 17 *sich bezahlt machen*
peak performance 18 *Höchstleistung, Hochtouren*
pedestrian 58 *Fußgänger/in*
peer 15T *Gleichaltrige/r, Mitschüler/in;* **~** *BE* 94V Angehörige/r des brit. Hochadels; **~ pressure** 13 *sozialer Druck (unter Gleichaltrigen)*
penalty 56 *Strafe, Bußgeld;* **~ charge notice** 56T *Bußgeldbescheid*
to **perform sth** 123 *etw aufführen, etw spielen*
performance, academic ~ 15 *schulische Leistung(en);* **peak ~** 18 *Höchstleistung, Hochtouren*

permanent 21 *dauerhaft, beständig;* 122 *unbefristet, fest;* **~ home** 51 *fester Wohnsitz*
permission 93 *Erlaubnis*
persistent 24 *beharrlich, hartnäckig*
perspective, *to* **get some ~** 16T *etw relativieren*
physical 12 *körperlich, physisch*
to **pick grapes** 25T *Trauben ernten*
to **picture sb/sth** 99 *jdn/etw abbilden*
picture, the big ~ 50 *das große Ganze*
pie chart 16P *Tortendiagramm*
place, in the first ~ 51 *überhaupt (erst), in erster Linie*
to **place high value on sth** 13 *großen Wert auf etw legen*
plate, number ~ 56T *Nummernschild*
to **play havoc with sth** 18 *etw komplett durcheinanderbringen*
pleasure 19 *Vergnügen, Annehmlichkeit*
plot 119T *Komplott*
to **plummet** 53 *abstürzen, stark fallen*
plunge, *to* **take the ~** 62 *den Sprung wagen, springen*
poet 45 *Dichter/in*
poetry 45 *Dichtung, Gedichte*
point 28 *Sinn, Zweck;* **~ of view** 16T *Perspektive, Blickwinkel;* **charging ~** 54 *Ladestation;* **exclamation ~** 130 *Ausrufezeichen;* **turning ~** 122 *Wendepunkt*
policy, area of ~ 91V *Politikfeld, Politikbereich*
politics pl 10 *Politik, politische Einstellung(en)*
polling station *BE* 96 *Wahllokal*
pollution, air ~ 56T *Luftverschmutzung*
poodle 47T *Pudel*
poor(ly) 17 *schlecht*
popular, national ~ vote 87 *landesweite Volksabstimmung*
popularity 11 *Beliebtheit*
populated 84T *bevölkert*
population 84T *Bevölkerung*
to **portray sb** 124 *jdn darstellen, jdn porträtieren*
posh 116 *nobel, vornehm*
positive, on a ~ note 48 *positiv*
to **postpone sth** 30 *etw vertagen, etw verschieben*
pothole 57 *Schlagloch*
poverty 121T *Armut*
power 91 *Macht, Einfluss;* **veto ~** 92 *Vetorecht;* **separation of ~s** 79 *Gewaltenteilung*
powerful 91 *mächtig, einflussreich*
to **praise sb/sth** 121T *jdn/etw loben*
precious 124 *wertvoll*
to **predict sth** 29 *etw vorhersagen, etw voraussagen*
prediction 29 *Vorhersage, Voraussage*
present 61 *gegenwärtig;* **~ moment** 12 *gegenwärtiger Zeitpunkt*
to **present an award** 99 *einen Preis überreichen*
president, *to* **run for ~** 87 *sich um die Präsidentschaft bewerben;* **vice ~** 84T *Vizepräsident/in*
presidential: ~ candidate 84T *Präsidentschaftskandidat/in;* **~ election** 79 *Präsidentschaftswahl*
press, quality ~ 115 *seriöse Zeitungen/Zeitschriften;* **freedom of the ~** 114 *Pressefreiheit*
pressure, peer ~ 13 *sozialer Druck (unter Gleichaltrigen)*
to **pretend** 124 *vorgeben; so tun, als ob*
to **prevent sb/sth from doing sth** 118 *jdn/etw daran hindern, etw zu tun*
pride 22 *Stolz*
primary 84T *Vorwahl*
prime minister 96 *Premierminister/in*
privacy 64T *Privatsphäre;* **invasion of ~** 101 *Verletzung der Privatsphäre*
probe, space ~ 116 *Weltraumsonde*
process, election ~ 84 *Wahlverfahren*
pro-choice, *to* **be ~** 81 *Abtreibungsbefürworter/in sein*
profession, *to* **pursue a ~** 25 *einen Beruf ergreifen*
professional 10T *beruflich;* 15 *professionell, hauptberuflich;* 22 *Fachmann/-frau*
to **progress** 121T *vorankommen, Fortschritte machen*
progressive 10 *fortschrittlich*
progressive 12T *schrittweise, stufenweise*
prominent 8 *auffällig, deutlich*
prone, *to* **be ~ to sth** 15 *anfällig für etw sein, zu etw neigen*
to **propel sb** 130 *jdn antreiben, jdn vorwärtstreiben*
proper 57 *richtig, echt, anständig;* 113 *ordentlich*
property 44 *Immobilie(n);* 129 *Eigentum*
proposal 23 *Vorschlag, Angebot*
to **protect sb/sth** 23 *jdn/etw schützen*
protection, data ~ 110 *Datenschutz*
to **provide: ~ sth** 59 *etw bereitstellen, für etw sorgen;* **~ for sb** 19 *für jdn sorgen*
provided 100 *unter der Voraussetzung, dass*
to **provoke sb** 117 *jdn provozieren*
proxy, by ~ 97 *durch einen Bevollmächtigten*
public: ~ facilities pl 118 *öffentliche Toiletten;* **~ service** 99 *Dienst an der Allgemeinheit;* **~ service broadcaster** 115 *öffentlich-rechtlicher Sender*
publication 117P *Veröffentlichung*
punishment 20 *Strafe, Bestrafung;* **threat of ~** 130 *Strafandrohung*
puppy 113 *Welpe*
purpose 56 *Zweck, Absicht;* to **serve a ~** 88 *einen Zweck erfüllen, zweckdienlich sein*
to **pursue a profession** 25 *einen Beruf ergreifen*
pursuit 23 *Aktivität, Beschäftigung*
to **put sth off** 19 *etw (auf später) verschieben*

Q

quality press 115 *seriöse Zeitungen/Zeitschriften*
question, *to* **raise a ~** 100 *eine Frage aufwerfen*
to **question sth** 88 *etw in Frage stellen*
to **quit sth** 31P *etw beenden, etw kündigen*
quite, not ~ 127T *nicht ganz, nicht direkt*

R

racket 19 *Lärm, Krach*
to **raise: ~ sth** 81 *etw* (Steuern usw.) *anheben;* **~ sb** 131T *jdn großziehen;* **~ a question** 100 *eine Frage aufwerfen;* **~ animals** 64T *Tiere züchten, Tiere halten;* **~ funds** 84T *Geld sammeln, Mittel beschaffen*

range 22 *Angebot, Auswahl, (Produkt-)Palette;* **mountain ~** 61 *Gebirge, Gebirgszug*
rank, taxi ~ 54 *Taxistand*
ranking 14 *Einstufung, Bewertung*
to **rant** 122 *losschimpfen*
rarel(y) 16P *(nur) selten*
rate 18 *Tempo*
to **rate sth** 11 *etw einstufen, etw bewerten*
rating 54 *Bewertung, Einstufung*
to **reach out (to sb)** 131T *sich an jdn wenden*
to **read** 112 *lauten*
rear end 12 *Hinterteil*
rebel 27 *Rebell/in*
reception 99 *Empfang*
recognition 56T *Erkennung*
to **recognize sb** 129 *jdn (wieder)erkennen*
records pl, **medical ~** 126 *Krankenakten*
recruitment 127T *(Personal-) Anwerbung, Rekrutierung*
to **refer to sth** 11 *sich auf etw beziehen*
to **reference sth** 117P *auf etw verweisen, etw zitieren*
referendum 79 *Volksabstimmung*
refresher 84T *Auffrischung*
to **refuse** 91V *sich weigern*
regard, with ~ to 82 *hinsichtlich, in puncto*
regardless of sth 15 *unabhängig von etw, ungeachtet einer Sache*
to **register** 96 *sich anmelden, sich registrieren lassen*
registration, voter ~ 88 *Wählerregistrierung;* **car ~ office** 56T *Kfz-Zulassungsstelle*
regular, at ~ intervals 129 *in regelmäßigen Zeitabständen*
to **regulate** 93 *regulieren, steuern*
to **rehearse sth** 28 *etw proben, etw einstudieren*
to **reject sb** 122 *jdn abweisen, jdn verstoßen*
rejection 127T *Ablehnung*
to **relate to sth** 26 *einen Zugang zu etw finden, etw mit etw anfangen können;* 131T *in Beziehung zu etw stehen*
to **relax sth** 12T *etw entspannen*
relaxation 12T *Entspannung, Lockerheit*
to **release sb** 118 *jdn auf freien Fuß setzen*

relevant, *to* **be ~ to sb/sth** 23 *für jdn/etw wichtig / von Bedeutung sein*
to **relieve sth** 16T *etw abbauen, etw lindern*
to **relocate** 118 *umziehen*
reluctant, *to* **be ~ to do sth** 19 *sich dagegen sträuben, etw zu tun; etw nur widerwillig tun*
to **rely on sb/sth** 18 *sich auf jdn/ etw verlassen*
to **remain** 79 *bleiben*
to **remind sb of sth** 46 *jdn an etw erinnern*
to **remove sb from office** 92 *jdn des Amtes entheben, jdn absetzen*
rent 49T *Miete*
rental 49 *Miete, Miet-*
repetition 67 *Wiederholung*
reporting 115 *Bereichterstattung*
to **represent sb** 97 *jdn vertreten, jdn repräsentieren*
representative 83 *(Parlaments-) Abgeordnete/r*
request, friend ~ 126 *Freundschaftsanfrage*
required, *to* **be ~ to do sth** 81 *etw* (aufgrund von Vorschriften) *tun müssen;* **~ by law** 96 *gesetzlich vorgeschrieben*
to **rescue sb** 22 *jdn retten*
to **resemble sb/sth** 64 *jdm/etw ähneln*
resident 22 *ortsansässig, vor Ort;* 51 *Einwohner/in*
response 18 *Reaktion*
responsibility to(wards) sb/sth 114 *Verantwortung jdm/einer Sache gegenüber*
responsible 127T *verantwortungsbewusst*
to **rest sth on sth** 12 *etw auf etw ablegen, etw auf etw ruhen lassen*
restricted 18 *beschränkt*
result, election ~ 84T *Wahlergebnis*
to **result in sth** 57 *etw zur Folge haben*
return, in ~ 94V *als Gegenleistung, im Gegenzug*
to **review sth** 9 *etw überprüfen, etw überarbeiten*
to **revolve around sth** 19 *sich um etw drehen*
reward 19 *Belohnung*
rewarding 25T *befriedigend, lohnend*
rhyme scheme 67 *Reimschema*
rich 47T (Farbe:) *satt*

ridable 45 *fahrbar*
ridiculous 27 *lächerlich*
right: ~ to vote 81 *Wahlrecht;* **civil ~s** pl 120 *Bürgerrechte;* to **exercise a ~** 91V *von einem Recht Gebrauch machen*
rigid 18 *starr*
rise 51 *Aufstieg;* **~ (in sth)** 50 *Anstieg (von etw);* to **be on the ~** 12 *(ständig) zunehmen, auf dem Vormarsch sein*
road surface 57 *Straßenbelag*
root 45 *Wurzel*
row 17 *Streit, Auseinandersetzung;* **blazing ~** 19 *erbitterter/wilder Streit*
royal 99 *königlich, Königs-*
rubbish 111 *Unsinn, Quatsch*
rule 120 *Herrschaft*
to **rule sth out** 31 *etw ausschließen, etw unmöglich machen*
rumour 117 *Gerücht*
to **run for president** 87 *sich um die Präsidentschaft bewerben*
run-down 49T *heruntergekommen, verwahrlost;* to **feel ~** 13 *sich schlapp fühlen*
rural 45 *ländlich*
rush, adrenaline ~ 61 *Adrenalinrausch*

S

sadly 18 *leider, bedauerlicherweise*
sarcasm 27 *Sarkasmus*
scale, large-~ 46 *großformatig*
scary 47T *unheimlich, furchteinflößend*
scenery 62 *Landschaft*
schedule 101 *Terminkalender*
scheduling 15T *Terminplanung, Zeitplan*
scheme 118 *Programm;* **hire ~** 54 *Verleihsystem;* **rhyme ~** 67 *Reimschema*
school, nursery ~ 31P *Kindergarten;* **trade ~** 15T *Berufsschule*
science, applied ~es pl 31P *angewandte Wissenschaften*
screen, acrylic ~ 47T *Plexiglaswand*
screenplay 26 *Drehbuch*
sea creature 62 *Meerestier*
secretly 57 *im Verborgenen*
see-through 118 *durchsichtig*
to **select sb/sth** 84T *jdn/etw auswählen*

self-sufficiency 22 *Eigenständigkeit*
selfish 15 *egoistisch*
Senate *AE* 83 *Senat*
senator 84T *Senator/in*
senior 99 *hochrangig*
sense: ~ of community 49T *Gemeinschaftsgefühl, -sinn;* **~ of humour** 47T *Humor;* to **make ~** 131T *einen Sinn ergeben*
to **sense sth** 57 *etw fühlen, etw spüren*
sensible 15 *vernünftig*
sensitive, *to* **be ~ to sth** 19 *auf etw empfindlich reagieren, empfänglich für etw sein;* **~ information** 129 *vertrauliche Daten*
to **separate sb/sth** 118 *jdn/etw (voneinander) trennen*
separation of powers 79 *Gewaltenteilung*
seriously, *to* **take sb/sth ~** 57 *jdn/etw ernst nehmen*
servant, civil ~ *BE* 94 *Beamte/-in*
to **serve a purpose** 88 *einen Zweck erfüllen, zweckdienlich sein*
service 23 *Dienstleistung;* **public ~** 99 *Dienst an der Allgemeinheit;* **armed ~es** pl 29 *Streitkräfte, Armee;* to **do community ~** 96 *Sozialstunden leisten;* **public ~ broadcaster** 115 *öffentlich-rechtlicher Sender*
session, parliamentary ~ 99 *Legislaturperiode*
to **set up business** 52 *sich (geschäftlich) niederlassen*
shade 131T *Schatten*
shame, *to* **be a ~** 47T *schade sein, eine Schande sein;* **S~ on you!** 119T *Schämen Sie sich! Schäm dich!*
to **shame sb** 67 *jdn an den Pranger stellen, jdn der Lächerlichkeit preisgeben*
share 79 *Anteil*
to **share sth** 61 *sich über etw austauschen, über etw sprechen*
shelter 22 *Tierheim*
to **shift** 61 *sich bewegen, sich verschieben;* **~ away from sth** 98T *von etw abrücken*
to **shine a light on sth** 131T *etw beleuchten*
to **shove sth** 16T *etw schieben, etw stecken*
to **show sth off** 131T *etw zur Schau stellen*
to **shut sth down** 119T *etw stillegen*
shutter 47T *Fensterladen, Rollladen*
shy 10 *schüchtern*
side, the bright ~ 13 *die positiven Aspekte*
to **side with sb/sth** 82 *sich hinter jdn/etw stellen, für jdn/etw Partei ergreifen*
significant, *to* **be ~** 115 *von Bedeutung sein*
signposting 48 orientierende Hinweise für die Zuhörer/innen in einem Vortrag
silly 10T *albern, doof*
similarly 30 *ebenso, in gleicher Weise*
simultaneously 19 *gleichzeitig, zur selben Zeit*
sin 112 *Sünde*
to **skim** 8 (Text) *überfliegen*
to **sleep in** 18 *ausschlafen, länger schlafen*
sleeping pattern(s) 18 *Schlafrhythmus*
to **slow sth down** 81 *etw bremsen, etw verlangsamen*
to **slump** 53 *absacken, stark zurückgehen*
smell 47T *Geruch*
snowball fight 11 *Schneeballschlacht*
social: ~ inequality 82 *soziale Ungerechtigkeit;* **~ welfare** 82 *Sozialhilfe;* to **fit in ~ly** 15 *sich anpassen, dazugehören*
society 12 *Gesellschaft*
soldier 57 *Soldat/in*
solely 123P *ausschließlich, nur*
to **solve sth** 59 *etw lösen*
space probe 116 *Weltraumsonde*
to **speak up for sb** 121T *für jdn eintreten, sich für jdn stark machen*
specific 30 *bestimmte/r/s*
specifically 18 *insbesondere, genauer gesagt*
speech, free ~ 115 *freie Meinungsäußerung;* to **give a ~** 99 *eine Rede halten*
speeding 58 *Geschwindigkeitsüberschreitung, zu schnelles Fahren*
spending history 126 *Kaufhistorie*
spontaneous(ly) 23 *spontan*
to **spot sth** 117 *etw erkennen, etw entdecken*
spray paint 47T *Sprühfarbe*
spread 119 *Ausbreitung, Verbreitung*
to **spread** 119T *sich verbreiten;* **~ sth** 119T *etw verbreiten*
stall, food ~ 49T *Imbissstand*
stance, *to* **take a tough ~ against sth** 82 *eine harte Haltung gegenüber etw einnehmen*
stand, *to* **take a ~ against sth** 46 *ein Zeichen gegen etw setzen*
to **stand sb/sth** 64T *jdn/etw ertragen*
standard, *to* **meet emission ~s** 56T *Emissionsgrenzwerte einhalten*
to **stare at sb** 27 *jdn anstarren*
state, emotional ~ 12T *Gefühlszustand;* **swing ~** *AE* 84T US-Bundesstaat mit hohem Wechselwählerанteil; **head of ~** 99 *Staatsoberhaupt*
station, polling ~ *BE* 96 *Wahllokal*
to **step down** 99 *zurücktreten*
to **stick to sth** 80 *an etw festhalten, bei etw bleiben*
stimulating 18 *aufputschend*
straight away 112 *sofort*
strain 130 *Druck, Strapaze(n)*
to **strengthen sth** 99 *etw stärken*
stress levels pl 12 *Stressniveau*
to **stress sb out** 16T *jdn stressen*
stressed out, *to* **be ~** 15T *(völlig) gestresst sein*
stressor 15T *Stressfaktor*
string, a ~ of events 57 *eine Reihe von Ereignissen*
structure 59 *Aufbau*
to **struggle: ~ to do sth** 62 *etw nur mit Mühe tun können; es schwer haben, etw zu tun;* **~ with sth** 122 *mit etw zu kämpfen haben*
struggle, sb finds sth a ~ 18 *jdm fällt etw (sehr) schwer*
stubborn 15 *stur, dickköpfig*
stunning 62 *atemberaubend*
stylistic device 67 *Stilmittel*
suburban 15T *außerhalb (des Stadtzentrums), am Stadtrand*
suburbs pl 15 *Stadtrand, Randbezirke*
to **suffer: sth ~s** 13 *etw wird in Mitleidenschaft gezogen*
suffering 12 *Leiden, Leid*
to **suggest sth** 18 *etw nahelegen, auf etw schließen lassen;* 59 *etw vorschlagen*
sunset 131T *Sonnenuntergang*
superb 47T *erstklassig, hervorragend*
superficial 131T *oberflächlich*

to **support your family** 66 *die eigene Familie ernähren*
support, financial ~ 119 *finanzielle Unterstützung*
supporter 84T *Anhänger/in, Unterstützer/in*
to **suppose:** to **be ~ed to do sth** 91V *etw (eigentlich) tun sollen*
Supreme Court *AE* 90 *Oberster Gerichtshof*
surface, road ~ 57 *Straßenbelag*
to **surge** 51 *sprunghaft ansteigen*
surgery 22 *Arztpraxis*
suspicious, *to* **be ~ of sb** 66 *jdm misstrauen, jdm mit Argwohn begegnen;* to **look ~** 129 *verdächtig aussehen*
to **swear at sb** 118 *jdn anpöbeln, jdn beschimpfen*
sweat 26 *Schweiß*
swing: ~ state *AE* 84T US-Bundesstaat mit hohem Wechselwähleranteil; **~ voter** 78 *Wechselwähler/in*
syllable 131T *Silbe*
to **sympathize with sb** 25T *für jdn Verständnis haben, mit jdm mitfühlen*

T

tabloid 101 *Boulevardzeitung, Massenblatt;* **the ~s** pl 101 *die Boulevardpresse*
to **tackle sth** 82 *etw bekämpfen*
to **take: ~ sb/sth seriously** 57 *jdn/etw ernst nehmen;* **~ action** 121T *Maßnahmen ergreifen;* **~ care of sth** 15 *sich um etw kümmern;* **~ office** 83 *sein/ihr Amt antreten*
to **tap into sth** 131T *einen Zugang zu etw finden, sich etw erschließen*
targeted advertising 129 *gezielte Werbung*
tax, *to* **collect ~es** 94V *Steuern eintreiben*
taxi rank 54 *Taxistand*
taxpayer 78 *Steuerzahler/in*
tear 101 *Träne*
to **tear sb limb from limb** 131T *jdn in Stücke reißen*
to **tease sb** 25T *jdn aufziehen, jdn necken*
to **tell: Time will ~.** 94V *Die Zeit wird es zeigen.*
temporary 21 *vorübergehend;* 47T *vorläufig, provisorisch*
to **tend to do sth** 16 *dazu neigen, etw zu tun*
tension 12 *Spannung(en), Angespanntheit*
tent camp 51 *Zeltlager*
term, on sb's ~s 19 *zu jds Bedingungen, nach jds Vorstellungen*
terrified, *to* **be ~ of sth** 9 *(fürchterliche) Angst vor etw haben*
textbook 26 *Schulbuch*
theorist, conspiracy ~ 119 *Verschwörungstheoretiker/in*
theory, conspiracy ~ 119 *Verschwörungstheorie*
thigh 12 *Oberschenkel*
though, as ~ 66 *als ob*
thought, food for ~ 25T *Denkanstöße*
threat: ~ (to sth) 13 *Bedrohung (von etw);* **~ of punishment** 130 *Strafandrohung;* **death ~** 119T *Morddrohung*
thrill 23 *Nervenkitzel*
to **tidy sth** 18 *etw aufräumen*
tight 24 (Geld:) *knapp*
time, at the ~ 127T *seinerzeit;* **sb has a hard ~ doing sth** 25T *jdm fällt es schwer, etw zu tun;* **T~ will tell.** 94V *Die Zeit wird es zeigen.* **~ traveller** 31 *Zeitreisende/r*
timeline 84T *Zeitplan*
tiny 131T *klein, winzig*
tone 67 *Tonfall, Ton*
toned 124 *durchtrainiert*
top, on ~ of sth 56T *zusätzlich zu etw*
to **touch on sth** 131T *etw* (Thema usw.) *berühren, etw streifen*
touching 67 *rührend, bewegend*
tough, *to* **take a ~ stance against sth** 82 *eine harte Haltung gegenüber etw einnehmen*
tour, guided ~ 46 *Führung, Rundgang;* **walking ~** 47T *Rundgang*
to **track sth** 115 *etw (nach)verfolgen*
track, *to* **lose ~ of sth** 131T *etw aus den Augen verlieren*
trade school 15T *Berufsschule*
traffic: ~ calming 58 *Verkehrsberuhigung;* **~ cone** 57 *Leitkegel, Pylon;* **~ control** 56T *Verkehrssteuerung*
to **transform sth** 49T *etw verwandeln, etw umwandeln, etw (grundlegend) verändern*
transit 56T *(öffentlicher) Verkehr, Stadtverkehr*
transport, urban ~ 45 *Stadtverkehr*
transportation, department of ~ 57 *Verkehrsbehörde*
to **treat sb/sth** 24 *jdn/etw behandeln*
tribe 111 *(Volks-)Stamm*
to **trigger sth** 13 *etw auslösen*
true, *to* **be ~ to sth** 66 *einer Sache entsprechen*
to **trust sb/sth** 114 *jdm/einer Sache vertrauen*
trustworthy 126 *vertrauenswürdig*
truth 56T *Wahrheit*
tuition fees pl 98T *Studiengebühren*
to **turn: ~ to sb** 122 *sich an jdn wenden;* **~ violent** 121T *in Gewalt umschlagen;* **Things ~ed out well.** 127T *Die Sache ging gut aus.*
turning point 122 *Wendepunkt*
turnout 79 *Wahlbeteiligung*

U

unaffordable 49T *unerschwinglich, zu teuer*
unannounced 119T *unangekündigt*
unbiased 115 *unvoreingenommen, neutral*
uncertain 84 *unsicher*
unconstitutional 91V *nicht verfassungsgemäß*
to **undergo sth** 18 *etw durchmachen*
underprivileged 23 *benachteiligt, unterprivilegiert*
understanding 127T *verständnisvoll*
unimpressed, *to* **be ~ by sth** 66 *sich von etw unbeeindruckt zeigen*
unique 62 *eigen, spezifisch;* 126 *einzigartig*
unity 99 *Einheit*
unless 117P *außer wenn*
unlike 51 *anders als*
unlovable 124 *nicht liebenswert*
unpredictable 61 *unberechenbar*
unrecognizable 51 *nicht wiederzuerkennen*
unsafe 57 *gefährlich*
unseparated lane 57 *nicht abgetrennte Fahrspur*
up, *to* **be ~ to sth** 115 *etw anstellen, etw machen, etw vorhaben*
upcoming 84T *bevorstehend*

Bildquellen

Cover: (Foto) Shutterstock.com / Lewis Liu; (Gestaltung & Produktmarke) Rosendahl Berlin - Agentur für Markendesign
S. 8/1: Shutterstock.com / Phovoir; **S. 8/2:** mauritius images / alamy stock photo / Rawpixel Ltd; **S. 8/3:** Shutterstock.com / VH-studio; **S. 9/1:** Shutterstock.com / Krakenimages.com; **S. 9/2:** Cartoonstock / Steven Smeltzer; **S. 9/3:** Shutterstock.com / Sunshine Seeds; **S. 10/Foto:** Shutterstock.com / Phovoir; **S. 10/Korea-, USA-Icon:** Shutterstock.com / Mint Fox; **S. 10/Football-Icon:** Shutterstock.com / cougarsan; **S. 10/Regenbogenfahne:** Shutterstock.com / sebastian ignacio coll; **S. 10/Faust-Icon:** Shutterstock.com / weberjake; **S. 10/Musik-Icon:** Shutterstock.com / Aratehortua; **S. 10/Kirche-Icon:** Shutterstock.com / Arizzona Design; **S. 10/Beten-Icon:** Shutterstock.com / weberjake; **S. 10/Krankenwagen-Icon:** Shutterstock.com / Arizzona Design; **S. 11:** Shutterstock.com / Lightspring; **S. 12/Smileys:** Shutterstock.com / paramouse; **S. 12/Foto:** Shutterstock.com / Krakenimages.com; **S. 15/Foto:** Lori Mann; **S. 16:** Shutterstock.com / Monkey Business Images; **S. 17:** Cartoonstock / Steven Smeltzer; **S. 21/1:** Shutterstock.com / SZBDesign; **S. 21/2:** Shutterstock.com / Viktoria Suslova; **S. 22/1:** Shutterstock.com / niall dunne; **S. 22/2:** Shutterstock.com / Sunshine Seeds; **S. 23/1:** Shutterstock.com / Joa Souza; **S. 23/2:** Shutterstock.com / Reimar; **S. 23/3:** Shutterstock.com / My Good Images; **S. 23/4:** Shutterstock.com / Versta; **S. 24/1:** Shutterstock.com / FANKS; **S. 24/2:** Shutterstock.com / Mick Fitzsimmons; **S. 24/3:** Shutterstock.com / Chanchai phetdikhai; **S. 24/4:** Shutterstock.com / icemanphotos; **S. 26:** Imago Stock & People GmbH / Mary Evans; **S. 27/1:** mauritius images / alamy stock photo / AF archive; **S. 27/2:** Imago Stock & People GmbH / Mary Evans; **S. 30/1:** Shutterstock.com / VH-studio; **S. 30/2:** Shutterstock.com / wavebreakmedia; **S. 31:** akg-images / ClassicStock; **S. 32/1:** Shutterstock.com / Serg Zastavkin; **S. 32/2:** Shutterstock.com / Roman Samborskyi; **S. 32/3:** Shutter-

stock.com / Roman Samborskyi; **S. 36/Sanduhr:** Shutterstock.com / Artem Novosad; **S. 39**: Shutterstock.com / Ivelin Radkov; **S. 41:** Shutterstock.com / artKULO; **S. 43:** mauritius images / alamy stock photo / Rawpixel Ltd; **S. 44/1:** Shutterstock.com / Elena Dijour; **S. 44/2:** Shutterstock.com / Monkey Business Images; **S. 44/3:** Shutterstock.com / Olivier Tabary; **S. 45/1:** Shutterstock.com / emperorcosar; **S. 45/2:** Shutterstock.com / Timelynx; **S. 45/3:** Shutterstock.com / Olga Danylenko; **S. 45/4:** Shutterstock.com / JuliusKielaitis; **S. 46:** Shutterstock.com / Elena Dijour; **S. 47/1:** Shutterstock.com / EQRoy; **S. 47/2:** Shutterstock.com / Ron Ellis; **S. 47/3:** Shutterstock.com / AC Manley; **S. 47/4:** Shutterstock.com / EQRoy; **S. 47/5:** Klein und Halm / Shutterstock.com / SevenMaps; **S. 49/1:** Shutterstock.com / Hotforphotog; **S. 49/2:** Shutterstock.com / Andriana Syvanych; **S. 49/Laura:** Shutterstock.com / vilaplaneta; **S. 49/Ben:** Shutterstock.com / BMPhotolab; **S. 49/Jorge:** Shutterstock.com / Alexandra Rotanova; **S. 49/Amahle:** Shutterstock.com / JKstock; **S. 51:** Shutterstock.com / emperorcosar; **S. 54/1:** Shutterstock.com / SC Image; **S. 54/2:** Shutterstock.com / Dmitry Kalinovsky; **S. 54/3:** Shutterstock.com / Timelynx; **S. 54/4:** Shutterstock.com / Jacek Chabraszewski; **S. 55/1-3:** Shutterstock.com / Kristina Rudkevica; **S. 55/4:** Shutterstock.com / deviyanthi79; **S. 55/5:** Shutterstock.com / robuart; **S. 55/6:** Shutterstock.com / curiosity; **S. 57/1:** Joe Linton / L.A. Eco-Village; **S. 57/2:** mauritius images / alamy stock photo / Eric Brown; **S. 58:** stock.adobe.com / @klaus rein / artfocus; **S. 60:** Shutterstock.com / fizkes; **S. 61/1:** Shutterstock.com / Nitr; **S. 61/2:** Shutterstock.com / Umomos; **S. 61/3:** Shutterstock.com / Martin Vlnas; **S. 61/4:** Shutterstock.com / Olga Danylenko; **S. 63/1:** Shutterstock.com / danceyourlife; **S. 63/2:** Shutterstock.com / Seita; **S. 64/A:** Shutterstock.com / Iconic Bestiary; **S. 64/B:** Shutterstock.com / Lemberg Vector studio; **S. 64/C:** Shutterstock.com / Oxy_gen; **S. 64/D:** Shutterstock.com / klyaksun; **S. 65/1:** Shutterstock.com / JuliusKielaitis; **S. 65/2:** Shutterstock.com / Mai_justrace; **S. 66/1:** Shutterstock.com / Olivier Tabary; **S. 66/2:** Shutterstock.com / Michael Overstreet; **S. 67:** Write About Now Media / Clementine von Radics; **S. 68/A:** Shutterstock.com / YummyBuum; **S. 68/B:** Shutterstock.com / miniwide; **S. 68/C:** Shutterstock.com / Vectorpocket; **S. 68/D:** Shutterstock.com / Disavorabuth; **S. 68/Step 1:** Shutterstock.com / r2dpr; **S. 68/Step 2:** Shutterstock.com / bearsky23; **S. 68/Step 3:** Shutterstock.com / Tukunen; **S. 68/Step 4:** Shutterstock.com / SurfsUp; **S. 68/Step 5:** Shutterstock.com / bsd; **S. 69/Step 6:** Shutterstock.com / Honza Hruby; **S. 69/Step 7:** Shutterstock.com / AnnIris; **S. 69/Step 8:** Shutterstock.com / BesticonPark; **S. 69/Step 9:** Shutterstock.com / BesticonPark; **S. 69/Step 10:** Shutterstock.com / popicon; **S. 69/Step 11:** Shutterstock.com / BUTENKOV ALEKSEI; **S. 69/Hinweiszeichen:** Shutterstock.com / Kovalov Anatolii; **S. 69/Personen:** Shutterstock.com / GoodStudio; **S. 70/1:** Shutterstock.com / Blan-k; **S. 70/2:** Shutterstock.com / AVIcon; **S. 70/3:** Shutterstock.com / Chippo Medved; **S. 70/4:** Shutterstock.com / Drk_Smith; **S. 72:** Shutterstock.com / BenzSuthep; **S. 73:** Shutterstock.com / In-Finity; **S. 74/Karte:** Shutterstock.com / Mega Pixel; **S. 74/Nadel:** Shutterstock.com / cosma; **S. 74/Foto:** mauritius images / alamy stock photo / Sally Anderson; **S. 75:** Shutterstock.com / Zlatko Guzmic; **S. 77:** Shutterstock.com / Monkey Business Images; **S. 78/1:** Shutterstock.com / Andriy Babets; **S. 78/2:** Shutterstock.com / Brent Eysler; **S. 78/3:** Shutterstock.com / Lorna Roberts; **S. 79/1:** Shutterstock.com / 24K-Production; **S. 79/2:** Shutterstock.com / Michal Kalasek; **S. 79/3:** Shutterstock.com / ESB Professional; **S. 79/4:** Shutterstock.com / Gergo Orban; **S. 80/1:** mauritius images / alamy stock photo / Kristoffer Tripplaar; **S. 80/2:** Shutterstock.com / Devi Bones; **S. 80/3,6:** Shutterstock.com / Handies Peak; **S. 80/4:** Shutterstock.com / Perfect 5hot; **S. 80/5:** dpa Picture-Alliance / AP / ASSOCIATED PRESS; **S. 80/7:** Shutterstock.com / Angyalosi Beata; **S. 80/8:** Shutterstock.com / Gregory Johnston; **S. 80/9:** Shutterstock.com / Ryan Rodrick Beiler; **S. 80/10:** Shutterstock.com / mark reinstein; **S. 82:** Shutterstock.com / Andriy Babets; **S. 83/1:** Shutterstock.com / 24K-Production; **S. 83/2:** Shutterstock.com / VADISH ZAINER; **S. 84:** Shutterstock.com / Freud; **S. 87/1:** stock.adobe.com / Ranta Images; **S. 87/2:** Shutterstock.com / StockLite; **S. 88/Parteiensymbole:** Shutterstock.com / Handies Peak; **S. 88/US-Karte:** Shutterstock.com / GG Digital Arts; **S. 90/1:** Shutterstock.com / Freud; **S. 90/2:** Shutterstock.com / vector toon; **S. 90/3:** Shutterstock.com / STRIPBALL; **S. 90/4:** Shutterstock.com / Freud; **S. 90/5,6:** Shutterstock.com / Design Collection; **S. 90/7:** Shutterstock.com / VOLYK IEVGENII; **S. 90/8:** Shutterstock.com / Freud; **S. 90/9:** Shutterstock.com / frozenbunn; **S. 90/un.li.:** Cornelsen / Julia Hintze; **S. 92/1:** Shutterstock.com / Chess Ocampo; **S. 92/2:** Shutterstock.com / Michal Kalasek; **S. 92/3:** Shutterstock.com / Christopher Penler; **S. 93/Executive:** Shutterstock.com / Freud; **S. 93/Legislative:** Shutterstock.com / Freud; **S. 93/Judicial:** Shutterstock.com / Freud; **S. 94/A:** Shutterstock.com / ESB Professional; **S. 94/B:** Shutterstock.com / Alex Segre; **S. 94/C:** Shutterstock.com / pcruciatti; **S. 94/4:** Cornelsen / Julia Hintze; **S. 95:** Shutterstock.com / Peter Hermes Furian; **S. 96/1:** Shutterstock.com / Ranta Images; **S. 96/2:** Shutterstock.com / ARENA Creative; **S. 96/3:** Shutterstock.com / CebotariN; **S. 96/4:** Shutterstock.com / fitzcrittle; **S. 99/1:** Shutterstock.com / Lorna Roberts; **S. 99/2:** Shutterstock.com / FiledIMAGE; **S. 102:** dpa Picture-Alliance / AP / AP Photo; **S. 103/1-4:** Shutterstock.com / kuroksta; **S. 103/5:** Shutterstock.com / artyway; **S. 103/6:** Shutterstock.com / maljuk; **S. 109:** Shutterstock.com / Brent Eysler; **S. 110/1:** Shutterstock.com / dotshock; **S. 110/2:** Shutterstock.com / Tom Wang; **S. 110/3:** Jenny Bienemann; **S. 111/1:** Shutterstock.com / Fatya Anggraeni; **S. 111/2:** Shutterstock.com / insta_photos; **S. 111/3:** Cartoon Stock / Maria Scrivan; **S. 111/4:** Shutterstock.com / Nicoleta Ionescu; **S. 112/Sterne:** Shutterstock.com / cougarsan; **S. 112/Herz:** Shutterstock.com / JosepPerianes; **S. 112/Feuer:** Shutterstock.com / Vector bucket; **S. 112/Smileys:** Shutterstock.com / cougarsan; **S. 112/un.li.:** Cartoonstock / HillaryAllison; **S. 112/un.re:** Cartoonstock / Keren Keet; **S. 113/Herz:** Shutterstock.com / JosepPerianes; **S. 113/Smiley:** Shutterstock.com / Vilmos Varga; **S. 113/Foto:** Shutterstock.com / dotshock; **S. 114:** Shutterstock.com / mipan; **S. 115:** Shutterstock.com / Fatya Anggraeni; **S. 116/1:** Shutterstock.com / ambrozinio; **S. 116/2:** Shutterstock.com / Robert Kneschke; **S. 116/3:** Shutterstock.com / heardinlondon; **S. 117/1:** Shutterstock.com / difugi creative; **S. 117/2:** Shutterstock.com / D Line; **S. 117/3:** Shutterstock.com / Francois Poirier; **S. 117/4:** Shutterstock.com / musmellow; **S. 117/5:** Shutterstock.com / schab; **S. 117/6:** Shutterstock.com / Cinderella Design; **S. 118/1:** Shutterstock.com / Ramon Espelt Photography; **S. 118/2:** Shutterstock.com / Ross-Helen; **S. 118/3:** Shutterstock.com / Sergio Yoneda; **S. 118/4:** Shutterstock.com / Joseph Sohm; **S. 118/5:** dpa Picture-Alliance / AA; **S. 119/1:** Shutterstock.com / Phil Pasquini; **S. 120/1:** Shutterstock.com / GiantSwing; **S. 120/2:** Shutterstock.com / E setiawan; **S. 120/3:** Shutterstock.com / kiciulla; **S. 120/4:** Shutterstock.com / pantid123; **S. 120/5:** akg-images / Studio Nippoldt; **S. 120/6:** Shutterstock.com / Uncle Leo; **S. 120/7:** Shutterstock.com / Hamdi Ujeb Addakhil; **S. 120/8:** Shutterstock.com / roseed abbas; **S. 120/9:** Shutterstock.com / Stock-Photo; **S. 120/10:** Shutterstock.com / Jovica Varga; **S. 121:** Shutterstock.com / Arthimedes; **S. 122:** Shutterstock.com / insta_photos; **S. 124/1:** Shutterstock.com / meunierd; **S. 124/2:** Cartoon Stock / Maria Scrivan; **S. 124/3:** Shutterstock.com / Stuart Jenner; **S. 126:** Shutterstock.com / Nicoleta Ionescu; **S. 127/1:** Shutterstock.com / DW labs Incorporated; **S. 127/2:** Shutterstock.com / AJR_photo; **S. 127/3:** Shutterstock.com / Stas Vulkanov; **S. 127/4:** Shutterstock.com / Syda Productions; **S. 129/ob.li.:** Shutterstock.com / La1n; **S. 129/Smiley:** Shutterstock.com / AyselDesign; **S. 130/1-3:** Jenny Bienemann; **S. 131:** Jenny Bienemann / David Kindler; **S. 132:** Shutterstock.com / olhahladiy; **S. 133/1:** Shutterstock.com / ANT 7; **S. 133/2:** Shutterstock.com / Telman Bagirov; **S. 133/3:** Shutterstock.com / Alexandr III; **S. 133/4:** Shutterstock.com / rungrote; **S. 133/5:** Shutterstock.com / archivector; **S. 134:** Shutterstock.com / Syda Productions; **S. 136:** Cartoonstock / Chris Wildt; **S. 137:** Cartoonstock / Len Hawkins; **S. 139:** Shutterstock.com / linear_design; **S. 141:** Shutterstock.com / Frenggo; **S. 144**: Shutterstock.com / Tom Wang; **S. 146/1-12:** Shutterstock.com / Pewara Nicropithak; **S. 163/1:** Shutterstock.com / Yindee; **S. 163/2:** Shutterstock.com / GoodStudio; **S. 164:** Shutterstock.com / Irina Strelnikova; **S. 165/1:** Shutterstock.com / N. Savranska; **S. 165/2:** Shutterstock.com / GoodStudio; **S. 165/3:** Shutterstock.com / Keji; **S. 167:** Shutterstock.com / tati._.9; **S. 168:** Shutterstock.com / EgudinKa; **S. 172:** Shutterstock.com / Vectorium; **S. 174:** Shutterstock.com / Artisticco; **S. 175:** Shutterstock.com / metamorworks; **S. 177:** Shutterstock.com / Artram

Textquellen

S. 18: Dean Burnett: Why Your Parents Are Driving You Up the Wall and What To Do About It, Penguin Books 2019; **S. 73:** Guardian News & Media Ltd 2020; **S. 102:** Emma Gonzalez, Washington, DC, 2018; **S. 107:** Longman Dictionary of Contemporary English, Langescheidt-Longman GmbH 2003; **S. 142:** Guardian News & Media Ltd 2021